Social Work: the Sc
Psychological Appr

to toil

Social Work: the Social Psychological Approach

Glynis M. Breakwell
Department of Psychology
University of Surrey

Colin Rowett
Social Work Department
Broadmoor Hospital

VNR Van Nostrand Reinhold (UK) Co. Ltd.

**Published by Van Nostrand Reinhold (UK) Co. Ltd.
Molly Millars Lane, Wokingham, Berkshire, England**

Library of Congress Cataloging in Publication Data

Breakwell, Glynis Marie.
   Social work, the social psychological approach.

   Includes bibliographical references and index.
   1. Social service — Psychological aspects. 2. Social psychology.
I. Rowett, Colin. II. Title.
HV31.B725   361.3'01'9   82-6931
ISBN 0-442-30519-2   AACR2
ISBN 0-442-30520-6 (pbk.)

Printed and bound in Great Britain by
Robert Hartnoll Ltd. Bodmin, Cornwall

Preface

This book was created to describe the social psychological approach (SPA) to the social work process. It has long been asserted that social workers need to understand and use social psychology in their practice. Yet the literature available to social workers has been limited. There have been no texts on social psychology specifically designed for social workers. Instead, social workers have been presented with various forms of individual psychology and macrosociology. There is, however, an important contribution which social psychology, the study of the individual in a social context, can make to the social work process. This contribution is the central concern of this book. Consequently, the book is seen as filling a fundamental gap in the existing social work literature.

The structure of the book is dictated by the belief that social workers and social psychologists should collaborate in evolving a social psychological model of social work practice. Such a model, the result of collaboration between a social worker and a social psychologist, is presented here. The book is addressed not simply to teachers and students of social work but also, specifically, to social work practitioners and to social psychologists besides all those who deal with social work problems. In addressing a wide audience, it is important to establish a lingua franca: social workers need to understand the basics of social psychology and social psychologists must understand the basis of social work practice. The structure of the book reflects an attempt to establish such a common foundation.

There are seven parts to the book. Part I comprises a single chapter, The Social Psychological Approach, which is vital to the subsequent arguments. This is an exposition of the SPA to the social work process, describing the components of the SPA which are elaborated upon in the course of the book.

Part II comprises seven chapters. Chapter 2, The Character of Social Psychology, draws the broad outline of the discipline, its history and methods. Chapters 3, 4, 5 and 6, in turn, describe the theories and findings of social psychology in areas of relationships, identity, groups and the environment. Chapter 7, on change, outlines the techniques effective in inducing personal and social change and the variables which impair or accentuate their impact. Chapter 8 rounds off this part with a statement of the 'Central Tenets of SPA Explanation and Analysis'; this includes a statement of how they may come to work in the social work process.

Part III, The Nature of Social Work, comprises Chapters 9, 10 and 11 which, in turn, describe the structure of social work, the organization of its professional bodies, and the demands placed upon social workers and the skills available to satisfy them.

Part IV, Theory Use, seeks to explain in Chapter 12 how social workers analyse their task and attempts to show how the SPA would lead to a more comprehensive understanding of their role as well as providing techniques which are effective in bringing about the attainment of social work objectives. Chapter 13, on the use of theory, is included in order to show how theories should be chosen and used by the social worker — among a plethora of competing theories, the rules for optimal usage are important.

Part V is devoted to showing the applications of the SPA. In this part there are seven chapters — on disablement, group homes, child battering, community work, mental illness, the use of the SPA by the client, and student supervision — which are designed to show the use of the SPA in practice in areas of central concern to social workers. Since the manner of usage of the SPA will depend upon the context and the nature of the problem, these chapters are designed to capture some of this flexibility and dynamism. Their structures and emphases vary, though all serve to explicate the SPA.

Part VI, Analyst Analyse Thyself, consists of Chapters 21 and 22 which represent attempts to show how the SPA can be used by social workers to analyse, explain and ultimately surmount the problems inherent in the position of their profession and in their own position within that profession.

Part VII, Theory into Action, portrays some of the strengths and weaknesses of the SPA model of the social work process.

The central object in writing this book was to show how the SPA is not just a non-directive orientation to social work like so many others which tell social workers what they should achieve but not how to do so. The SPA model of the social work process provides the tools of analysis and the means of explaining social work problems which can then be used to inform the evolution of strategies of intervention and controlled change designed to cope with those problems. Social psychology provides the seeds of a whole body of techniques which can be central to social work practice; this book scrapes the surface of this potential.

The authors are grateful to John Wiley & Sons Ltd. for permission to publish Chapter 21, which is based on material previously published by them in G.M. Breakwell (Ed.) *Threatened Identities,* © 1982.

The views expressed are solely those of the authors and should not be taken to represent the views of the Department of Health and Social Security.

Glynis M Breakwell & Colin Rowett
Oxford
September 1981

Contents

Part I
The Social Psychological Approach

1
The Social Psychological Approach

Even if social work has proved a promiscuous suitor and inconstant mistress, the history of alliances between social work and psychology is venerable. Social work has flirted with, lovingly embraced, become married to and finally divorced itself from various branches of psychology in its time. Nevertheless, these shifting alliances have had certain characteristics in common. They have been similar in form and, to some extent, in content.

The form of these alliances is characterized by a strict dichotomy of roles. Social workers play the part of 'the practitioner'; psychologists play the part of 'the theorist'. The practitioner and the theorist are engaged in very different enterprises, based on different values and played by different rules. Practitioners are in business to assuage or solve the clients' problems and to do so within the legal and moral constraints placed upon them by the institutions for which they work. Theorists are in business to observe, and then describe, patterns of events in the world about them; in the hope that, ultimately, they will describe causal relationships between events and come to be able to predict their occurrence. The practitioner needs to act in order to change events, the theorist needs to watch in order to understand them. Of course, despite their different objectives and methods, the activities of practitioner and theorist are in some ways compatible. Certainly a relevant theory can inform practice. It may help the practitioner to see a specific problem against a broader backdrop, it may indicate the likely course of developments and it may suggest where, when and how intervention might be possible. Effectively, the practitioner takes the theory and puts it to work. This is exactly what social workers have been doing with psychological theories for over half a century. It has meant that there has been a unidirectional flow of expertise: from psychology to social

1

work. There has been a marked absence of any real collaboration either in the production of theory or the initiation of techniques of intervention. Social work has acted the part of the asset-stripper: those aspects of psychological theory which prove useful are retained, the rest are piled on the scrap heap. This utilitarian attitude has led social workers to deal only with fragments of theories, notably those fragments which are compatible with the needs and values of the moment. Moreover, they are eclectic in their pragmatism. There is no principled objection to using a bit of behaviourism and a slice of psychoanalysis in the same morning and with the same client. As long as it works, it is justified.

There is an obvious problem with this sort of alliance between social work and psychology. Social workers treat the discipline of psychology like a supermarket where theories fill the shelves like cans; they take the can, open it (often without understanding the cooking instructions), devour the contents and all too frequently suffer the indigestible consequences. This piecemeal selection is a hit and miss affair. Some cans look good due to prominent packaging; others are missed because they are on inaccessible shelves. When random work with the can opener leads to miserable results, its after-effect can be the abandonment of all theory. Disillusionment with the very process of theorizing takes over. People throw away their can opener and resort to intuition or fieldwork legend to guide their actions. This phenomenon of disillusionment leads to doubt about whether the supermarket method is best. Perhaps the strict dichotomy of roles between theorists and practitioners is inappropriate. Perhaps it would be more appropriate for psychologists and social workers to collaborate in the development, evaluation and implementation of theory. Possibly the grow-it-yourself method is more likely to lead to the social work good life. True collaboration involves the mutual exchange of knowledge and skills. It necessitates theorists and practitioners working as equals in a joint enterprise. This is turn, of course, demands that both groups are more sensitive to the values and needs of the other. It requires psychologists to examine the conditions under which social workers have to use theory and expects that social workers will learn how theories are created and evaluated. Perhaps this is too great a change in orientation to be hoped for just yet but this book was produced with the ideal of true collaboration in mind.

While the traditional form of alliances between social work and psychology has been from the supermarket-customer mould, the sort of psychology chosen for use by social workers has been similar on certain dimensions. Now this might seem, at first sight, a strange claim since social work's favourite and most long-lasting alliances over the years have been with psychoanalysis and behaviourism. Superficially at least, two stranger and more dissimilar bedfellows would be difficult to find. Psychoanalysis, positing a model of man founded on the battle of the instinctual duo, libido and Thanatos, against a plethora of ego defence mechanisms lodged in the unconscious, envisages the adult personality to be the inevitable result of infantile psychosexual development. Behaviourism, positing a model of man free of instincts and the unconscious where the individual is the malleable product of responses to stimuli, envisages the adult

2

personality to be situation-specific, the result of cumulative patterns of reinforcement. Of course, this merely caricatures these two schools of thought. It is not within the remit of this book to examine their tenets in depth or the fruits of their alliances with social work; other writers have done this, notably Yelloly (1980) on psychoanalysis and Jehu (1967) and Jehu *et al.* (1972) on behaviourism. Nevertheless, it can be seen that the models of man that psychoanalysts and behaviourists adopt are fundamentally different. Yet they are ironically similar in that they are individualist. They are both theories of the individual taken out of social context; they ignore or minimize the importance of the social processes which mould and give meaning to thought, feeling and action. They thus seek to understand and explain the individual without reference to the processes and structures of the surrounding society. It is an exercise akin to seeking to understand how water is transformed into steam without reference to the nature or source of heat. The resultant understanding is partial; the explanation is incomplete.

It is, however, hardly surprising that social work should find 'individualist' variants of psychology attractive. Social work, itself, has been until very recently 'individualist' in orientation. The object of intervention has been the individual's problem, the target for change the 'problem individual'. Of course, in considering the relationship between individualism in psychology and individualism in social work, the chicken and the egg problem arises. Social work, being individualist in orientation, may have then chosen individualist brands of psychology. But alternatively, the choice of individualist psychology may have pushed social work towards individualism. In truth, it seems unlikely that there is any unilinear causal relationship. It seems much more likely that the relationship is dialectical. Regardless of its genesis, an individualist social work found individualist psychology amenable to its ethics and objectives and, most importantly, to its world view. Moreover, it should be remembered that the choice was not exactly free. Until relatively recently most psychology which would be available to social workers was individualist. The growth of social psychology has been relatively slow and only certain limited aspects of it have been publicized widely. Social work can hardly be criticized for choosing paradigms which seemed to have greater maturity and which were easily available and already claimed therapeutic viability. The fact that no blame should attach to old choices does not, of course, mean that they should be maintained unchallenged especially as social work changes in response to altered legislation and demand. The prime objective of this book is to show what social psychology is and how social work can use it. The new alliance suggested is different in both form and content from its predecessors: it is based on active collaboration in implementing the data and theories of social psychology.

It is envisaged that social psychology can be useful to social work on two distinct levels. The first level is in the analysis of the problems of a client or a client group. Social psychology here can form the frame of reference for the analysis of the origin, course and consequences of a problem presented by a client or a group of clients. It may suggest apposite points of intervention and

3

what form intervention may take. Moreover, it may offer ways of erecting a reflexive understanding of the social worker's own role in the problem. The second level is in the analysis of the position of the profession of social work and the position of the individual social worker. At both these levels, the potential alliance between social work and social psychology is outlined in later chapters.

1.1 The Model of the Social Psychological Approach

It should be emphasized now, as it will be throughout the book, that no specific theory from within the remit of social psychology is being advocated here. Instead, it is the generic *social psychological approach* (SPA) to the analysis of a problem, the person presenting the problem and the social context in which it resides which is being advocated. The exact parameters of the SPA are the subject of the remainder of the book but in the rest of this chapter the object is to outline the model of the SPA to the social work process. But before going on to that a disclaimer needs to be made. No claim is being made here for the primacy of the SPA to the analysis of social work problems. There are other orientations based on various economic, political and social ideologies and theories to the analysis of such problems which are of considerable value and importance. The point is that the SPA fills a gap between the broad macrosocial perspectives offered by sociology and the narrow individualism of psychology tied to the medical model. More importantly, it provides pragmatic tools for intervention which analysts based in other theoretical or ideological traditions can use. The SPA dictates a way of looking at the world but it does not dictate what you see. Most importantly, the SPA actually carries prescriptions for action based on the analysis it instructs. Current orientations to analysis in social work merely tell the social worker what should be achieved but give few clues about how it should be achieved. Social workers have to resort to inadequate grafts of techniques from a variety of disciplines. These are not integrated. They fit together badly. The effect is similar to what happens when a child drops a pile of different jigsaw puzzles and the pieces from different puzzles get mixed up; attempts to solve any of the puzzles are then made even more difficult, every effort produces mismatch and distortion because the pieces from different sets demand different rules of solution. The SPA offers an *orientation to analysis and a series of techniques of intervention*. It thus suggests what the social worker should do and how that should be achieved. It is therefore a step towards eradicating the discrepancies which exist between what is demanded of the social worker and what the social worker knows how to achieve.

The SPA model of the social work process has three stages. Each stage is outlined below but all are described in detail in later chapters.

Stage I Analysis or Description

This entails the definition or description of the problem facing the social worker at each of four levels:

4

(i) the intrapsychic — the thoughts, feelings and actions of each individual
   involved in the problem;
(ii) the interpersonal — the relationships between individuals involved;
(iii) the intragroup — the structure and processes of any groups involved;
(iv) the intergroup — the relationships between any groups involved.

There are specific targets for description at each of these levels:

(a) identity
(b) relationships   These are the identifiable elements in
(c) groups   the problem
(d) environments

Each of these targets should be analysed at each of the four levels. So that, for
instance, an individual's identity processes can be described in terms of intrapsychic dynamics, relationships, group memberships, and relationships
between groups that are important to the individual. In fact, this can be done
for each target zone which means that the pattern of description can be very
complex (see Fig. 1.1).

Level of Analysis or Description		Target of Analysis
Intrapsychic		Identity
Interpersonal	Each level can be used	Relationships
Intragroup	with each target	Groups
Intergroup		Environments

Fig. 1.1

The descriptions may involve the use of information-gathering techniques
widely used in social psychology:

(i) the interview;
(ii) observation — both participant and non-participant;
(iii) questionnaire and survey techniques;
(iv) archival data, e.g. case histories, police records, community newspa-
    pers.

Stage II   Explanation

Having described the salient characteristics of the problem it is necessary to
seek out the processes which are involved in its genesis and its maintenance. It
may be that processes which cause the problem are not synonymous with those
which maintain it. Effectively, the social worker who wishes to eradicate the
problem is primarily concerned with the processes which maintain it since these
are the processes which must be annulled or diverted if change is to be brought
about.
   The SPA designates four processes as central to all social behaviour and thus
central to the social work problem:

(i) construal
(ii) consistency

5

(iii) comparison

(iv) conformity

Many social psychological theories have these four processes as the core of their explanations. The social worker must choose between the different theories in order to explain the dynamics of the problem. The means of evaluating a theory and choosing the right one or ones for the social work process are discussed in Chapter 13.

Stage III Change

The social psychological theory chosen to explicate the dynamics of the problem will indicate the features of the situation which need to be changed if the problem is to be ameliorated. But it is important to realize that the social worker has to decide upon what would be the optimal result of any change induced before embarking on any intervention. The social worker may set up goals for change autonomously or in collaboration with the clients or other professionals. It is not of great significance how the goals are established, the fact that they should be established is of greater importance. How the goals are established only becomes important when this is itself an objective for the social worker. For instance, some social workers feel that client collaboration in the specification of goals of intervention is vital. Once the goals are established the SPA would indicate that in order to achieve them *the social worker must direct intervention at certain target zones (equivalent to the targets of description) — identity, relationships, groups and the environment. Altering the processes of these target zones is the object of intervention.*

The form of intervention will be shaped by knowledge of the way in which processes of construal, consistency, comparison and conformity control social behaviour. The social worker, informed by the theory chosen to explicate this particular problem, seeks to employ these processes to bring about change. Specific theories about the induction of personal and social change can be employed to direct intervention strategies.

Reflexivity

This is not really a stage in the process so much as an orientation which should be adopted throughout the other three stages described above. Reflexivity is demanded of the social worker in the SPA. The social worker must be self-consciously aware of his or her own role in the problem and in the process of change. This awareness has two aspects:

(i) understanding the impact of the social worker on the clients and the problem's dynamics;

(ii) understanding the impact of the problem upon the social worker.

Both impacts are analysable in exactly the same way that the problem itself is analysable — through the use of levels of analysis and of explanatory processes. Since the social worker is often the very channel through which persuasion and coercion work to bring about the desired change in the situation, it is vital to understand how this channel works. It should be emphasized here that reflexivity does not refer simply to the social worker's understanding of himself or herself. It refers to an understanding of the 'self' in interaction with others while in the occupational role of social worker. This is a very different sort of understanding from awareness of the 'self' in a vacuum.

It is fairly important in adopting the SPA to the social work process to realize that reflexivity changes analysis, explanation and strategies of change. Moreover, each of the three stages in the process are tied together in a feedback loop. So they can be represented in a cybernetic flow chart (Fig. 1.2).

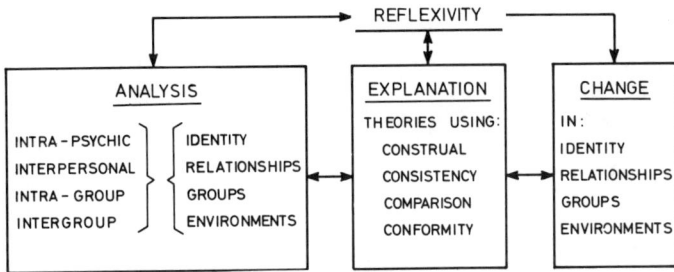

Fig. 1.2   The model of the SPA to the social work process.

In the following chapters each element in this model of the SPA to the social work process is described in detail. The purpose here has simply been to inform the reader of the integrated model.

Part II
The Nature of Social Psychology

2
The Character of Social Psychology

In seeking to describe the fundamentals of the character of social psychology, three dicta need to be remembered:

(i)   the character of social psychology changes across time;
(ii) the character of social psychology changes according to location;
(iii) the character of social psychology depends on the individuals involved in its study and development.

Since all of these three forces for variation in the character of the discipline act simultaneously and frequently interact with each other to instigate change, it can be seen that capturing the essence of social psychology might be likened to capturing free-flowing mercury: difficult.

Bearing in mind this warning that generalizations which make social psychology seem in any way static or homogeneous should be regarded with suspicion, it is possible to go on to make generalizations, which may be grouped under four headings:

(i)   the subject matter of social psychology;
(ii) the theories of social psychology;
(iii) the methods of social psychology;
(iv) the crisis of social psychology.

2.1   Subject Matter

Proshansky and Seidenberg (1970) argued that the definition of a field of enquiry can be either descriptive or theoretical. According to them descriptive definitions designate the kinds of events subject to analysis and study, whereas theoretical definitions designate the observed phenomena. Obviously any such clear-cut dichotomy is simply a convenient fiction. More often than not theoretical presuppositions predetermine in the social sciences what phenomena will be studied *and* can, in fact, bring such phenomena into existence by drawing a boundary around a set of social activities and then labelling them a phenomenon. In such a situation, any attempt to describe a discipline through descriptions of the phenomena it studies will immediately carry theoretical considerations into the discussion. An example might help here: one of the central topics for study by social psychologists is attitudes, yet the notion that 'attitudes' exist derives directly from specific social psychological theories. The point here is that an 'attitude' is both something to be studied and an explanatory concept which is an integral part of social psychological theory. This sort of duality means that in describing the subject matter of social psychology it is difficult to avoid immediately introducing perhaps unwanted theoretical overtones. These overtones are undoubtedly audible in the generalizations about subject matter outlined below.

In fact, it is possible to provide generalizations about the subject matter of social psychology at two levels: the idealized and the realistic. At the idealized level, it is what social psychologists believe they should be studying which would be described. At the realistic level, it is what social psychologists actually *do* study which would be described. Descriptions at both levels are necessary in order to understand the social psychological approach completely.

Allport in his lucid and comprehensive chapter for *The Handbook of Social Psychology* (1954, 1968) entitled 'The Historical Background of Modern Social Psychology' pointed out that 'the key problem of social psychology — man's social nature — is both ancient and persistent'. When the task of social psychology is defined as the analysis of 'man's social nature' it can be argued that Plato was a social psychologist, together with all other great social, political and economic theorists since his time. Of course, the alternative is to admit that such a vague specification of the task is tantamount to no specification and to demand more. Nevertheless, it gives us the first idealized generalization about the character of social psychology.

Generalization 1

   Social psychologists study individuals in their social context.

Ideally, social psychologists are not interested in the individual alone deprived of his or her social environment. In fact, there is a strong feeling that, as Krech *et al.* (1962) put it, '. . . every man lives in a social world, and no psychologist can study the behaviour of an asocial man' (p. 7). The idea is that even when the individual is physically isolated from others, they and the society they form remain a psychological presence for the socialized individual. However, it would be equally true to say that ideally social psychologists are not interested in examining society and its processes without regard to individuals. In 1902,

10

Cooley seems to have captured what was to be at the base of social psychology; he said:

> A separate individual is an abstraction unknown to experience, and so likewise is society when regarded as something apart from individuals. The real thing is Human Life, which may be considered either in an individual aspect or in a social, that is to say a general, aspect; but is always as a matter of fact, both individual and general.

This tendency to see the Individual and Society as dialectically related and consequently as a single target for analysis may arise from the dual paternity of social psychology. The term social psychology originated in 1908 when two books with that title were published. One was written by William McDougall, normally regarded as a psychologist, and sought to explain social behaviour in terms of personality based on instincts. The other was the product of a sociologist, Edward Ross, who deemed that social behaviour was determined by situational constraints which generated imitation and irresistible forces of 'suggestion'. Thus social psychology had one progenitor in psychology and the other in sociology and it has found itself peripheral to both major disciplines. Psychology has its social psychologists and sociology has its social psychologists. The social psychology taught on psychology courses is very different from that taught on sociology courses and the two wings of social psychology rarely come together. In practice, the social psychologists in the psychology camp concentrate on the Individual and those in the sociological camp, where they survive, on Society. Thus, the idealistic view of the subject matter of social psychology begins to crumble; few can maintain the pretence that they study the Individual in Society in any grandiose way.

In practice, social psychologists have pared down the task facing them by restricting their subject matter to what are considered tractable problems. A second, more realistic, generalization about the subject matter of social psychology can therefore be specified:

Generalization 2

Social psychologists study social influence processes.

Allport (1954) is explicit about this:

> . . . social psychologists regard their discipline as *an attempt to understand and explain how the thought, feeling, and behaviour of individuals are influenced by the actual, imagined, or implied presence of other human beings.* (p. 5, italics from the original)

Many other writers have reaffirmed this emphasis that social psychology is about the analysis of 'the influence that people have upon the beliefs or behaviour of others' (Aronson, 1976, p. 5). They include the authors of most of the student texts on social psychology (e.g. Hollander & Hunt, 1976; Newcomb *et al.*, 1975; Steiner & Fishbein, 1965; Wrightsman, 1972). Hollander and Hunt (1976) are perhaps most insistent upon the connection between this emphasis on social influence processes and the broader aim of understanding the individual in social context:

> Social psychology is a field of study which attempts to understand social behaviour. In particular, it studies influence relationships either between individuals, or with respect to groups, institutions, and society. The distinctiveness of social psychology arises from two features: first, its essential focus upon the *individual* as a participant in social processes; and, second, its concern with the *analysis* of these processes, through appropriate research methods, to provide explanations rather than mere descriptions. (p. 2, italics from original)

In effect, the analysis of such social influence processes necessitates the identification of the spheres in which they operate. There has been a marked tendency to regard each of the spheres of their operation as a separate area for social psychology. So Raven and Rubin (1976) could describe the areas of social psychological study thus: people alone and together; liking, disliking, friendship and aggression; cooperation and competition; interpersonal power; the structure of groups and the effect of group membership on individual behaviour; group performance and leadership; and intergroup conflict and cooperation. Although not exhaustive, this is a realistic and representative sample of the areas in which social psychological study takes place.

2.2 Theories

Wrightsman (1972) stated:

> Social behaviour and interpersonal relationships are conceptualized by various theories. In psychology, a theory is a set of conventions, created by the theorist, as a way of representing reality. Thus no theory is given or predetermined; each theory makes a set of assumptions about the nature of the behaviour it seeks to describe and explain. In addition to such assumptions, a theory contains a set of empirical definitions and constructs (concepts). While social psychological theories clearly differ from each other with regard to assumptions, constructs, and emphases, all such theories serve common purposes, one of which is to organize and explicate the relationships between diverse bits of knowledge about social phenomena. (p. 5)

From this it is clear that, although social psychological theories may be created in the same way and may be designed to serve similar ends, they are in substance very varied.

Generalization 3

There is no single integrative theoretical framework in social psychology.

Diversity of theories is the order of the day and there is no common language of descriptive or explanatory concepts that all theorists will agree upon. Without an overall integrative framework, there has been a tendency towards ever greater fragmentation with mini-theories, which are in reality no more than odd hypotheses, evolving to explain very narrow social behaviours in highly

12

specific contexts. Frequently, such hypotheses are directly derived from a single experimental context; they fit that experiment. The problem then arises when a directly contradictory hypothesis is derived from and supported by a slightly different experimental context. The two contradictory hypotheses then both have empirical backing and their relative usefulness cannot be consensually established. Often, the dilemma could be resolved if the two competitive hypotheses could be shown to fit under the umbrella of a larger theoretical framework which specified the circumstances in which each could be said to operate optimally. However, there are few theorists who carry such umbrellas. Thus a fourth generalization is possible:

Generalization 4

Social psychology is littered with mutually exclusive hypotheses about social behaviour, all of which seem to have some empirical support.

Much of the substantive content of these theories or hypotheses will be examined in later chapters and it is inappropriate to do that here. However, there are one or two observations which can be made here about their substantive content. In most of these theories the idealized target for social psychological study 'the individual in social context' is approached only tortuously. The targets for explanation are specific social behaviours or events and the explanations themselves are virtually invariably lodged at the level of the individual. The cognitions and the motives of the individual are seen to be the prime determiners of action. Global explanations of social action which might span from the analysis of individual dynamics through to the exploration of societal processes are simply not available. Social psychology may have been bred from both psychology and sociology but it does not unite them, even theoretically, in itself. The theorist will opt for one path or the other: the individual or the society, and once that decision is made the level at which the explanation is lodged follows. The choice of path by the theorist is, of course, not random. The path chosen depends obviously to some extent upon the character of the individual theorist and upon his or her past experiences. It was no mere chance happening that Jews who fled to America from Fascism in Europe in the 1930s should have studied the origins of racial prejudice and authoritarianism (Adorno *et al.*, 1950). The individual experiences of the theorist seem to explain the choice of subject for study in many cases. However, they do not truly elucidate why the theorist will choose a particular level of explanation. This seems to be much more closely tied to the sociopolitical context within which the theorist works and the intellectual tradition with which it is invested.

Recent exchanges between the social psychologists of the West and those of the Soviet Union have provided poignant evidence of the importance of sociopolitical context for the theorist. Strickland (1979) in reporting on a conference where East and West social psychologists met for the first time in any numbers for over 50 years describes how difficult communication between the two sides was. There was, in fact, a twofold language barrier: the expected semantic one and an unexpected conceptual one. Concepts basic to the Western view of social psychology simply did not exist in the Eastern analytical frame. Concepts founded on notions of individualism and autonomy were not used in the Soviet social psychology; just as concepts based on collectivism and total interdependence did not find their way into Western social psychology. Thus the dominant ideologies of each society had infiltrated the theory building of their respective social psychologists. This is not surprising. After all, social psychologists are a product of their society and no matter how hard they try they can never be objective observers of it. Dominant ideologies will determine the level of analysis and the level of explanation they adopt.

There is a further fundamental influence on the level of explanation adopted that should also be mentioned. Social psychologists largely exist within academic communities that have their own powerful élites and intellectual traditions. If a new theorist is to gain acceptance and credence he or she must gain it from these élites which administer the tradition. Morawski (1979) describes this system at some length and very interestingly. The most that can be said here is that the structure of social psychological communities tends to be a force for conservatism and against innovation or diversity. This means that once a level of explanation is adopted, it tends to stay. The effects of two distinct intellectual traditions, shepherded by their professional élites, can be seen in the contrast between American and European social psychology. In the States, social psychology pursues the ideal of positivist empiricism; it is founded on highly controlled experiments with individuals or artificial groups. In Europe, particularly on the Continent, the emulation of the physical sciences has always been less ardent. Social psychology in the States became tied to the behaviourist traditions while in Europe it has lain inside a complex network of psychoanalytic, symbolic interactionist and Marxist tines. No claim should be made here that these two traditions never cross-fertilize; indeed they do and many a hybrid has resulted. The point is that there are identifiably distinct traditions separated by the Atlantic and the result is a series of very different social psychological theories.

Generalization 5

Social psychological theories are highly dependent upon the sociopolitical context from which they spring. They are also tied to the intellectual traditions of the communities in which their originators reside.

Being responsive to the demands of dominant ideologies and the impelling social problems of the moment, social psychology has wandered from the straight and narrow like the drunk that cannot walk the policeman's straight line. There is little continuity across time in the research of social psychologists even within a single community. In America, the 1900s saw an emphasis on research on groups with explanations focusing on coercive social forces; the 1920s and 1930s saw a move to the examination of the individual and explanation in terms of personality and attitudes; the 1940s and 1950s saw the pendulum swing back towards investigations of the behaviour of collectivities and

14

explanations based on situational constraints; and the 1960s and 1970s allowed for growing interest in the relationships between groups and explanations centred on large-scale processes. Such progress through fads and fashions has not permitted the accumulation of an integrated body of knowledge or theory. The charm of social psychology might be said to lie in the fact that any aspirant theorist can try his or her luck. New theories blossom like desert flowers after rain, and they fade as fast. Without the masterplan to integrate their efforts social psychologists work furiously but all too often in different directions. Instead of taking up the digging of the tunnel where the last person left off, each starts a new tunnel. Mining disasters are not uncommon.

Generalization 6

Social psychological theorists do not learn the lessons of their discipline's past failures.

In fact, the final generalization in this section on theory really originates from the fact that social psychologists in the main have a very poor sense of history — whether their own or anyone else's. Social psychological theories tend to deal with social phenomena as if they were in a temporal vacuum. The phenomenon for analysis is sliced out of time, out of its place in history. Most frequently, the use of experimental manipulations means that the event had no place in history anyhow. By doing this, social psychology loses the sense of how events and processes are connected in time. Theories in social psychology are so chronically bound to their own sociopolitical context because they do not trace phenomena in time and place. Yet in order to understand a social phenomenon it is vital to know how it changes in the long term. For instance, in order to understand conformity, it is necessary to know not just under what conditions an individual will conform now but also whether those same conditions would have induced conformity ten years ago or will do so in ten years time because if they do not it might just be possible to say that the nature of conformity is changing. If our theories could then seek an explanation for the change in the nature of conformity we would not only get closer to a dynamic theory of social processes, we would also be able to locate the individual in a changing social context. A move to this form of historicism would not be difficult; it would simply mean that replications of past research should be treated with respect and where they generate findings incompatible with those expected the question should be asked: 'Does this mean that people's responses to this situation are genuinely changing?' Until that happens, social psychology will remain historically naive.

Generalization 7

Social psychological theories are atemporal.

2.3 Methods

In talking about the 'methods' of social psychology, we are really talking about

15

the tools and techniques which are used to describe and explain social behaviour. Since social psychology professes to be a science these techniques rely heavily on the empiricist model of enquiry. That is to say, social psychologists rarely indulge in armchair theorizing; they traffic in data and evidence rather than assertion and assumption. When assertions are made they should, at least ideally, be supported by data. Thus the process of theory building goes something like this: the theorist observes a social phenomenon and wants to know why it occurs (the phenomenon might be that young mothers with infants in prams take more risks in crossing the road than other pedestrians); intuitively the theorist may think this phenomenon occurs for a particular reason (these young mothers believe drivers will be more likely to give way to a pram); the theorist then has to test this notion (it is necessary to gain access to the prampushers' reasons for crossing the road in the way they do). If the notion is supported by the data, the theorist might go on to build more elaborate notions around it (for instance, that young mothers feel themselves to be a specially indulged class which encourages them to feel invulnerable, etc.). However, if the data falsify the original explanation, it has to be amended. The data may then provide clues as to the real explanation. Alternatively, the data gathered may have been narrowly testing a particular explanation and fail to provide any further clues. If this is the case, the process may start over virtually from scratch. Theory building at its best is thus a cyclical process: moving from hypothesis to evidence back to hypothesis to start over again.

The social psychologist's methods for gathering evidence and testing hypotheses are varied. Secord and Backman (1964) argue that they can be hung along a continuum from the purely experimental to the purely non-experimental methods. Experimental and non-experimental methods vary primarily in the degree of control exerted by the investigator over the behaviour observed. In experiments, the investigator tends to have almost complete control: normally, the investigator will choose who takes part in the experiment; the investigator will design the experimental situation, determining what happens to the people during the experiment; and will then control the channels through which these people are allowed to respond to the experiment. Such experiments are created to rest hypotheses about cause − effect relationships. In order to do that, the experimenter will introduce the hypothesized cause and observe for the expected behavioural effect; this can then be compared with behaviour in situations where the 'cause' is not introduced. Of course, in order to ensure correct causal inferences, the experimenter has to exclude all other causes of response variation. This often means that experimental situations are highly contrived and artificial; they simplify the context and potential expression of a response to the point where it becomes unrecognizable. As Tajfel and Fraser (1978) point out:

> The major advantages of experiments are in the relative simplicity of their logic and results; these are also their major disadvantages, since only too often simplicity turns into blatant over-simplification. (p. 12)

Moreover, the experimental method is known to have other serious defects.

16

These are discussed at length in Badia *et al.* (1970) and Sommer and Sommer (1980). It is enough here to say that they centre upon the fact that experiments in which the subject matter is people and their behaviour do not work like those in the physical sciences. A chemical in a chemistry experiment is hardly likely to be aware that it is being experimented upon. People are eminently aware that they are in an experiment normally, even if they do not know its purposes. This fact of their awareness influences their behaviour. It can be argued that they cannot behave in an experiment in exactly the way they would behave outside it.

The simple fact that they are in an experiment impinges upon their every action. They may try to do what they think is socially desirable or what the experimenter would like them to do. Alternatively, they may try to guess what the experiment is all about and make sure they behave in an unexpected fashion just to be difficult. No matter what reaction they have to the experience of being in an experiment, the central point remains: their responses are not uncontaminated by that experience. Thus the information gained from the experiment is in some senses contaminated and one has to question how far it is justifiable to generalize from experiments to behaviour outside them. Under experimental conditions, in an artificial setting while trying to out-guess the experimenter, you might hypothetically be willing to kill your father-in-law; but would you really do it?

Some of these difficulties are overcome by non-experimental methods. Non-experimental methods involve no manipulation of events by the investigator who merely observes and records (with varying degrees of stringency) naturally occurring relationships. There are two major areas of difficulty in the use of non-experimental methods: the problem of measurement and the problem of causal inference. The problem of measurement is really very simple. Non-experimental methods do not require the investigator to create or control the context in which observations are made, nor do they require him or her to pre-determine what sort of behaviour is permissible. However, in order to measure effectively the response to that context some sort of intervention will be necessary. This intervention may simply be at the level of the investigator being present during the response, but it may involve interactions between the investigator and the respondent (in interviews, for instance, when the respondent has to describe the response) and these may be highly structured (as in the use of questionnaires). Where such structures are imported, it is no longer reasonable to assume that the investigator is merely reporting naturally occurring behaviours. Measurement techniques shape behaviour because they channel it and are selective in what bits of it they consider. In so far as this happens in the use of non-experimental methods, then the results are contaminated by the procedure that gathered them. It is no longer possible to claim that such results reflect with total lucidity the 'natural' situation and no longer reasonable to generalize from them to events outside the investigation. The second problem is that of causal inference. Non-experimental methods will normally allow the formulation: 'X precedes Y'. The investigator observing X and Y, observes X invariably to precede Y; that is to say their occurrence is correlated. However, to use an old saw, correlation does not equal causation. Simply because they co-vary in occurrence does not mean that X causes Y, or Y causes X. In fact, both may, for instance, be the product of some third event: Z. Alternatively Y may cause A which in turn causes X, when Y alone could not cause X. The point about the non-experimental method is that, because it does not provide room for the manipulation of possible causes, it can only provide evidence of correlations not causal relationships. This is of course a drawback for a discipline that seeks to specify cause and effect. Thus the non-experimental method while providing data which are grounded in real events, provides data that are not easily interpretable.

Generalization 8

Social psychologists rely on empirical methods; all of which are flawed.

Each method or technique has its strengths and weaknesses. Data from archives, surveys, field studies, 'natural' experiments, field experiments, and laboratory experiments can always be in some senses valid and invalid simultaneously. Luckily, each technique tends to have its own strengths and weaknesses and these are not identical to those of other techniques. Thus, a series of techniques, each flawed in a different manner, when used in unison can provide a more complete understanding of a phenomenon than any used in isolation. Increasingly, social psychologists are turning to the mixed method approach. They are even beginning to see the advantages of truly integrated methods.

Generalization 9

Social psychologists are aware of the inadequacies of their methods and are seeking remedies.

2.4 The Crisis of Social Psychology

Unfortunately, sometimes the remedies are worse than the illness. Being aware that they have no integrated macro-theory and no integrated mosaic of method, social psychologists have for some time now felt considerably ill at ease. The 'crisis' of social psychology has been one of self-doubt. Really the term 'crisis' is a misnomer. The threat is chronic rather than acute. Its expression is typified by the publications of the early 1970s (Harré & Secord, 1972; Israel & Tajfel, 1972; Armistead, 1974). It was a time of self-castigation on many fronts. Experiments, when not considered mere frippery — fun and games in the laboratory, were labelled 'dehumanizing' because manipulations frequently involved the deception and demeaning of those involved. Any other sort of research without immediate practical or policy implication was deemed pointless. Theory without ideological commitment was scorned and any which failed to take account of social processes was demoted. It would be wrong to

18

imply by the use of the past tense that this process of self-criticism is at an end. However, its first full flush of youth has faded. It has mellowed into a more constructive phase.

Dissatisfaction with the ethics and the logic of experimentation has led to greater reliance on non-experimental methods. Most particularly, it has led to the belief that the investigator and those investigated need to cooperate in order to understand the phenomenon under scrutiny. Those investigated are not called 'subjects' and are not subjected to manipulation. They are treated as equals in the research process — or ideally so. When the investigator wishes to know why a person acts in a particular way, he or she asks that person. Of course, this may mean that it is now the turn of the investigator to be deceived. That is the risk the investigator using this ethogenic or ethnomethodological approach has to take and risks can be minimized in a number of ways. The real point is that this approach encourages the researcher to deal with the problems which are of importance to those under research because then they will cooperate more readily; which encourages the researcher to examine the political and pragmatic implications of the research; and this, in turn, predisposes the researcher to locate the resultant theory at a wider social level. On the whole, social psychologists adopting this approach are keen to capture knowledge not for its own sake but because it enables individuals and societies to grow and change. Such people tend to believe in humanistic psychology and phenomenology.

One important point about what is in some quarters called the 'new social psychology' should be noted. Ethogenics encompasses an approach to data gathering and an orientation towards those who are investigated; it does not have any single underlying theory or explanation of social behaviour. Some of those who adopt it take over the dramaturgical model of Goffman (e.g. 1971) but this is not a theory, merely an extended metaphor for description.

The self-doubt of the early 1970s did lead to theoretical developments. Particularly, it led to a revival of emphasis on the individual taken in social context. Tajfel (1978), Moscovici (1972), and Doise (1978) have led the way towards causal accounts of social behaviour in terms of overall social processes and against explanations in terms of general laws of individual motivation. Thus the move has been from explanation in individual terms towards explanation in terms of the social processes of groups and social categories (Tajfel, 1981).

Simultaneously, those social psychologists whose work had typified the highly controlled, individualist research of the 1960s have broadened their perspective. They have not dropped what is valuable about the experimental method but they no longer focus on small fragments of social behaviour decontextualized. They are now examining the processes involved in whole 'social episodes' (Forgas, 1979) and are analysing complete 'social situations' (Argyle, et al., 1981).

With this greater width of perspective has come a certain degree of retrenchment. Yet people have begun to defend the experimental method:

Success or failure depend largely upon the quality of the ideas (or theories) from which an experiment derives. Good ideas (or interesting theories) often lead to experiments which expand our knowledge and provide new *hints* about the texture of our social life; trivial ideas (or theories) lead to trivial or silly experiments. This simple truth applies with equal force to other methods of research in social psychology. . . .' (Tajfel and Fraser, 1978, p. 12. © Henri Tajfel and Colin Fraser, 1978. Reprinted by permission of Penguin Books Ltd.)

Moreover, there is some idea that it is not a social psychologist's job to analyse the context of individual and group action. The analysis of the social, political and economic context of action should be performed by sociologists, political scientists and economists, respectively, or so the argument goes. As Eiser (1980) puts it, the social psychologist is 'not a Jack of all trades' (p. xiii). Increasingly, the criticized — having made their initial concessions — are turning to the attack. They question whether their critics have actually provided any substitutes for the institutions of experiment and systematic theoretical analysis which they attacked. Since the critics are relatively unproductive in terms of research, these are telling retaliations.

Thus the pendulum swings slowly back and forth or, rather, the spiral cycles upwards because criticisms are not just forgotten, they are incorporated in ever more complex structures. Ultimately, it is rather difficult to decide who follows the 'new social psychology' and who the 'old'; the two mingle indistinguishably. Perhaps this process of amalgamation across time is the solution to the 'crisis of social psychology'. It is strange that two perspectives, like the ethogenic and the experimental, can initially appear so mutually exclusive and yet grow together, becoming more alike until they lose their individual identities. Perhaps this is an overstatement and yet this process of compromise is strong: the radical, changing the establishment, is changed by it.

Generalization 10

The crisis of social psychology generated new types of theory and research which are now being assimilated into the establishment view.

2.5 Character or Silhouette: Concluding Remarks

The sketch of social psychology above captures something like its silhouette rather than its character. It is a perfunctory and oversimplified representation of its multiple personalities. Nevertheless, the unique *social psychological approach* to the understanding of people's behaviour can be seen there. It is founded on the dual belief that social behaviour and networks can be profitably analysed and effectively explained. It is grounded in empiricism. It seeks to be socially relevant and is increasingly associated with an action orientation.

Any discipline which attempts to explain why people act the way they do and seeks to predict their actions is valuable for a social worker. Any discipline which explicitly applies itself to social problems is even more valuable to a social worker. But any discipline which, having analysed those problems, is willing to speculate about remedial measures is indispensable to a social worker. The contention is that social psychology is such a discipline. Overstating the case in this way is, of course, designed to infuriate readers just enough so that they read on.

Thus far, it is the general properties of social psychology that have been considered. In the remaining chapters in this part of the book, an attempt will be made to describe some of the most central substantive findings and theories of social psychology.

3

Relationships

Social psychologists have been concerned with three central questions in their study of relationships between people:

(i)   how people form their impressions of others when they first meet — the *process of impression formation*;

(ii) what leads people to like or dislike others — the *process of interpersonal attraction*;

(iii) how long-term relationships develop — the *process of interpersonal commitment*.

The answers to each sort of question have considerable value for the social work process and are therefore summarized below. It should be noted that this summary is highly selective, dealing with key concepts and theories. The reader wishing to delve further in this area might begin with Robert Hinde's (1979) sensible review *Towards Understanding Relationships* and then sample the collection of readings in Duck (1977) and Huston (1974).

3.1   The Processes of Impression Formation and Attribution

The processes of impression formation and attribution tend to go hand in hand. Impression formation is the process of forming judgements about the qualities or characteristics of other people. Attribution is the process of assigning causes or reasons for actions or events; it focuses upon attempts to explain behaviour. The connection between these two processes is quite obvious: we often infer a person's characteristics from the way he or she acts and the reasons

22

for such action; moreover, we often use what we believe to be a person's characteristics to explain why he or she behaves in a particular way. For instance, take the case of Kathy who hits Alan after he has made certain sexual advances towards her. The observer who did not know Kathy might conclude from this scene that she was a young woman who believed in propriety, and that this was her salient characteristic. The observer who knew Kathy of old and had come to believe her to be aggressive might take a very different line and assume that the attack on Alan could be explained in terms of it being yet another example of Kathy's aggressive character. The impressions you have of others and the attributions you make about them are thus interwoven.

Impression formation and attribution processes are obviously important in the social work process. A social worker is continually meeting new people and is expected to deal with them. To act effectively, the social worker has to be able to form a reasonably accurate impression of the new client quickly. An almost instinctive assessment of the client's characteristics is undertaken immediately. This is, of course, only a preliminary assessment; the effective social worker will set up a series of hypotheses about the client that can be tested in later meetings and the assessment will be modified accordingly. Nevertheless, this 'first impression' can be vital because it can predispose the social worker to regard the client in particular ways and relate towards him or her in a limited fashion. The danger of 'first impressions' is that they can act as 'self-fulfilling prophecies'. In other words, a social worker having decided when first meeting a client that he was, for instance, too simple-minded to handle his own finances might never give that client an opportunity to handle his own money; in such a situation, the client has no chance to prove the social worker wrong and, more importantly, may actually become incapable of dealing with money matters due to lack of practice or declining self-confidence. The social worker, therefore, has to monitor the impact of 'first impressions'. The same could be said of attribution processes. The social worker is continually faced with the task of explaining why people behave in the way they do. Explaining why a problem exists is fundamental to its solution. Understanding why Jane, who is 16, is prostituting herself may improve the chances of stopping her doing so. Yet attribution, like impression formation, has its dangers. Explanations can be attractive and even mesmeric without being in the slightest degree correct. Where explanations are evolved, they have a strange power to mould our future perception of the problem, so that only events or acts which can be encompassed within the existing explanatory framework are noticed or invested with importance. Again, the social worker has to be wary and monitor this process of attribution. Monitoring both processes is facilitated when one knows something about how they work.

Impression Formation

The process of forming judgements about the qualities of other people is continual. Throughout the course of social interaction, evidence is gathered and judgements are made. This process is necessary because we need to be able to

23

predict what others will do and understand why they do it. Having an image of what a person is helps us to deal with him or her largely because it promotes anticipation; it enables us to organize and select information and predisposes certain sorts of response to that person.

The impressions formed about others obviously depend upon how they present themselves and how they behave. However, impressions are not simply founded on what there is objectively to see about a person. People, notoriously, do *not* see all there is to see about others. They are selective about the sort of information they will accept as permissible evidence. Selection is guided by: (1) sets of assumptions about 'human nature'; (2) stereotypes and prototypes; (3) personal constructs. All three influences on selection and inference will be discussed below. Throughout it should be remembered that impressions are a function of the interaction between what there is to 'see' and how it is 'seen'.

1. Assumptions about 'human nature' are harboured by most people, they are sometimes glorified by the label 'philosophies'. Such assumptions can normally be expressed in the format: 'all people are good at heart'; 'Man is perfectable'; 'everyone is ultimately selfish'; or 'humans are rational beings'. The precise content of these dicta about 'human nature' varies but they represent global beliefs about mankind. They are developed sometimes from personal experience, at other times they are simply adopted from those with whom we are intimate or those we respect. They act to shape expectations. If it is assumed that 'everybody is good at heart', in the last resort the villain is expected to be retrievable — if only the right efforts are made.

People are rarely forced to change their philosophy of 'human nature'. Even when it is shown repeatedly to be wrong, such a philosophy is maintained. The person believing it will often simply not perceive evidence which falsifies it, whereas evidence which supports it is avidly collected. Expectations derived from the philosophy which are disconfirmed are simply forgotten or, more subtly, such expectations are reinterpreted so as to appear to be confirmed.

Impressions of others are formed within the framework of the philosophy. The pressures to 'see' people in ways which confirm the philosophy are strong. The more fiercely a person believes a philosophy to be correct, the less chance there is for objectivity in judgements about others. Of course, not everyone holds such a philosophy about human nature or, at least, not everyone has such a well-formulated picture of the rest of humanity. Unfortunately, there are other factors which confound objectivity and these can be said to operate for everyone.

2. Stereotypes and prototypes confound any chance of objectivity in the perception of others.

Stereotypes. Wrightsman and Deaux (1981) define stereotypes as 'relatively rigid and oversimplified conceptions of groups of people in which all individuals in a given group are labelled with the so-called group characteristics' (p. 72). An example of stereotypy here might highlight its key features. Someone might hold a stereotype of feminists which depicted all feminists as unattractive, aggressive, domineering and sexually abnormal. The first thing

24

to notice is that the stereotype ignores the fact that there are many brands of feminism ranging from the radical to the moderate. The stereotype acts to dichotomize women: there are feminists and there are those who are not. Secondly, the stereotype attributes characteristics to *all* feminists. The stereotype acts to obliterate individual variability. *All* feminists are unattractive, aggressive, domineering and sexually abnormal. Once a woman has been categorized as a feminist the stereotype indicates what one should expect. Thirdly, the characteristics which form the stereotype are boldly drawn and simplified. Stereotypes rarely use subtle concepts.

The oversimplicity of stereotypes is indicative of what has been regarded as their prime function: simplifying the processing of information. They are said to work in the following way: a new person enters our life, we categorize them as belonging to a particular group of people, once the group is identified we do not have to explore their personality further because the stereotype comes into play and we assume that they possess a certain set of characteristics like all members of the group. The stereotype saves us time and energy; since we know all feminists are unattractive and aggressive, we do not need to gather information about the one we have in front of us. In a world full of brief meetings and inadequate information, the stereotype can be adaptive.

The stereotype has a further function. A stereotype can act to legitimate the *status quo*; it can be used as a rationalization for the state of relations between two groups. For instance, the stereotype held by whites about blacks in the USA just before the Civil War served to support slavery. Negroes were pictured as childlike, irresponsible, and incapable of self-determination. The stereotype 'explained' why they should be enslaved: it was for their own good, after all they could not be expected to look after themselves. In similar vein, women have suffered from the stereotype that they are indecisive, emotional, and childlike. Here, again, the stereotype is used to deprecate the subordinate group and, thereby, sustain their subordination.

The painful irony of these situations is that those with power develop a stereotype of themselves which is imposed on the people that are subordinated. Blacks and women not only accepted the white man's stereotype of their own groups but they accepted his glorification of his own group. Until the growth of the Black Power movement and the Women's Liberation movement, blacks and women seem to have failed to evolve stereotypes which might protect themselves. They actually adopted stereotypes of the white male which proclaimed his superior intellect, morality and emotional stability.

Breaking the power of a stereotype is an extremely difficult thing to do. The stereotype acts as a filter though which experiences are channelled. Experiences which challenge the stereotype are filtered out. Markedly, stereotypes have implicit behavioural prescriptions and proscriptions. The man who accepts the stereotype of feminists which was portrayed above is unlikely to seek their company, in avoiding feminists he is unlikely to gain information which disconfirms the stereotype and the stereotype sustains itself. The stereotype can also work in another way. If feminists are believed to be unattractive, then the person can make a syllogistic error of assuming unattractive women to be feminists. In fact, Goldberg *et al.* (1975) showed that, where no other information is available, people will say that unattractive women are more likely to be feminists than attractive ones. Moreover, Jacobson and Koch (1978) found that many people believe unattractive women endorse feminism because they lack other goals. This is a nice example of how a stereotype is double edged: one should avoid feminists because they are unattractive, etc., and one should avoid the unattractive because they are feminists. The chances of disconfirming the stereotype dwindle rapidly. There is one further important feature of stereotypes which hampers their eradication. Stereotypes are often applied inconsistently. So, for instance, a stereotype might be: 'all Scots are tight-fisted' but there is no insurance that it will be applied every time one meets a person from Scotland. People are keen to make exceptions to their stereotypical rules. Thus, 'all Scots are mean' might be the stereotype, then the person holding that stereotype meets Jimmy; Jimmy is a Scot but Jimmy is *not* mean. If the rules of logic applied, the stereotype should be abandoned since it has been shown to be wrong: if Jimmy is not mean but is a Scot, then not all Scots can be mean. However, the rules of logic are not applied and the rules of stereotypy are. The stereotype is not applied to Jimmy and the reason is that Jimmy is not thought of as a Scot. So long as Jimmy is not categorized as a Scot the stereotype is dormant. It is almost as if because Jimmy is not mean, he cannot be conceived of as a Scot. The implicit challenge to the stereotype is deflected. This deflection or evasion tactic is very common. When there is no way in which we can reconstrue someone's behaviour so as to confirm our stereotypes, we reconstrue the social category to which they belong instead. The attractive, unaggressive, submissive, and sexually normal feminist is just no feminist!

Prototypes. Cantor and Mischel (1977, 1979) coined the term 'prototype' and it connotes something similar to Wegler and Vallacher's (1977) ideas about the existence of implicit personality theories. The notion is that people carry prototypes or implicit personality theories around with them. These are abstract representations of personality types. So a person might believe that there is a type of personality which could be labelled 'extrovert'. A certain set of traits might be said to comprise this personality type. The 'extrovert' type might comprise those who are sociable, socially skilled, dominant, afraid of being alone, insensitive to the feelings of others, etc. People who believe that such a personality type exists, it is argued, will organize the information they have about new acquaintances in terms of the typology.

Just like stereotypes, prototypes can ease the process of impression formation since they allow information to be classified and once it is classified offer pre-packaged patterns of inference which should be drawn from it. However, again just like stereotypes, prototypes introduce certain distortions into impression formation. Prototypical reorganization of information about a person will lead to the exclusion of certain parts of the information. Snyder and Uranowitz (1978) illustrated this beautifully in a carefully controlled experiment. Subjects in their experiment read an extensive narrative about the life of Betty K. concerning her childhood, education, and choice of career. After reading it, one-

26

third of the subjects were told that Betty was lesbian; one-third were told she was heterosexual; and the others were given no information about her sexual preferences. One week later, all of the subjects were asked to recall what they could of Betty's early life. Subjects who had been given information about her sexuality distorted recall to match what they knew of her later sexual preferences. Those who had been told she was lesbian 'remembered' more incidents suggesting homosexuality. Now, this experiment could be said to illustrate the operation of a stereotype or a prototype. The label is less important than the power it had to filter the information recalled.

3. *Personal constructs* are also a basis for classifying people. The theory of personal constructs was put forward by Kelly (1955) and has been effectively summarized by Bannister and Fransella (1971). The definition of a personal construct is no simple matter. 'A construct is essentially a discrimination which the person can make' (Bannister & Fransella, 1971, p. 40). In essence, a construct exists to pinpoint a dimension on which it is possible to differentiate between phenomena. The construct system is the network of such dimensions along which the person experiences the world. Constructs are not necessarily tied to verbal labels: a discrimination may be made between two phenomena which have no linguistic tag. Constructs are invariably bipolar; they have positive and negative poles. For example, good versus bad; young versus old; truth versus lie; or big versus small. Their bipolarity is not necessarily logical, it is *psycho*logical; so that someone might use the construct tree versus street. Constructs are arranged in the system in pyramid fashion: more comprehensive constructs subsuming those which are more specific at each new level, until, at the top, there are a limited number of core concepts. Thus the pyramid might be as shown in Fig. 3.1.

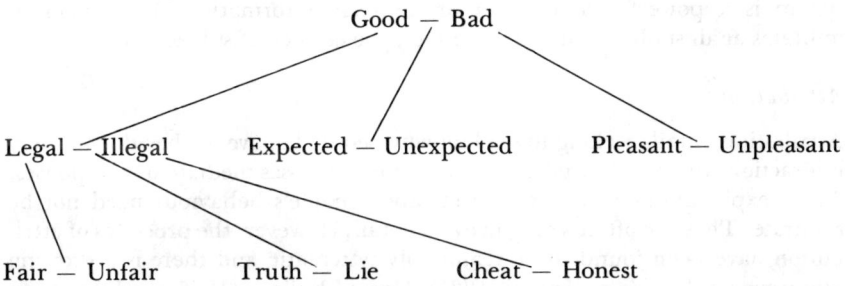

Fig. 3.1

Kelly argues that each person's construction system is composed of a finite number of these dichotomous constructs and that each system is unique. Different patterns of experience lead people to differ in their patterns of construal. The essential purpose of the construct system is to enable the person to predict what is likely to happen. Kelly believes that man acts as a scientist might in construing the world: constructs are used to predict events, those which are effective are maintained and those which are not are changed. The elaboration

27

of the construct system takes place in such a manner as to ensure that the potential to predict and anticipate events is maximized. The system is subject to continuous modulation so as to maximize its predictive power. Even so, some constructs, once established, are unlikely to change, for example, right versus left refers to a construct which is unlikely to change. Experience will demand that some constructs are changed, for example, Right versus Left. The capital letter has strange powers!

Since constructs are fundamental to the individual's psychological processes, people with similar constructs are supposed to function in a similar way psychologically. According to Bannister and Fransella (1971, p. 30) such 'people are similar because they construe, i.e. discriminate, interpret, see the implications of events, in similar ways'. Kelly sees interpersonal interactions in terms of people attempting to understand each other through attempts to fathom each other's construct systems. The more similar the systems, the easier the interaction. Shared constructs translate into shared meanings, facilitate communication and liking.

The importance of construct systems for impression formation is clear. The construct system forms the framework within which a person is categorized and described. The complex, subtly differentiated system will call forth an impression which is itself complex and multifaceted. The simple system will permit an impression formed along only a limited number of dimensions. Core constructs will be central to the impression because people are evaluated on these dimensions first. The person whose core construct is Fascist versus Socialist is likely to form a very different impression of a person than someone whose key construct is tennis player versus cricketer. In short, the construct system determines what is seen to be important and how it is interpreted. Like philosophies of human nature, stereotypes and prototypes, the construct system is a powerful determiner of impression formation. Like them, it militates against objectivity. It is, in fact, the essence of subjectivity.

Attribution

Attribution entails seeking to explain why people behave as they do. In every interaction with another person, attribution processes mediate our responses. These explanations of our own and other people's behaviour need not be accurate. They are often wrong in every detail. However, the processes of attribution have been found to be reasonably systematic and there is a growing literature on them (e.g. Antaki, 1981). Harold Kelley's (1967) work has been seminal in the area. He argued that in making attributions, we look for systematic patterns of relationships and infer cause and effect from these patterns. Basically, we look for co-variation between phenomena: 'an effect is attributed to one of its possible causes with which, over time, it varies' (Kelley, 1967, p. 108).

Kelley postulates that there are three types of cause: (1) actor; (2) entity; and, (3) circumstances. The actor is the person whose behaviour one wishes to explain. The entity is the person with whom the actor interacts. The circum-

28

stances are the situational variables which surround the interaction. The decision about which of these three possible causes for the behaviour is the actual cause is based on three types of information: (1) consensus; (2) consistency; and, (3) distinctiveness. Consensus information indicates how many other people behave in this way. Consistency information indicates whether the actor behaves in this way regularly. Distinctiveness information indicates whether this type of behaviour on the part of the actor is specific to interactions with this particular entity.

Kelley argues that the origin of the behaviour is said to lie with the actor when consensus is low; consistency high; and distinctiveness low. For instance, a father hits his infant daughter. The explanation for the father's behaviour would have to revolve around something about his character if: no one else hits the child (consensus low); he hits her regularly (consistency high); and he hits not only her but his other children (distinctiveness low). However, where consensus, consistency and distinctiveness are all high, the observer is likely to conclude that the entity is the origin of the behaviour. So, if other people besides the father hit the child (consensus high); and the father hits the child regularly (consistency high) and only hits this particular child (distinctiveness high), we are likely to conclude that the child is in some way the cause of the behaviour. Circumstances are used to explain events where consistency is low. If the father hits the child only very rarely, we look to see what special circumstances surround the event and tend to attribute his behaviour to them.

This is, of course, a rather nice, rational model of how we come to explain events. It is founded upon a problematic assumption however; it assumes relevant information is available yet it is probable that it will not be. Kelley does take account of this weakness. He suggests that we deal with the problem of insufficient information by developing 'causal schemata'. Causal schemata are ready-made sets of beliefs about what causes certain types of behaviours. For instance, experience in social work might lead to the evolution of a causal schema which indicated that when a father hits a child, the father is responsible for the action and this might be in turn founded on a whole substratum of beliefs about child battering. The point is that these causal schemata short circuit the need for a rational appraisal of the information. They are the easy way out. Of course, the social worker cannot really afford to take such an easy way out. In making attributions, the social worker has to filter out the effects of causal schemata.

Certain types of bias which enter the attributional process are well documented and are worth noting because they are extremely likely to affect the social work process. The first concerns what are called actor — observer differences. If called upon to explain someone else's behaviour, we tend to overemphasize the actor as the cause of his or her own behaviour (Ross, 1977). In doing this, we tend to ignore consensus information (e.g. Nisbett & Borgida, 1975). So that even when we know that other people behave in the same way in that situation, we still attribute the actor with responsibility for his or her actions. As a corollary to this, when called upon to explain our own actions, we tend to regard them as situationally determined (Jones & Nisbett, 1972). It is almost as if we want others to take the responsibility for their actions but are unwilling to shoulder our own responsibility.

Other factors influence actor – observer differences. The observer of an act is even more likely to attribute the actor with responsibility if the act affected the observer in some way or if the observer believes the act was intended to have such an effect (Jones & Davis, 1965). For instance, the social worker who believes a client attempts suicide as a 'call for help' is likely to believe the client responsible for his or her own actions; situational variables are likely to remain unconsidered. Construing suicide as a 'call for help' means that it is seen as an act intended to influence the social worker or someone similar. It pushes attributions towards the actor rather than towards the entity or the circumstances. The nature of the relationship between the actor and the observer is also of importance in shaping attributions. If a relationship is positive then when the actor does things which are evaluated positively by the observer these are seen to be due to the actor's disposition or character. However, if the relationship is negative then when the actor does things which are regarded as good they are attributed to the situational constraints surrounding the behaviour (Regan *et al.*, 1974). Again, in this process, the way in which people strive to maintain their believe systems about others is visible.

There is one other area where much information about attributional processes has been accumulated: on attributions of success and failure. From the mass of data in the area there is, perhaps, one salient feature of interest to the social work process. This concerns a difference between men and women in their attributions about their own behaviour. Men, when they are successful, attribute success to their own qualities (their skill, intellect, etc.). However, when they are unsuccessful, men attribute failure to circumstances (the difficulty of the task, extraneous events, etc.). On the other hand, women who succeed explain it in terms of luck or circumstances and only when they fail do they invoke their own qualities as explanatory. The male tactic is adapted to generate unrealistic self-satisfaction; the female tactic is designed to generate unrealistic self-distrust. Neither tactic is optimally adaptive. This is particularly true in the social work process where realistic self-appraisal is vital.

In discussing the processes of impression formation and attribution above an effort has been made to highlight the factors which confound objectivity. Most social workers would agree that some semblance of objectivity in the appraisal of people is fundamental to the social work process. The social worker cannot allow presupposition and prejudice to take over. Yet, all of the evidence above indicates how very difficult it is to control these subversive forces. Indeed, it appears that perception is founded upon them because it needs to be selective.

The key to control of these forces lies in understanding how they work. The beginnings of understanding can be gleaned from current social psychological work — some of which is summarized above. Taking the SPA to impression formation and attribution in the social work process leads to: understanding how they operate; the conscious manipulation of them; and, the self-conscious placement of them into the process of problem analysis. The focus, as always with SPA, is to give a means of analysing the problem and prescriptions about how to deal with it. Self-conscious, rational social work demands that the social worker monitors the processes of impression formation and attribution. The tools with which these processes can be analysed have been outlined above.

There is one further thing that probably should be made explicit, although it is implicit in everything above. The social worker engages in forming impressions of the client and making attributions about his or her behaviour but it should never be forgotten that these are two-way processes. The client is also forming impressions and making attributions. These will determine how the client responds. They will also, therefore, interact with whatever conclusions the social worker has derived. It is therefore not sufficient for the social worker simply to monitor his or her own impression formation and attributional processes, some attempt must be made to monitor those of the client. Only by doing this can the social worker forestall the worst misunderstandings which the client may be conceiving.

3.2 The Process of Interpersonal Attraction

Interpersonal attraction is the process whereby one person comes to like another. On the basis of research, it is possible to say under what circumstances the odds are in favour of one person liking another. These can be arranged under seven headings:

(i) We like those who have similar beliefs, values and personal characteristics to ourselves.
(ii) We like those who satisfy our needs — mutual liking tends to develop when needs are complementary, so that both parties get what they want from the relationship.
(iii) We like those who are physically attractive according to our cultural norms — this tendency is mitigated by a countervailing tendency to seek out those who are about as attractive as we think ourselves to be.
(iv) We like those who are competent and intelligent — this concept of competence extends to include those who are socially skilled, we like those who know how to deal 'properly' with social interactions (Cook, 1977).
(v) We like those who are pleasant to us.
(vi) We like those who reciprocate our liking — this can result in a spiralling effect towards ever greater liking.
(vii) We are more likely to like those who are in geographical proximity to us (Mita et al., 1977).

Three types of theory have been proffered to explain the process of interpersonal attraction. They are not contradictory, in truth, they appear to build upon each other. They are: (a) reinforcement-affect theory; (b) social exchange theory; and, (c) equity theory.

Reinforcement-Affect Theory

This is the simplest of the three. It was proposed by Byrne and Clore (1970; see

31

also Byrne, 1971). They argued that we come to like those who give us rewards and dislike those who punish us. The reason is simple: rewards are associated with positive affect, the source of rewards becomes similarly associated with positive affect, i.e. liking. The opposite is true for those who punish us because punishment is associated with negative affect. Consequently, as long as one knows what acts as a reward and what as a punishment, the theory can predict when attraction will occur.

Social Exchange Theory

This is an extention of the reinforcement-affect theory because in it Thibaut and Kelley (1959) argue that attraction is a two-way process. Any relationship involves rewards and costs. Where rewards exceed costs, liking will result. However, this simple calculation is confounded somewhat by other factors. For instance, liking will only result if the differential between rewards and costs exceeds a certain expected level. Also, if greater differential rewards are available from alternative but mutually exclusive relationships, then liking will not result. Liking becomes a matter of maximizing personal gains.

Equity Theory

Many people faced with the two formulations above pointed out how naively simple they are in their assumptions about the economic, rational model of man. Walster *et al.* (1978) took the theorizing one step further. They argued that in forming friendships we consider not simply our own rewards and costs but also those of the other person. They showed evidence that people seek to balance their own rewards and costs and those of the other person. Friendship and liking is most likely to occur when these are equitably arranged; hence 'equity theory'. The implication is that we neither like to exploit our friends nor be exploited by them.

The major problem with both the empirical studies and the theories of inter-personal attraction reported above is that they deal only with the initial phases of attraction. They set the scene for understanding the first skirmishes in the relationship but nothing more. In the social work process, relationships that are of importance have normally been long established. The sorts of information that social psychologists have about long-term relationship are limited but they are considered below and it is worth bearing in mind that at the time of writing this is a rapidly expanding area of study.

3.3 The Process of Long-Term Commitment

Thibaut and Kelley (1959) describe the stages of a relationship: sampling; bargaining; commitment; and institutionalization. This four-stage process is typical of other descriptions which have been offered (Levinger & Snoek, 1972; Murstein, 1977). During the sampling phase, selection of possible friends or partners takes place and surface variables are of prime importance (e.g.

physical attractiveness and proximity). In the next phase, the selected people indulge in bargaining; assessing the potential profits which can be made from the relationship. If both parties are satisfied that their profit margins are reasonable, a commitment to the relationship is made. The final phase entails the institutionalization of this commitment. At this point, the importance of social roles and social norms is greatest. The commitment is shaped into its institutionalized forms by these roles and norms (e.g. marriage may institutionalize a commitment between two people prescribing socially acceptable roles for each partner).

The development of the relationship is characterized by a movement from concern with external features of the other person to concern with internal factors (such as beliefs and values) (Kerckhoff & Davis, 1962). This is paralleled by an increasing willingness to engage in self-disclosure; telling the other about one's most private and intimate thoughts and feelings. This self-disclosure has to be carefully timed. Kelvin (1977) has described how dangerous mistimed self-disclosure can be because it lays the person open to exploitation — material and emotional. Yet people are willing to take this risk because self-disclosure within what is perceived to be a caring relationship allows individuals to get positive feedback about themselves and in this way to validate the most central aspects of their self-concept. Consequently, total self-exposure entails a lot of stress and can be justified only by total faith in the other person. It signifies an immense investment in the other person. It is preferable if such investments are mutual; the balance of power is then more even and the relationship is perceived as equitable.

As people come to share experiences and feelings in this accelerating pattern of self-disclosure, they simultaneously tend to become behaviourally interdependent. They are often together, doing things with or for one another. Under these circumstances, there is reason to believe that close friendship may entail changes in the personal construct systems of both parties. Similarity in construct systems may have been influential in attracting them to each other in the first place. Duck (1977) has argued that thereafter similarity in constructs may facilitate communication and, within the process of self-disclosure, may encourage the growth of new understanding. This may mean the extension and elaboration of the construct systems. It may even mean growth in similar directions.

All of this paints rather a pleasant picture of the development of relationships; implying somehow that they grow bigger and better every day. Of course, this is not true. In fact, many relationships break down. Some break down early in their development before the processes of self-disclosure and common construal have evolved. Others break down after these processes have run their course. Relationships break down for many reasons. Perceived inequities seem common reasons (one person feeling they are always giving and the other always taking). Women have been found to be more sensitive to the state of a relationship under these circumstances (Hill et al., 1976), they are also more likely to end such a relationship (Rubin et al., 1978).

Many relationships which have broken down in reality continue to run with the cracks papered over because the costs of allowing the cracks to show would be too great. Breaking a relationship can mean losing many of the support structures for one's identity. In some cases it can mean material hardship but in all cases it means social hardship. Couples, particularly married couples, evolve a joint social identity, a joint network of friends and joint behavioural patterns. When this is considered in relation to the evidence that such couples grow to construe the world in very similar ways, the depth of the problem introduced by break-up is easily seen. Couples would rather avoid the problems even where the relationship itself is no longer satisfying. The spin-offs from a relationship can outweigh the relationship itself. In effect, some sort of compromise has to be reached between expectations about how satisfying the relationship itself can be and the profits it provides tangentially. Once the compromise is reached, the relationship can then enter equilibrium. Swenson (1978) compared a large sample of married couples who ranged from newly-weds to those who had been married over 60 years. Over time the expression of love for each other declined steadily, so did affection, moral support, interest and concern for each other. However, the consolation was there too: over time the problems in the relationship steadily declined. Compromise and equilibrium seem to typify these relationships.

All of the work on the breakdown of relationships serves to emphasize something which is consistently ignored when talking about their development: the importance of the social context of the relationship. Relationships develop within specific social structures that are organized around certain social norms and dominated by particular social groups. Relationships will be predicted upon their context. In societies where homosexual relationships are illegal, the forms available for the development of contacts between two men will be constrained. If those men want a homosexual relationship, they will be particularly constrained. But even those who do not want a homosexual relationship will be constrained by social expectations; any hint, no matter how incidental, of homosexuality needs to be expunged from their relationship. Such social norms control not only the manner of a relationship but also with whom it is possible to have a relationship. So, for instance, at certain times, in certain places, friendship between black and white people has been unthinkable.

Seeing a relationship as a process of growth which must be contextualized is necessary for the social work process. All too frequently, the social worker sees a relationship for the first time when it is in crisis. Under such circumstances it is difficult to trace its development and its impact on those involved. Yet this is vital to an understanding of how to deal with the crisis. Seeking to understand the stages in growth of the relationship and delineating its social context are useful in the process of analysing the crisis. The brief outline above of the social psychology of long-term relationships is designed to pinpoint where information from the client may be useful. In resolving a conflict between a couple, focusing upon their common identity support system and their communalities in construal can be of considerable value. Emphasizing what they stand to gain and what they stand to lose in the break-up can crystallize their understanding of the implications of their actions. Implementing principles of equity may move them back into synchronization. The action strategies which a social worker can derive from the social psychological analysis of relationships are numerous. The propriety and relevance of each can be assessed only in relation to a specific problem. Some of their applications are described in Part V of this book. The important thing to remember is to use the evidence *and* theories of social psychology as a foundation for both analysis and intervention.

4
Identity

This chapter will be concerned with six issues relating to identity:

(i)   What is identity?
(ii) What is the relationship between personal and social identity?
(iii) What effects does the need for self-esteem have?
(iv) How are 'spoiled identities' managed?
(v)   What effects do threats to identity have?
(vi) How can understanding identity affect the social work process?

Since the social psychological literature on identity is vast and the room available in which to discuss it here minute, extensive pruning has been necessary. Material has been selected which seems to have immediate relevance to the social work process. However, there are more comprehensive guides available (Burns, 1979; Breakwell, 1982) for the reader whose appetite is whetted.

4.1   What is Identity?

Confusion stalks, like a wolf in the woods, through the literature in this area. Largely, this is because:

(i)   people use different labels to refer to the same phenomenon (e.g. identity, self, character, personality, etc.);
(ii) labels are used inconsistently; this happens in two ways:
    (a) two theorists will employ the same label but define it operationally and theoretically in two quite distinct ways;
    (b) a single theorist will employ the same label in two different places in

his or her writings and in the second it will connote something slightly, or even totally, different from its first meaning;

(iii) the phenomena with which theorists are dealing are complex and multi-faceted; they sometimes believe that they are dealing with the same facet as someone else when, in fact, they are dealing with something which is subtly different.

These factors lead to confusion because people who believe that they are speaking a common language, because the words sound the same, cannot actually communicate effectively. It is as if two people were talking about apples and the conversation is going along well; they agree that apples are useful, easy to store, and relatively inexpensive but it is important to keep them away from damp. It is only when one participant mentions that she has just purchased some new software for her 'apples' that the other might begin to doubt whether they are, in fact, both talking about the same thing: the sort of apples that fall from trees into the lap of budding physicists rather than the sort of apples that those same physicists might use to compute the gravitational pull of the moon. An apple is a type of fruit and a type of computer. Now it is relatively easy to detect that sort of semantic misunderstanding but not so easy when the word refers to a highly complex, abstract entity like identity. This is why it is so important to understand what is meant by the word 'identity' in the following discussions.

The words 'identity' and 'self-concept' will be used interchangeably. The important thing to remember is that they both refer to *a dynamic process and its continually changing products rather than a static entity*. Identity is simultaneously a process and the products of that process. Mead (1925) characterized this duality of identity when, having argued that 'we reflect, we are conscious, we are aware of self', he concluded that the self has two components: 'I' and 'me'. 'I' acts. 'Me' observes and reflects on the actions of 'I'. 'Me' monitors what 'I' does, evaluates it, and changes it. 'Me' represents the process of self-consciousness; 'I' is the product of that process and its interactions with the phenomenal world.

The identity process entails having an awareness of our separation from others and the uniqueness of our consciousness. The identity process acts to integrate our experiences, relate them to each other and fit them into place in our cumulative biography. The identity process, because it interprets each new experience against the backdrop of our past, is the anchor for our continuity over time. It carries our expectations about ourselves, derived from past patterns of behaviour, and records when they are not met. In doing so, the identity process maintains our awareness of ourselves as purposive agents: actors with intentions who have responsibility for our own actions.

It is vital to remember that this self-awareness is always located in a social context. The individual's identity is a social product. It is only through social interaction that the person comes to develop knowledge of his or her identity. Charles Horton Cooley (1902) proposed the notion of the 'looking glass' self. He argued that we understand what we are by observing what others think about

37

us. Effectively, he insisted, self-awareness originates in what we see of ourselves reflected from others — hence the mirror imagery. George Mead (1925) extended this line of argument but took a developmental perspective. Children learn how to behave from watching the people who surround them. They imitate the behaviour of people who are important in their lives — 'significant others' as Mead called them. This imitation extends to the way they are themselves treated. They treat themselves as others treat them; they come to see themselves as others see them. 'Taking the role of the other,' the child learns an appropriate identity for that social context. But this process does not cease with the passage from childhood. Adults continually monitor the impression they make on others, establish whether it is congruent with the self-image and respond with change when inconsistencies arise. Videbeck (1960) demonstrated experimentally how sensitive people are to their image in the eyes of others. Subjects in the experiment rated how good they felt they were at oral communication prior to reading a poem out loud before an 'expert'. This 'expert' (who was a confederate of the experimenter) told half the subjects that they were good and half that they were bad at oral communication. This assessment was independent of actual performance. At the close of the session, subjects again rated their own conception of their ability. The results show that when pre- and post-experiment self-assessments are compared the 'expert's' opinion is influential. The subjects changed their own assessments of their ability to match those of the 'expert'. This was true regardless of whether their actual performance showed the 'expert' to be wrong. However, the 'expert' had less effect on those about whom he was critical than on those he praised.

This qualification in the Videbeck findings is important because it emphasizes that not all information about the self reflected from others carries equal weight. According to Gergen (1971) both the characteristics of the appraiser and the appraisal determine the extent of its impact on self-conception.

The appraiser — to have effects must have importance for the individual (be what Mead called a 'significant other') and must be considered an expert justified in passing judgements. Moreover, the appraiser must be seen to take detailed account of what the individual does and give an individualized appraisal; this is known as personalism. When the appraiser has no personal significance and no claim to expert knowledge, then the appraisal has little power to change self-conceptions. The same is true if the appraiser appears to ignore important evidence about the individual's behaviour or fails to recognize what the individual regards to be unique aspects of his or her case. The importance of this information for the social work process is obvious. Social workers wishing to influence a client need to establish themselves not just as 'experts' but need also to personalize their assessments.

The appraisal — needs several characteristics to be maximally effective:

(i) It needs to be *consistent* — fluctuations in the content of appraisal causes it to be discredited.

(ii)   It needs to be relatively *simple* — changes in self-conception are difficult, simple categorical statements about what change is necessary are
the most easily assimilated.

(iii) It should be used *continually* — lengthy exposure to a message increases
its impact.

(iv)   It should be versed in *positive terms* — praise and flattery have more
effect than abuse in changing self-conceptions.

(v)   It should not be *too discrepant* with the individual's self-appraisal — an
appraisal made by someone else which is totally at variance with one's
own appraisal is likely to be ignored because it is not seen as credible.

This again is information valuable to the social worker, it says something about
how to make one's message persuasive as an instrument of change.

4.2   What is the Relationship between Personal and Social Identity?

The emphasis above upon the importance of others in the construction and
maintenance of identity through the identity process moves naturally into questions about the relationship between personal and social identity. For a long
time, social psychologists have accepted that there is a dichotomy between
personal and social identity. Personal identity refers to those intimate and
private aspects of the person which are central to the person's sense of autonomy and uniqueness; it is the fulcrum of the person's sense of continuity and
consistency across different social contexts. Social identity refers to the public
self which is derived from the person's membership of different social groups
and categories and occupancy of various roles; it is the sum of all those different
faces the person puts on to meet the world. Personal identity, if not constant, is
slow to change, growing organically through assimilation and accommodation. Social identity changes with the social demands; there are many 'social
selves' within each of us which can be taken off the shelf and paraded before an
audience at our command and often at the audience's command. New 'social
selves' can be added to the repertoire with ease. James recognized this almost a
century ago:

> A man has as many social selves as there are individuals who recognize him and carry
> an image of him in their mind. (James, 1890, p. 294)

Although some social psychologists still accept this strict dichotomy of personal and social identity (e.g. Harré, 1982), it is increasingly under attack
(Breakwell, 1982). In analytic terms the dichotomy may be useful if the individual is examined at a single moment in time. Taking a slice out of time and
examining the individual one might be able to say: 'this is her personal identity'
and 'this is her social identity'. However, the distinction becomes blurred and
ultimately invisible when the individual is considered across time. This is
because social identities become personal identities over time. People learn to
play a part to suit their social circumstances but after a while they are no longer

39

pretending to fit the part, they take on the characteristics of the part and the part becomes 'part' of them. The personal identity assimilates the social identity. Taking an evolutionary or developmental perspective, there is no dichotomy between personal and social identity. They are both part of the identity process.

How does a social identity come to be assimilated into the personal identity? This can be answered by examining the importance of 'roles'. Society is a formal, hierarchical structure which allots people to specified positions within the structure. Each of these positions has a more or less clearly defined role attached to it. The role is the behaviour which is expected of the occupant of that social position. So for instance, a doctor holds a certain social position and is expected to fulfil a particular role. The same is true for positions not associated with occupation in the narrow sense, e.g. wife, mother, daughter, great-grandmother — all have roles attached. The role carries prescriptions for behaviour (i.e. the ideal behaviour for someone in that position) and expectations about the attributes of someone occupying that position (i.e. the ideal identity for someone in that position). People commonly strive to get others to conform to role expectations, whether in their behaviour or their attributes. Individuals who fail to conform are subjected to considerable social pressures. The role can, therefore, play an important part in directing behaviour. Hunt (1976) argued that 'large parts of individual social behaviour are formally determined and have little to do with specific intrapsychic aspects of the behaviour' (p. 288). He goes on to say that where a role is particularly prominent in a person's life, taking up a large part of his or her time, the person will 'invest' large amounts in it. It will then be central to the person's 'view of things'. Attempts will be made to augment its clarity, resist any change in it and it will dominate behaviour. The person comes to see himself or herself virtually totally in terms of the role. Other people see the same image; and they serve to reinforce in their behaviour and attitudes the importance of the role. Thus, women, who once saw themselves as potential actresses, authors, painters, etc., may come to see themselves solely as wife and mother. Those around them may see them only in these lights too. The role and the expectations of those around her control her behaviour and her self-expression. If Mead and the symbolic interactionists are right, personal identity must change to be consistent with social identity in such situations. Seeing herself behave in certain ways and seeing others respond to her in certain ways — the ways congruent with *being* a wife and mother — the woman can only conclude that this is what she *is*. The social context reforms the personal identity.

It would be inappropriate, however, to assume that all roles have dramatic impacts on personal identity. Roles performed for brief periods and in which the occupant has no emotional investment will have little impact. Moreover, personal identity is reasonably resistant to change. One of the central factors influencing change is the need for self-esteem.

4.3   The Effects of the Need for Self-Esteem

Self-esteem is central to the dynamics of the identity process. If there is one consistent finding in social psychology it is that people wish to believe that they
have personal worth. James (1890) argued that personal worth was an absolute
quality and dependent upon objective measures of success or failure. Veblen
(1958) suggested that personal worth is not measured in absolute terms but in
relative terms: we assess ourselves in relation to others. Festinger (1954) formalized the suggestion in an article entitled 'A Theory of Social Comparison
Processes'. In it, Festinger claimed that people need to validate their attitudes
and beliefs. Normally, they do this against objective evidence. When there is
little factual evidence they turn to other people and test whether their beliefs
and attitudes are congruent with those of other people. As we have seen above,
the attitudes and beliefs of others are vital in establishing the self-concept.
They are also vital in establishing self-esteem. They are important in two ways:

(i)   As comparitors — in assessing our personal worth we compare ourselves
      with others; it is therefore important to choose the right comparitors,
      ones that are relevant, respected and not too different from ourselves.
(ii) As assessors — our own assessment of our personal worth is strongly
      influenced by what others think of us.

Self-esteem is so important that people are careful to encourage others to see
them in a positive light. This entails *impression management*. Impression management involves projecting a particular image of one's self to others. Goffman
(1971) posits that social interaction is a theatrical performance in which each
individual acts out a part — a 'line'. A 'line' is a carefully chosen set of verbal
and non-verbal acts designed to express one's self. The 'line' shifts from situation to situation. It is created to gain social approval. If it is successful, the person is said to be 'in face'; if it is not, the person is 'out of face'. The point which
Goffman wishes to emphasize is that these performances involve all participants in a mutual commitment to work to keep each member of the interaction
'in face'. Only by keeping 'in face' can the interaction continue without embarrassment. Face-saving devices are used to manage embarrassments; *faux pas*
are ignored or reinterpreted (e.g. aggression is 'not understood' or interpreted
as a joke). The reason for this 'face-work' is simple — only by keeping the interaction going can all concerned get a share of the social approval that is inherent
in this sort of arena.

Impression management is a highly skilled activity. It requires a clear awareness of how others interpret actions and a wide range of self-presentation skills.
It also requires an ability to act in ways which need not be in accordance with
the way in which we conceive of ourselves. For instance, impression management may necessitate a whole series of lies, and if honesty is fundamental to our
self-concept, there will be tension between our acts and our self-conception.
The skilled impression manager has to tolerate that strain. Of course, it entails
risks. It is possible to come to believe one's own performances, especially when
people treat us as if we are what we pretend to be. The distinction between the

public and private realities gets lost along the way. The image is no longer managed, it is managing.

Snyder (1979) has shown that some people are skilled managers of impressions. Such people monitor themselves and take careful note of their effects on others. They regard themselves as flexible and adaptive; they can control the expression of their emotions through purposive and accurate use of non-verbal cues; and they seek out information about others. They play a controlling role in social interactions and are good at detecting attempts by others to manage impressions. Elliot (1979) showed such people are keen to know well in advance what sort of situation they are entering. They are sensitive to group norms (Snyder & Monson, 1975) acting in a conforming manner with conforming groups and a non-conforming manner with non-conforming groups. As one might imagine, their actions indicate little about their attitudes or feelings.

Christie and Geis ((1970) labelled this pattern of behaviour 'Machiavellian-ism' (for obvious reasons) and invented a scale to measure this tendency. They found that such people are actually very effective in influencing others. What is more, they are not easily influenced themselves. They gain personal satisfaction from the sheer act of manipulation and are willing to violate almost any social norm for self-gain. The interesting thing is that this sort of orientation has been shown to be operative in children as young as ten years of age. High 'Mach' children normally have high 'Mach' parents, so it can be predicted.

One of the prime functions of impression management is to gain social approval. It therefore comes into play most often when someone has just lost social approval or anticipates that it will be lost. Schneider (1969) showed that people engaged in more impression management after they had failed in a task. When anticipating failure, people will do a little anticipatory management of their image. For example, when expecting to fail on a test or in an interview, people will publicize reasons why they could not possibly be expected to suc-ceed. Everyone who has ever stood with others outside an examination hall will be able to picture the character who comes up to describe in lurid details how he got drunk last night and every night for the preceding week and can hardly expect to write his name let alone pass the exam. This is anticipatory manage-ment. Characteristically it serves to shift the blame for failure from the indivi-dual to the circumstances. In attributional theory terms, the person shifts from dispositional to situational attributions.

Impression managers have one obvious strategy open to them in their search for social approval: this is *ingratiation*. Jones (1964) described four ingratiation tactics:

(i) Compliments — flattery. This tactic is only effective if it can be made to seem spontaneous and credible. Flattery has been shown to be most effective with those who are insecure. But it must be discriminating flat-tery. The person who compliments everyone is undiscriminating and his or her compliments devalue themselves.

(ii) Conformity to the opinions or behaviour of the target. Again credibility is important and can be attained by the selective application of agreement with the target. Undiscriminating agreement with all the target does or says will simply lead to the label of 'yes-man' and devaluation. However, selective agreement gives the appearance of judicial appraisal. Of course, it is then vital only to disagree on matters of slight importance while agreeing consistently on everything that matters to the target.

(iii) Self-enhancement — the object here is to praise oneself in such a fashion that the target recognizes your worth. But the praise must be modulated to vibrate optimally with the target's sense of self-worth. A secure target will receive your efforts after self-glorification with tolerance and may even accept some of what you say. An insecure target does not want to be surrounded by people superior to himself or herself, so self-praise needs to be minimized. Self-deprecation may be the order of the day.

(iv) Rendering favours — these again have to be carefully disguised so as to appear not to have an ulterior motive.

One might argue that ingratiation cannot be very effective since people are aware of all these techniques and can guard against them. There are two replies to this. Firstly, very few people actually sit down to make themselves conscious of how others try to ingratiate themselves. Secondly, and this accounts for the former, people like to be ingratiated. There is a strong motive not to notice that others are attempting to ingratiate you; every ounce of vanity pushes that recognition away. Ingratiation techniques work.

In describing these impression management techniques no evaluative stance has been adopted. There is no point in saying impression management is good or bad. Impression management is a skill and it can be used for both good and bad ends, it is not an end in itself. Social workers will find that they have to deal with people who are highly skilled in the techniques of impression management; many of these will not be clients but other professionals. In order to deal with them effectively, it would be useful to possess these skills oneself. In these cases, practice normally makes perfect.

There is a further aspect of this question about the ethics of impression management which needs to be considered. Self-esteem is important to healthy psychological functioning. Low self-esteem is related to 'field dependency' (Witkins *et al.*, 1962) which is associated with conformity to situational demands (Wylie, 1961). High self-esteem leads to field independence and consistency of behaviour across situations. It is associated with a feeling of integration and satisfaction. If impression management can bring such positive results through securing self-esteem, its value has to be recognized.

High self-esteem, once achieved, tends to reduce the need for impression management. People with high self-esteem care less about what others think of them. Such people tend to select out information from the environment which supports their self-concept. They learn rapidly and forget slowly things which are self-gratifying.

4.4 How are 'Spoiled Identities' Managed?

When self-esteem and social approval are so important, the obvious question becomes: 'what happens when social approval is not forthcoming?' Those who are stigmatized find themselves in this position. The term *stigma* in the original Greek was used to refer to the bodily signs said to symbolize something unusual and bad about the moral status of their bearer: the mark of a slave or criminal. The stigma forewarned that this person should be avoided, especially in public places. Goffman (1976) describes how the meaning of stigma has changed though it still carries implications of social unfitness. He argues that any attribute, physical, psychological or social, can become a stigma when associated with a disparaging stereotype. Having only one leg, having been a mental patient, having been a Fascist can all be stigmata. Being stigmatized leads to a 'spoiled identity' in Goffman's terms, the individual has lost social approval.

Faced with this situation, the stigmatized has a series of options which largely depend on the nature of the stigma. Stigmas can differ in their degree of visibility. Disfigurement is normally more visible than a history of incarceration in mental hospitals. Visible stigmas lead to the identity being immediately *discredited* whenever the person meets someone. When the stigma is not apparent, Goffman argues that the identity is not discredited but potentially *discreditable*. It is only when the identity is discredited that it is regarded as 'spoiled'. Discredited and discreditable identities lead to different forms of adjustment. Moreover, the types of adjustment made depend to a large extent on whether the stigma is innate or the result of trauma. The effects of being born a dwarf or of losing one's sight after an accident will be very different. The dwarf is virtually socialized into the art of dealing with stigma, the person blinded has all the skills to learn. The dwarf learned the single stigmatized identity; the blind person has to relearn an identity, replace the old with the stigmatized identity. The results of these very different processes obviously have to be very different in themselves.

Where a visible stigma leads to a discredited identity, Goffman suggests there are two alternatives open:

(i) to play the role of the stigmatized as specified by others;
(ii) to withdraw and engage in self-definition of role.

To Play the Role

This really means playing the game by the other fellow's rules. People have certain expectations about what behaviour any particular stigma will lead to. Playing the role means confirming their expectations. It can mean that the stigmatized person gains social approval. If social stereotypes are fulfilled, the stigmatized is seen as less threatening. There is a considerable amount of evidence now that stigmatized people act out what is expected of them. Braginski, *et al.*, (1969) showed that schizophrenics in psychiatric hospitals play out complex impression management performances to project images of incompetence. By fulfilling expectations they forfend changes in the regime.

This happens in non-institutional settings too. Farina *et al.* (1971) showed the power of others' expectations. They took a group of ex-mental patients and asked them to talk to a stranger. Half were told that the stranger knew of their psychiatric history, the others were told that the stranger knew nothing about them. In fact, the stranger was never told anything about the patient's history. When interviewed after the experiment, those who had thought the stranger knew their history said that they felt less appreciated, found the task more difficult and felt they performed worse than did those who thought the stranger knew nothing. Even more importantly, objective observers of the experimental interaction, who knew nothing of either the psychiatric history of those participating nor which experimental condition they were observing, felt that those who had been led to believe that the stranger knew their history were significantly more tense, anxious and poorly adjusted than the others. This experiment shows that simply believing that another person knew their psychiatric history changed both their self-perception and their behaviour. The vital thing here is that the other person does not need to have any particular expectations about the stigmatized, the strangers knew nothing about the patients and could not have been transmitting their expectations to them through subtle cues since they had none to transmit. It is the stigmatized who carries a set of beliefs about what others expect and when they are triggered by the belief that the others know of the stigma, they change behaviour and self-perception.

Living up to what you perceive to be the expectations of other people can be an arduous business. This is particularly so when part of the stereotype leads you to be treated as a non-person — someone to be ignored, avoided or treated as an object without pride or privacy. People often treat the stigmatized as if they had no power over access to themselves. This is especially easy with the physically handicapped who can be man-handled 'legitimately'. But it extends to others too. The disfigured can be quizzed about the origin of the flaw and it can be done publicly. It is almost as if personal questions are permissible because it is 'obvious' that they should be seen to reflect concern, sympathy and pity — all very righteous emotions. The stigmatized tend to resort to one of two ways of dealing with this onslaught: they withdraw or they employ bravado. Physical withdrawal is often not possible and the withdrawal often used is psychological; expressed in anger or disdain. Bravado frequently entails the use of humour — black comedy in the sense that it is normally directed against the stigma and plays upon the audience's sense of pity or guilt.

Redefinition of the Self

Such a redefinition of the role of the stigmatized can come about through: (1) individual withdrawal and (2) joining a group the object of which is to change the social representation of that stigma. The second option is of prime importance. The group can comprise other people with the stigma or can involve people accepted as 'courtesy' members of the stigmatized group. Such groups need not necessarily achieve their objective of changing the public image of the

45

stigma but they can still have beneficial effects. Simply belonging to a group of similar people or people who are supportive can mitigate the impact of the 'spoiled' identity because it can act as an arena for the pursuit and attainment of social approval. Simply gaining such approval can result in effective redefinition of the self, even if the stigma remains and its public identity is unchanged.

Where the stigma is less visible, a discreditable identity evolves. Here the key is uncertainty as to its status because at any time the secret can be discovered and identity discredited. Much of the time and energy of such stigmatized people is spent in maintaining the secret. This process is known as 'passing' — getting people to believe you are something that you are not. The arts of impression management discussed earlier are vital here. But the stakes are high. The costs of discovery are great. The tension can be severe and it means that this form of adjustment is unstable. Of course, successive successes in 'passing' encourage belief in the illusion. Both the stigmatized and those deluded may come to believe the illusion totally. In some cases, this may result in the eradication of the stigma. For example, the homosexual who consistently plays 'straight' may actually come to be 'straight'.

Some understanding of the tactics used by the stigmatized is useful for the social work process. The use of the SPA in dealing with the stigmatized is central to several of the chapters in Part V. But it is important to remember in this that it is not simply the reactions of the stigmatized which need to be analysed but also the reactions of the social worker. The processes of impression formation discussed in Chapter 3 will operate to control how the social worker sees the stigma. The social worker needs to analyse how these processes affected his or her responses. It is further necessary to examine how these interact with the habitual and transient strategies of the stigmatized to determine their behaviour at any one time. The accent, as throughout in the use of the SPA, is upon self-conscious analysis in the social work process.

4.5   What Effects do Threats to Identity Have?

People battle to maintain their identity and to achieve social approval for it. Yet they are under continual pressures to adapt to new situations which entail different identity requirements. Certain sorts of situations are particularly threatening to identity. Three of these will be discussed here:

   (i)   conditions of alienation
   (ii) role conflict
   (iii) marginality

Conditions of Alienation

Fromm (1955) said that alienation occurred when a person 'has become, one might say, estranged from himself'. Horney referred to it as 'an alienation from the real self' (1950). Phenomenologically, Gergen (1971) describes it as 'a noxious feeling arising when overt actions are detached from or inconsistent with underlying conceptions of self (p. 87). Accordingly, he sees the sources of alienation as being: (1) dissonance among self-concepts; (2) behaviour which violates identity aspirations and which consequently leads to dissonance and frustration; and, (3) behaviour which is unrelated to the person's most salient ways of viewing the self. Alienation is on the increase, therefore, because in our society all three sources are thriving. They thrive because, in such a society, the number and type of relationships are increased and each new relationship puts new demands on the person, requiring unique adaptations.

Seeman (1959) talked more about the actual experience of alienation. Alienation has five components: (1) powerlessness; (2) meaninglessness — entailing a lack of certainty about what to believe; (3) normlessness — entailing the absence of accepted rules or rituals; (4) isolation — entailing becoming estranged from the remainder of the social world and not subject to its rewards or punishments; and (5) self-estrangement — entailing the inability to find activities which are self-rewarding. The alienated do not, therefore, expect social reinforcement from others and are not capable of generating self-reinforcement. They are beyond the need for social approval since the entire business has lost meaning. Alienation of this sort has been shown to be tied to handicap and to criminality. Alienation is also associated with increasing age. Pensioners often show signs of alienation: withdrawal from others; low self-esteem; and maladaptive self-centration. It is also a recognized consequence of both role conflict and marginality which are discussed next.

Role Conflict

Hunt (1976) describes how role conflict can occur. Where individuals occupy more than one social position role conflict can occur and is most frequent in settings where normative guidance is inadequate (contexts Durkheim and Merton would regard anomic). The conflict can be of two kinds: (1) a condition in which the individual *experiences* the simultaneous arousal of two or more incompatible behavioural tendencies — wants to behave in two quite different ways at the same time; and (2) where the objective social requirements demand simultaneously responses from the person which are mutually exclusive or incompatible — in this case the individual is not necessarily aware that the conflict exists, all demands may not be equally obvious to him or her.

The following circumstances are thought conducive of conflict:

(i)   When the individual occupies two positions, which entail quite different roles which are incompatible, conflict ensues if both roles are invoked in a single situation.

(ii) When a single role is imbued with mutually exclusive role expectations, e.g. the family which expects their adolescent child to be both submissive and autonomous set up role conflict.

(iii) When the individual has one stereotype of the role attached to a position he or she occupies but recognizes that others have quite different and incompatible stereotypes of that role.

(iv) When the role enactment conflicts with role expectations — i.e. when the individual does not act in a way which conforms with his or her expectations of how someone in that role should act.

(v) When some aspect of the role is incompatible with aspirations that are not related to the role, e.g. there are strong role expectations that certain professional groups will not strike in pursuit of pay increases, yet this code is incompatible with attempts to secure an affluent lifestyle.

In any of these circumstances role conflict can occur. Such conflict represents a threat to established identity patterns and has to be managed. Frequently, faced with such threats, people become acutely aware of the danger of changing anything about their self-conception. Bannister (1981) claims that this results in their taking refuge in a rigid, inflexible and inappropriate notion of themselves. This is not really 'management' of conflict, it is more a matter of blocking it from awareness. The conflict is unchanged but one pretends it is not there; it is the syndrome of the ostrich with its head in the sand.

There are at least two other typical response syndromes: the lemming and the chameleon syndromes. Lemmings run from conflict, the syndrome involves vacating positions which cause role conflict. This may be a very sensible strategy but has dangers. All roles are subject to conflicts in some degree. If the person develops a preference for dealing with role conflict by exit from the role, the need to change roles can become an habitual problem. Moreover, exit from the role is sometimes not feasible. It is a strategy only of value where social mobility is possible. The chameleon syndrome involves quite the opposite tactics: chameleons deal with role conflict by seeking to be all things to all people, complying with all the conflicting role demands. This syndrome can be as debilitating as the others. The essential feature of role conflict is that demands are being made which *cannot* all be fulfilled simultaneously. The chameleon who tries to fulfil all of them will inevitably fail. But the tactic may succeed for a time because audiences for different roles can be kept separate and information about other performance can be restricted. As long as the chameleon can control the audience and the information given it, he or she is in business. Of course, these tactics are really only useful when conflict is externally defined. It is less easy to cope with role conflict which results from incompatibilities between one's own expectations of self and perceptions of behaviour. The chameleon syndrome in that case can mutate slightly: resulting in a process where the self is re-conceived as the context and demands change. Such re-conception of the self is not real change, it is still part of the chameleon syndrome because the changes are transient and purely utilitarian. They operate at a superficial level to justify behaviour. Instead of fooling others, they fool oneself.

Marginality

Marginality is, in some senses, a specific type of role conflict. Park (1928) first formulated the 'marginal man' notion and it was later elaborated by Stonequist (1937). They were really talking about people who found themselves trapped

48

between two social groups or two distinct cultures. People who had some affiliation with both groups or both cultures and could, therefore, be totally accepted by neither. The offspring of racially mixed marriages are considered to be in the marginal position. The second generation immigrant occupies a marginal position between two cultures: that of the homeland and that of the New World. Park, and later Stonequist, argued that people in these sorts of positions develop a particular network of personality characteristics. These characteristics include 'spiritual instability, intensified self-consciousness, restlessness, and malaise' (Park, 1928). These are relatively difficult predictions to test since the terms are ill-defined. However, the research which has been done offers no support for the suggestion that there is a 'marginal personality type' (Goldberg, 1941; Antonovsky, 1956). Most importantly, claims that marginality leads to higher rates of suicide, delinquency, crime and 'derangements of the nervous system' have proven fallacious (Golovensky, 1952).

The key to dispelling much of the confusion surrounding the effects of marginality lies in making a simple distinction: between the marginal experience and the marginal position. People can occupy a marginal position, for instance, as second generation immigrants, without being brought to experience marginality. The experience of marginality only happens if those surrounding the marginal reject him or her. The marginal position is only experienced if mediated through rejection. It is only when marginality becomes a central feature of experience that it will shape identity, because identity is a product of what others think of the individual. Hitch (1982) describes this symbolic interactionist approach to marginality effectively.

The marginal who experiences public rejection has to deal with a serious threat to identity. Rejection may mean being evicted from important social networks and will not be taken lightly. The marginal in this situation has two types of strategy which are logical options though they may not both be practical: (1) the individual tactics; and (2) the group tactics.

Individual tactics. These involve changing the way in which the self is seen by others in order to retrieve acceptance. They basically entail attempts to 'pass'; to get people to believe that one is not a marginal. Obviously, some sorts of marginality are more easily camouflaged than others; this was mentioned earlier when discussing stigma and marginality is, after all, a form of stigma. When 'passing' is too difficult, group tactics tend to be used.

It is important to recognize that even successful attempts to 'pass' have repercussions. In an experimental study of 'passing' Breakwell (1979) found that subjects who 'passed' successfully into a group behaved differently from those who were 'legitimate' members. Ironically, the 'passers' showed greater conformity to group norms and were more ardent in their praise of the group than the legitimate members. This effect occurred even though 'passers' believed their illegitimate status to be unknown.

Group tactics. The marginal may respond to social rejection by seeking new social contacts which will offer support to a threatened identity. When a number of marginals are simultaneously rejected, they can come together to form a cohesive new social group of their own. Such a new group deflects attributions of marginality because the marginal is a real member at last. However, the establishment of a new group need not be the end of the problems. The new group itself may be 'marginal', deprecated by other groups and accorded no social status. If this is the case, the marginals who form its membership will gain little kudos from it. They may simply have moved from the ghetto of personal marginality to the ghetto of group marginality. Of course, a group in this position has more power than the individual to manipulate its social representation and act to persuade others to belie their prejudice. The marginal group can seek a public voice and strive for recognition of its worth. But in order to do this it must maintain the cohesiveness of its membership and this is not easy if membership has minimal benefits. Some will wish to leave the group because it cannot offer them social status. Others will leave because membership actually acts as a further stigma that aggravates existing problems. Maintaining membership in these circumstances requires some of the powers of persuasion and coercion considered in Chapter 7.

When both types of strategy, individual and group, fail, the marginal is likely to find his or her social identity collapsing. Self-esteem is destroyed and alienation can result. Marginality is the sort of threat to identity which combines some of the worst aspects of role conflict and stigmatization.

4.6 Understanding Identity Dynamics and the Social Work Process

Analysis of the dynamics of identity has two implications for the social work process: changes in interpretation and changes in strategy.

An Interpretive Framework

Knowledge of the dynamics of identity provides a framework for the interpretation of one's own and other people's behaviour. Behaviours are not viewed as individuated responses to stimuli, they are seen as part of a whole schema which reflects the identity of the actor. Knowledge of identity dynamics facilitates behavioural predictions. Actions are seen within the frame of impression management and role occupancy. They can be predicted on the basis of the individual's effort to impress and gain self-esteem and on the basis of his or her conformity to role expectations. People whose identities are 'spoiled' or 'threatened' also behave in predictable ways, as described above. Such an interpretive framework and such powers of prediction are of considerable value in the social work process. The social worker who can outline the identity dynamics of a problem has a greater chance of predicting developments, anticipating events, and thus is more likely to be able to cope. Prediction is fundamental to achieving social work objectives.

Knowledge of identity dynamics can shape the strategies used by social workers in two directions: (1) by showing how to change identities; and, (2) by showing how to change the social representation of an identity.

Changing identities. One of the central features of all that has been said above is that identity is not static, it is a dynamic process; in the search for self-esteem through social approval, others have a vital role to play in the construction of identity. Knowing this, the social worker can embark in a self-conscious attempt to change identities. The target for change can be the social worker's own identity or that of others.

Rogers (1951) argued that one of the most powerful ways of changing anyone's self-concept was to offer them a chance to explore themselves in a non-threatening and accepting environment. Rogers' major assumption was that the self-concept could change directly. When the self-exploration was conducted in an environment full of social approval, the individual was supposed to be able to face inconsistencies, assimilate what others might think, and refashion the self-concept. Rogerian therapy has been used extensively for three decades and still has many disciples; it can be seen as the theoretical foundation for many encounter and therapeutic group techniques. However, Ziller (1973) has argued that the self-concept is a complex organized schema and cannot change directly. It changes through a series of stages: first, attitudes, then values, after that behaviour, then roles and only then will the self-concept change. Ziller's (1976) 'helical theory of personal change' posits that changes in the lower level constructs gradually result in modifications in constructs of greater complexity and centrality. Hence, if the self-construct is to be changed, it can only be changed through affecting the lower level constructs first. On the basis of this theory, the social worker who wished to influence a client to change would not simply offer an accepting environment and sit and wait for the client to indulge in self-exploration (à la Rogers) but would actively set about influencing attitudes and values. Ziller's theory is much more in tune with the social psychological approach than many others. It has clear action implications for the social work process: change through changing attitudes and values, not to mention behaviour and roles. Some of the techniques of bringing about such change are discussed in Chapter 7.

Changing social representations. This strategy does not entail actual change in an identity, simply a change in the way it is represented socially. Effectively, this means impression management. Both the social worker and the client may need to learn how to do this. The social worker may need to manage the impression the client or other professions form. The client may wish to manipulate what all others see, including the social worker. Techniques for management have been discussed above. One of the most obvious trends in impression management has not been mentioned however. This is social skills training (Trower *et al.*, 1978). Social workers are already actively involved in training various parts of their clientele in 'social skills' — how to behave in an interview for a job with young unemployed; how to be assertive with depressives; and, how to smile at the right time with schizophrenics. So there is nothing new in asking social workers to train in the skills of impression management. It is perhaps novel to ask them to see this as part of an overall analytic framework which revolves around identity dynamics.

Changing social representations may involve not only restructuring how an individual manages his or her impression, but on a larger scale, it may involve changing the impression the individual makes by changing the impression made by the group to which he or she belongs. Strategies which may be used to do this are discussed in Chapter 7 and more of the complex matters of group dynamics are discussed in the next chapter.

Knowledge of the dynamics of identity and the use of this knowledge in the analysis of a problem and in deriving strategies to cope with the problem are central to the social psychological approach to the social work process. In Part V, examples of its operation are given.

5
Groups

The analysis of groups is central to the social psychological approach. A broad outline of this analysis is presented below. The key issues fall under three headings:

(i)   The nature of groups
(ii) Intragroup dynamics:
    (a) the nature of group membership
    (b) the importance of norms and conformity processes
    (c) group decision making:
        1. 'groupthink'
        2. influence and dominance hierarchies
        3. communication networks
        4. factors influencing the quality of decisions
    (d) leadership
(iii) Intergroup dynamics:
    (a) explanations of conflict and cooperation between groups:
        1. the conflict of interests model
        2. the social identity model
    (b) reducing intergroup conflict:
        1. superordinate goals
        2. the GRIT proposal

The fourth and final part of this chapter will discuss the implications of the SPA analysis of groups for the social work process.

5.1 The Nature of Groups

Many definitions of this term 'group' are available in the literature. Some define groups mainly in terms of interaction among two or more individuals (Homans, 1950); others stress the notion of role differentiation (Greer, 1955); and most emphasize shared goals (Shibutani, 1961). Sherif (1966) produced a definition which typifies the majority. A group is:

> . . . a social unit that consists of a number of individuals (1) who, at a given time, stand in status and role relationships with one another, stabilized in some degree, and (2) who possess, explicitly or implicitly, a set of norms or values regulating the behaviour of individual members, at least in matters of consequence to the group. (p. 62)

The 'matters of consequence to the group' were considered to be goal attainment. The Sherif definition, although typical, fails to mention two important features of groups which Smith (1967) emphasizes:

> A group is defined here as (1) the largest set of two or more individuals who are jointly characterized by (2) a network of relevant communications (3) a shared sense of collective identity, and (4) one or more shared goal dispositions with associated normative strength. (p. 141)

Sherif focuses attention on the role structure within groups and the norms which maintain that structure and facilitate goal attainment. Smith introduces the need to consider communication networks between people and their 'shared sense of collective identity' when examining groups. Both perspectives are necessary in order to get a clear picture of what a group is and how it functions.

However, it is worth emphasizing that such analytic definitions tend to cloak the vastness of the diversity in types of groups which exist. Groups come in all shapes and sizes, from the family group to the racial group. Such groups vary along a whole series of dimensions:

(i)   Size — from two to thousands or more.
(ii) Length of life — from a few minutes to millenia.
(iii) Permeability of boundaries — the ease with which people can join and leave the group: some groups are easy to enter and leave (e.g. a group talking sociably around a bar); some are easy to enter but not to leave (e.g. the army); some are difficult to enter but easy to leave (e.g. élitist social clubs); and, some are difficult to enter and difficult to leave (e.g. secret societies like the Ku Klux Klan).
(iv) Origin of membership — in some groups membership is ascribed, people have no choice about their membership (e.g. racial groups); in other groups membership is achieved, people choose to join and seek admission (e.g. membership of a professional association).
(v)   Degree of bureaucratic organization and strictness of the status hierarchy — in some groups there is little bureaucracy, in others a vast structure; in some groups there are no status differentials between members, in others there is a complex and rigid status network.

54

Although these are separate dimensions, they tend to co-vary: high levels of bureaucracy being tied to high levels of status differentiation.

(vi) Cohesiveness — the degree to which individual members like each other and act as a single entity; this is associated with how far members identify with the group. Some groups lack cohesion and their members feel minimal group allegiance. Others are strongly cohesive and individual members lose their sense of a separate identity virtually completely.

(vii) Frequency of intragroup communication and its nature — communication takes place on many levels (verbal and non-verbal) and through various media (direct face-to-face through to codes bounced off satellites); groups differ in the channel of communication adopted and in the extent to which it is used.

(viii) Nature of goals — goals themselves vary along many dimensions but three of these are vital in determining a group's structure:

    (a) their complexity — greater goal complexity is associated with greater bureaucracy, more status differentials, etc.

    (b) their duration — short-term goals generate quite different group structures — greater permeability of group boundaries, less bureaucracy, etc.

    (c) their origin — some goals are specified by the group itself (indeed a group may crystallize around the desire to achieve a particular end), other goals are imposed upon the group by outside powers (this is particularly so when the group is part of a broader organization). Self-selected goals encourage cohesion among members.

Each group can be described in terms of each of these eight dimensions separately. However, positions along these dimensions tend to co-vary. There could be said to be two 'types' of group which represent opposite ends of the group spectrum: the concrete group and the conceptual group. Concrete groups and conceptual groups do not differ on all of the dimensions described above. But they differ on central dimensions. Concrete groups have specified goals, they have status hierarchies and bureaucratic structures, they have communication networks which are frequently used, they have members who identify with their group and are known to each other, and these groups have a sense of their own history. Conceptual groups have no goals, no status hierarchy, no communication between members (who remain anonymous), membership is ascribed not chosen, and boundaries are impermeable. Most groups can be arranged on a continuum which runs from the perfect 'concrete' group to the perfect 'conceptual' group. Most groups would fall between the middle and the 'concrete' end of this continuum. Nevertheless, examples of the 'conceptual' group do exist. Breakwell (1978a) describes the creation of conceptual groups by advertising campaigns. Such campaigns erect groups around a product; all people who consume the product are said to be group members. Such 'groups' are then attributed with positive characteristics. The advertisers play upon the fact that people seek self-esteem and can gain it from accepting membership of a 'group' which has been made to appear attractive. Of course, in advertising the process goes one stage further: membership of this attractive group can only be maintained we are told by purchasing and consuming the relevant product. So group affiliations are used to sell the goods. The point is that these 'groups' have no rules or roles (other than the consumer role), no goals, and no need for communication between members. They exist primarily within the concept system of those upon whom they are imposed; hence the label 'conceptual groups'. Even though these groups are not tied to any common set of social interactions they have the power to motivate behaviour and strangely enough the power to control allegiance. Members of conceptual groups created by advertising feel allegiance to their group and feel identification with other group members — they feel they would like other group members and are similar to them. The important thing to remember about conceptual groups is that membership is ascribed (imposed on people by others — through a process of labelling them members) and yet it still motivates allegiance. Given this fact, conceptual grouping can be a serious measure of social control. The conceptual group serves those who erect and impose it, not necessarily those who form its membership.

Having spent so much space elaborating upon how diverse are the different structures of groups, one would be forgiven for thinking that little could be said about how groups, as a whole, function. Yet this is not true. Much can be said about the general dynamics of group processes. Certain sorts of processes seem to go on in all types of groups regardless of their position on the eight dimensions described above. Nevertheless, like all generalizations, the ones below need to be treated cautiously.

5.2 Intragroup Dynamics

In this section the discussion revolves around what goes on *inside* groups.

The Nature of Membership

Membership of a group can be a complex process. It entails a transaction between the individual and the group. The individual receives the benefits of membership which may be material or psychological. In return, the group receives the individual's allegiance and abilities. Individuals tend not to join groups which cannot provide material or psychological benefits and, if possible, leave groups which cease to provide them with such benefits. Groups restrict entry to those who serve the groups' ultimate ends. Thus both the individual and the group have standards which are applied to membership.

For the individual such standards are embedded in what might be called the 'internal criteria' of membership (Breakwell, 1976). The individual has certain knowledge and beliefs about what a group can provide. In addition, the individual has certain aspirations and expectations about what can and should be gained from membership. A membership will be attractive if it can offer satisfaction of these aspirations and expectations.

For the group such standards are embodied in 'external criteria' of membership. The group expects members to possess certain characteristics. Expectations are sometimes transformed into explicit rules of entry: then only people possessing the relevant characteristics can gain entry. Often expectations are not formalized but operate just as effectively through mores and stereotypes; unless the candidate for membership complies with these unwritten rules of entry, the path is barred.

For membership of a group to be satisfactory for the individual the external criteria and internal criteria need to be compatible. Where the individual believes that the group wants one set of things from its members and the group actually wants something quite different there is trouble brewing. Unless the individual can reconstrue the situation, the membership is founded on misunderstanding and is consequently open to attack. The position of many social workers may provide a pertinent example. An individual may believe that the only important qualification for being a good social worker is talent in solving the problems of clients. That individual, having had some success with solving other people's problems might claim to be a good social worker. However, it is unlikely that social workers as a group would accept this as the criterion of membership of their professional group. It is more likely that this person would be told that it is necessary to have formal training in social work to join the professional group. This is an example where internal and external standards clash: the problem solver believes that he or she is a member of the group, the group will not accept him or her. An individual's response in this situation largely depends on whether the rejection is deemed legitimate; that is to say, it depends on the credence with which the 'external criteria' are viewed. If rejection is perceived as legitimate, it will be seriously considered and the individual may change his or her behaviour in order to comply with its requirements. If it is perceived as illegitimate considerable effort will be put into changing the 'external criteria' (Breakwell, 1976, 1978b). Of course, this clash between 'internal' and 'external' criteria can operate in the opposite fashion with the individual claiming not to be a member and the group insisting that he or she is a member. This might apply in the case of any sort of deviance. For instance, the person who had daily conversations with the devil in the local bus stop might not consider him or herself to be mentally ill. However, his or her psychiatrist might have other ideas about what characteristics suited someone to join the group of the mentally ill. Similarly, someone labelled 'criminal' by society might have a more idiosyncratic view of criminality, excluding his or her own behaviour from any such category. He or she would not then consider him or herself a criminal but would be considered a criminal by others. Again the clash of internal and external criteria is fundamental. In this variant, the importance of the clash is tied to whether others can impose membership on the individual. If the group can envelop the individual without permission the consequences can be serious. The individual is unlikely to be able to maintain an idiosyncratic set of internal criteria of membership in the face of the extensive pressures to conform operating inside the group.

Whether the incompatibility of internal and external criteria results in unaccepted eviction from the group or undesired absorption into the group, the effects on the individual are likely to be extensive. If the individual has substantial emotional investment in the membership or in avoiding membership the impact will be greater. The result is likely to be a change in self-concept and in self-esteem. In a sense, the incompatibility is a challenge to the validity of the individual's whole construct system. It queries whether the individual is interpreting and predicting the world accurately. This sort of threat to the construct system leads to revisions and, in the meantime, self-doubt. The revisions are, of course, not always directed inwards. Occasionally, such experience will lead the individual to challenge the existing 'external' criteria. This normally occurs when 'external' criteria can be characterized as unjust or illegitimate on the basis of comparison with other social institutions. Thus, for instance, the 'external' criteria of the US airforce exclude homosexuals from membership. This exclusion, accepted since the inception of the force, has been challenged since homosexuality has come to be accepted within other social groups. The challenge has been based on the assertion that if equality of opportunity is afforded homosexuals elsewhere in society, they should receive it in the airforce. Such a move in response to incompatibility is, however, very risky because the person issuing a challenge to the 'external' criteria must expect the group to defend itself from the implicit attack on its norms and standards. In a way, making the overt challenge to the group's 'external' criteria involves burning one's boats. The individual making the challenge virtually precludes any chance of re-entering the group through 'passing' (i.e. pretending the incompatibility does not exist) or through genuine attempts to change the internal criteria. If the challenge fails the person is either stuck on the outside of the group wanting to get in or on the inside wanting to get out.

Of course, in some cases membership is unproblematic: internal and external criteria are compatible. But it is worth remembering that membership is not an all or nothing process even then. An individual will retain aspirations and expectations about the group and, if the group fails to fulfil them, affiliation will decay. Membership is a process of exchange; unless the exchange continues to be satisfactory to both parties concerned, the bond joining the group and individual will be lost.

The Importance of Norms and the Conformity Processes

Emile Durkheim observed that whenever individuals collectively face an out-of-the-ordinary situation or problem that allows for numerous alternative interpretations or modes of attack, they develop a common interpretation or a common way of meeting the problem. Subsequently, such *répresentations collectives*, as Durkheim called them, affect the experience and outlook of the individuals with reference to the situation or the problem. The group's collective interpretation becomes dominant, it is the standard or *norm*. Norms help the individual to cope with new information or occurrences; they offer a standard frame of reference, a yardstick for interpretation and evaluation.

58

Norms help to disambiguate information because they focus attention on specific aspects of it, they indicate what can or should be ignored.

The power of group norms should not be underestimated. They exert mighty conformity pressures. Individuals find it difficult to resist the norm. The norm indicates the 'correct' way of viewing the world and the individual who does not agree is considered deviant by the group; moreover, the individual is likely to accept this verdict of deviance. A classic experiment by Solomon Asch (1956) indicates the power of the norm. Groups of subjects were presented with a series of cards, on each card there were four lines: the standard line (s) and three comparison lines (a, b, and c). The subject's task was to say which of the three comparison lines was similar in length to the standard line. The task was easy since the correct match was obvious. However, Sherif arranged the group so that in each (and they ranged in size from 2 to 19 subjects) there was only one naive subject. All the rest had been asked by the experimenter to give the same incorrect response. The subjects gave their answers in turn and the naive subject was normally second to last in answering (last in the dyads). Sherif found that one-third of the subjects under these conditions gave the incorrect answer that other group members had given. These subjects faced with a choice between giving the correct answer and that required by the norm were dominated by the norm. The power of the norm was evident so long as there were at least three other subjects who responded identically. Replications of the experiment throughout the 1950s and early 1960s confirmed the finding. Recently, however, there has been some discussion about whether such dramatic conformity effects would still be found. Some argue that during the 1970s people in the Western world grew less rule-bound and grew to care less about what others thought. Autonomy and self-esteem seem to militate against conformity.

Nevertheless, certain circumstances have been said to engender conformity within a group:

(i) Where there is little discrepancy among the opinions of group members — the number of people who are already deviants as regards the group norms is important; the more existing deviants, the more likely someone is to resist conformity pressures.

(ii) Where the opinion concerned is very important to the smooth functioning of the group — if it is important there is less chance of deviance being tolerated.

(iii) Where the group is cohesive — if individuals in the group like and respect one another they are more likely to conform to a group norm.

(iv) Where certain personality types are involved — the authoritarian, those low in self-esteem, the self-blaming, those high in the need to affiliate, the less intelligent, the anxious, and those with low tolerance for ambiguity are more likely to conform.

(v) Where there are superordinate norms of conformity — some cultures prize group conformity, others prize autonomy for the individual.

(vi) Where *deindividuation* is strong — this refers to the tendency that people have to lose their sense of their own personal identity in a group. Le Bon

59

(1896) first described this tendency in crowds, in which people will lose their sense of personal responsibility, allowing emotion to rule intellect, and accepted social restraints fail to function. This loss of restraint seems to go hand in hand with the feeling of anonymity. Zimbardo (1969) showed this in a simple experiment. Subjects were brought into a room and seated in a small group. They expected to be taking part in an experiment where they were to administer electric shocks to a person in another room and they believed the purpose of the experiment was to test their 'empathic ability' since they were asked to rate the person's reactions to the shocks. In fact, no shocks were given but the subjects saw film of a woman pretending to be hurt by their shocks. In one experimental condition, the women subjects were clearly identified: they wore their own clothes, wore a name tag, were introduced to each other, etc. In the other condition, the women wore loose white garments, had a hood over their heads, and were not introduced. This latter condition was considered likely to introduce a sense of anonymity. The hypothesis was that 'anonymous' subjects would feel less sympathy or empathy with the suffering of the woman they 'shocked' and would give a greater number of shocks. Both hypotheses were confirmed. This loss of restraint associated with deindividuation reinforces the tendency to conform with group norms.

People do sometimes withstand group pressures to conform: exhibiting 'reactance' or anticonformity. Some deviants can maintain resistance for a considerable time if they resort to another group for support. In such cases, the deviant does not use the group which labels him or her deviant as a means for self-evaluation; another group is used as the standard against which to compare behaviour and beliefs. In such a way, the deviant can maintain a positive self-image by disregarding rejection.

If the deviant can hold out in this way and can be consistent, then there is a possibility of changing the group norm. Faucheux and Moscovici (1967) and Moscovici *et al*. (1969) demonstrated the power of two persistent and consistent deviants on a group norm. The task was a colour discrimination problem. Subjects were pretested to establish that they had perfect colour vision and the colour slides had been tested to ascertain that some were consistently seen to be blue and others green. Subjects, in groups of six, were shown slides. The slides were blue. Two of the group had been briefed by the experimenter to say these slides looked green. Under this condition, 32% of all naive subjects were led to report that the slides were green even though they were clearly blue. This experiment was taken to expose the power of the persistent minority. Most interestingly it showed their power not simply in public but also in private. After the initial phase of the experiment, subjects did a further set of judgements about more slides but this time alone. Even alone there was a clear tendency for subjects to judge blue slides as green after exposure to the minority viewpoint. Moreover, those who had resisted the influence of the minority in public were even more influenced in their later private judgements. In public they upheld the majority norm, in private their judgements were bent by the minority norm. If minorities can get people to express their changed perceptions publicly it comprises an enormous breakthrough. Public complicity in the

60

promulgation of a new norm represents much greater commitment.

Within the group, the deviant can be a force for change. But the deviant first needs to stand outside of the group's conformity network and, second, needs to be consistent. The deviant who wants social approval from the group which is to be changed will never succeed nor will the one whose message is too complex or apparently inconsistent. The cardinal rules for the person who wishes to change group norms are (1) maintain emotional autonomy and (2) be simple and consistent.

Social workers often administer the pressures that a group can exert upon the deviant. Social workers often find themselves in the role of deviant wishing to change the system. They, therefore, see the process of conformity from both sides. Even then it is not easy to sit back and take an analytical look. The discussion above is designed to encourage such an analytical look.

Group Decision Making

'Groupthink'. Janis (1976) coined the term 'groupthink'; it

> refers to a deterioration of mental efficiency, reality testing and moral judgement that results from ingroup pressures (p. 407)

Janis argued that the overt agenda of a group might rank rational decision making very highly but the covert agenda ranks it second to the desire to maintain group cohesiveness, solidarity and intragroup friendliness. Janis explored decision making in a series of political fiascos (like the escalation of war in Vietnam by President Johnson, the Bay of Pigs Incident under President Kennedy and the Watergate affair) to prove his point. The decision-making process in these contexts showed six major defects:

(i) The groups limited themselves to a few alternative courses of action without a full survey of alternatives.
(ii) Members failed to re-examine initial decisions from the standpoint of non-obvious drawbacks that had not originally been considered.
(iii) Courses of action initially considered to be undesirable were neglected, never considering whether they had any non-obvious gains associated with them.
(iv) Outside expert evaluation of the group's decision was not sought.
(v) Only evidence to support their chosen course was sought, other information was ignored.
(vi) Little time was spent in discussing how the decision might be affected by bureaucratic inertia, sabotaged by political opponents or derailed by the media.

In such groups, loyalty to the group is of uppermost importance and represents the highest morality. Loyalty requires that each member avoid raising controversial questions or voicing doubts, questioning weak arguments or suggesting problems. The group represents a cohesive, self-sustaining organism and members need to conform to remain within the safety of its clutch. Other people outside the group are wrong or wicked. The group can do no wrong, anything it decides is regarded as morally good. Dissidents are seen to be traitors and wicked. This perception of outsiders legitimates atrocious treatment of those not in the group.

The symptoms of groupthink are at their height in times of stress where the decision may actually challenge the safety of the group in some way.

It should be emphasized that 'groupthink' is not reserved for government leaders and their minions. 'Groupthink' can happen in any group, particularly in any group under pressure to make critical decisions. Social work groups are thus prime breeding grounds for 'groupthink'. The symptoms should be carefully monitored:

(i)   illusions of invulnerability of the group;
(ii)   collective efforts to rationalize decisions even after they are shown to be inappropriate;
(iii) an unquestioning belief in the group's inherent morality;
(iv)   stereotyped views of the 'enemy' as too evil to warrant genuine attempts to negotiate with them;
(v)   emergence of self-appointed 'mind guards' who seek to protect group leaders from thoughts that might damage confidence in the group's decisions.

'Groupthink' can be prevented. It is important to build into groups a self-critical norm — encourage the expression of doubts and criticisms. The use of certain self-appraisal rituals is helpful — a time for second thoughts can be instituted (so that people having had time to think about the decision might bring forward new doubts or new information and this could be done in a less formal atmosphere than the first decision); also when making suggestions people can be asked to give all alternative solutions with their relative pros and cons; and, finally, experts who are not group members should be asked to join sessions on a selective basis. It obviously helps if the leader of the group can maintain an unbiased stance during deliberations so that no attempt can be made by followers to ingratiate themselves by supporting the leader's position in an unreasoned way. If possible it helps if the group can be subdivided and each subgroup works independently on the problem, then when the whole group reforms there is less singularity of allegiance and greater diversity of approach. These are, of course, only a few of the measures which might be taken to prevent 'groupthink'. The first step along the path to prevention is to recognize its existence.

Influence hierarchies. Groups normally have a 'pecking order'. Schjelderup-Ebbe (1938) described this phenomenon in relation to chickens: chicken A pecks B and C; chicken B pecks only C; and C pecks no one. A is most dominant in that pecking order, B next and then C. Pecking orders operate in human groups. Zander *et al.* (1957) showed one operating in the social structure of a mental health team composed of a psychiatrist, clinical psychologist and psychiatric social worker. These experimenters interviewed about 150 teams about their power relations. There was agreement that the psychiatrists were at the top of the power hierarchy with the psychologists second and social workers at the bottom. Interestingly this affected communication patterns in the teams: psychologists and social workers displayed a strong tendency to communicate up the hierarchy — to the psychiatrists — and limited themselves to comments they felt might obtain liking and support for themselves from the psychiatrists. Kelley (1951) argued that upward communication substitutes for upward mobility which is impossible to gain in reality.

The tendency for those higher in the power hierarchy only to communicate with their fellows in positions of power means that others have little chance to influence policy even though they attempt to do so by directing much of their efforts at the powerful. The tendency of the least powerful to fail to communicate with each other acts to reinforce their powerlessness because they do not come together to present a unified front with a single loud representative voice. Lack of communication leads to lack of cohesiveness which leads to lack of social power. The circle is vicious. It can only be broken if those in the least powerful positions choose to respect each other and act together.

Communication networks. The pattern and content of communication in groups has been studied extensively by social psychologists; there is only room to consider two methods of study here:

(i)   the Bales Interaction Process Analysis;
(ii) communication network analyses.

(i)   *The Bales Interaction Process Analysis* is a method for studying communication in groups. It was developed by Bales (1950) and requires an observer to observe and classify group interactions according to a pre-established category system. The classificatory frame is given in Table 5.1. The observer has to note who says what type of thing to whom.

Bales noted a typical structure for interactions in decision-making groups: they start with concern for the task — establishing what the group's goals are (during this time when task-relevant information is exchanged a differentiation of roles occurs with some more active in giving suggestions); as time passes and fatigue or problem difficulty has its impact, irritation and hostility set in and these will be met by efforts at reconciliation on the part of certain members which can result in the restoration of group solidarity and a return to task orientation.

Interventions which are designed to shape the development of the discussions should be made well before irritation grows. Strategic interventions work best early in the discussion and are most effective if regularly reiterated.

(ii) *Communication network analysis* involves the analysis in the laboratory of communication patterns that are carefully manipulated. Bales' technique can be used anywhere as a means of generating information and an understanding of how a particular group works, it is therefore useful in the social work process. Network analysis is not practicable as a technique but the findings that have been generated are valuable insights into how one might maximize the efficiency of intra-organizational communication.

63

Table 5.1 Bales' Interaction Process Categories

(Reproduced from R.F. Bales (1950) *Interaction Process analysis: a method for the study of small groups*, by permission of The University of Chicago Press. Copyright 1950 by the University of Chicago. All rights reserved.)

A Social – emotional area: positive reactions	1. Shows solidarity, raises other's status, gives help, reward.
	2. Shows tension release, jokes, laughs, shows satisfaction.
	3. Agrees, shows passive acceptance, understands, concurs, complies.
B Task area: attempted answers	4. Gives suggestion, direction, implying autonomy of other.
	5. Gives opinion, evaluation, analysis, expresses feeling, wish.
	6. Gives orientation, information, repeats, clarifies, confirms.
C Task area: questions	7. Asks for orientation, information, repetition, confirmation.
	8. Asks for opinion, evaluation, analysis, expression of feeling.
	9. Asks for suggestion, direction, possible ways of action.
D Social – emotional area: negative reactions	10. Disagrees, shows passive rejection, formality, withholds help.
	11. Shows tension, asks for help, withdraws out of field.
	12. Shows antagonism, deflates other's status, defends or asserts self.

With careful manipulation of setting it is possible to establish what pattern of communications works best and under what conditions. The manipulations involve bringing subjects into a laboratory and seating them in isolated cubicles. They can communicate only by way of written scraps of paper passed to each other through slots. In this situation, it is possible to control who can communicate with whom by closing or opening slots. The situation is highly artificial and yet not totally unrepresentative of chains of communication in highly stratified organizations where procedure dictates lines or channels of communication.

These sort of researches have largely focused on a single factor: how *centralized* the network of communication is. A centralized network is one in which a single person is key and all communications pass through that person, as if the person were a switchboard operator. Bavelas (1950) found that in a centralized network simple tasks could be dealt with effectively and quickly. Simple problems could be solved because the central person was capable of integrating all relevant information coming from all sources of communication and come to the right conclusion. However, where problems were complex and required more than a single person to deal with the information, the centralized network was inefficient. Errors made by the central person could not be filtered out by others because no one else had all the information. With complex problems it is best to have a system where communication is integrated. The centralized system has other disadvantages: the peripheral group members feel isolated and never feel they understand what they are working towards, they consequently become less satisfied with the group. Such findings are worth bearing in mind in organizing social work teams since these tend to be 'centralized'.

Factors influencing the quality of decisions. Each of the three areas already considered is likely to influence the quality of group decisions but there are other important factors. These can be summarized:

(i) The quality of decisions will be improved if all members accept a common goal; they all need to be working for the same end.

(ii) The quality of decisions will be improved if the task is divisible — that is to say if the task can be broken down into component parts such that each person can contribute a certain expertise to the solution of particular elements.

(iii) The quality of decisions will be improved if status differentials are not allowed to cloud judgements — that is if it is accepted that someone low in the hierarchy may have just as good an idea as someone higher in the power structure.

(iv) The quality of decision making will be improved if communication patterns are shaped according to the nature of the problem — centralized networks for simple problems; more diffuse networks for complex problems.

(v) The quality of decision making will be improved if the size of the group is tailored to the problem — there should be just enough people involved in order for them each to have a task to do, superfluous people waste energy and time and resources.

(vi) The quality of the decision making will improve if the group encompasses a number of different types of people (i.e. if it is heterogeneous) though they must form a reasonably cohesive band.

(vii) The quality of decision making will improve if the leader is good — what is meant by a good leader is discussed below.

Leadership

Stoghill (1974) described the cluster of traits associated with the *effective* leader:

a strong drive for responsibility and task completion, vigour and persistence in pursuit of goals, venturesomeness and originality in problem solving, drive to exercise initiative in social situations, self-confidence and sense of personal identity, willingness to accept consequences of decisions and actions, readiness to absorb interpersonal stress, willingness to tolerate frustration and delay, ability to influence other persons' behaviour, and capacity to structure social interaction systems to the purpose in hand. (p. 81)

However, as Hollander and Julian (1976) pointed out leadership is a process which depends on the interaction between the leader, the followers and the situation (which includes things like group size, resources, task in hand, etc.). Suedfeld and Rank (1976) provided a rather neat illustration of this point in their study of revolutionary leaders. They hypothesized that revolutionary leaders would need to be cognitively simple and categorically simple-minded in their approach to problems prior to the revolution and more sophisticated and broader after the revolution to deal with world politics. Their data support the hypothesis: only those leaders who became more complex in style remained in power after the revolution, the others were lost. The situation and the following determine the sort of leadership which is required. Leaders need to fulfil the expectations of their followers if they are to maintain support but this must not be done at the cost of their perceived competence. A leader must conform to group norms and be competent in solving the group problems if his or her legitimacy is to be assured. In this the individual's actual beliefs or abilities are less important than his or her *perceived* beliefs and abilities. The followers need to believe in the leader if the leader is to be able to influence them. The leader's influence is maximized where followers indulge in 'identification', treating the leader as an ideal person, someone to be emulated and admired. This does happen, particularly in times of crisis, when group members require reassurance and absolute truths.

Fiedler's *contingency model of leadership* is probably the best known social psychological analysis of leadership (Fiedler, 1967). The model has four basic components:

(i) Leadership style — leaders are said to vary along a continuum which runs from 'task orientation' to 'interpersonal orientation'; some leaders are more concerned with the completion of a the group's task than in its membership, others feel the relationships among members are the vital thing and the task is secondary.

(ii) Leader – member relations — this refers to how far the leader is liked and respected.

(iii) Task structure — the structure of a task is characterized along three dimensions: goal clarity, solution specificity, and decision verifiability; when all three are high, the task is highly structured and much activity relating to it is predetermined.

(iv) Position power — this refers to the authority invested in the position of leader within the group: some have great positional power (e.g. the Prophet in the Mormon religion), others have very little and depend upon manipulating agreement and approval.

Fiedler argued that different patterns or constellations of these factors are most effective. So, for instance, task-oriented leaders are most effective in *very* favourable or *very* unfavourable circumstances; that is, where they have either strong position power, good leader – member relations and a clear task structure or where this position is totally reversed. Relationship-oriented leaders are most effective in conditions which are moderately favourable, unfavourable and where the leader's influence and power are mixed or moderate.

The implications of Fiedler's work is that to make a leader more effective it is not necessary to seek to change that person's character or even style, it is rather necessary to change the situation or choose the right situation for that person to operate in. Fiedler *et al.* (1976) called this process 'leadermatch'. Such a solution is, of course, appropriate where mobility is feasible. When it is not, Fiedler's model gives less cause for optimism and resorting to attempts to change leadership styles may be more economical. Perhaps for the social work process both means of optimizing the value of leadership might be implemented.

5.3   Intergroup Dynamics

Explanations of Conflict and Cooperation between Groups

There have been two major social psychological theories evolved to explain conflict and cooperation between groups:

(i)   the conflict of interests model;
(ii) the social identity model.

The central tenets of both are given below.

The conflict of interests model. This explanation of intergroup conflict was evolved by Sherif (1966). His argument is simple: when two groups compete to attain a single objective or when they have different but mutually incompatible objectives, intergroup hostilities will result and norms of discrimination develop. Such norms legitimate the derogation of the outgroup and tend to cement affiliation to the ingroup. Sherif (1961) had shown empirical support for this notion when he created short-term groups and provided them with conflicting goals. Once the groups were established and their conflict of interests made explicit, Sherif was able to sit back and watch norms of discrimination take over.

There is a corollary to this argument which is that when groups have to cooperate in order to achieve goals desirable to both, discrimination and hostility will decline. Again Sherif found this occurred in his experimental groups. He called these mutually desirable goals 'superordinate goals' and claimed that their introduction militated against intergroup conflict.

From this it would seem that intergroup hostilities are bred of real competition to attain goals. In itself this is little more than a statement of common sense. It is hardly a theory of group conflict. Most importantly, a distinction must be drawn between what constitutes a *sufficient* cause for conflict and what is a *necessary* cause. The conflict of interests is undoubtedly a sufficient cause but its status as a necessary cause has been challenged. Tajfel (1978) has argued that group hostility and norms of intergroup discrimination do arise when *no* overt conflict of interests has occurred.

The social identity model. Having challenged the Sherif model, Tajfel went on to make a counter-proposal which has become known as the social identity model. Firstly, a series of studies were conducted in order to establish what were the minimal conditions of categorization which would evoke ingroup affiliation and outgroup deprecation. These studies (Tajfel, 1970; Tajfel *et al.*, 1971) showed that the mere act of classification is sufficient to arouse biases in favour of the ingroup. In the studies, subjects were arbitrarily divided into two groups, in some with no effort to disguise the fact that the division was random, and yet it was found that the groups had power to command the allegiance of so-called members. No explict or even implicit conflict of interests was necessary; no interindividual similarity of ingroupers; no actual or even anticipated interaction between group members is required; discrimination against outgroupers still occurs. These results have received repeated confirmation (Doise *et al.*, 1972; Doise & Sinclair, 1973; Tajfel & Billig, 1973). Such groups are almost perfect 'conceptual' groups; cognitive entities. Yet they can motivate behaviour and shape attitudes.

In such groups, where there are no group goals let alone competition with an outgroup for the goal, Sherif's model simply fails to explain discrimination and hostility. Tajfel proposed an alternative type of explanation. He suggested people derive their social identity from group memberships and wish to possess a positive social identity because this secures self-esteem. They consequently wish to belong to groups which can contribute to their self-esteem because they are high in status or power. In situations where the standing of a group is ambiguous, like in conceptual group experiments, its members seek to establish its superiority. By establishing their group's superiority they effectively establish their own superiority. Thus the other group is deprecated and their own glorified. Within this framework, hostility between groups is seen as the natural consequence of the drive that individuals have for a positive social identity.

Of course, like all explanations that ultimately resort to the use of needs or drives as the motive forces for action, this model is tautological. It represents a sort of intermediary explanation of the phenomenon. It is necessary to explain the need for a positive social identity before the theory becomes free of circularity. This has not been done. Nevertheless, the social identity model does highlight the fact that explanations simply in terms of conflicts of interest which have been offered for intergroup conflicts are inadequate.

Reducing intergroup conflict

Social psychologists have proposed two ways to reduce intergroup conflict:

Introduce superordinate goals. This was suggested by Sherif and has already been shown to work in some circumstances. However, even when such goals can be effectively introduced, they tend to reduce conflict only for the period during which the groups need to work jointly to achieve the goal. After the superordinate goal is attained, the groups return to their earlier hostilities. The superordinate goal therefore seems to be a relatively temporary means of conflict reduction, but can be useful nevertheless.

The GRIT proposal. This was suggested by Osgood (1962) and was designed for use in international relations. However, it can be used effectively at the intergroup and interpersonal levels too. GRIT stands for Graduated Reciprocation in Tension Reduction. In essence the suggestion is that the escalation of hostilities between groups can be forestalled or decelerated by the use of a graduated peace offensive. Such an offensive would consist of one side in the conflict acting *unilaterally* to defuse the situation (for instance, by restricting armament production or by exchanging valuable economic resources or services). The acts of unilateral peace must be substantial enough to engender trust and invite reciprocation. In fact, the side using this tactic should act and then explicitly invite reciprocation. But it is essential that the graduated plan should be continued regardless of whether reciprocation occurs in the earlier stages or not. It is essential that the other side should be told what to expect in advance and that acts are consistent with what they have been told. Publicity about these efforts is important since it can motivate the other side to make sure it is not seen to be in the wrong by failure to reciprocate. However, these conciliatory acts must be accompanied by explicit firmness if there is any sign that the other side are taking advantage. Consequently, unilateral conciliatory acts from a position of power are most effective. There is considerable experimental support for the effectiveness of GRIT as a technique (Pilisuk & Skolnick, 1968).

5.4   The Analysis of Groups and the Social Work Process

The group matrix is always a vital determiner of the individual's feelings and actions. In the social work process it needs to be continually considered. A social work problem may develop as a consequence of intragroup or intergroup dynamics. The social work solution to the problem may lie with manipulating intragroup or intergroup dynamics — even when the source of the problem does not lie in the group processes. Moreover, it is worth remembering that groups themselves have problems which may be brought to the social worker or community worker (some of these issues are considered in Chapter 17). For these reasons the social worker needs to understand something of the dynamics of group membership and intergroup relations.

The reflexive use of the SPA also dictates that the social worker should analyse his or her own group memberships and the relationship of social workers as a group to other groups (both professional and client groups). Chapters 22 and 23 attempt such an analysis.

Throughout Part V of this book, the importance of group processes to the social work process is illustrated and emphasized; they operate to shape the analysis of the problem and its solution. The SPA theories and evidence described above are meant to provide a simple introduction to the nature of these group processes. More information is available in Cartwright and Zander (1968).

6
Environment

The preceding discussions of identity, groups and relationships have ignored the importance of the physical environment. The purpose of this chapter is to examine the importance of the physical environment as a determiner of social behaviour. A simple-minded notion of the 'physical environment' is a sufficient starting point: it is the natural and artefactual world in which we live. It comprises the mountains and meadows, cities and cemetries, monasteries and mudhuts, chairs and crockery, roads and railways. The physical environment is the space and the inhabitations of space which surround us.

All social life takes place in the physical environment and it would be a gross error to believe that the physical environment is an irrelevance in the analysis of social life. Our social activities are not only contained by the physical environment, they are also constrained and structured by it. Much social behaviour depends on having an appropriate physical context and appropriate material resources. When the context or resources are missing or inadequate, social behaviour is necessarily modified. This is, of course, obvious. It is impossible to play squash without a squash court or swim without water. Perhaps there are other examples more relevant to social work practice. It may be impossible for unemployed young people to meet socially if there is no place set aside for them to gather. The place may be a street corner or it may be a youth centre or an amusement arcade. Unless they have somewhere to gather where their presence as a group is regarded as legitimate, their attempts to meet are fragmented and when successful are very threatening to others. Thus, the young people on the street corner, who gather there because there is nowhere else for them to go, are seen as 'gangs', 'layabouts', and 'undesirable'. They are targets for abuse and are frequently moved on by the police often simply because it is not their 'place' to be there rather than because of anything they do. There are many other examples of how the absence of particular resources in the physical environment or their peculiar location shape social behaviour. Take the hypothetical case of the disabled pensioner who has no personal transport and is thus relatively immobile. He (She) would like to see other people; he (she) has always been outgoing and likes dealing with others. Ideally, he (she) and his (her) social worker would like him (her) to attend a day centre where he (she) could meet others effectively. The only problem is that the nearest day centre is 15 miles away. The simple facts of his (her) immobility and the distance of the centre can mean the isolation of the man (woman). The more complex facts of inner city life might even mean that he (she) is deprived of company even within the narrow confines of his (her) own tower block. His (Her) physical environment traps him (her) just as effectively as the spider's web traps the fly. It is unnecessary to go on with other examples, all of our everyday experiences indicate the truth of the assertion that contexts and resources have a fundamental impact on social behaviour and on consequent attitudes or emotions.

It goes virtually without saying that the process can operate in reverse: people change the physical environment. They do it intentionally, for instance when they build cities or airports or canals, and they do it incidentally when they pollute the seas and the stratosphere. On the one hand, people change the physical environment to suit themselves; on the other hand, in the very act of inducing that change, they set in motion a series of chain reactions over which they have no control or very little and which may change the environment in ways which far from suit their instigators. One may drop a pebble into a pool to get rid of it but the ripples that result when it breaks the surface may be far from desirable.

The interaction of people with the physical environment is very complex. It is certainly no simple unidirectional causal relationship. People do not simply control the environment; no more than the environment simply controls them. The interaction has to be seen as a process which is continual and never ending: people bend to the environment and the environment bows to them. Change on the part of either may not be explicitly negotiated but it is clearly ultimately the result of compromise.

The social worker, in analysing a problem situation and in choosing an intervention strategy, must take the physical environment into consideration. Upon occasion, the physical environment may be fundamental to a client's problems. For example, physical isolation may be at the root of a client's problems because it means he or she cannot get to the shops to feed him/herself regularly. However, it is more frequently the case that the physical environment merely mediates other reasons for a client's problems. Thus, for instance, a social worker may find himself or herself dealing with a family which has no cohesion, where the parents fight and the children are pawns in the battle. It may be the case that many of the difficulties seem to stem directly from their inadequate accommodation: it is small, overcrowded, noisy, and in a difficult area. In such a case, it is easy to pin the problem on the physical environment. However, that may be the wrong thing to do. An essential question has to be answered before

72

the physical environment can be considered the fundamental source of such a family's problems. Why are they in such accommodation? If the answer is something to do with the poverty of the family and this poverty is due to the unemployment of the parents at a time of economic recession then there are other causes for the client's problems. Poverty may be the fundamental source of the problems, the physical environment mediates this poverty but it is not the source of the problem. The physical environment often acts as a mediator in the evolution of problems.

In most cases, the analysis of a client's problem will entail consideration of the physical environment even when it is not implicated as a 'cause' of the problem. This is because the manipulation of the physical environment may be the route to the solution or at least amelioration of the problem. For instance, a divorcee may be being harassed by her ex-husband. The physical environment may have nothing to do with her problem. Nevertheless, a change in the physical environment may assuage her problem. The change may be as simple as removing her telephone or as drastic as changing her accommodation. Either way, the manipulation of the physical environment can alleviate a problem that it had nothing to do with generating.

So, the physical environment is important to the analysis of the problem by the social worker; it may be implicated in both its cause and in its solution. But the physical environment is also important to the very *process of social work* itself. Social work, like all other social behaviour, takes place inside a physical environment and the impact of this physical environment on what the social worker can do should not be ignored. From both the client's and the social worker's point of view the physical environment in which their interchange takes place is important. It will influence how the social worker perceives the client and how the client perceives the social worker. Some of the aspects of this synchronous process of influence will be described below.

Essentially, the central arguments above can be summarized by saying that the physical environment can have four roles in the process of social work. It can:

(i) be a determiner of a problem or it can mediate the determination of a problem;

(ii) be manipulated in order to bring about the amelioration or solution of a problem;

(iii) act as a context to the analysis of the problem and thereby influence the conclusions drawn;

(iv) influence the way in which the client perceives the social worker and the social worker's actions.

In order to understand these four roles it is necessary to consider some of the theories and data of environmental psychology. The single major characteristic of environmental psychology might be said to be its lack of a unifying framework. There are innumerable studies of the effects of specific environments on specific behaviours or attitudes in specific people. Many of these are reported in such texts as Heimstra and McFarling (1978), Porteous (1977), Rapoport

(1977) and Altman (1975). The reader wishing further material might refer first to these texts. However, here, it has been necessary to be selective and the selection has been on the basis of what might be useful to social workers in practice.

6.1 Privacy

Altman's (1975) model of the environment and social behaviour is of considerable practical value and will forms the basis for much of the ensuing discussion. Altman argued that the key concepts in understanding how people operate in the physical environment are privacy, personal space, territory and crowding. Altman postulates that privacy is of primary importance. He defines privacy as 'selective control of access to the self or one's group' (p. 18). Privacy is important because, as Westin (1970) pointed out, it serves four functions:

  (i)   personal autonomy
 (ii)   emotional release
(iii)   self-evaluation
 (iv)   limited and protected communication

Privacy enables individuals to relax from social roles and expectations; they can behave as they wish, say what they like to whomever they like, assess themselves and plan the future. Of course, people do not need privacy all the time. But everyone needs privacy sometimes. The task before most people is to optimize privacy: to have as much as is desired but no more and no less. Too much privacy can turn into isolation; too little privacy can be like living in a goldfish bowl, being continually on show. Of course, different people have differing demands for privacy. Some desire privacy most of the time, others need privacy only occasionally. No matter what the absolute level needed, if there is a disparity between what is desired and what is achieved the individual will be dissatisfied.

In order to achieve the desired level of privacy, various mechanisms come into play. Two of these are central: personal space and territory. These will be considered in turn.

6.2 Personal Space

According to Sommer (1969) 'personal space refers to an area with an invisible boundary surrounding the person's body into which intruders may not come. . . . Personal space is not necessarily spherical in shape, nor does it extend equally in all directions . . .' (p. 26). Goffman (1971) emphasized the vital feature of personal space: within it 'an entering other causes the individual to feel encroached upon, leading him to show displeasure and sometimes to withdraw' (p. 30). Personal space is effectively mobile territory appended to the individual. When it is breached the individual's sense of personal control

74

is threatened, anxiety and stress result and may be followed by flight or aggression.

How we come by our sense of personal space is not really known. We are not born with it. Young children have no clearly delineated personal space. It seems that they have to learn about where the boundary between oneself and others should lie. Parents are instrumental in this process. They often explicitly instruct their children on the appropriate distances to maintain from others in different social situations. This instruction begins early in the socialization process. By adolescence, the personal space system is well established.

Since personal space is a function of the socialization process, it is hardly surprising that it is subject to individual and cultural variations. The research on individual variations of particular interest to social workers is probably that on people with personality disorders or social – emotional disorders; for example, schizophrenics, psychotics, neurotics, and drug addicts. Such people seem to have different self/other boundary systems from most people.

Research indicates that schizophrenics prefer to maintain greater distances from other people than do those who are not psychiatric patients and the distance they maintain is more variable (Horowitz et al., 1964). As their clinical state improves, the personal space requirements of such patients become more similar to those of non-patients (Horowitz, 1968). The same sort of need for a greater personal space is shown by children with social and emotional disturbances (Weinstein, 1965; Fisher, 1967; DuHamel & Jarmon, 1971; Newman & Pollack, 1973). Kinzel (1970) examined the personal space requirements of prisoners and found that violent prisoners required four times as much space as non-violent prisoners. Altman (1975), after reviewing the evidence, concludes:

> Abnormality, in any of several forms, is associated with either (1) greater interpersonal distance from others or (2) greater variability in distance kept from others. (p. 71)

A central question for the social worker who deals with people who are 'abnormal' in some sense is, 'How do others react to those with abnormalities or defects?' Kleck et al. (1968) demonstrated that people maintain a greater distance from those labelled as having some type of social stigma (e.g. amputees, epileptics, or mental patients) than the non-stigmatized. Moreover, greatest distances were maintained from those with non-visible stigma (e.g. epilepsy and mental illness). The tendency to wish to distance oneself from the handicapped, whether mental or physical, is quite general (Wolfgang & Wolfgang, 1971; Comer & Piliavin, 1972) and begins early in life (Lerner, 1973). Physical distancing of 'deviants' seems to be part of the process of self-protection people engage in.

It seems then that in interacting with 'deviants' the normal rules of exchange and placement do not work. The reason for their failure lies in the nature of the interaction between the 'deviant' and the 'normal'; neither party can be said to be solely to blame for their dysfunction. The 'deviant' could be said to push the interactive system slightly out of kelter but this is then magnified and accentuated by the response elicited from the 'normal'. The lubricant of social

75

interchange is thus not refurbished and friction is likely because neither party really knows which rules are operative. Of course, the social worker who is aware that this breakdown is a possibility has every chance of avoiding it. Such avoidance requires the social worker to pay attention to the demands for personal space that a client in this category may make and to be responsive. It may often mean curbing personal reactions: the social worker may find his or her own personal space invaded or ignored and may have to endure this. The key to controlling what might seem like instinctive reactions in these situations is a simple awareness that the reaction is likely. The key is *anticipation* and this can only be achieved through a high degree of *self-awareness*.

Quite apart from individual differences in personal space requirements, there are cultural differences. There are, for instance, marked sex differences. These are reviewed by Altman (1975), he concludes:

> the thrust of the data is that males have larger personal-space zones than females and that people generally maintain greater distance from males than from females. (p. 74)

It should, however, be added that these sex differences are affected by the age and ethnic group of those interacting and the situation in which they interact. The differences become blurred quite quickly. Nevertheless, they are worth bearing in mind. For instance, the female social worker may find that her personal space is being encroached upon because a male client expects women to need less space. The irony may lie in the fact that when not acting in an official capacity the social worker would expect to have a smaller personal space than the men around her, but when acting officially her authority adds a larger shell to the personal boundary. What to her as a woman would not be an encroachment, to her as a social worker is an encroachment.

The same sorts of misunderstandings are likely to emanate from other cultural differences in personal space boundaries. The evidence about differences between ethnic groups is not simple and is contradictory. Massive generalizations like 'Arabs require less personal space than Americans' (Watson & Graves, 1966) are worthless for social work purposes; so are statements like the middle class requires greater distancing than the lower socioeconomic groups (Scherer, 1974). They are worthless because they are often based on inadequate evidence and on data derived from samples in atypical situations. Most social workers have their own 'patch'; an area they know well and whose occupants are familiar to them. If social workers are to take account of cultural differences in personal space, it is wise to do so through observing their operation on the ground, in their 'patch'. The observing social worker can build up a picture of the personal space requirements and, indeed, other non-verbal mechanisms of his or her clientele. Such information is valuable in avoiding misunderstandings. If the social worker understands the client's system of personal space signals, there is less chance that either will encroach upon the other.

Amidst all this talk of individual and cultural differences in personal space requirements it should not be forgotten that there are situational constraints on the operation of personal spacing mechanisms. Personal space requirements are sensitive to the nature of an interaction and to the purpose of an interaction. When the person with whom we interact has similar views to ourselves, is liked, and has favourable personal attributes (like high intelligence or high prestige), we allow greater proximity (Altman, 1975, pp. 82–83). If the interaction requires self-disclosure (as in a counselling session) greater proximity is preferred. In fact, Haase (1970) found that distances of 30 to 50 inches were preferred by subjects in counselling situations. Being too far away, even only 66 to 88 inches, led to a feeling of less warmth and satisfaction. Moreover, Albert and Dabbs (1970) found that people listen most attentively to a message from a speaker about 4 feet away and are most open to persuasion from that distance. All of this seems to imply that the social worker should take care to optimize physical distance from a client taking into consideration individual, cultural and situational factors. However, in doing so, it is necessary to understand that violation of personal space need not simply be a matter of getting too close to someone physically. Violations may entail the use of inappropriate body positions (for instance, leaning forward with sudden intensity during a discussion can serve to make a point with emphasis, but often it does so because it indicates potential intrusions into the other's personal space). Alternatively, violations may operate at the symbolic level (for instance, staring at another can be regarded as a threat or challenge). The social worker needs to anticipate how his or her actions will be interpreted in the negotiation of personal space in order to optimize the interaction with the client.

In using this notion of personal space to inform social work practice, it is important to recognize that *both* the client and the social worker have a concept of their own personal space. Either can find that they are viola*ting* or viola*ted*. The art of effective interaction lies in monitoring the exchange of space, whether at a physical or symbolic level, and ensuring an equilibrium that offers security to both parties. The social worker who feels uneasy in an interaction with a client might do well to establish in what ways the equilibrium has been disturbed. Reinstituting the equilibrium oils the wheels of effective communication which is a fundamental skill of social work.

6.3 Territory

Personal space is the mobile territory that an individual has appended to his or her person. People also have more static territories — geographical areas that are personalized and are marked in some way so as to show they 'belong' to the individual. Such territories are normally defended against encroachment. Altman (1975) describes three sorts of territories: primary, secondary and public:

(i) 'Primary territories are owned and used exclusively by individuals or groups, are clearly identified as theirs by others, are controlled on a relatively permanent basis, and are central to the day-to-day lives of the occupants.' (p. 112)

(ii) 'Secondary territories are less central, pervasive, and exclusive . . .'
(p. 114)
(iii) 'Public territories have a temporary quality, and almost anyone has free access and occupancy rights.' (p. 118)

Examples of these three sorts of territory might be: primary territory — the individual's house; secondary territory — the individual's local pub; and public territory — the individual's local park.

The social work process often involves the social worker entering the client's primary or secondary territories. Upon occasion such entry is permissible because the client invites the social worker in or because the client believes that the social worker's job legitimates temporary access even though no explicit invitation has been extended. On other occasions, entry will be seen as a violation and may even be viewed as 'contaminating' the territory or rendering it impure.

Such violations and contamination of the client's territory, especially primary territory, can have serious consequences. An individual's identity often gets bound to territory. The territory facilitates privacy and allows for the functions of privacy to be fulfilled (as was mentioned earlier). Much of the purpose of privacy involves ensuring the security of the individual's identity. Privacy gives the opportunity for self-evaluation and self-inspection which are vital if an effective identity is to be maintained. Privacy also gives the opportunity for intimacy with others who are valued and who value us; again providing a vital support structure for identity. If the territory is violated, privacy is lost and identity is threatened. The link between identity and territory is expressed in other ways too. In one's own territory it is possible to express one's identity. By choosing this piece of furniture rather than any other, or that painting rather than another, or those curtains and no others, the person imbues the territory with an identity of its own which is in turn an expression of that person's identity. We mould our territories to suit our identities and they can tell the careful observer much about us. Thus the territory acts simultaneously as a harbour where maintenance work is done on the identity and as a medium through which that identity is symbolized. As a result, any violation of the territory can be a dual threat to identity: putting both its maintenance and expression at risk.

The social worker who violates a client's territory may be endangering much of value. Yet violations may be absolutely necessary; it may be the social worker's legal responsibility to force entrance to a territory. In such situations, there are one or two things to remember:

(i) Expect the client to warn you that you are violating the territory — warnings take many forms (verbal and non-verbal) but they serve a single purpose: the reinstigation of boundaries and they are easily identified when they are sought.

(ii) Expect escalation of warnings and, perhaps, a shift into actual aggression if the violation is extended over time or is located in particularly intimate territories.

78

(iii) The negative effects of violations can be ameliorated by the use of certain rituals — for instance, small things like waiting to be asked before sitting down in a client's living room.

(iv) Take time to understand what the territory symbolizes to the client and be wary of assuming the client 'sees' it in the way you do — this is important because a territory which symbolizes nothing more than squalor to the social worker may reflect a life's work to its occupant (this will be considered again later in the discussion of habituation).

(v) Expect to feel a certain amount of psychological stress when called upon to violate a client's territory and do not over-react to it (do not interpret it as a sign of personal inadequacy, such a response is quite predictable).

Bearing these five things in mind, it is possible to minimize the impact of violations.

Thus far, the discussion has centred on the client's territory, whether primary or secondary, and there has been no mention of the social worker's territory. Yet interactions with clients do take place in the social worker's territory: in the office or interview room. Admittedly, these may not be regarded as primary territories. Nevertheless, they are arenas in which the social worker has a degree of investment and with which he or she is identified. Occupants normally personalize their office in some fashion. They like their desk in a certain place, they like their chair in a specific relationship with other chairs in the room, they like the window open and they like to be close to it, they dislike noise around them, etc. A client entering this personalized environment is expected to conform to the rules of that environment: not to move the chairs, not to close the window, not to whistle distractingly, etc. The client who breaks the rules is violating the territorial powers of the social worker. This can be extremely disconcerting for the social worker who has not realized how much he or she depends on having the environment just so and under control. It changes the balance of power slightly or at least adjusts the fulcrum of initiative in the interchange. This may, of course, be beneficial, giving the client the initiative. However, in fact, the client will rarely take the initiative in the social worker's territory or, at least, not effectively. The client is more likely to be subdued by the symbols of the social worker's authority and legitimacy which are embedded in the territory: the desk, the forms, the records, and all the bureaucratic paraphernalia. Sometimes, subduing a client is desirable, particularly if the client is irate or dissatisfied. But at other times, the last thing that the social worker wishes to do is subdue the client. In such instances, it is useful to know what sorts of environments are least likely to subdue or subordinate. Data, already discussed in the section on personal space, indicate that maintaining a certain level of proximity facilitates interchange (4 feet seems about right). Interchange is made more formal if a desk intervenes between the participants. The social worker who comes out from behind the desk is less likely to subdue the client. Placement of chairs is important: they should not be opposite each other rather they should be at right angles so that interactants have to turn slightly to talk and look each other in the eye. Untidy offices are seen as small and constraining but give an informal air to the interchange which may be desired. There are many other features which might be considered: decor, the route of access, noise levels, the permeability of the territory to others during the interchange, etc. More details can be found in Heimstra and McFarling (1978), Chapter 3.

Of course, a social worker will rarely have much leeway to change the context in which he or she works. Substantial changes in decoration and structure are likely to be the responsibility of the employing agency and are likely to be determined by economic considerations. However, the social worker will have control over certain aspects of furniture layout and these should be manipulated to optimize their impact on the client and to serve a useful purpose in facilitating interaction.

The emphasis above has been upon primary and secondary territories and yet public territories can be of vital importance in the social work process. Two types of public territory are institutions (like elderly people's homes and mental hospitals) and neighbourhoods; some of the dynamics in each are considered below.

Institutions

It is important to realize that institutions tend to become total worlds for their inmates, who have no other territory. Inmates in psychiatric hospitals and in old people's homes have lost their earlier territories and have to carve out new ones inside the institution. Territory inside the institution is difficult to keep because it is difficult to mark it as one's own; after all, the inmates know that the institution as a whole is a public territory, they know that they have no legal jurisdiction over it. This means that inmates' efforts to mark out patches of territory for themselves can be haphazard and can operate only in trivial areas (though they may not seem trivial to the inmates). For instance, the old people's home's inmates will lay claim to particular chairs as 'theirs' and no one else is allowed to use them (Lipman, 1967, 1968); removing the chairs can precipitate a crisis. Another sort of example comes from Hereford *et al.* (1973). They reported how nine institutionalized retarded adults who had a long history of night bedwetting were placed in less dense sleeping arrangements; each bed was given more room and was bounded by a painted mark indicating its space. They found that there was a marked decline in bedwetting under the new layout. It is not really possible to establish whether the change in amount of bed territory was directly a determiner of the decline in bedwetting. It may simply be that both events were correlated with and generated by other simultaneous changes. However, the researchers suggested that under close living conditions, where there were no real territories, bedwetting may have served as a means of marking territory, when territories were marked in other ways bedwetting proved no longer necessary. If they are right and bedwetting serves territorial purposes just as urination serves to mark the territory of other animals, it may have important implications for those families battling with an enuretic child. Social workers involved with such families might consider the total

80

environment that surrounds the child and examine whether a small change in territorial definitions might solve the problem. It seems preferable to consider this, at least as a preliminary, before resorting to aversive therapies aimed at behaviour modification.

Where these efforts to mark out territory in an institutional setting fail, the process of institutionalization (the loss of personal identity and autonomy) is accelerated. To some extent, this would be reason enough for social workers to intervene when possible to support the client in territorial exploits. However, the social worker is restricted by the resources available; it may be impossible to provide ecological niches for even a small proportion of an institution's inmates. Nevertheless, even though knowledge of the processes of territoriality in such settings may not lead to specific ameliorative action strategies, the knowledge is valuable. Understanding something of the process should militate against the misinterpretation of a client's behaviour and needs.

Neighbourhoods

The definition of a neighbourhood is not easy to produce, it is simplest to think of it as a district within which a community resides. People tend to think of their neighbourhood as their territory. Membership of the neighbourhood can be very important to the individual and a family. People feel allegiance to their neighbourhood even when in objective terms it could be called a slum. Some of the strongest neighbourhoods are in inner cities and they are poverty-stricken, crime-ridden, jobless places without recreational or educational facilities. Fried and Gleicher (1972) studied Boston's West End slums. They describe the strong sense of belonging which residents felt and the strong social ties and friendship network which encircled the area. In such communities, the primary territory of the home is extended on to the streets and the external environment becomes a part of the home with many personal and social activities taking place in the street. Similar results have been found elsewhere (see Rapoport, 1977, pp. 96−100 for a review of these studies). This means that urban renewal has its problems: the dislocation of territory and the destruction of social networks.

Social workers involved in moving families or individuals from one neighbourhood to another need to be aware of this problem. A situation which the social worker perceives as unpleasant may be completely satisfactory to the occupants. This is not to romaticize the slum it is rather to recognize that the social worker and client may have different values and different expectations. When the social worker claims the priority of his or her values and expectations, it can breach basic territorial allegiances which the client feels. In understanding the client's acceptance of what seems to the social worker unacceptable, the concept of 'habituation' is useful. People are adaptive. People change to deal with new situations. More than this, they sometimes change without ever knowing it. They get used to the situation which surrounds them and think nothing of it. If the situation is habitual, they habituate. Events of a certain type may initially appal us (e.g. lurid report of child molestation or a rat found swimming in our toilet) but if they are frequent enough we grow accustomed to them, they lose their power to shock or even concern, and ultimately we hardly recognize them when they happen. This is the process of habituation. Thus the inequities of life in the slums are hardly perceived — except when there is a change in the expected pattern of events (for instance, when unemployment pushes people towards greater poverty). It is difficult for the social worker to see through the eyes of habituation. Perhaps it is inadvisable to try because it would dissuade the social worker from seeking change. Yet change is problematic.

Attempts at urban renewal have come up against many problems. The problem of breaking old neighbourhood loyalties is only one. Other problems seem to arise from the sort of public housing which has been created to replace these so-called slums. The physical characteristics of such buildings, until quite recently high-rise developments, do not favour either social relations among residents or normal family activities. Individual familial housing units tend to be small and insulation against noise from outside or other rooms is minimal. The front door to an apartment often opens onto a corridor which is seen as a public thoroughfare and this weakens the occupants' willingness to use it for social interaction. Interaction between parents and children is reduced by the separation of the home from places where play is permitted and this reduces parental control over the behaviour of offspring. Such developments are characterized by what Newman (1973) calls an absence of 'defensible space'. They are surrounded by space which is not considered to be the responsibility of any particular group and this space is not subject to effective surveillance by any protective agency. The result, according to Newman, is a higher incidence of crime against property and persons in these areas. Moreover, criminals are more likely to escape detection because people do not know their neighbours well enough to be able to identify an intruder. Since most people are anonymous in these areas, the intruder is unremarked.

The picture of these inner city developments is therefore not a pretty one, especially when one adds to the mixture above the fact that most of the occupants will be drawn from the poorest and least educated groups in the community. It is a cocktail that most social workers will be knowledgeable about, many of their clients will come from such developments. The social worker has little power to influence housing policy of course. The social worker deals primarily with the consequences of such housing policy and battles with the symptoms rather than the causes of problems in this area. Even at the level of mitigating symptoms, some knowledge of causes is valuable. Thus the discussion of public housing above is not considered wasted.

6.4 Crowding

Personal space and territoriality have been described as mechanisms designed to achieve privacy. When they fail, achieved privacy will be less than desired privacy and the individual or group will feel *crowded*. This notion of crowding

82

is fundamentally a psychological concept. Crowding occurs when the individual has to deal with *an excess of undesired social contact*. The key word here is 'undesired'. A person need not feel crowded in the midst of a packed football terrace, even though he stands like a sardine in a can, because he desires this social contact. On the other hand, a person can feel crowded on a deserted beach because he or she sees just one other person on the horizon. This emphasis on the desirability of social contacts separates the experience of being crowded from the sheer density of other people. Of course, high density increases the likelihood of interpersonal contacts and the likelihood of interference with various boundary-control mechanisms but it is not synonymous with crowding. Whether such increased contacts are perceived as undesirable is dependent upon the nature of the environment and the expectations held of it; the nature of the people involved and the attitudes held about them; and the nature of the contacts and their duration. Where one person feels crowded, another will feel isolated because it is a function of a very subtle assessment process where many factors are taken into consideration.

Studies of responses to crowding show it to be correlated with high anxiety and stress levels (Smith & Haythorn, 1972), greater hostility to other people and to the environment (Paulus *et al.*, 1975), greater avoidance of social interaction (Valins & Baum, 1973) and, over lengthy periods, with lower levels of performance on problem-solving tasks (Sherrod, 1974). Some of the other correlates of crowding are discussed in Altman (1975, pp. 184–192).

There are various theoretical perspectives used to understand crowding. Stokols (1976) categorizes them:

(i)   stimulus overload theories;
(ii) behavioural constraint theories;
(iii) ecological theories.

The three types of theory focus on different levels at which crowding can operate. The stimulus overload model postulates that people can only deal effectively with a certain level of stimulus input, when that level is exceeded information can no longer be processed efficiently, and the person wishes to reduce stimulation. This is a theory concerned with tolerance levels of the individual's psychological equipment for assimilating and accommodating to stimuli. When overload occurs social behaviour changes: there is withdrawal from social interaction to prevent stimulation. Milgram (1970), a leading exponent of this view, argues that city dwellers are overloaded and adopt various strategies to keep input to a manageable level. For instance, the urbanite is unwilling to interact with another unless it is absolutely necessary and this results in what has been labelled 'bystander apathy' — ignoring others in distress who need help. According to Milgram, the entire prepackaged nonchalance of city dwellers to their fellows is a symptom of stimulus overload; one which has been refined to an art form and crystallized in what amounts to an etiquette of the streets.

The behavioural constraint theories assume that the effects of crowding are so perturbing because crowding curtails the freedom which people have to act in a way they wish (Proshansky *et al.*, 1970). The ecological theories, stemming from Barker (1968), centre on the idea that each context has a certain number of niches or places for people where they can play a role; when the number of people exceed the number of niches there is 'overmanning'. Crowded environments are overmanned environments. Both of these theories deal with the social consequences rather than the causes of crowding. Both emphasize how crowding will constrain social behaviour.

In many ways, the three theoretical perspectives are compatible rather than competitive. Taken together they portray something of the operation of crowding at the psychological and the social levels. As magnifying glasses through which behaviour can be analysed these theories have considerable value for the social work process. First, they enable the social worker dealing with clients in crowded environments to anticipate something of the clients' reactions. Second, they encourage the social worker to analyse those reactions against the broad backcloth of the clients' environment. Third, they channel thoughts about the possible means of helping the client; an assessment of the environment must be a precursor to any decision about the sort of strategy to use. Perceiving the client as a cog in the machinery of the environment may seem distasteful to someone who believes in the free will and potential to change that a client has. Yet, for the purposes of analysis, a mechanistic orientation can work wonders. Contextualizing a response has advantages because seeing it in isolation may make it meaningless or, worse still, may endow it with meaning that it does not have. The woman who locks herself in the lavatory for an hour every day may be regarded as 'mad' and her behaviour non-adaptive if her context is ignored. But if the behaviour is contextualized — she lives in a crowded flat with young children, she has no private territory, she is pestered by noisy neighbours, etc. — escape to the lavatory becomes not only sensible but logical too. The social worker who knows something of the dynamics of crowding is unlikely to decontextualize such a behaviour and this transforms the way that behaviour is analysed. A problem behaviour is less likely to be seen as originating in the individual, it is more likely to be seen as originating in the relationship between the individual and the environment. Dealing with the problem in the social work process becomes a matter of evolving strategies to change that relationship between individual and environment and this may mean changing the environment rather than the individual. In fact, the social worker adopting this perspective is much more likely to locate his or her intervention simultaneously at a series of levels: affecting the individual, the family, the community and the environment (this notion of multiple levels of analysis and intervention is central to Chapter 12).

6.5 Conclusion

The social work process must take account of the physical environment because it can (i) determine or mediate the determination of a problem; (ii) be instrumental in solving a problem when manipulated effectively; (iii) influence the way the social worker relates to the client and the problem; and (iv) influence the way the client responds to the social worker.

The concepts of privacy, personal space, territory and crowding are useful in the organization of the large amount of data available on environmental psychology. These concepts can be used effectively in analysing social work problems and in evolving strategies to overcome them.

7

Personal and Social Change

The primary function of the social work process is to instigate and shape patterns of personal and, sometimes, social change. The change may be physical or economic, psychological, social or even political. Social workers are involved in administering and designing change on all these planes. In dealing with a single client change on each level may be desirable. Take for example the hypothetical case of a young family man who is paralysed from the waist down after a car accident. At the physical level the social worker may be involved in ensuring the man has a wheelchair and is furnished with various aids for the disabled around his home. At the economic level the social worker may be asked to sort out his disability benefits. At the psychological level the social worker may be instrumental in leading the man to accept his disability and cope with family life. At the social level the social worker may need to counsel his friends and relatives on the implications of his disability. At the political level the social worker may be involved in attempts to change council policy on the provisions for disabled shoppers in the local town centre. At each level the social worker is involved in change and it is worth remembering that change at one level will have repercussions on other levels. Most changes have simultaneous reverberations at both the personal and social levels.

In the preceding four chapters on the nature of relationships, identity, groups and the environment the emphasis has been upon providing a framework necessary for the analysis of social work problems. They have served to outline the SPA to the analysis and interpretation of social phenomena and have delineated some of the central findings of this analysis. In doing so, they have introduced hints on how social workers may use the analysis in their prime role as agents of change. However, there has been no explicit discussion thus far of what might constitute the most effective strategies for the introduction of change. The purpose of this chapter is to rectify this omission. The object here is to discuss the social psychological research upon how change can be brought about.

Personal and social change basically entails change in the attitudes and/or the behaviour of individuals or groups. Attitudes and behaviour are, of course, functionally related though they are not by any means always positively correlated. Much effort has been expended by social psychologists in attempting to establish what makes attitudes change and how those changes are related to changes in behaviour. The structure of this chapter reflects the emphases of this work.

7.1 The Nature of Attitudes and their Relation to Behaviour

Many social psychologists have argued that attitudes have three basic components: the cognitive, the affective or emotional, and the behavioural (Katz and Stotland, 1959; McGuire, 1969). The cognitive component comprises the beliefs the individual holds about the attitude object (i.e. the person or object to which the attitude appertains). For instance, an attitude towards the mentally ill might entail a belief that they are 'dangerous'. The affective or emotional component consists of how the individual feels about the attitude object: on the positive side such feelings may include respect, admiration or sympathy; on the negative side they may include hatred, contempt or fear. The behavioural component refers to the action tendencies towards the attitude object; the anticipated action implications of the attitude. For instance, an attitude toward the mentally ill which held that they are dangerous and to be feared is likely to include a behavioural tendency to avoid such people.

Obviously, this oft repeated assertion that attitudes have these three components can be confusing. It is fine when the components gell together in the expected manner as in the above example, however, often they do not. Sometimes beliefs and feelings are quite at variance with what the person holding the attitude intends to do and actually does. In a classic study, LaPierre (1934) showed that people do not act in a manner consistent with their expressed beliefs and feelings. He found that hoteliers who had claimed that they would not give rooms to 'members of the Chinese race' when faced with a Chinese couple wanting a room gave them one. Moreover, the couple were afforded completely satisfactory service during their sojourn in these hotels.

Ajzen and Fishbein (1980) have suggested that this sort of confusion can be avoided if the term 'attitude' is restricted and used only to refer to the evaluative dimension, to indicate liking or disliking of the object or person. Then the other two dimensions are labelled separately as beliefs (referring to the cognitive component) and as behavioural intentions (referring to the intended actions) (Fishbein & Ajzen, 1972). This allows them to generate a formal model of the relationship between behaviour and these three constructs.

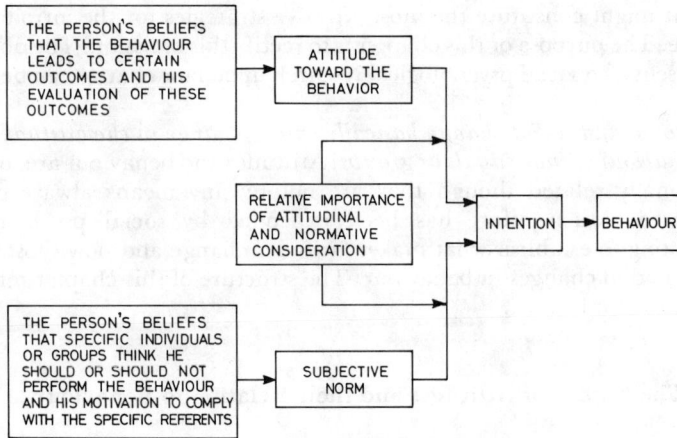

```
┌─────────────────────┐
│ THE PERSON'S BELIEFS │
│ THAT THE BEHAVIOUR   │        ┌──────────────┐
│ LEADS TO CERTAIN     │───────▶│ ATTITUDE     │
│ OUTCOMES AND HIS     │        │ TOWARD THE   │
│ EVALUATION OF THESE  │        │ BEHAVIOR     │
│ OUTCOMES             │        └──────────────┘
└─────────────────────┘

                        ┌────────────────────┐
                        │ RELATIVE IMPORTANCE │      ┌───────────┐   ┌───────────┐
                        │ OF ATTITUDINAL      │─────▶│ INTENTION │──▶│ BEHAVIOUR │
                        │ AND NORMATIVE       │      └───────────┘   └───────────┘
                        │ CONSIDERATION       │
                        └────────────────────┘

┌──────────────────────────┐
│ THE PERSON'S BELIEFS      │
│ THAT SPECIFIC INDIVIDUALS │        ┌──────────────┐
│ OR GROUPS THINK HE        │        │              │
│ SHOULD OR SHOULD NOT      │───────▶│ SUBJECTIVE   │
│ PERFORM THE BEHAVIOUR     │        │ NORM         │
│ AND HIS MOTIVATION TO COMPLY       └──────────────┘
│ WITH THE SPECIFIC REFERENTS│
└──────────────────────────┘
```

NOTE: ARROWS INDICATE THE DIRECTION OF INFLUENCE

Fig. 7.1 A model of reasoned action. The arrows indicate the direction of
influence. (From Icek Ajzen and Martin Fishbein (1980) *Understanding
Attitudes and Predicting Social Behaviour*, © 1980, p. 8. Reprinted by
permission of Prentice-Hall, Inc., Englewood Cliffs, NJ.)

Fig. 7.1 depicts this model. Ajzen and Fishbein (1980) called it 'a theory of
reasoned action'. The theory is based on the assumption that human beings are
usually quite rational and make systematic use of the information available to
them in making their decisions about how to act. They consider actions of
social relevance to be under volitional control. The person's intention to act in a
certain way is therefore viewed as the immediate determinant of that act. The
implication is that it is possible to predict behaviour by establishing the actor's
intentions.

The model claims that intentions in turn are a function of two basic determinants: the attitude towards the behaviour; and the subjective norm about
the behaviour. The attitude towards the behaviour is simply the person's
positive or negative evaluation of performing the behaviour. The subjective
norm is more complicated; it refers to how the individual perceives the
prescriptions of society about that behaviour. The subjective norm reflects
whether the individual believes society would approve or disapprove of such
behaviour. Generally speaking, the individual will intend to act in a certain
way if the act is positively evaluated by the individual and is perceived to be
positively evaluated by society (or at least that part of society important to the
individual). Of course, when these two determinants are at variance, their
relative strength becomes important: in some instances personal feelings will
have priority; in others social constraints will hold sway. In order to predict
intention and thus behaviour it is imperative to know the relative weights
allotted to these two determiners.

Attitudes and subjective norms are both a function of beliefs — though different types of belief. Attitudes are determined by what the person believes about the outcome of acting in a particular way: if it is believed that the act will result in benefits, it is associated with a positive attitude; otherwise, it is associated with a negative attitude. Subjective norms result from beliefs about what other individuals or groups consider desirable behaviour; what others are believed to think will only matter if the individual is motivated to comply with their values.

The model has the advantages of being simple and operational. Ajzen and Fishbein have shown that if these determiners of action are carefully measured behaviour can be predicted. Moreover, they have found that manipulations founded on the precepts of this model will achieve attitude and behavioural change. This approach to attitude change will be considered below.

7.2 Theories of Attitude Change

There are various attempts to explain how attitudes change. Learning theorists (e.g. Staats, 1968) have explained the process in terms of changing patterns of reinforcement: an attitude will be dropped when it no longer elicits rewards for its holder. Most explanations have a more cognitive orientation. Sherif and Hovland (1961), for instance, evolved 'social-judgement theory' to explain attitude change. Sherif argued that attitudes cannot be represented by a single point on a scale, rather, they consist of a range of acceptable positions. Each attitude is surrounded by a range of other different views which are acceptable but their acceptability declines as they shift further from the original attitude. Attitude change occurs within these tolerance limits. When a persuasive communication is received it may be effective in changing the attitude if it prescribes a shift within the tolerance limits; otherwise, it will not effect change. In predicting attitude change the obvious problem then lies in establishing the tolerance limits, this is not easy and prediction on this basis is unwieldy. Relatively speaking, the social-judgement theory has had less attention than other cognitive theories as a consequence. The cognitive-consistency theories dominate the scene. This family of theories state that people wish to see the world as orderly and consistent. When inconsistencies are perceived people try to eradicate them. One of the ways of doing this is to change one's attitudes when they are inconsistent with either each other or with behaviour or events. The consistency theories see attitude change as an attempt to retrieve an orderly relationship between attitudes and between attitudes and experiences. There are three consistency theories:

(i)   dissonance theory
(ii) congruity theory
(iii) balance theory

Dissonance Theory

Dissonance theory was proposed by Leon Festinger (1957) and is concerned with the relationships between two or more 'cognitions' (items of information — any knowledge, opinion or belief about the environment, oneself or one's own behaviour). He postulated that the relationship between cognitions could be consonant or dissonant. Consonance occurs when one cognition follows from or is implied by the other. Consonance is likely in four types of situation: (1) when cognitions are logically consistent; (2) when thoughts, feelings and actions are congruent with social rules and expectations; (3) whenever specific instances are consistent with more encompassing rules or principles; and (4) when a cognition is consistent with past experience. Similarly, dissonance occurs whenever these conditions do not hold true. The overall degree of dissonance varies as a function of the number and importance of dissonant cognitions as a proportion of the number and importance of consonant cognitions. Sherwood *et al.* (1969) formalized this proposition:

$$\text{Dissonance} \; = \; \frac{\text{Importance and number of dissonant cognitions}}{\text{Importance and number of consonant cognitions}}$$

The existence of dissonance is important because it is believed to be an aversive state and people try to avoid it. Avoidance involves changing the cognitive system to retrieve balance between its components. Attitudes which engender dissonance will be open to change.

Dissonance theory generated much research and two paradigms were particularly favoured: the free-choice situation and the forced-compliance situation. In the free-choice situation, people were offered several alternatives (all of which were similarly attractive or unpleasant so there was little to differentiate between them in objective terms). The subject has to choose one. Dissonance theorists argue that this choice entails dissonance: the subject chooses one of a series of very similar alternatives and needs to rationalize the choice, that alternative has to be regarded as better than the others or else their choice is incomprehensible. Subjects is this situation generally claim the alternative they chose was superior to the others on some dimension and hold to this attitude even though the alternatives are objectively of similar worth. Knox and Inkster (1968) showed how this operates in a nice little study. They showed that bettors who had actually placed a bet on a horse had greater conviction that their horse would win than bettors who were about to place a bet but had not yet done so. The simple fact of having made the commitment to the horse by the bet improved its attractiveness. This is known as post-decisional dissonance and is something we are all familiar with. Its likelihood and magnitude depend on: (1) the relative attractiveness of alternatives to start with — if they are unequal dissonance is unlikely; and (2) the similarity of the consequences of the alternatives — if their consequences are very similar there is little chance of dissonance.

In the forced-compliance situation people are induced to openly say something that conflicts with a private conviction or belief. If the public statement cannot be retracted dissonance is likely to involve the alteration of the original belief. For instance, a person may be compelled to argue the case for the legalization of cannabis and privately believe that cannabis is harmful; this will create dissonance. To reduce the dissonance the person must either retract the public statement or change the private belief. If retraction is impossible then the only option is to change the belief. This is regarded to be a prime reason for attitude change — the person is placed in a position where actions incompatible with the attitudes are required and, thereafter, has to rationalize the act through changing the attitudes. However, dissonance will only result in this sort of situation if the person takes responsibility for the initial public statement or act. If the person feels that he or she acted in that way only because constrained by external circumstances, attitudes will not change because the action can be rationalized in terms of the external constraint. Thus if someone is paid to act in a counter-attitudinal fashion it will have little effect on their attitudes. They must feel that they chose to act in that way for dissonance to occur and attitudes to change. But when people do feel they have chosen their course of action then counter-attitudinal role playing can be a potent force of attitude change.

It should be said that dissonance theory has received considerable criticism. Bem (1967, 1972) claims that all of the experimental results which dissonance theory is said to explain could be explained more simply by assuming that people infer their attitudes from their actions. Bem argues that attitudes do not determine behaviour but are rather *post hoc* rationalizations of behaviour. If a person behaves in a certain way (e.g. eating ten cream cakes at a sitting), that person observes himself and assumes that he likes the object of that behaviour (i.e. the cream cakes).

Nevertheless, dissonance theory points to an important phenomenon for anyone interested in instigating change: attitudes can be influenced by shaping behaviour — role playing is an effective means of changing attitudes as long as the role is undertaken voluntarily. The social worker using role play to train social skills might also use it to change attitudes.

Congruity Theory and Balance Theory

These two theories should be described together because congruity theory grew out of balance theory. Fritz Heider (1946, 1958) was the first to develop a theory about the ways people view their relationships with others and with their environment. He limited his analysis to the relationship between two people and a single aspect of the environment. P is the person on whom the analysis focuses, O is some other person, and X is the environmental entity (a belief, thing, idea, attitudinal object). Heider posited that people wish the relationships between these three to be *balanced*. The relationships were characterized in terms of the valence of bonds between the three: positive or negative evaluations. For a triad to be balanced all three bonds have to be positive or one positive and two negative; otherwise, there will be imbalance and this produces tension and generates forces to restore balance. Heider used triangular diagrams, like those shown in Fig. 7.2, to express the bonding pattern among triads. They can be translated easily. Take pattern 1 for instance. P likes O, P likes X and O likes X (it should be noted that X never has likes or dislikes being an entity rather than a person). P might be the client, O might be the social worker, and X might be an alcoholics' rehabilitation scheme. In this triad there is no pressure for change, no imbalance; attitudes will not change. But take another example, pattern 5: P likes O, O likes X, but P does not like X. The client likes the social worker, the social worker likes the rehabilitation schemes, but the client does not. This triad is unbalanced and is likely to change. The social worker will hope that the change is in the direction of moving the client towards liking the rehabilitation project but there is a possibility that balance will be restored by the client losing respect for or liking of the social worker. The existence of imbalance and its implications are thus important. Examining relationships in terms of balance can be useful as a predictor of tensions. However, it does not predict what changes will occur. In a sense, the model is too simplified to be of practical use. Relationships are always more complex than the triad could imply. The triad is simply a heuristic device which crystallizes some of the tensions of more complex relationships.

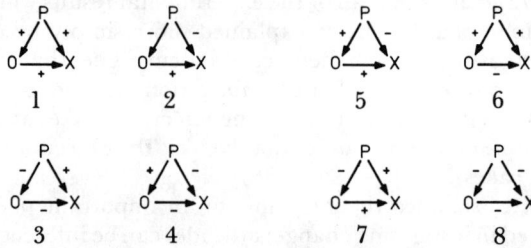

Fig. 7.2 Heider's balance theory. (Reprinted by permission of Elsevier North Holland Inc., from 'The concepts of balance, congruity and dissonance', by R.B. Zajoric, *Public Opinion Quarterly* 24, 280−296, copyright 1960 by The Trustees of Columbia University.)

Congruity theory is an extension of balance theory and filters out some of the more blatant simplicity of its predecessor. Balance theory assumes that when P finds imbalance there will be a change in his or her feelings about either O or X but not both. Congruity theory assumes that change in the feelings towards both may occur. Congruity theory was proposed by Osgood and Tannenbaum (1955) and is concerned exclusively with attitude change which occurs when some source (S) makes a statement about some object (O). P is taken to be the attitude holder. Again take an example, P (the client) likes the social worker (S) but is against O (all homosexuals). If the social worker (S) were then to make a statement in favour of homosexuals, the client would experience incongruity: someone liked, likes something disliked. Thus far congruity theory maps directly on to balance theory. However, congruity theorists argued that, given incongruity, the nature and direction of attitude change will depend on the intensity of the original feelings. If the client's (P's) original feelings towards the social worker were of only moderate acceptance and feelings against

92

homosexuals very strong, then congruity would be restored by coming to dislike the social worker. However, if the position were reversed: strong liking for the social worker and mild distaste for homosexuals; then the congruity would be restored by changing the attitude towards homosexuals. Osgood and Tannenbaum argued that the intensity of feelings (what they called associative or dissociative bonds) could be measured and thus the direction of attitude change predicted.

If Osgood and Tannenbaum were right and such feelings can be measured on a simple scale from $+3$ to -3 then their work is of use to social workers who might be able to estimate how likely their statements were to change the client's attitudes.

There is one final family of theories evolved in social psychology to explain attitude change: *the functional theories*. These contend that attitudes are formed and maintained to satisfy ulterior motives and needs. Katz (1960) claimed four functions are served by an attitude: (1) adjustive — maximizing rewards and minimizing punishments; (2) ego-defensive — protecting people from unpleasant truths about themselves and the world; (3) value-expressive — proclaiming the individual's values to the world; and (4) knowledge — assistance in making sense of the world. Kelman (1958) suggested that attitudes evolved to serve different functions would not all be changed by the same methods. Value-expressive attitudes would be changed by showing attitudes to be inconsistent with values. Adjustive attitudes would be changed by altering the reward — punishment contingencies. Knowledge attitudes would be changed through the provision of new information and re-education. Ego-defensive attitudes would have to be shown to fail to provide adequate support.

In a sense, the functional theories of attitude change are the most amenable to practical implementation: they give clear statements about what type of strategy should change which type of attitude.

It is time now to return briefly to Ajzen and Fishbein's (1980) theory of reasoned action and its implications for attitude change. They argue that since beliefs are the determinants of attitudes, it is beliefs which should be changed if attitudes are to change. The message designed to change beliefs should consist of two parts: the *arguments* and the *evidence* for the argument. When the object is to change behaviour as well the message will include recommended actions too — *the more specific the recommendation, the better the chances of success*. In shaping the message it is vital to attack primary beliefs about the performance of the target behaviour. So it is necessary to specify the set of primary beliefs which serve as the potential determinants of a given attitude and behaviour. These beliefs concern the perceived consequences of performing the behaviour. To be effective the message must influence these primary beliefs and influence enough of them to change the attitude towards the behaviour. As long as there is a strong relationship between attitude, intention and behaviour (see Fig. 7.1) this will then change behaviour. Ajzen and Fishbein showed the superiority of this change technique over one which did not attack primary beliefs in a study of alcoholics. They were trying to persuade these alcoholics to take treatment. With one-third of the group, they attacked primary beliefs about therapy in a positive appeal — stressing the positive consequences of signing up for treatment. With one-third, they attacked primary beliefs about therapy by stressing the negative consequences of failure to sign up for treatment. With one-third, primary beliefs about therapy were not attacked — the evils of drinking were attacked and therapy was offered as a means of overcoming these problems. Ajzen and Fishbein (1980, p. 231) compared the impact of these messages on the attitudes and behaviour of the alcoholics. Attitudes towards therapy in both groups who had appeals which attacked primary beliefs about therapy improved and they were actually more willing to undergo therapy. This occurred regardless of whether the appeal was positive or negative. Those given the 'traditional' appeal about the evils of drink hardly changed their attitudes towards therapy at all and were unwilling to enter therapy. It seems that Ajzen and Fishbein are pointing to something very important when devising strategies to change attitudes and behaviour. The attack must be focused on the specific origin of the attitude or behaviour and must be directed at achieving a specific type of change. The message must be tailored carefully to its ends if it is to be successful. Some of the features affecting the success of persuasive messages are considered below.

7.3 The Process of Persuasion

Persuasion entails getting someone to do something, feel something or believe something when he or she resists doing, feeling or believing that thing. There is no strict dichotomy between persuasion and coercion. They blend into one another along a continuum. Persuasion is more likely to be used to label a process of change if the individual changed comes to accept the change; coercion is used when the change is wrought but not accepted. Social workers primarily rely on persuasion although they have powers to coerce under various legislation.

The process of persuasion has been extensively studied by social psychologists. Four factors are thought to be important:

(i) the source of the persuasive message;
(ii) the message;
(iii) the context;
(iv) the recipient.

The Source

An individual's or a group's power is a function of social influence — the ability to shape another's behaviour. Raven and Rubin (1976) describe three types of power: (1) informational; (2) reward and coercive; (3) expert, referent and legitimate. Informational power is based on providing information which changes behaviour. For instance, Rokeach (1971) provided individuals with information which showed that their values and attitudes were inconsistent and these people changed their attitudes: the simple provision of new information instigated change. Reward and coercive power involves forced compliance.

The individual wielding this type of power must keep those who are to be influenced under surveillance so that any transgression can be punished. Expert power relies on possessing information which is needed and restricted and the origin of which is obscured. Referent power capitalizes upon the fact that the person (or group) which wields it is respected and admired; people who respect you are more likely to do what you tell them to do. Legitimate power primarily stems from an individual's status within the social structure. Invested with legitimate power the individual can say what 'ought' to be done and has a right to do so. If the source of a message has any of these sorts of power, the message will be persuasive and capable of eliciting change.

Without power *per se*, it is important for the source of a persuasive message to be perceived as credible and trustworthy. For instance, people are more likely to be influenced by an appeal for change if they believe the person making the appeal has no reason to lie — for example if they overhear the appeal when they believe it is not being made for their benefit. Credibility and trustworthiness interact with the attraction of the source. The more attractive the source, the more influence he or she has. However, in some instances this can backfire: dissonance theory would predict that an unattractive source may change attitudes because the auditors cannot explain why they should bother listening unless they agreed with the message, certainly they cannot explain their listening in terms of the attraction of the speaker. Smith (1961) had a set of army reservists listen to a message designed to get them to eat grasshoppers. The message was either delivered by an attractive person or an unattractive one. The attractive source caused more grasshoppers to be consumed but the unattractive source led subjects to believe that those they did eat were really quite nice. The effects of the characteristics of the source are obviously complex!

The Message

Three aspects of the message seem vital: (1) its content; (2) its organization; and (3) its medium.

Content. Two aspects of the content of messages have been extensively studied:

   (i) one-sided versus two-sided presentations;
   (ii) fear arousal in the message.

   (i) One-sided versus two-sided presentations. A one-sided presentation puts one side of the argument and ignores counter-arguments. This is effective when the audience already agrees with the message and when the audience is not particularly clever; a two-sided argument discusses opposing views, which is effective when the audience is initially against the ideas carried in the message or when the audience is intelligent. The 'inoculation' theory proposes that a two-sided argument should include the opposition's views in a watered-down form and this will lead to inoculation against them in the future; the audience is effectively being given the disease in a weak form and being given time to develop what Harrison (1976) called 'cognitive antibodies'.

95

(ii) Fear arousal. Many persuasive messages are designed to arouse fear and take the form 'if you do not do this then something terrible will happen to you'. Most of the public health campaigns use this format. Yet the effects of fear arousal are not clear-cut. Fear can act to inhibit change: high anxiety impairs learning; fear may make the source of the message unattractive and so act against its persuasiveness; and fear elicits avoidance, the message which is fear-arousing may be too fearful to contemplate. McGuire (1969) argued that there is a curvilinear relationship between fear and persuasion: no fear, no motivation for change; great fear, avoidance of the message; but moderate fear, change. The optimal level of fear is difficult to establish and is very much dependent upon the initial levels of anxiety of the target. For the anxious even a small amount of fear arousal in the message may make them seek to avoid it. It is also worth remembering that people adapt to fearful situations and events. A message which initially illicits fear may soon lose its power to do so. A further factor should be considered: different levels of fear may be needed for different sorts of change. Short-term, immediate change can be induced by high fear arousal; long-term changes are best instigated through moderate fear messages. The use of fear may sound unethical; far too manipulative. But, in fact, fear is harnessed to enforce virtually every social or moral code. We use it whether we will or no. The information above is proffered in the hope of encouraging the humane and efficient use of the power of fear.

Organization of the message. Again two features have been studied: (i) order effects; and (ii) forewarning effects.

(i) order effects. In lengthy messages, primacy and recency effects operate: early parts of the message are remembered and the parts near the end are remembered, the bit in the middle is lost. The implication of this is clear: keep the message short or put the important things in early or very late.

(ii) forewarning effects. These arise when the audience is told that an attempt will be made to change its attitudes. The consequences of forewarning are unclear. It can lead to resistance or persuasion but the second is more likely if the audience can be made to feel that the forewarning implies that no underhand manipulation is being attempted: this enhances the trustworthiness and attractiveness of the source.

The media. The agency or means of presenting the appeal can be important. Face-to-face presentation is most effective; then, TV or films; then, audio presentation; and, least effective, the written word. Lamm (1967) had subjects in one room participate in a discussion while subjects in other rooms either watched or just listened. Discussants showed most shift in their attitudes about the topic discussed, observers next most and listeners least. Face-to-face interaction is likely to have greater impact because the source can tailor the message to the specific audience's reactions and has more channels of communication available (the use of non-verbal and verbal channels).

96

The Context

One aspect of the context of the persuasive act has been seriously studied and this is the extent to which distractions are important. Most messages are delivered in real life in highly distracting circumstances with the TV on, the telephone ringing, the bath running, the children screaming, the police appearing, etc. Therefore this information on the impact of distraction is important. Strangely, distracted audiences show more attitude change after an appeal. Distraction may bring this about because it prevents the audience evolving counter-arguments to that proposed in the appeal; or because in distracting circumstances people have to listen harder to get the message and, having done so, have a certain investment in it (in dissonance terms, to ignore it having worked to get it would generate dissonance); and, if the distraction is nice it can result in the message being associated with positive feelings and thus facilitate persuasion. This seems to imply that distraction has its effects by hindering the reception of the message but facilitating yielding to the message. This is important, if true, because it indicates that complex messages will not be effective under distracting conditions. In fact, Regan and Cheng showed this to be the case: simple messages were enhanced by distraction; complex messages hindered.

The Recipient

Psychologists sought for years to define the 'persuadable personality'. It is safe to say now that there is no such thing. There are no personality types who are easy to persuade. The characteristics of the recipient interact with the nature of the source, message and context in determining change.

However, in any community there are what Katz and Lazarsfeld (1955) called 'opinion leaders'. These are people who act as filters of public messages. Most people are not influenced directly by the public media, they are influenced by direct contact with another person who promotes an idea. The opinion leaders, however, are influenced directly by the public media (TV, radio, newspapers, etc.) and thus act as bypass channels of influence. What they fail to pass on to others will not be passed on. In shaping a programme of influence, the opinion leaders should consequently be prime targets.

The persuasion process is most effective when the persuader can control each of the four components interacting in the process. However, that is rarely, if ever possible. It would really necessitate the removal of the person to be persuaded from the normal social context which supports existing attitudes and behavioural patterns. Of course, this can happen when the person is institutionalized. It can also happen on a more temporary basis when the person joins a 'growth group'. 'Growth groups' go under many names: T-groups, encounter groups, experiential groups, sensitivity groups, etc. They vary in structure and in underlying rationale. Verny (1974) and Rowan (1976) provide good introductions to groups of this sort. The use of such groups in the social work process has also been explored extensively (Douglas, 1978, 1979). It is, therefore, inappropriate to devote much space to their description here. Nevertheless, they should be considered fertile ground for the persuasion process. Such groups evolve norms of self-exposure and self-exploration and the power of norms to evoke conformity has been discussed earlier — few resist the group. A group that lasts for any time can create a new world for participants with new standards and new expectations. The group leader, if it is a directed group, therefore has considerable power to direct change by moulding group norms and patterns of interaction. Systematic research on the impact of such groups is in its infancy but Shaw (1976) concluded that the discrepancy between perceived and ideal selves of participants declines; participants perceive changes in their behaviour and attitudes as a result of the group experience; observers report perceptible changes in the overt behaviour of participants; and, under some conditions participation can result in severe psychological disturbances. The implications are clear enough: such groups are powerful influences for good and potentially for bad.

7.4   The Process of Coercion

The process of coercion is not easy to describe because there is little research upon it. The absence of research is, of course, a natural consequence of the nature of coercion. Someone or some group capable of coercion is capable of excluding researchers from the process. There are, however, more journalistic descriptions of coercion. Watson (1980) for instance describes the torture and 'brainwashing' techniques used during international and civil wars. The communists during the Korean war were particularly successful in their coercive methods: about one-third of the American prisoners were induced to collaborate with their enemy. These methods included eight major variants: (1) enforcing trivial demands — the object here is to introduce the habit of compliance; (2) demonstrating the omnipotence or omnipresence of the captors — this suggests the futility of resistance; (3) giving occasional indulgences — providing some positive reason for compliance and impairing the habituation to deprivation; (4) threats — designed to cultivate anxiety, dread and despair; (5) degradation — tends to make prisoners concerned with very basic needs rather than higher ideals such as loyalty; (6) control of perceptions — this entails control of the environment, all aspects of which can be made monotonous in order to foster introspection, eliminate distractions and emphasize the predicament; (7) isolation — encourages dependence on the captor for social stimuli and deprives the victim of the support system of a group which results in intense concern with the self, again militating against group loyalties; and (8) induced debility and exhaustion — through starvation, physical hardship and emotional strain which weakens mental and physical resistance. All of these variants were used in some form.

Resistance to these sorts of coercive techniques can be taught and the prime method seems to be simply to give a person experience of such techniques.

It is noticeable from the description above that coercive techniques rely massively on removing the individual from the social group, making the individual doubt his or her group's power, introducing threats to self-esteem and social identity, and supplanting the old norms of behaviour with new ones. To this extent, such measures are not dissimilar to what happens in any total institution (e.g. mental hospital, prison). Providing new group loyalties is also part of the process. Since the Chinese Revolution, China has used 'revolutionary colleges' to retrieve those who are in political error. The training in such colleges has three stages. The first stage involves the dissident being placed in a ten-man study group together with other dissidents. The group is expected to discuss its hatred of the old regime and the experiences of members. The group is lectured on ideology and new purposes. The second stage involves a shift to more personal and emotional topics and the dissident is expected to adopt the correct ideological stance. Recalcitrant group members are publically threatened and humiliated. The second stage is designed to engender fear and submission. The third and final stage begins when the dissident submits and confesses his errors. He has to produce a signed confession of 5000−25 000 words which is read to the group and subject to painful revisions. When the confession is finally accepted by the group, the dissident gains emotional relief, the group is again supportive. The dissident gains readmission at the cost of autonomy. Such training takes the encounter group principle through to its logical conclusion: the manipulation of the individual.

Techniques of coercion which are founded upon social psychological processes have been emphasized but there are other methods, including the use of drugs which change behaviour and simple physical control. These are, in a sense, less interesting. The social psychological methods of coercion are more interesting because in watered down versions we are all subjected to them, in our families and in our primary groups.

Describing coercion and persuasion separately may have implied that they are seen as distinct. In fact, they blend into one another and are used in concert regularly. Regimes which use coercion are fond of persuasive techniques and use them particularly within their public media. The use of propaganda machinery is common. 'Propaganda' means simply 'that which is to spread'. It uses censorship: the doctoring of information to control opinions and encourage inappropriate conclusions. Concealment of the source of a message can be an important part of censorship since knowledge of the source will shape the interpretation of the message and its power to influence. Propaganda also involves the use of derogatory or inflamatory language to shape public opinion. Propaganda works best if the mass media and interpersonal contacts work in the same direction: the individual is most influenced when friends and fellow group members confirm what is said in the media. Insecure individuals or those in marginal or inferior social groups are prone to be influenced by the media propaganda particularly if it offers any crumb of kudos for them.

In its milder forms propaganda shades down into rhetoric. Rhetorics are biased patterns of argument, they rely on invoking ingroup loyalties and outgroup deprecation, and can be employed to manipulate intergroup relations. Some of the ways in which rhetoric has been used by and against social workers and their profession are described in Part VI. Rhetoric is important because it can set the parameters of intergroup and interpersonal comparisons by establishing images for groups and people. It is also important because, unlike propaganda, it does not need a massive government or bureaucratic organization to generate it. Individuals can effectively evolve rhetoric and through using it consistently and persuasively they can change the images of individuals and groups. In Chapter 22 some recommendations are made about the ways in which social workers might use rhetoric to improve the image of social work. It could equally well be used to change the public image of a client group.

7.5 The Social Work Process and Change

Social workers are expected to generate change. Yet often no one, including the social workers, is sure about what should be changed or how it should be changed. The SPA to change says something about both what and how. It provides a conceptual framework: it is attitudes and behaviour which are to be changed. Then it provides some information about how to induce change: the processes of attitude change, persuasion and coercion. It is essentially showing how *first level social work skills* can be mapped on to *second level skills* in order to meet the demand for change. The information above indicates what one needs to achieve in order to maximize the potential for changes, earlier chapters on relationships have indicated this can be achieved through paying attention to identity, relationships, groups and the environment.

There has been a heavy accent upon manipulation in all that was said above. This was deliberate: social workers need tools to do their job, SPA has tools to offer — but the social workers who use them pay a price: they have to take the responsibility for bringing about change. Any professional using the tools of that profession manipulates clients and manipulates others on behalf of the clients. Social workers who have effective tools and skills must come to terms with the prospect of manipulation both for and of the client. Otherwise, social workers will only fool themselves when they claim to be agents of change.

8
Central Tenets of SPA
Explanation and Analysis

The purpose of this chapter is to crystallize some of the more important themes which are woven through previous chapters. It is these themes which are elaborated upon in later chapters. Here they are delineated in their simplest and most concrete forms.

The prime object of the SPA is the analysis and explanation of the experience and behaviour of individuals in social context. Analysis and explanation are two distinct processes. *Analysis entails the examination of a phenomenon in order to ascertain its detailed constitution and structure*; it involves the resolution of the whole into its component elements. Analysis is essentially a process of description. Analysis of a phenomenon may be the first step along the path towards explaining it but analysis is not synonymous with explanation. *Explanation entails the description of how a phenomenon came to exist*; it involves the specification of the precipitating conditions or causes. With reference to the experience and behaviour of individuals in social context, the processes of analysis and explanation can operate at four levels:

1. the intrapsychic — with phenomena whose realm of operation is within the single person;
2. the interpersonal — with phenomena whose realm of operation lies in the interaction and relationships between people;
3. the intragroup — with phenomena whose realm of operation lies within the group;
4. the intergroup — with phenomena whose realm of operation rests in relationships and interactions between groups.

These levels are quite distinct. But it should be recognized that processes operating at these different levels interact. The experience and behaviour of individuals can be analysed and explained at any one or any number of these four levels.

An illustration of how this might work would be useful.

The event: a man (A) rushes into a room where another man (B) is sitting and attacks him. This event can be analysed and explained at each of the four levels (see Table 8.1).

Table 8.1

Level	Analysis	Explanation
1. Intrapsychic	The thoughts, feelings, and specific actions of A are described.	A is a hyperaggressive character, unstable, often in trouble.
2. Interpersonal	The constituents of the relationship between A and B are the targets for discovery.	A and B are enemies because they are in competition for the respect of a girl.
3. Intragroup	The roles A and B play in their group(s) are targets for discovery.	A and B are enemies because they are in competition for the dominant position in their group.
4. Intergroup	The object is to discover whether A and B have different patterns of group membership.	A and B are enemies because they are leaders of opposing groups.

It should not be assumed from the example that these four levels operate only in the analysis and explanation of the behaviour of individuals; the activities of groups can similarly be subjected to multi-levelled analysis and explanation. For instance conflict between groups can be *analysed* in terms of the actual intergroup hostilities; the impact on groups taking part; the influence upon interpersonal relations; or the consequences for each individual. Similarly, the *explanation* of intergroup conflict can be lodged at each or any of the four levels: the madness of one man may explain it; the animosity of particular individuals may engender it; the structure of a single group may precipitate it; and the status of intergroup relations may initiate it. Sometimes, *factors at all four levels need to be considered* in the analysis and explanation of the event.

It should also not be assumed that analysis and explanation are always founded on the same level when addressed to an event: a detailed analysis of the event at the interpersonal level may be paired with an explanation purely in terms of intrapsychic dynamics. For instance, the analysis may describe the deterioration of a marriage and the explanation may be totally concerned with the thoughts and feelings of one partner. It is not uncommon in the social work process to find quite extensive analyses of events (case histories can cover a family's entire recent history — including its relations with various social institutions like the police or medical services) tied to explanation at a single level (predominantly behaviourist or psychoanalytic interpretations).

The SPA requires that an event or problem should be analysed at each of these levels and explanations of it at each level should be considered. There are instances where all four levels are not necessary, but in the vast majority of cases they are. The social worker adopting the SPA should consider each level in turn and consider the relationships between the processes operating at these distinct levels.

The SPA indicates what are the key targets for analysis and the key processes in explanation. The *key targets for analysis* have been discussed in detail in previous chapters; they are *identity, relationships, groups, the environment and change*. When faced with an event or problem requiring analysis, SPA requires certain questions, focused on these target zones, to be answered:

(i)   What does the event/problem imply for the identity of those individuals or groups involved?
(ii)   What does it mean about and for the relationships of those involved?
(iii) What group structures and processes are involved?
(iv)   What role does the physical environment play in the action?
(v)   What processes of personal or social change are involved?

The analysis required by these questions is extensive but it has large pay-offs: a comprehensive understanding of the event/problem and through it indications of how change may be wrought.

The SPA posits that certain *key processes* should be considered in the explanation of an event/problem. There are four key processes.

Construal

The construal process is the way in which people make sense of the world. Construal involves assimilating information, categorizing it according to a classification system evolved through experience, and endowing it with personal meaning. Construal is the fulcrum of the subjective world and, since people only perceive the world through their subjectivity, it is a prime determinant of experience and action. The construal process determines how we see what we see and how we think we should respond. It is, therefore, fundamental to any explanation.

Consistency

People seek stability. They wish to maintain their thoughts, feelings and actions in a state of equilibrium. Inconsistencies between any of these three elements results in distress because inconsistency threatens the person's ability to predict experience and thus understand it. The consistency process is, there-

103

fore, a strong motive force; pushing the individual to think, feel and act in ways which are consistent with what has gone before. The consistency process explains much human activity.

Comparison

People seek to validate their understanding of the world. When possible, they use objective evidence in order to confirm their understandings. If this is not available, they compare their understandings with those of other people: a process of social comparison. As long as the process yields consensus the understanding is validated.

People seek self-esteem and self-validation. Here again the comparison process has a fundamental role to play because esteem is not an absolute but a relative property. Value is a social construct and the individual's value is socially defined. The value of any particular individual will depend upon how he or she fares in comparison with other people. The person establishes his or her own value in comparison to others and self-esteem is calculated on the basis of this comparison.

The comparison process is continual — we continually assess our position relative to others. Moreover, the process of comparison emphasizes the benefits of distinguishing oneself from others. Comparison gives rise to attempts at *differentiation*; efforts to make oneself distinct in valued ways. Attempts at differentiation will, themselves, become important determinants of behaviour both of individuals and groups. The process of differentiation is a prime determiner of personal and social change because when old differences diminish new differences will be developed.

Conformity

The process of conformity is founded in two sources. The first concerns the desire that people have to receive social approval which is necessary in some form if self-esteem is to be maintained. People conform in order to receive social acceptance. The second concerns the desire people have to enforce conformity upon others. People pressure others to conform (to think, feel, or act as expected) so that their expectations can be met and their construals verified, the need for consistency sated, and favourable comparisons maintained. The conformity process is as a consequence very strong: individuals have good reason to conform; society has good reason to demand them to do so.

Each of these four processes will go on simultaneously to determine thought, feeling and action. However, it should not be thought that they necessarily act in unison. *They can be in conflict*. Fulfilling the requirements of consistency may be at variance with satisfying conformity demands, for instance. For example, a woman joins a women's group which insists that members should not do domestic chores for their spouses, the woman has always done such chores: conformity to group norms and consistency to personal rituals are in conflict.

Where the processes come into conflict it has to be resolved or else the individual will not function effectively. The processes themselves initiate change but conflict between them is a more powerful motivator of change. Such change will involve an adjustment in the relative salience of each process in that particular context. In the case of the woman who faces conflict between conformity and consistency the problem may be resolved by not doing the domestic chores on those nights when she goes to the group: conformity dominates in the time closest to the group context; consistency reasserts itself in the meantime. Of course, in the long run, this changed pattern of behaviour will alter what is regarded as consistent behaviour. After some months of group membership, the woman may regard it as inconsistent to do the chores on certain nights. The initial change operates to alter the parameters on which the processes work.

Central to any understanding of these processes is the recognition that the individual exists in a changing social world and that these processes must assimilate and accommodate the individual to that changing world. The processes deal with change and seek stability. The dialectic of change and stability is consequently central to their operation. Change in the individual or group is a function of the interaction between a new social context and these four processes. Moreover, change can be a function of the relationship between these four processes. Thus, two equations for change can be postulated:

Change $= f$ (Novelty of context $\times$ Social psychological processes)

and

Change $= f$ (Construal $\times$ Comparison $\times$ Consistency $\times$ Conformity)

The techniques for inducing personal and social change described in Chapter 7 are really *designed to manipulate the operation of these four processes.*

8.1 SPA Explanation and Analysis and the Social Work Process

It will be argued in Chapter 12 that problems faced in the social work process should be analysed at each of the four levels: intrapsychic; interpersonal; intra-group; and intergroup. It is proposed there that the intervention strategy chosen by the social worker should be accommodated at the level at which the problem can be most adequately analysed. Thus intervention strategies might be at any of the four levels. However, the chosen level will depend largely upon the explanatory processes which most adequately explain the problem. Tracing the operation of the processes of construal, consistency, comparison and conformity is an essential means of understanding and explaining the problem.

The preceding chapters in this part of the book have been designed to show just how these processes manifest themselves in relation to the key targets for analysis: the identity, relationships, groups, and environment.

The social work process requires not simply the analysis and explanation of the problem, it also requires techniques for dealing with the problem. Where the processes of construal, consistency, comparison and conformity can be harnessed, they are the means of dealing with the problem. Chapter 7 describes how these processes can be implemented to generate personal and social change. The social work process should employ these methods to deal with problems. Chapters in Part V attempt to show how this might work.

The SPA to social work would therefore result in a process in a series of stages:

(i) Analysis of the problem at four levels: intrapsychic; interpersonal; intragroup; and intergroup; and in terms of four key targets: identity; relationships; groups; and environment.

(ii) Explanation of the problem in terms of processes of construal, consistency, comparison and conformity.

(iii) Intervention in order to generate change using techniques based on the motive power of construal, consistency, comparison and conformity.

Part III
The Nature of Social Work

9

The Structure of Social Work

Describing how a particular occupation is structured is usually fairly simple and uncontroversial. Certainly, if the occupation were medicine, dentistry or nursing there would be little difficulty. Accounts of their respective career hierarchies and employing bodies, even supplemented by discussion of their professional associations, the demands made upon them and the skills used in meeting those demands, though perhaps a little staid in their predictability should be easy to produce and would probably receive a general nod of agreement from the particular practitioner concerned. Furthermore, should that information then be presented to the general public, it is unlikely that it would provoke any surprise. Achieving this important degree of congruity between the way its members and the public perceive the structure and function of a service organization depends on a number of such factors as:

  (i) a fairly high level of agreement among the members themselves about how their profession is structured and what its functions are;
 (ii) a structure that has been established for some considerable time;
(iii) having organizational and professional functions the public find acceptable;
 (iv) powerful rhetoric from within the organization to convey the appropriate imagery of itself to outsiders;
  (v) the existence of receptive media who accept the professed rhetoric more or less at face value.

Social work meets few of these criteria. The basic difficulties experienced by social workers in achieving congruity centre on the following areas.
  1. Though most social workers work in local authority social services depart-

107

ments even this basic information is not generally known. A poll commissioned by the National Institute of Social Work Working Party on the Role and Tasks of Social Workers (as reported by S. Weir in *New Society*, 7 May 1981) found that only 27% of a national quota sample of 994 people in Great Britain aged 16 or over knew that most social workers are employed by the local authority.

2. Local authority social services departments are highly structured but differ considerably in the form the hierarchical structuring takes. Knowing how one social services department is structured, though giving a good idea of the size and complexity of the bureaucracy involved, cannot be immediately generalized to the neighbouring local authority.

3. Social workers do not all work in local authority social services departments. They are also employed by local authority education departments as education welfare officers or 'social workers in education'. The Probation and After-Care Service increasingly employs probation officers who hold the Certificate of Qualification in Social Work, the basic social work qualification, after having completed their training on courses shared with student social workers seconded from local authorities. Social workers are also employed by such central government departments as the Department of Health and Social Security to work in the four Special Hospitals, and by the Department of Employment to work in their various rehabilitation units. There are also considerable numbers of social workers who, though paid by social services departments are permanently deployed to various hospital settings, GP practices, child guidance clinics, residential establishments for such groups as children, the elderly, the mentally handicapped, and the physically handicapped, and to various types of day centre. Further, considerable numbers of qualified social workers are employed by the numerous voluntary agencies that have proliferated in recent years. Finally, an increasing contingent of social workers are moving into the area of private practice, on either a part-time or full-time basis, being paid by clients for various specific services.

4. Local authority social services departments, by far the largest single employer of social workers, have only been in existence for a little over a decade. Formally created by the Local Authority Social Services Act 1970, they are only recently beginning to settle down into recognizable and predictable patterns, and the actual work performed at field level is still in the throes of being evaluated for its worth by professionals in other fields, by the media and the clients.

5. General agreement has not been reached among social workers themselves about what they should be doing and how they should be doing it: their goals and techniques. There are a number of factions within social work expressing very different and at times completely contradictory views of these issues.

6. Public acceptance of what they do is important to the members of any 'people occupation'. The public after all, is supposed to be the reason for the occupation's existence. Doctors and nurses, by and large, perform relatively simple and understandable tasks. They give injections, perform operations, identify physical malfunctions and prescribe physical treatments. If the com-

plaint gets better or is improved, then they have performed their task properly. If the problem gets worse, then a second opinion is sought. If it continues to deteriorate, then it is 'incurable', that is, there is no known technique that will combat it. In such instances it would be most unusual for the doctor to receive the blame: he has used all the techniques known to him. The techniques are inadequate, not the doctor. It might, in fact, be argued that a profession is identified by the techniques available to its practitioners.

Social workers are largely without readily understandable techniques and operate in areas where there is usually little or no agreement over what constitutes the complaint. It is not surprising that the public's acceptance of what they do has been so limited. The National Institute of Social Work poll, however, indicates that perhaps the tide is changing a little: 60% of the sample who had had personal contact with a social worker (29% of 994) were 'satisfied' with the help or information given (22% were dissatisfied, 18% didn't know).

7. Social work has always suffered from its inability to develop a powerful collective voice to put across to the media and the general public what social work is all about. The largest professional association for social workers, the British Association of Social Workers (BASW), represents only a small proportion of the potential membership. Despite having made a number of significant advances and achievements in its decade of existence, it has communicated only a few of these to the main body of social workers and to outsiders (see Chapter 10).

8. Dealing in essentially moral issues, social work must be something of a godsend to the purveyors of mass media images. It meets a number of the basic criteria for good copy — it has heroes, villains and victims, has been uneasy about speaking in its own defence, and if stereotypical media images are to be believed is apparently manned by wishy-washy liberals. Like most stereotypes these images contain an element of truth, and it is this element of truth-telling that sticks like gristle in the teeth of the majority of social workers who lead fairly sedate lives, carrying out highly complex tasks with scant reward or recognition, and who cannot by the remotest stretch of the imagination be described as naive do-gooders, radical anarchists or some other social fantasy figure.

Social work, then, has failed to disseminate accurate information about itself to outsiders for a number of reasons, some of which are postulated above. As a result there is a mismatch between the image attributed to social work and the reality that lies behind the image. The purpose of the rest of this chapter is to try and achieve greater clarity by edging the outline of the image and shading in the reality. The current structure of social work will then be placed in historical context, and finally, consideration will be given to one or two of the major issues that faces the social worker in the organization.

9.1 Social Work: The Image

Social work is clearly not a homogeneous occupational grouping. Social workers are employed in a wide range of settings and utilize a variety of different methods to try and achieve sometimes alarmingly disparate goals. However, such distinctions are more apparent to practitioners themselves than to outsiders. Social work as a whole, whether social workers like it or not, does have an image ascribed to it by the media, the general public and by other professions. Obviously the 'media', the 'public' and 'other professions' covers a variety of sins, and there will be differing attitudes within each grouping towards social work. Furthermore, a difficulty arises in the absence of sufficient research data from which to draw reliable conclusions. However, there is some documentation from which to offer a few somewhat cursory comments about the type of imagery each group accords to social work, comments that do bear some relationship to the experiences of practitioners in the field.

Media Imagery

The press, particularly the tabloid newspapers, seem to have taken a dislike to social workers, while making little other than implicit comment on social work itself. The most common source of newspaper coverage follows the various inquiries that have taken place over recent years into the circumstances surrounding the deaths of young children, usually either directly at the hands of their parents, or indirectly as a result of parental neglect. Social workers have frequently been involved at some stage with such families. Although social workers have never killed the child themselves and other professionals are frequently involved with such families, it is usually the social worker who is judged. Take, for example, the case of Malcolm Page, a 14-month-old boy who died from hypothermia and malnutrition in his parents' home. The headline in the *Daily Star*, 28 March 1981, was: 'Six Social Workers . . . But Still Baby Died in Squalor'. The first line of the ensuing article commented: 'Tragic baby Malcolm Page was doomed to die surrounded by incompetent social workers'. The article goes on to imply that despite six social workers being involved, four case conferences being held, and the family being known to the local authority concerned for some three years prior to the child's death, social workers were at fault in not removing the child from home sooner. The only comment attributed to BASW was that BASW 'described Malcolm's death as an unfortunate combination of circumstances'. In addition the article contained comments on the failure to attribute blame: 'The GP who chaired the Committee . . . said they did not want to apportion blame but denied there had been a whitewash — even though the report did not blame the principal social worker involved and shied away from blaming anyone'. On the fate of the main social worker concerned: 'She was later transferred to another office to gain further experience'.

Notwithstanding the actual truth of the case, and of the reporting standards of the particular newspaper involved, the imagery of social workers contained in this article is clear: social workers are inexperienced, incompetent, unaccountable and indecisive, and their professional organization minimizes their errors.

110

Public Imagery

The National Institute of Social Work poll referred to earlier, despite various methodological failings, is one of the few pieces of research on the general public's (as opposed to the client's) knowledge of and attitude toward social workers. In general the findings are surprisingly positive. Table 9.1 goes some way towards indicating that social workers are more likely to be seen as 'caring people doing a difficult job' than 'soft-hearted do-gooders' or 'long haired revolutionaries'.

Table 9.1   Which of these phrases, if any, would you use to describe social workers?

N = 994 National Quota aged 16 or over. Respondents could give more than one answer. (© *New Society*, 7 May 1981, reproduced by permission.)

	%
1. Caring people in a difficult job	48
2. There to help people find their own solutions to practical or emotional problems	41
3. There to ensure that people get their rights	24
4. There to encourage local people to help neighbours in need by voluntary action	22
5. Soft-hearted do-gooders	7
6. A sop to society's conscience	6
7. Long haired revolutionaries	2
8. None of these	6

People were not quite sure, however, where these caring people came from. About one in three placed them in local authority or social services, 10% thought they were employed by the civil service, 2% considered them to be in the voluntary or independent sector, and some saw them as being completely self-sufficient.

Interestingly there seemed a marked difference between what the people thought social workers did, and what they believed they should do. Social workers were seen as dealing mainly with families experiencing problems, children in difficulty, old people and 'people who can't cope with life'. On the other hand, the public considered that social workers should work with disabled people as the main priority, followed by helping poor people get their rights and helping people with emotional problems (Table 9.2).

Table 9.2 Which of the Following Should Social Workers Do as Part of Their Job?

$N = 994$. (© *New Society*, 7 May 1981, reproduced by permission.)

	%
1. Visit disabled people to investigate their needs	76
2. Help poor people get their rights	64
3. Help people with emotional problems	54
4. Decide whether a child should go into a home	41
5. Look after old people in old people's homes	40
6. Control and supervise disruptive teenagers	32
7. Decide on compulsory admission of mentally disturbed people to hospital	24
8. Campaign for a zebra crossing on a busy road	16
9. None of these	3

Imagery from Other Professions

It is probably fair to say that most of the professions who regularly work with social workers disapproved of the consequences of the Seebohm recommendations for the reorganization of the structure of social work which resulted in the Local Authority Social Services Act 1970, and that their image of social work and social workers continues to be influenced by those consequences of the reorganization which affected them directly. Thus Little and Burkitt (1975) writing on behalf of the Society of Clinical Psychiatrists circulated questionnaires in 1972 ($N = 77$) and 1975 ($N = 86$) to its members, seeking to elicit their views on the quality of social work service to psychiatric patients before and after the 1970 reorganization. They concluded that:

> . . . very large majorities: 1. reported a deterioration in quality; 2. considered this due to fundamental defects in the Seebohm Report, or its application, rather than to teething troubles of a new service; 3. found that generically-trained social workers without practical psychiatric experience . . . were virtually useless when requested to work with a psychiatric patient.

Here social workers are useless to psychiatrists because the changes of employer and training methods are seen as minimizing psychiatric expertise.

Maggie Fogarty (*Social Work Today*, 10 June 1980) solicited comments from a range of professional associations about social workers, supplemented by comments from a number of individuals. The organizations contacted reflected a fairly wide cross-section of opinion — the Police Federation, the Health Visitors' Association, the Royal College of Nursing, the National Union of Teachers, the Social Work Service of the Department of Health and Social

112

Security, and the British Medical Association. Her conclusion was interesting in that the other professions seemed to indicate their acceptance of the existence of social work within their network while simultaneously holding a number of criticisms about social workers as people:

> In all, the attitudes of the professions and professionals towards social work . . . shows a chiefly positive attitude. No-one questioned the need for social workers or that there should be restrictions on recruitment. Criticisms about age, inexperience and failure to communicate sometimes degenerated into stereotyping . . .

Although there would seem to be some evidence for the view that social work has carved out a niche among other professions, there would seem to remain a certain amount of dissatisfaction both with the effects of reorganization on previous specialisms and with social workers as people.

Summary

Social work, unlike most of the other people professions, has failed to achieve congruity between its actual structure and functions and how its structure and function are perceived by outsiders. There are a number of possible explanations for this, some of which are outlined. The imagery of social work held by the media, the general public and other professions varies according to the focus of interest, although it is similar in its failure to acknowledge a biased perception and in the degree of mismatch between perceived social work structure and function and the actual tasks performed by social workers. In the next section we examine the reality in more detail.

9.2 Social Work: The Reality

The two most important factors in the lives of the majority of social workers, who are employed by local authorities, are the structure of the organization that pays their wage and the tasks they are obliged to carry out by law.

The Structure of Local Authority Social Services Departments

Local authority social services departments were established in 1970 as a direct consequence of the Local Authority Social Services Act. The Act attempted to meld into one organization statutory duties previously held by three different departments — children's, welfare and health. Since 1970 a number of additional pieces of legislation have been enacted which have increased the duties of social services departments.

Considerable autonomy was left with each local authority at the time of the reorganization to devise the particular structure it found most suitable. Accordingly no two local authorities are exactly alike. However, the majority are reasonably similar in terms of the number of levels within the hierarchy and in the general divisions of responsibility between administration, training, fieldwork, domiciliary and residential facilities. To give a flavour of a social

DIRECTOR

DEPUTY DIRECTOR

ASSISTANT DIRECTOR | ASSISTANT DIRECTOR | ASSISTANT DIRECTOR

PERSONNEL | SPME UNIT | PROJECT GROUP | DIRECTOR SUPPORT | Finance & Administration

WEST DIVISION (AS EAST DIVISION) | EAST DIVISION

Logistics | Finance | Secretarial & Information

OPERATIONS MANAGER

AREA MANAGER | STAFF OFFICERS | TRAINING & DEVELOPMENT MANAGER

TEAM MANAGERS | PRINCIPAL HOSPITAL SOCIAL WORKERS | TRAINING & DEVELOPMENT OFFICERS | DIVISIONAL ADMINISTRATION OFFICER

TEAMS HOSPITAL BASED

TEAMS | Transport | Logistics | Office Service

DOMICILIARY | RESIDENTIAL & DAY CARE | FIELDWORK

SOURCE: ESSEX SSD FACTSHEET 2 13/5/81

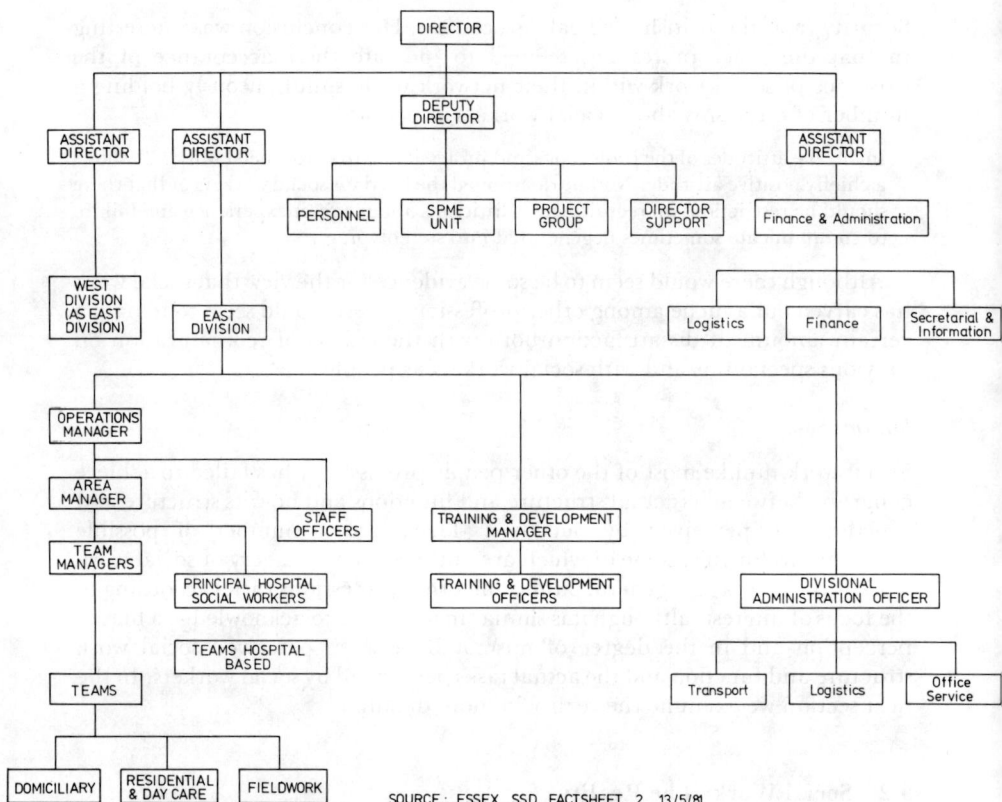

Fig. 9.1   Structure of East Sussex SSD. (From *East Sussex SSD Factsheet 2*, 13 May 1981)

services department structure, Fig. 9.1 sketches the structure of part of East Sussex social services.

With a budget of over £27 million, the 3000 staff (whole time equivalent figures) (of whom some 250 are social workers) of the department are attempting to provide a wide range of services to a population of some 655 000. These services are categorized under seven broad headings: fieldwork and administration; services for the elderly (homes, day centres); services for children (residential homes, foster parents, day nurseries, playgroups, childminders); services for mentally handicapped (homes, day centres); services for mentally ill (day centres); services for physically handicapped (aids, adaptations, day centres, sheltered employment, orange parking badges); and 'other services' (home help, meals on wheels, telephones). The Social Services Committee has gone some way to specifying its goals:

1. To promote and sustain the independence of individuals and families by helping

114

them to:
   (a) recover, where possible, their impaired physical, mental, emotional and social functioning;
   (b) reduce the handicapping effects of disability;
   (c) adapt constructively to living with disability;
   (d) avoid deterioration in their capacities.
2. To invest time and resources in prevention, i.e. to ensure that help is given early enough to avert or postpone the need for more comprehensive and costly services.
3. To adopt a strategy of care in the community.
4. To use residential care more positively as an integral part of a range of services aimed at promoting independence, and, where possible, enabling individuals to return to life in the community.
   (Source: Report of East Sussex Social Services Committee, December 1977)

Social workers, then, are part of a complex whole: a bureaucratic organization attempting to distribute services paid for out of public money to people in need while simultaneously avoiding the recipients' dependence and assisting them to return to independent living. Decision making is structured and accountable; financial considerations are important; service delivery is not solely left to social workers.

Algie (1971) considered that the overall objective of reorganization was to improve service effectiveness, and that this overall objective could be subdivided into service objectives, economic objectives and professional objectives ('to increase the status of the social services profession'). Economic and service objectives seem to have been fairly successful, but there has been general failure to achieve the professional objectives, a point that will be developed further in Chapter 10.

The example of the structure of one particular authority hopefully gives a flavour of the scale of social work. Social work is big business. In 1976—1977 some £32 056 million were spent on social services, which is 52% of all public expenditure and 26% of the entire national income. Of this sum, £1208 million were spent directly on personal social services, normally operationalized through a social services department in each local authority (Source: Byrne & Padfield, 1978). In 1977 social service departments together employed some 260 000 staff of whom approximately 100 000 were probably called social workers of one form or another, though by no means all held a Certificate of Qualification in Social Work. Table 9.3 provides a breakdown of staff numbers in local authority social services departments.

The Legislative Framework of Local Authority Social Services

Stroud (1975) lists a number of the statutory duties that have devolved to social services departments. These may be summarized as:

1. To arrange for the adoption of children.
2. To supervise children placed for adoption and assist the courts in decisions about adoptions.
3. Registration of childminders and supervision of children placed with them.

Table 9.3 Local Authority Social Services: Numbers of Staff

(Reproduced from *Community Care*, 16 April 1981, by permission.)

	1974	1977
All staff in social services departments	236 000	266 000
1. Fieldwork staff including trainees, welfare assistants, community workers, management and supervisors	22 674	25 700
2. ATC staff	6 000	7 000
3. Staff in day centres for the mentally ill, elderly and physically handicapped	3 700	5 600
4. Day nursery staff	9 200	9 800
5. Home helps	87 000	92 000
6. Residential staff for elderly and physically handicapped	58 000	64 000
7. Homes' staff for mentally disordered	4 600	7 300
8. Staff for community homes for children and young people	23 700	27 400

4. Approval and supervision of all places where children live away from their parents (with the exception of boarding schools). A particular concern with children's homes and foster homes.
5. Provision of substitute homes for children deprived of a normal family life.
6. Providing advice, guidance and assistance to families where there is a risk that a child might have to be taken into care.
7. To provide reports to juvenile courts where care proceedings are envisaged.
8. To supervise children placed on supervision orders and to provide care and treatment for those on care orders.
9. Provision of aids to the disabled.
10. Provision of opportunities for occupation and recreation for the disabled.
11. Provision of residential accommodation for those in need of care and attention through old age, disability or other special circumstances.
12. Provision of facilities to prevent the onset of mental illness.
13. Provision of a home help service.
14. Provision of a meals service to the ill, aged or disabled.
15. To survey the needs of the elderly and disabled and inform them of the services available.

16. To provide social work services to the health service, particularly in hospitals and child guidance clinics.

Clearly the range of responsibilities and the authority delegated to social services, particularly to social work staff, is enormous. The implications of such demands on social workers will be examined in detail in Chapter 11.

9.3 Social Work: The Historical Background

So far, then, we have compared the image with something of the reality. The purpose of this section is to explain something of the origins of contemporary social work, as its history contains the seeds of many of its current dilemmas.

A conventional starting point is not to take a starting point and argue that social work is a form of altruistic behaviour that is endemic to man as a social animal; it became linked with the growth of the established Church in the Middle Ages, formalized with the development of the Poor Laws, and made necessary by the effects of the Industrial Revolution in creating structurally disadvantaged classes in which the government had no wish to intervene. The development of Friendly Societies, which offered friendship and limited financial help to the poor, and charitable societies designed to meet most conceivable social needs, necessitated ordering and structuring to avoid chaotic and patchy services.

The Society for Organizing Charitable Relief and Mendicity was established in 1869 to meet this need. Concerned about the deteriorating effect they believed disorganized charity was having on the morals of the poor, they attempted to organize the promotion of financial and material assistance by defining proper areas of competence, devising and executing 'scientific' methods of social casework and educating and reforming the recipients of relief so that they might regain their ideal state of being independent, self-respecting individuals. Thus the Charity Organisation Society (COS) combined practicality with Victorian work-ethic morality. Perhaps its biggest single contribution to later social work practice was in the coining of the word 'casework' to mean the disciplined, organized and consistent means of dealing with individuals in need, and in employing full-time caseworkers to put the ideas into practice. C.S. Loch the Secretary of the COS from 1875 until 1913 was its driving force, a devout believer in systematic assessments of needs and in the Christian goodness of the objectives.

Casework was directed towards two more client groups by the turn of the century — hospital patients and criminals. The COS began introducing its trained caseworkers into the hospital service in 1895. Called almoners, that is, official distributors of alms, their original purpose was to prevent the abuse of the hospital by persons able to pay for medical treatment. Despite this simple control function, almoners slowly developed in numbers, confidence and professional altruism, eventually providing the rudiments of a social service to patients in hospitals throughout the country. Early specialisms developed rapidly, particular interests between the First and Second World Wars seem to have been in tuberculosis and venereal disease.

In 1876, 47 years after the establishment of the first police force, the Church of England Temperance Society recruited the first police court missionary. Precipitated by the 1824 Vagrancy Act which allowed for the prosecution of idle and disorderly persons, rogues and vagabonds and incorrigible rogues and therefore brought large numbers of petty offenders before the courts who were uninfluenced by deterrent sentences, the missionaries were required to help persons convicted, but given only a token sentence, to lead a good and useful life.

Originally intended to work with drunkards, the number of missionaries grew until by 1900 there were over 100, working with a range of offenders, though mainly drunkards, children and petty criminals. The 1887 Probation of First Offenders Act formalized the notion of probation as part of English law, and increased the level of importance attached to the work of the missionaries who eventually developed into the current Probation and After-Care Service.

By the turn of the century the three strands, caseworkers, almoners and missionaries, were expanding rapidly and becoming incorporated in a more general social movement seeking greater equality between the classes, characterized by the establishment of the Fabian Society, and the work of such individuals as Florence Nightingale, Octavia Hill, Thomas Barnardo, Charles Booth, and Sydney and Beatrice Webb. Social services were being seen less as a form of charity and more as basic rights which should be available to all the citizens of a civilized country. Though well behind most other European countries, Britain passed a number of pieces of legislation reflecting the change towards a less primitive form of altruism:

1907   Probation of Offenders Act. Founded the probation service.
1908   Children Act. Juvenile courts for young offenders.
1908   Old age pension scheme.
1910   Establishment of employment exchanges.
1911   National Insurance Act; payments as a right when sick or unemployed in return for contributions.

Caseworkers, probation officers and almoners were becoming caught up in legislation, officially recognized, and given certain prescribed tasks to carry out. The tool they were expected to use was known and considered acceptable: social casework. Essentially an administrative technique, social casework was in many ways tailormade for the early demands placed upon it — recording decisions, systematizing approaches, collecting basic information and monitoring outcome. No hint was apparent of a significant change in technique that was to occur with the dissemination of Freud's theories and clinical findings in the 1920s. Responsible not only for the creation of an additional casework strand — psychiatric social work — psychoanalysis spread rapidly throughout the new welfare network. Not only did it have the pleasantly high status overtones of medicine, but perhaps more importantly by

118

locating the core of the individual's problems in the individual, took the emphasis away from a more open-minded analysis of the social factors relevant to a particular individual. A system received a theory and became an occupation: or at least it did for one small group of individual caseworkers. Most of the rest found themselves fairly rapidly enmeshed in the fine fabric of state welfare provision:

1930   Poor Law Reform Act introduced state funding for social workers and certain statutory duties.
1948   National Assistance Act repealed the poor law, transferring the responsibility for the care of the children and the elderly to the local authorities.
1948   Children Act established a new local government department, manned by social workers. For the first time social workers were functionally autonomous, self-managed, and headed by a Children's Officer.

The separate branches of social work had established their own associations fairly rapidly — Hospital Almoners' Association 1903, National Association of Probation Officers 1912 and the Association of Psychiatric Social Workers 1930. The original body, COS, remained as a charity until 1946 when it became the Family Welfare Society, partly state funded and concerned almost exclusively with intrafamilial difficulties.

It is unclear when the term 'social work' was first introduced, though it seems likely to have occurred in the 1920s as an attempt to devise a catch-all term for the various branches of an original single body, branches which had gone their own way but had no wish to deny their common origins. It is unfortunate perhaps that nothing more precise could have been devised, but then again 'general practitioner' means very little either: what is used as a technique is perhaps more efficient as a means of distinguishing one job from another, than the job name in itself.

A number of attempts had been made to unite the various professional bodies, and in 1936 The British Federation of Social Workers (BFSW) had been created, an organization which attempted to bring together some 12 different social work bodies in the shape of a federation. The opportunity for members to join the BFSW on an individual basis was proposed but only qualified social workers were allowed to do so. In 1951 however, the individual members of BFSW formed their own organization, the Association of Social Workers, with the aim of unifying their profession under the banner of casework method. In 1965 a Committee on Local Authority and Allied Personal Services was convened, and its report under the Chairmanship of Lord Seebohm (1968) recommended the abolition of distinctions between the various forms of welfare provision and their unification in one single generic social service department in each local authority, whose purpose was to provide:

a community based and family oriented service, which will be available to all . . . . The new department will have responsibilities going beyond those of existing local

119

authority departments, but they will include the present services provided by children's departments, the welfare services provided under the National Assistance Act 1948, educational welfare and child guidance services, the home help service, mental health social work services, other social work services provided by health departments, day nurseries, and certain social welfare work currently undertaken by some housing departments. (Seebohm, 1968)

These recommendations were incorporated in the 1970 Social Services Act, and 'one door on which to knock' came into being. This nearly reached completion in 1974 when hospital social workers also became employees of the local authorities, though probation officers have remained resolutely independent since their formation; in practice, employers and professional body. In 1970, the British Association of Social Workers (BASW) was formed to replace previous associations, and though never attracting more than a minority of all social workers, remains the strongest professional voice within social work. For a fuller discussion of BASW see Chapter 10.

Table 9.4

ALTRUISM CHRISTIANITY/ RELIGION	ADMINISTRATION INDUSTRIAL REVOLUTION	FRIENDLY SOCIETIES CHARITABLE SOCIETIES	1869 COS CASEWORK

1907 PROBATION OFFICERS 1895 ALMONERS 1924 PSYCHIATRIC SOCIAL WORKERS	1948 CHILDRENS OFFICERS	1951 BRITISH FEDERATION OF SOCIAL WORKERS	1970 SEEBOHM BRITISH ASSOCIATION OF SOCIAL WORKERS
CASEWORKERS	CASEWORK		GENERIC SOCIAL WORKERS

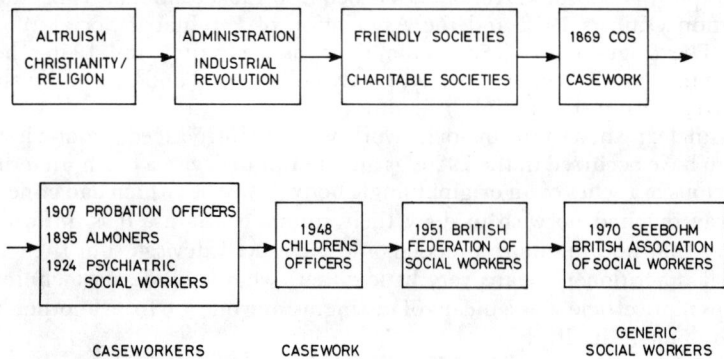

Historically social work has developed as shown in Table 9.4. Note the shifting emphases between method and state-determined job role; the move from the original method (casework) to the current role (generic social worker). Social workers are now left to use whatever technique they choose to meet a particular difficulty. A problem arises, of course, with increasing evidence that social workers are largely ineffective *regardless* of the technique they use, but are valuable in the role they fill. This leads to an interesting question about social workers themselves: who becomes a social worker, and how are they trained? After all, presumably not everyone wishes to carry enormous responsibility for other people without any effective means of influencing the situation one way or the other.

Social workers have been trained in a university setting since 1903 at the London School of Economics: the form of their training, its status and value have always been in dispute. In a survey of 250 social workers carried out by

120

Gallup in 1981 (*Community Care*, 16 April 1981), 6% considered their training prepared them for the job very well; 23% well; 44% adequately, 24% badly and 3% very badly. Apparently then over one-quarter of sampled social workers felt themselves inadequately trained. Despite the dissatisfaction with it, training has always been encouraged. The 1959 Younghusband report on social workers in the local authority health and welfare services recommended urgent increases in the numbers of 'trained' staff and urged a rapid expansion in the training system. In 1962 the new Council for Training in Social Work offered a certificate in social work to those successfully completing a two year course of approved study usually in a college of education or polytechnic. With the 1970 reorganization came an added boost to training. The Central Council for Education and Training in Social Work (CCETSW) was created by statutory instrument in 1971, and superseded all previous social work training bodies. A QUANGO, council members must be approved by the Secretary of State (Department of Health and Social Security), who directly appoints 8 of the 64 members. The Certificate of Qualification in Social Work (CQSW) became the basic qualification for all social workers. CCETSW effectively unified the training for all social workers, including probation officers. By 1977 some 80 institutions offered training leading to a CQSW, producing some 2500–3500 social workers a year. In Paper 15.1, February 1977, CCETSW stated that no central syllabus was to be laid down but all courses should cover:

   (i)   principles and practice of social work;
   (ii) supervised practice in social work;
   (iii) applied social studies, including
         human growth and behaviour
         social policy, social administrative and social services
         aspects of the social services relevant to social work

and added that 'the student's training should be designed to prepare a social work practitioner who can work effectively with clients'.

Perhaps the biggest single fundamental deficit in social work training is the absence of a substantive theory which applies to the context in which social workers practice; together with an associated technique for putting the conclusions from such a theoretical analysis into practice. Part of the reason for writing this book is to make a contribution to this goal by offering an integrated approach that slices through theory and practice, and raises the possibility of monitoring work, evaluating output and achieving goals. It is with the latter aim that greatest conflict might arise.

A precise statement of social work goals is rarely attempted: normally they are left to drift in a sea of morals whipped by a gale of crises. In many ways this is perhaps an understandable state of affairs, as it obscures a potential fundamental clash between the values of an individual and the values of his/her employers. As we will see later, there is some evidence to indicate that social workers tend to value individual worth, the responsibility of the group to care for its members, basic rights, change, dependence on others, the ability of culture to outweigh the effects of heredity, and diversity. BASW in *The Social Work Task* (1977) lists a code of ethics which nicely confuses values, ethics and principles but nevertheless seems to be advocating 'the recognition of the value and dignity of every human being . . . the profession accepts a responsibility to encourage and facilitate the self-realisation of the individual person'. In other words, BASW implies that the social worker must defend the rights of the individual when those rights are threatened. As polemic this is stirring stuff. In practice, however, a fundamental and obvious problem arises. With values like these, what structure could possibly provide adequate support, administration and resources to social workers in a way that did not threaten any individuals' rights to self-realization? It is in this area, in the potential if not actual clash between values, structures, goals and controls, between social workers and social service departments that greatest confusion occurs.

Social services departments are bureaucratic. They operate largely according to set procedures, are funded by the taxpayer, and monitored by the government and local council. There is a strong element of political control (compare the values of the Labour and Conservative Parties with those of most social workers and see which Party will advocate social work growth and which will attempt to reduce its influence). Promotion is dependent on 'good behaviour'; directors may or may not have a social work qualification; all resources are controlled by managers and administrators, not social workers. It is not surprising, as Nina Toren (1972) found, that the employing organization rather than professional training is the greater determinant of a social worker's professed values. How social workers resolve or fail to resolve this important fundamental value conflict is open to speculation: little researched, it is part of the underlife of social work.

9.4   Some Current Issues

The Role and the Person

A theme throughout this chapter has been the generally high level of confusion that seems to have developed between the social work role and the social worker. Time and again when asked their views of 'social work' people proceed to describe 'a social worker', normally in a manner that reflects their particular prejudices.

Given the largely statutory nature of the social work task, it is perhaps surprising that greater interest seems to be directed toward the person doing the task than to the task itself. Few people concern themselves with evaluating the character and physical appearance of particular doctors and nurses: what they do is much more important. Of course it is in the area of 'technique' that a central difficulty has arisen for social workers. Most other professions have specific techniques they utilize; techniques more or less restricted to themselves, quantifiable and open to evaluation. By choosing their central technique as 'the use of self in interpersonal relationships' social workers have put their very 'selves' on the line, to be examined and evaluated. Unlike a technique, the 'self' is not constant between social workers, is not quantifiable, and can only be evaluated on moral grounds. Criticisms of social work in a sense include both the person and the role under the catch-all category of 'self'. Unless social work can disentangle its self from itself outsiders will continue to evaluate people rather than methods — something that can only be to the long-term disadvantage of social work as a whole.

Values and Social Workers

Social workers, as we have seen, have a statutory duty to work with handi-capped, mentally ill, abnormal, deviant, immature and deprived people. Each of these terms is the result of a value judgement, and the existence of social work as an occupation reflects a series of complex value judgements made by the various groups in power. Such judgements centre on the attitude it is considered a civilized society should exhibit towards its structurally deprived members, and on how it should attempt to encourage conformity from them to the dominant social norms that have led to their alienation and deprivation in the first place. From the outset then, two mutually antagonistic value sets have been present in social work. BASW in *The Social Work Task* considered that social workers are influenced by values from four different sources:

(i)   Societal values. 'The role of statutory agencies, such as local authority social services departments, is not just to provide care and to express society's compassion . . . it is also to impose societal norms and to ensure conformity.'

(ii) Personal values.

(iii) Professional values. 'Whatever a social worker's personal values, as a social worker he is expected to be governed by values which are accepted by social workers and acceptable to the public generally as appropriate to that role.'

(iv) Agency values. 'Agency values will be reflected in organizational, pro-cedural and policy decisions taken by élite individuals and groups . . . and these values will influence the social workers employed by that agency.'

All in all, a fairly clear statement of whose value system local authority social workers are expected to hold — the dominant ones in society and in the employing agency. Now, if the value systems of the dominant social group and the employing agency are congruent with those held by the social work pro-fession as a whole, and if in turn most social workers hold personal values con-sistent with their professional values, then social workers should experience a high degree of job satisfaction and low levels of cognitive dissonance. This does not seem to be the case (*Social Work Today*, 10 June 1980; Kakabadse & Worrall, 1978).

What then are the professional values which should 'ideally' underpin social work practice? BASW's views seem to be fairly similar to those of the Central

Council for Education and Training in Social Work (1976), and outline five fundamental social work values:

(i) respect for persons; and/or
(ii) respect for life — particularly valued are the right to self-determination (to be able to choose and carry out the chosen action) and 'to be able to formulate and follow rules or general social norms' (CCETSW, p. 28);
(iii) acceptance — continuing to value a person because of his inherent worth;
(iv) confidentiality;
(v) individualization — each person's experiences are unique, and this should be recognized.

Thus 'ideal' professional social work values would seem to rest rather uneasily with the values that typically emanate from large-scale bureaucracies. Senior administrators might find it difficult to devise policies that permit self-determination for all, while recognizing that the needs of no two individuals are identical. As we have seen, however, BASW seems quite prepared to straddle two incompatible value systems.

What about social workers themselves? Being expected to hold incompatible professional and agency values would seem to necessitate selecting people for training with rather strong superordinate value systems. Unfortunately there has been little research on the values held by social workers so the question cannot be properly answered. McLeod and Mener (1967) studied the values of some 293 American social workers, and notwithstanding the considerable structural differences between American and British practice, came up with one or two interesting findings. Examining first the literature on 'social work philosophy' they concluded that there were ten major value dimensions, each arranged on bipolar continuum:

1. Security — satisfaction v. struggle suffering and denial. Individuals must have security and satisfaction of basic biological and cultural needs.
2. Group responsibility v. individual responsibility. The group has responsibility for the welfare of its members.
3. Interdependence v. individual autonomy. Individuals are interdependent with other members of the group.
4. Innovation — change v. traditionalism. A willingness to accept change.
5. Cultural determinism v. inherent human nature. Human nature is culturally determined and is amenable to change by altering the environment.
6. Individual worth v. system goals. A belief in the worth and dignity of the individual.
7. Diversity v. homogeneity. Diversity of ideas, values and life styles has a positive value, almost synonymous with democracy.
8. Individualization v. stereotyping. Every individual is unique and important and should not be stereotyped.
9. Relativism — pragmatism v. dissolutism — sacredness. The scientific

124

method and a pragmatic approach are of value in solving problems.
10.   Personal liberty v. societal control. Every individual has the right to direct his or her life as free from arbitrary external controls as possible.

The trained social workers in the sample adhered only to the first seven items, in the priority order listed. Stereotyping was acceptable, scientific method was not favoured, and the need for social control was accepted. The general 'feel' of the value system is of social workers seeing themselves helping to provide a basic minimum of physical and financial care to individuals on a personally tailored basis, with concern and compassion, but without expectations of being involved in 'scientific' evaluations or in structural change.

If there is any overlap with the value systems of British social workers then the critics who label social workers as 'long haired revolutionaries' seem to be a little off beam. Personal values seem to be roughly congruent with agency values, though these in turn seem to be incompatible with professional values.

Social workers might usefully decide on which side of the fence they want to stand. Are professional social work values to be abandoned and agency values substituted? Or are professional values to be adhered to and an attempt made to change agency and personal values? Or, indeed, should a more honest compromise be reached and social work strive to achieve some form of compartmentalization within the social services department, achieving a placid pool of consistent personal and professional values within the turbulent waters of agency expediencies? Whatever is decided, care must be taken not to adopt an excessively fatalistic stance. Without wishing to minimize the inherent difficulties, we saw in Chapter 7 that change is theoretically possible. If social work cannot change its own structure to suit itself, whatever form that might take, how much hope can it have of influencing the lives of others?

9.5   Conclusion

Chapter 9 is concerned with the structure of social work. An initial distinction was made between the image outsiders have of social work, and of its actual structure and function. The incongruity of these two factors was stressed and a number of possible explanations for this discrepancy offered. By placing the structure of social work in historical context the sources of a number of these confusions were pointed out. Finally, two of the many issues facing contemporary social work were outlined: the general confusion between the social work role and the person filling the role; and of the potential clash between values held by social workers, those put forward as the values that should be held by social workers, and those values usually considered acceptable in a large-scale bureaucracy.

Perhaps one of the most powerful reactions to an analysis of the structure of social work is the sense of the sheer size, complexity and demanding nature of the task that has been allotted to social work by the State. In Chapter 11 we examine in more detail the types of demand that are made on social workers and at the skills social workers have culled or developed to meet those demands. But to round off the social work picture, Chapter 10 contains an account of the development of social work as an aspiring profession, with particular reference to the major professional social work association, the British Association of Social Workers.

10
BASW and Social Work

Examining the growth of a professional association is, at the best of times, a chancy activity. When the profession has itself seemingly failed to achieve general consensus among its own members about what they should actually be doing for a living, then such an evaluation shifts to the even riskier business of trying to gather together multitudinous and disparate threads and knitting them into something approaching an intellectually and visually satisfying whole. No claim is made that what follows is in any way comprehensive; it is an inevitably biased account of the formation and development of the British Association of Social Workers (BASW), together with a consideration of some of the major issues that BASW members seem likely to have to grapple with in the immediate future.

Perhaps surprisingly, very little seems to have been written on BASW as an organization. The only sources of any substance are McCarthy (1980) and an issue of *Social Work Today*, 1 July 1980), a weekly magazine published by BASW itself. In this edition the editor monitored the preceding decade of BASW's history in diary form, supplemented by a series of interviews with all five past chairmen (each chairman serves for a two year period), and by an article from Chris Andrews, General Secretary of the Association from 1974 to 1980. The mood of the issue might be described as one of determined optimism, perhaps best encapsulated in the following comment from the General Secretary:

> The role of BASW is crucial. It has led the way in matters relating to confidentiality, ethics, setting a target date for ending the appointment of unqualified persons to social work posts, career grades, accreditation, a General Social Work Council, and in defining the social work task. The association, too, through its advice and representa-

tion services is able to assert the value of professional standards in instances when conflict arises between these and other considerations. The tragedy is that many have yet to be persuaded of the value of all this, both inside and outside social work. . . . (*Social Work Today*, 1 July 1980)

BASW represents itself as being successful and valuable, while simultaneously admitting that most social workers and members of the general public are not convinced that this is in fact the case. Why this unhappy state of affairs should have developed is open to a plethora of speculations, though three possible explanations can be immediately postulated:

(i)   BASW is deceiving itself. Others recognize that it has not achieved what it has professed to achieve, and therefore, denigrate the source of the misinformation.
(ii) BASW has made significant achievements in the areas specified, but these are not considered important by most social workers and most outsiders.
(iii) BASW has simply failed to communicate properly its undoubted achievements. Criticisms of the Association are made from ignorance rather than from the basis of accurate knowledge.

The contention here is that each of these postulates plays a part in helping to explain the curiously alienated position the British Association of Social Workers has created for itself: a professional organization typically representing itself as 'The Voice of Social Work' which has never managed to attract more than 10 000 or so members from its inception in 1970 to date. That is despite the increase in its potential membership during the decade from some 20 000 to something in the region of 100 000 (Table 10.1). Now it might be argued at this stage that it does not really matter what has happened to the British Association of Social Workers over the past ten years — in failing to attract membership it is *a priori* of minimal interest to most social workers and therefore a detailed comment on BASW's state of health is unwanted and would be considered by most social workers to be of little or no concern to them. In a sense that argument is unanswerable: the assertion here is that having a professional association is usually considered to be a desirable state of affairs, much to be encouraged, and the success or failure of any particular association is therefore some form of indicator of the strength, power and coherence of the profession concerned. Obviously such an assertion is predicated upon a belief that social worker either is a profession or should be a profession. Much has been written on both aspects of this notion of professionalism in social work, though no unequivocal conclusion has been drawn. Indeed, social work is such a fluid occupation, changing its structure and function so frequently, it is difficult to develop the perspective given by analysis of a lengthy period of stability within an occupation. However, there would seem to be a number of fundamental questions that need to be asked and answered about professionalism and social work, that provide a framework to the later discussion.

128

Table 10.1   British Association of Social Workers Membership 1971–1978

(From British Association of Social Workers' Annual Reports.)

Year	Total membership (Members + Associates + Students)	Lapsed membership
1971	8 539	—
1972	10 589	1045
1973	11 492	1387
1974	11 393	2135
1975	10 918	1886
1976	10 415	2352
1977	10 035	1675
1978	9 724	1020

10.1   What is a Profession?

Despite the voluminous literature on the subject there seems to be no clear definition available. However, there does seem to be general agreement that there is a distinction between professionalism, however defined, and professionalization. Millerson (1964) reviewed the existing work, largely sociological, on professionalism and found that there were six elements most commonly considered to be related to professionalism, from a total of 23 elements produced by 21 different writers. The six elements were:

(i)   skill based on theoretical knowledge;
(ii)   the provision of training and education;
(iii) a well developed organization;
(iv)   the existence of a code of conduct;
(v)   testing of the competence of members;
(vi)   provision of an altruistic service.

With some fairly slight variations these elements seem to coincide fairly well with the views of later writers. There are obviously a number of difficulties with such a trait approach to the analysis of professionalism. The most obvious one is that the traits are themselves derived from analysis of occupations generally considered to be professions, such as medicine and the law, thereby providing a circular argument — professions are what are generally considered to be professions, and therefore few other occupations ever receive the stamp of professionalism. However, trait analysis is useful in that it gives some insight into those characteristics generally taken to comprise professions, as long as the traits identified are not seen as representing anything other than current social perceptions of professional groups.

Professionalization is the process it is assumed occupations must exhibit if they are to become professions. It therefore relates directly to the trait approach. Wilensky (1964) argued in favour of a chronological sequence, as follows:

(i)   a full-time occupation is created to provide a specified service;
(ii) training is established, usually connected with a university;
(iii) a professional association is formed;
(iv) a legal monopoly of a particular skill is achieved;
(v)   a formal code of ethics is evolved.

Although there has been some disagreement over the order of the different stages (Johnson, 1972), the overall process seems to have received a certain credence.

One further aspect of being a profession must be taken into account — expectations are made that certain standards of behaviour will be upheld by each member of the profession. Such expectations centre on the professionals' independence, autonomy, respect for the clients' confidentiality, and high level of technical skill.

10.2   What is Bureaucracy?

Social services departments are typically referred to as bureaucracies by their critics, with an implicit assumption that bureaucracies and professionals are incompatible bedfellows. The classification of a bureaucracy is that of Weber who argued that it was a particular form of organization exhibiting the following main characteristics:

(i)   a hierarchical authority structure based on official position rather than individualism;
(ii) a system of rules governing the rights and duties of these positions;
(iii) a detailed system of rules for dealing with each case;
(iv) a clear-cut and highly specialized division of labour;
(v)   impersonal social relations with management based on files;
(vi) officials recruited to a salaried career with security of tenure based on technical qualifications.

Although there are clear similarities with the structure of social services departments there are also marked differences. The major difference lies in the location of the effective power in the organization. In a classical bureaucracy those whose role is to control how the organization functions are in a structural position that enables them to do so. In social services departments this is not necessarily the case. The fieldworker can have a considerable degree of autonomy, in some isolation from his hierarchical superiors, who are often not social workers but administrators. This has led Smith (1970) to term social work a 'front line organization', that is, one where power is effectively wielded by fieldworkers even though authority officially exists in a formal hierarchy. Although there will always be a shift away from the formal organization of power in a bureaucracy to more informal sources, the degree of power invested in fieldworkers as implied by Smith, though it might well have been applicable at the time of writing, shortly before the Seebohm reorganization, has been superseded by the consequences of Seebohm which have led to a direct increase in the amount of control management hierarchies are now able to hold over their fieldworkers. The demands of the media in particular have led to an increased tendency for social services departments to develop more formal rules and specialized division of labour, if only to help protect themselves from attack. The net result is that social services departments are becoming increasingly identified with the classical Weberian concept of the bureaucracy.

Of course, that is not necessarily a bad thing. Toren has argued that bureaucracy is only inimicable to social work when two 'core qualities' are threatened: the development and application of social work knowledge; and the social worker's commitment to place the interests of the client above all others. She considers that social work has a number of attributes conducive to bureaucratization, a short training period, no theoretical knowledge base, feminization, and recruitment from the lower classes (as compared presumably with the selection policies of the four 'great' persons' professions — the law, medicine, the ministry, and university teaching). She further argues that bureaucracy can in fact offer a number of benefits to both clients and consumers — reliability and fairness for the client; distancing and defence against the client's demands for the social worker. It might also be postulated, said Toren, that bureaucracies provide social controllers with a hideaway from the issue of social reform!

10.3 Where does Social Work and the British Association of Social Workers fit in?

The foregoing discussion goes some way towards indicating that social work is now only a semi-profession (with no theoretical base, universal code of conduct, or universal testing of members' competence). However, it seemingly aspires to become a full profession and has moved some way along the professionalization process, with most of its members working in a bureaucratic organization.

Two final issues therefore merit discussion — whether it is desirable for social work to become a full profession, and if it is, whether a social work professional is appropriately employed within a bureaucracy, in the form of a social service department which is almost certainly likely to remain the chief employer of social workers. These two issues provoke a range of discussions but they can be usefully narrowed down to two arguments — professionalism v. unionism; and bureaucracy as opposed to some other form of organization more appropriate to the fundamental precepts on which social work is based. It is in relation to these two arguments that the development and growth of the British Association, the largest professional association, for social workers, needs to be examined. But first we will consider the historical context; the development of professional associations in social work before BASW; and the generation of BASW itself. Much of the following is based on the work of McCarthy (1980).

The need for professional status seems to have been felt from the earliest days of social work. As specializations proliferated from the turn of the century to the Second World War so did the number of professional social work associations. Thus 1903 saw the establishment of the Hospital Almoners' Association, 1912 the National Association of Probation Officers and 1930 the Association of Psychiatric Social Workers. Despite a general recognition of similarities between the disparate branches the diverse backgrounds and methods of each specialism militated against unification. A first attempt to pull together the threads was generated in 1936 by the formation of the British Federation of Social Workers which managed to collect together 12 different associations under the one banner, associations representing such seemingly incongruous specialisms as almoners, moral welfare officers, psychiatric social workers, family caseworkers and probation officers. However, the British Federation of Social Workers ran on the principle of each member group remaining effectively independent. A later amendment to the constitution allowed individual membership to qualified social workers and their increasing number led to the formation of the Association of Social Workers in 1951, which superseded the British Federation of Social Workers. The aim of the Association of Social Workers was to unify social work as a profession by encouraging generic training and the ideology of casework. In some ways this reflected a general striving to achieve the status and relative independence previously attributed to the Association of Psychiatric Social Workers. The projected natural development towards this goal was probably substantially amended by the intervention of the Labour Government in the late 1960s and early 1970s into the large scale rationalization of the personal social services. Seebohm recommended a generic social work service based in local authority social services departments; the 1974 Local Government Reorganization Act incorporated the hospital social workers under social services department control, leaving only probation officers outside social services department influence and under the jurisdiction of the Home Office. This massive reorganization and incorporation of the vast majority of social workers into one type of organization broke down the remaining resistances to unification among the professional associations. In 1970 the British Association of Social Workers was formed and incorporated most of the pre-existing associations with the notable exception of the National Association of Probation Officers which remains independent.

British Association of Social Workers, 1970–1980

The birth of the British Association was not greeted with unanimous enthusiasm, and a number of the grievances aired at the time have remained with BASW throughout its infancy. Some of the more important of these were as follows:

1. The registration of the Association under the Companies Act and its automatic debarring from being a trade union. The whole area of unionization will be discussed later, provoking as it did a fundamental change in BASW's

constitution in 1978—1979 and the establishment of the British Union of Social Workers.

2. The desire to use BASW as a driving force to achieve a stronger professional base for social workers. Jacka (1973) cataloguing *The Acco Story* put it simply: 'The main motivation was professional. This was the way the rapidly growing but still young professions of various sorts of social worker could make their professional voice heard. . .'.

For some of the pre-existing associations, however, absorption into BASW meant a loss of professional control. Both almoners and psychiatric social workers had already established professional registers which were lost in the merger with the British Association. Particularly disconcerting to these associations was the later realization that BASW was too weak to introduce professional control over all its members. BASW's (1981) evidence to the National Institute of Social Work Inquiry contains a strong recommendation for a registration scheme of qualified social workers with a minimum of two years' experience.

3. None of the previous associations had succeeded in controlling the right to practice, and to date no social work organization has been able to influence the recruitment policy of employers. This was, however, viewed as an important possible spin-off from amalgamation.

4. BASW failed to control the awarding of social work qualifications, which was vested in the Central Council for Education and Training in Social Work in October 1971, an independent body with statutory authority created to promote training in all fields of social work. The Central Council took over the responsibilities of the former Central Training Council in Child Care, the Council for Training in Social Work and the Recruitment and Training Committee of the Association Council for Probation and After-Care. With 8 places on the 53 place Central Council, BASW is the largest single voice, but is by no means the controlling influence. Social work qualifications, therefore, effectively remain under state control, a blow to an aspiring profession.

5. At the outset BASW membership was restricted to qualified social workers, consistent with the search for professionalism. However, despite a rapid increase in the number of qualified social workers and hence potential members of the Association, the expected growth in membership did not occur. In fact, in the four years 1975—1978 membership actually fell despite the award of over 15 000 Certificates of Qualifications in Social Work (see Table 10.2).

The search for new membership, perhaps combined with pressure to avoid charges of élitism led to the 1978 Annual General Meeting resolving to extend membership to 'any person occupying a post in which in the opinion of Council a qualified social worker would be employed', a significant retreat from professional aspirations. Ironically, the expected increase in membership has not so far materialized, perhaps because BASW attempted to cover its options by recommending to employers that all designated social worker posts should be occupied by qualified practitioners by 1982.

Table 10.2

(Reproduced from P. McCarthy (1980) *Unionism and Professionalism in Social Work*, M.Sc. thesis, University of Oxford, by permission.)

Year	Membership of British Association of Social Workers	Number of Certificates of Qualification in Social Work awarded
1975	10 981	3582
1976	10 415	3981
1977	10 035	4039
1978	9 724	3780

The Structure of the British Association of Social Workers

The structure of BASW has changed substantially in the last two years, largely attributable to the financial crisis of 1978–1979 (to be discussed later). Initially, however, the structure was more complex than the relatively simple structure of the recent reorganization. Basically BASW was controlled by an elected council, and run on a day-to-day basis by the triad of Chairperson, General Secretary and Treasurer. Each Chairperson could serve a maximum of two years, though the General Secretary could continue until resignation, once appointed. In practice the five Chairpeople worked with only two General Secretaries during the decade.

BASW was divided into three large units and a number of smaller discrete groups. The three large units were:

1. The Standing Committees, consisting of
    (i)   Education and Training
    (ii)   International Relations
    (iii) Membership
    (iv)   Parliamentary, Public Relations and Social Policy
    (v)   Professional Development and Practice
    (vi)   Salaries and Service Conditions
    (vii) Publications
2. National Committees
    (i)   Physical Illness and Handicap, later to become General Health
    (ii)   Mental Health
    (iii) Family and Child Care
    (iv)   Treatment of Offenders
3. Special interest groups, which have varied substantially, and not all are currently in existence:
    (i)   Poverty
    (ii)   Geriatric, later to become Ageing

        (iii) Child Guidance
        (iv) Renal
        (v)   Intercultural
        (vi) Groupwork
        (vii) Gynaecology and Obstetrics
        (viii) Residential
        (ix) Social Work in Education
        (x)   Sexuality
        (xi) Haemophilia
   4. In addition, there have been such groups as:
        (i)   Law Panel
        (ii) Disciplinary Board
        (iii) National Executive (from 1974). Previously the General Purposes
              and Finance Committee, which had not in fact been prescribed by
              the constitution.
        (iv) And a recent proliferation of panels concerned with the law, public
              relations, social contexts, related agencies and so on.

BASW's policies were disseminated among branches in each region of the
country (69 in 1981), and 'each branch shall elect annually a Chairman, Secretary, Treasurer, such other Officers as it thinks necessary, a Branch Committee, a representative or representatives to the Regional Commitee and deputies
for such representatives' (BASW by-laws revised 28 October 1972).

In practice then the British Association started out with a comprehensive
and complex structure, effectively presuming a much higher membership and
hence financial and power base than it was in fact to receive. Its early years were
also marked by unexpectedly large profits from *Social Work Today*. Some of
the retrospective comments of BASW Chairpersons and General Secretaries
contained in the BASW anniversary issue of *Social Work Today* (1 July 1980)
convey something of the sense of failure, desperation and resolute optimism
that the clash between the original high hopes and subsequent events has
produced.

Kenneth Brill (General Secretary 1970–1974): 'BASW just cannot be at one
and the same time a substitute for NALGO [the National Association of Local
Government Officers], a pressure group for consumers, and a warm
professional club.'

Kay Richards (Chairperson 1974–1976): 'My chairmanship began with
external ambivalances, internal uncertainties and a commitment to improve
the associations' capacities to enhance the standard of social work and to influence social policy.'

Janie Thomas (Chairperson 1976–1978): 'There was much that was sound
and good; but two interrelated things immediately disturbed. One was the
financial problem of the association. The other, the declining membership.'

Chris Andrews (General Secretary 1974–1981): 'In 1970, a professional
identity was emerging which asserted the primacy of professional factors in the
practice of social work. Whatever his employment agency a social worker had

135

skills which stemmed from a common core. The formation of the British Association of Social Workers itself is testimony to this mood.

In 1980 very little progress is discernible in the march towards social workers controlling their own destiny. A social work qualification is still not seen as an essential prerequisite for many top social work posts, even in social work training. It is arguable that politicians, administrators, managers and trade unions exercise more influence over social work than do social workers themselves. Social workers can never enjoy complete professional freedom but clients are likely to be better served by workers answerable to colleagues for their practice competence than by poodles masquerading as professionals.'

So What Went Wrong?

The British Association has had a number of positive achievements. It has developed a wide range of contacts with such groups as the Personal Social Services Council, various government departments, political parties, trade unions, pressure groups, voluntary associations, and so on. It has international connections and is a member of the International Federation of Social Workers. It has submitted evidence to a range of Select Committees and Royal Commissions and provides a range of interest groups for the members of its 69 or so branches.

However, the first decade seems to connote failure rather than success, even to BASW officials. So what went wrong? Although it is early to identify clearly the significant dynamics of an association as complex as BASW, a number of factors can be postulated to have had a detrimental effect:

1. Failure to recruit and retain membership. McCarthy postulates four possible explanations.
   (i) Dissatisfaction with BASW. The Association is seen by some social workers as having been established to complete the process of professionalisation and has failed to do so.
   (ii) Anti-professionalism. Some social workers hold the opposite belief: professionalism is seen as a harmful monopolistic oligarchy that damages the client. McCarthy implies that this view is correlated with radical social work. This, however, is unlikely to be the case, given the considerable volume of literature from radical social workers stressing the potential of a profession to achieve radical change (Epstein, 1970, 1968; Rein, 1970).
   (iii) Bureau professionalism. Since most social workers work for bureaucratic social services departments there is no opportunity for the achievement of full professional status. The best that can be hoped for is a type of bureau professionalism, that is humanizing a bureaucracy. BASW is not considered essential to such a role.
   (iv) Status frustration. General frustration at being prevented from achieving professional status by external factors (CCETSW, universities, bureaucracy) has been focused on the Association.
2. Failure to recruit basic grade membership. BASW remains an association largely consisting of senior social workers and above, presumably

those people for whom professionalism has greater career immediacy.

3. The development of unionization. Although it is possible to be a member of both the Association and a trade union there is some evidence that unionism, particularly joining NALGO, is seen as an alternative to joining BASW by a number of social workers. McCarthy indicates that some 22% of social workers are members of NALGO, though they constitute only 5% of NALGO branch membership. BASW's attempt to develop its own union, the British Union of Social Workers, in 1978 seems to have failed to attract more than cursory interest.

4. Financial difficulties. The Association's Annual Report 1979–1980 outlines 'a shattering financial and organisational crisis'. Losses of some £4000–5000 per week in 1979 were largely brought on by inflation overtaking subscriptions, which were in any case continuing to decline, and by *Social Work Today* being no longer able to generate sufficient income to both finance itself and the *British Journal of Social Work* and subsidize the Association. Narrowly avoiding bankruptcy, the Association survived by adopting a number of drastic measures:

A sophisticated budgeting system has been introduced; a financial adviser appointed; a comprehensive review of the Association's staffing and salary structure undertaken: membership records and other information have been computerised; and a management board for *Social Work Today*.'
Elwyn Jones (Chairman 1978–1980), *Social Work Today*, 1 July 1980.

5. Creation and adherence to a specious definition of the social work task which was always incompatible with a desire for professionalism.

Some Concluding Comments and Speculations on the Future of the British Association

Social work in one form or another has striven for the status that is usually taken to follow from successfully progressing through the professionalization process from its very beginning. Each branch of social work generated its own form of professional association, the majority of whom merged with BASW largely in the hope of furthering the cause of professionalism which it was believed would be to the ultimate benefit of the client, as well as to themselves.

Social work as a whole can best be described as a semi-profession in that it has achieved some but not all of the clothes of the full profession. It is perhaps distinguished by its so far unsuccessful attempt to integrate professionalism within the bureaucracy of the social services department. There is no reason to believe, however, that a social work profession contained within a bureaucracy would inevitably be a definition of the impossible. Theoretically there is a potential for developing the notion of the professional social work bureaucrat. An 'applied social scientist' perhaps?

The British Association has been at the forefront in the striving for professionalism. Despite having made a substantial contribution to the advancement of social work in certain circumscribed areas — communication with higher level managers, policy making and so on — it has failed to pass through most of

137

the major developmental stages of a professional association. Its most important deficits lie in its failure to provide an adequate definition of the social work task, to hold membership, to compete with unionization and to manage its own finances.

Speculating about the future of an organization radically restructured after recent/crises is hazardous. However, there would seem to be in very general terms at least five superordinate and somewhat mutually exclusive goals BASW may aim for:

1. To become a public relations association for high level social services department managers and bureaucrats.
2. With a completely different definition of the social work task — based on the skill of analysing problem situations and translating theory into practice to effectively intervene in them — to be at the forefront in the development of a more rigorous applied social science approach within social work.
3. To degenerate into a loose conglomerate association attempting to ride a multitude of struggling horses and 'guide' them in the direction the vector force is taking them anyway.
4. To ally itself to a more radical approach to social work encouraging social change and stressing a political commitment.
5. To become the social work equivalent of the Civil and Public Servants Association, a professional association for social service bureaucrats.

It is clear that the ideas developed in this book would indicate that the second option should be the one that is pursued by BASW. Unless BASW contrives to rescue itself from its current dilemmas along the lines indicated, then it seems reasonable to surmise that it will either degenerate into further confusion and ultimate sterility or will be transformed into an organization receiving even less support from the majority of social workers than it has so far received. Either way, it will have failed to fulfil the high expectations of its progenitors.

11
Demands and Skills

According to BASW (1981) 'the commitment of social work is to strike as creative a balance as possible between the demands of peoples' environments and their coping abilities' (para. 3.2). Social work is seen as a mediator between the needs and interests of the state and those of the individual. Therefore social workers must presumably hold the belief that such a reconciliation is possible, and that if it is not then the State will accept responsibility for its disadvantaged members. Such an argument seems consistent with Davies' (1981) view that 'Social workers are the maintenance mechanics oiling the interpersonal wheels of the community' (p. 137). Although squirting oil into dark corners is occasionally beneficial in that it may lubricate a few rusty parts, it does not necessarily guarantee that the vehicle will be roadworthy, nor does it demand any skill other than the ability to point the oil can in the right general direction. As we will see shortly adequate response by social workers to the demands made upon them necessitates far more than the use of maintenance skills. Social workers need to have resources that will enable them to deal adequately with client problems of all types. Fobbing the client off with the occasional service might keep the mechanic in business for a short while but leads to general dissatisfaction and ultimate bankruptcy. Unless social workers demonstrate not only the ability to diagnose a fault but also begin to develop skills to identify and carry out the necessary repairs, then the elderly, poor and handicapped clients who make most of the demands may question the wisdom of taking their problems to grease-monkeys when what they really needed was a design engineer.

11.1 Demands

As social workers are employed in such a wide range of settings and experience demands that differ in type, intensity and frequency, it would be somewhat unreasonable to expect all social workers to have the skills necessary to meet effectively all the demands placed upon them. There are no limits to distress or expectations of help, nor, increasingly, are there many corners of contemporary living that have escaped the pseudopods of legal encroachment. Although social workers are themselves among the first to point to the general dearth of useful pragmatic knowledge available to the caring professions, and are keen to emphasize that involvement with a problematic social situation does not necessarily assume a responsibility for solving the problem, nevertheless at some point or other social workers must be seen to meet at least a substantial proportion of the demands placed upon them if for no other reason than to justify their continued existence. In the fight for financial resources it will increasingly be those agencies who can demonstrate their ability to perform their allotted tasks satisfactorily that will receive the funds. The time is long past when good intentions, obvious compassion and willing hands are considered sufficient social work skills to justify the huge sums of money that are increasingly being placed within the grasp of the personal social services. Social workers might usefully identify those skills available to them which are capable of meeting the demands and acknowledging those areas where skills are inadequate. Before we give more detailed consideration to social work skills, it is essential to outline more clearly the demands that generate their necessary development.

The point was made earlier that social workers are employed in a suprisingly wide range of agency settings. A social worker in the intake team of a London borough social services department is likely to experience a much greater frequency and breadth of demand bombardment than is a practitioner employed in a specialist voluntary agency sited in a rural area. Moreover, neither will experience exactly the same type of demands as those made on a social worker employed by the Department of Health and Social Security to serve in a high security Special Hospital housing mentally abnormal offender patients. Demands are weighted in different areas according largely to the type of agency. A simple basis from which to examine some of the demands faced by social workers is to divide them into three broad and interrelating types:

(i)   formal demands;
(ii) expectation demands;
(iii) organizational demands.

Formal Demands

Formal demands are those that necessarily require a response from the social worker of one form or another. They can be classified into two groups according to source — legal demands and client demands. Demands made on social workers in the form of specific legal requirements are extensive and well

140

documented (see, for example, Roberts, 1978), and are usually manifested in clear procedural schemata laid down for the social worker to follow by the employing agency. Thus the law relating to the compulsory admission of mentally disturbed citizens to a psychiatric facility is fairly clearly outlined in the 1959 Mental Health Act, and employing agencies usually provide the practitioner with supplementary and highly detailed procedures designed to ensure that the practitioner acts in accordance with both the spirit and the letter of the law. Similarly, the criteria for the imposition of a care order on a child are legally fairly precise, and the social worker is obliged to work to them when making application to a court.

Client demands are taken to be those formal demands the client makes of a social worker. These can range from a request for the provision of a telephone, a parking disc, or aids for the disabled, to a demand for help with controlling an unruly child or a dementing grandparent. Sometimes of course the client does not have a clear idea of exactly what he or she needs, and sometimes what the client thinks is required might not necessarily be consistent with an analysis of the original problem. In both these cases it falls to the social worker to clarify the demands being made. However, once the analysis of the demand is completed either by the client, the social worker, or both in collaboration, the social worker has necessarily to respond, either by attempting to meet the demand, or by deciding to refer the demand to a more appropriate agency, or by acknowledging that the social worker and/or the agency cannot meet the demand.

Expectation Demands

Not all demands are amenable to ready analysis; some remain largely concealed in the form of expectations. In most social work settings expectation demands will come from three main sources — the practitioner, the client and the agency.

Expectations are fairly difficult to evaluate, but such research as is available indicates the existence of what might be called the phenomena of expectation clash between clients and their social workers (Mayer & Timms, 1971). It is not unusual for clients to come to meetings with the social worker having already attributed the cause of the problem to a particular factor, usually some form of material deficit. The expectation is, therefore, that the solution to the problem will lie in material terms. The social worker on the other hand, largely on the basis of past training, may be more inclined to attribute the cause of the problem to dispositional variables in the client. The expectations of the practitioner are centred on the need to tackle the client's personality, usually the emotional component, rather than with attempts to engage in a search for material or structural change on the client's behalf. Not unreasonably, such a clash of expectations can lead to feelings of dissatisfaction. The client can feel dissatisfied with the social worker for having failed to provide an appropriate service. The social worker can feel dissatisfied with the client for not having presented an appropriate demand. Both client and social worker can feel dissatisfied with

141

themselves for having failed to meet the expectations of the other. Communication has broken down. The breakdown has not occurred at a purely interpersonal level, however. At least part of the explanation for the development of expectation clash lies in the failure of social work to develop an adequate rhetoric, a means of communicating the particular image of its structure, function and techniques it wishes to put across to outsiders. Clients have one image of social work; social workers, unfortunately, tend to have another. The use of rhetoric by social workers is developed further in Rowett and Breakwell (1982).

The relationship between the social worker and the employing agency is coloured by the development and retention of mutual expectations. The social worker expects support from the agency for decisions made, actions taken, and resources offerred; and for the opportunity to achieve such personal and professional development as might be desirable. Agencies such as social services departments might hold expectations of their workers that include having agreement with the declared role and function of the agency, showing obedience to agency procedures, and performing the allotted social work task to a certain minimum standard.

Expectation demands such as these can powerfully influence the social worker's self-perception, interaction with clients and performance in the agency. Not usually specified, expectation demands are in some ways the most powerful type of demands in their ability to generate feelings of extreme anxiety and dissatisfaction that do not have ready explanation and therefore parameters for their resolution.

Organizational Demands

Organizational demands are those, either at a formal level or at the level of expectation, that the employing agency makes on the social worker. Such demands therefore range from the formality of contractual job descriptions, adherence to the law, and the following of agency procedures, to expectations that the social worker will not have sexual intercourse with the clients while on duty and will not take part in organized activities protesting about the function of the employing agency.

How organizational demands are experienced by the social worker will depend in part on the type of agency concerned. By and large, large social services departments make a higher level of demand on their fieldworkers than do most voluntary agencies. It might indeed be argued that the increasing uneasiness felt by a number of social workers employed in social services departments stems in large measure from what they perceive as disproportionate emphasis on meeting organizational demands at the expense of client demands and at the expense of the professional demands they would wish to make of themselves.

Each type of demand is inter-related and usually difficult to tease apart. Legal demands, though apparently specific on paper, usually leave an amount of leeway for interpretation in practice by both the agency and the worker. In,

142

for example, cases of child abuse (see Chapter 16) the formal and expectation demands of the employer, usually but not always a social services department, are increasingly dominating social worker response to such cases. At times, these demands surround the social worker with a more rigid straitjacket than does the law itself. When the client is taken to be the child, attributed expectations tend to consist of normative adult beliefs of what form of parental care is in a child's best developmental interests. If the clients are the parents, expectations can range from beliefs about the need to receive some form of professional help to some form of punishment.

There are numerous occasions when the differing sources of demands generate conflict. One of the most common for local authority employees is when the expectation demands of the employer at the level of the locally elected social services committee are largely political and conflict with the traditional liberal and humanitarian background of most social workers. The attitude of the Labour Party towards welfare provision is usually taken to be more liberal and universalist than is that of the Conservative Party. On a very basic level the social work strike of 1978–1979 shook the aspiring profession to the roots when large numbers of social workers ignored the demands of their employers to maintain a service to the clients, and took strike action to further their claim for better pay and conditions.

The demands made on social workers must be seen in the context of how response to those demands is conceived and structured. A number of studies have attempted to examine what social workers actually do on a day-to-day basis, and as such have implicitly and sometimes explicitly provided an account of the demands made and the response proffered (Wetton, 1976; Wiltshire Social Services Dept. Research Unit, 1975). One of the most interesting of these studies is that by Goldberg *et al.* (1977). They examined one year's referrals to an area office in Southampton, part of Hampshire Social Services Department, serving a population of some 73 000 living in a mixture of neighbourhoods '. . . from a bedsitter/lodging, grey type of district near the docks, through fairly stable "respectable" working-class neighbourhoods, to owner-occupied housing in tree-lined avenues'. The area office was divided into three teams — the intake team of five and a half social workers and a part-time occupational therapist, headed by a senior social worker, and two long-term teams of six social workers and two social work ancillaries. The majority of the referrals were dealt with by the intake team who were expected to assess the referral and if necessary undertake short-term work of three months or less. Cases requiring a longer committment were passed on to the long-term teams.

From 1 February 1975 to 1 February 1976 the intake team received some 2500 referrals representing about 2000 cases, an average of about 50 referrals a week. A referral was defined as '. . . any incoming case requiring some social work input which is neither currently allocated nor on the agency review caseload'. 75% of all referrals were closed within two months. The major formal client demands were classed as shown in Table 11.1:

143

Table 11.1

(Reproduced from E.M. Goldberg, R.W. Warburton, B. McGuinness and J.H. Rowlands (1977) *British Journal of Social Work*, **7**, 257−283, by permission.)

Main problems given at first referral	No. of cases	%
Physical disability/illness/ageing	614	30
Financial/material	337	17
Housing/accommodation	217	11
Child behaviour/family relationships, etc.	284	14
Mental/emotional disorder	152	7
Delinquency	296	15
Other	119	6
	2019	100

Thus most demands came from the elderly, the frail and the disabled. Although care must be taken not to generalize these findings too extensively, they are probably consistent with the experience of large numbers of social workers employed by local authorities.

There was a fairly clear relationship between mode of referral and type of problem. Those who experienced financial and material troubles, usually single people or young married couples, and to a lesser extent those with housing problems, made contact on their own initiative. About half of the frail, elderly and physically disabled clients were referred by health agencies; almost all 'delinquents' were referred by the police; and those with mild behaviour or family relationship problems were referred by a range of agencies. It was found that 40% of all clients made a request for a specific service, usually practical; approximately 30% made fairly vague requests related to various financial, personal and legal problems; and the remaining 30% consisted of clients who for one reason or another merited a more thorough evaluation and assessment — normally child abuse cases or situations where the elderly were at risk.

The demands made on this office were therefore fairly intense, represented a wide range of client need, and presumably reflected a high level of expectations. Response to the demands required, potentially at least, an ability to analyse social and personal problems at a sophisticated multiplicity of levels, and the ability to utilize skills ranging from methods of controlling wayward youngsters to means of relieving difficulties in the ascribed identities of the physically disabled. All of this occurred against a background of legal requirements, unclear expectation demands from the clients, and agency demands putting a limit on the length of involvement, the resources available, and the expected effectiveness of the techniques used. Do social workers have the skills to cope with the demands made on them? One-third of the social workers in the sample felt dissatisfied with what they were able to achieve.

In the next section we look more closely at what constitutes a 'skill', what

144

skills are available to social workers, and at what form social work skills should take.

11.2 Skills

A skill is only of use if it satisfies the demands made upon it. Although a psychoanalyst might well be able to work as a building labourer, skill in psychoanalysis is unlikely to be of help in the design and construction of the house. Too frequently social workers are placed in situations where their skills are either inappropriate or simply not effective. Part of the difficulty rests in the area of semantics. Such terms as skill, method, approach, role, technique, knowledge, practice and orientation are often used without adequate definition and frequently as though they were interchangeable. In the interests of clarity *a skill will be taken to constitute expertise in a prescriptive technique which results in a demand being met.*

In other words, a social worker is 'skilled' only when having analysed the problem, he or she is capable of demonstrating expertise in a technique that prescribes how to achieve the desired goal or goals. As we will see in Chapter 12 demands usually arise from and operate within a number of different levels. It is therefore necessary for the analysis to predict this by itself operating on multiple levels. Each level of the analysis might lead to the generation of a different goal or series of goals, each necessitating the use of a different skill. This notion of multiple level analysis should be born in mind throughout this chapter and will be developed further in Chapter 12.

A second definitional problem arises with the use of the term 'technique'. *A technique is usually defined in terms of a conglomerate of actions that attempt to achieve a desired goal.* It differs from a skill only in that the notion of skill implies having expertise in a particular technique. A skill, then, is possessed by a person, and it is a characteristic of the person. A technique is a means of achieving an end, not embodied in a person.

Social work 'skills' can be seen to be divided into three broad categories according to how close they come to the notion of a skill proper — first level skills, second level skills, and at the third level, orientations. Such a conceptualization not only facilitates grater clarity in an analysis of social work skills but also provides it with a sense of purpose. If social work is to be of use to anyone it must be effective, and its primary concern must therefore be with the development of effective techniques.

First Level Skills

First level skills are the building blocks of other skills, without them the social worker could not become skilled in more complex techniques. First level skills are concerned with the development and maintenance of relationships, the ability to communicate effectively with other people, and the skills necessary to operate within a particular agency setting. These three facets seem superficially consistent with the views of Haines (1975), who terms them, respectively, relationship skills, transactional skills and organizational skills. Table 11.2 outlines Haines' summary of what he considers to constitute these three skill areas.

There are, however, three fundamental points of departure between Haines' conceptualization and that offered here. Firstly, Haines considers the skills listed to be *the* social work skills, not the prerequisites for the development of other skills. Secondly, his use of the term 'skill' seems to encompass a whole gamut of phenomena, from descriptions of 'desirable' behaviour from social workers to comments on client behaviour that might cause problems for the social worker attempting to practise these appropriate skills, for example, 'listening'. Thirdly, Haines fails to describe the framework within which these basic skills have to operate. There seems little point in, say, achieving expertise in 'relationships' without having some idea of what constitutes an ideal relationship. In Part II of this book fundamental information for the development of third level skills has been provided in the discussions on identity, relationships, groups and the environment.

The point should also be made that an essential component in the development of first level skills is to be able to be reflexive. In other words, the social worker needs to be able to understand something of her or his own identity, relationships, group memberships, and interactions with the environment before first level skills can be used in work with clients.

Haines also suggests that these three skill areas constitute a common core of expertise to be used by all social workers which distinguishes them from other professional groups. This elevation of first level skills to constitute the distinctive characteristic of social work is consistent with BASW's notion of the use of self as the unique element in social work. Of course, first level skills are *nothing of the kind*. They are required by all people professionals regardless of discipline. They are the basis of practice not its ultimate development; the prerequisites for the appropriate use of social work techniques not the techniques in themselves.

Once the notion of first level skills being in some way unique to social work is abandonned a clearer and hopefully more productive attempt can be made to examine the more complex skills social workers seem to require to deal with the complex demands made of them. After all, few clients cease to become clients merely because they have developed a relationship with a social worker, with whom they can communicate, and who is capable of working effectively within the context of the employing agency. What matters is how that relationship and communication can change the dynamics of the problem situation.

Second Level Skills

A second level skill presumes the existence of a first level skill, and consists of having expertise in a more complex prescriptive technique. All second level skills currently used by social workers originate from other disciplines. They have been adopted and usually adapted by social workers in their search for

146

Table 11.2 First Level Skills

(Reproduced from J. Haines (1975) *Skills and Methods in Social Work*, by permission of Constable Publishers.)

Relationship skills

1. *Management of Relationships*	2. *Creation and Use of Relationships*
Initiation	Individuals
Maintenance and development	Pairs
Termination and transfer	Families
Crisis intervention	Groups
	People in the environment
	Organizations in the environment

Transactional skills

1. *Communication*	2. *Overcoming Problems*
Observing	Language
Receiving	Irrationality
Listening	Apathy
Interpreting for oneself	Silences
Responding	Mental disorders.
Questioning	Alien cultures
Interpreting to others	Alien value systems
Summarizing	Intuition
Planning action	

3. *Management of Transactions*

Dimension(s)
Venue
Frequency
Length

Organizational skills

1. *Agency Membership*	2. *Management*
Teamwork	Clerical staff
Collaboration within the agency	Ancillary workers
Collaboration with other agencies	Volunteers
Using consultation	Promotion of organizational change
Using supervision	Management and development of own resources

3. *Administration*

Reports and records
Statistics and data collection
Preservation of confidentiality
Taking decisions

Work load management — planning of priorities and work programme techniques that might effectively meet some of the demands made upon them. The level of expertise with which they are utilized varies between individual social workers; and one of the unfortunate consequences of attempting to extract skills from their theoretical context is that they are occasionally used in situations contra-indicated by their theoretical origins. There is little point, for example, in attempting to practise some form of psychoanalytically-derived therapy with the majority of social work clients, nor in utilizing reality therapy with someone suffering from an active psychosis. Less extreme and probably more common examples are the use of bereavement therapy following the loss of a limb, and the extension of network analysis to include middle class couples with diffuse families.

Table 11.3 lists a number of second level skills occasionally used by social workers: the originating discipline; the focus of concern; and some of the source texts. Contained in Part V of this book are the bare outlines of some of the techniques, but the reader is directed to the source texts for full elaboration of the precise techniques involved.

Table 11.3   Second Level Skills

	Skill	Source discipline	Focus of concern	Further reading
1.	Behaviour modification	Psychology	Interpersonal	Jehu (1967) Skinner (1959) Herbert (1981)
2.	Psychoanalysis	Neurophysiology	Intrapsychic	Freud (1975) Yelloly (1980)
3.	Psychotherapy	Psychology	Intrapsychic Interpersonal	Rogers (1951) Cox (1978)
4.	Personal construct therapy	Psychology	Intrapsychic	Kelly (1955) Bannister (1980) and Fransella
5.	Transactional analysis	Psychiatry	Intrapsychic Interpersonal	Berne (1964)
6.	Reality therapy	Psychiatry	Intrapsychic	Glasser (1965)
7.	Network analysis	Sociology	Interpersonal Intragroup	Bott (1957)
8.	Crisis intervention	Psychiatry	Intrapsychic Interpersonal	Caplan (1960) Lindemann (1944)

The Third Level: Orientations

At the third level, *orientations entail non-prescriptive ways of looking at a*

148

problem. These orientations contain no specified techniques for inducing change. In fact many of what are regarded as techniques in social work are in truth merely orientations.

Four such orientations have developed more or less chronologically with the expansion of social work — casework, groupwork, community work and integrated methods. The first three are essentially statements of interest, foci on the particular types of problems a social worker should be interested in. Casework derives from the systematic recording techniques of the Charity Organisation Society, supplemented by a later stress on the intrapsychic and to a lesser extent interpersonal levels of analysis encouraged by psychoanalysis and psychotherapy. Focused on the individual, it is essentially a means of recording interaction between a particular client and a particular social worker. Although it necessitates the use of first level skills, casework does not as such prescribe action and cannot therefore be viewed as anything more than an orientation.

Groupwork is closely entwined with the psychotherapy boom of the 1940s and 1950s, underpinned in large measure by psychoanalysis and humanist psychology. Extensively developed in America it provides an 'emotional' experience in a structured group setting. Although it can be a powerful means of changing an individual's behaviour, the orientation itself does not prescribe what to do in order to achieve specific desired changes.

Community work tends to adopt a different level of analysis to both casework and community work, concerning itself more with structural analyses of particular communities and their effects on certain stigmatized or disadvantaged members of the community. Not linked to any particular theory or technique, it tends to glean most of its input from sociological research findings. Chapter 17 provides a more detailed discussion of community work.

Finally, and most recently, there has been the development of the integrated methods orientation, usually attributed to the work of Goldstein (1973) and Pincus and Minahan (1973). Based on a simple notion of biological systems theory, it attempts to subsume the three earlier approaches under the general banner of systems analysis. Essentially an attempt to provide a more comprehensive type of problem analysis operating on a number of different levels, it does not in itself prescribe the use of particular techniques. As such it remains at the third level, an orientation rather than a second level skill.

We might end this section on the different types of 'skills' available to social workers by summarizing schematically as shown in Fig. 11.1.

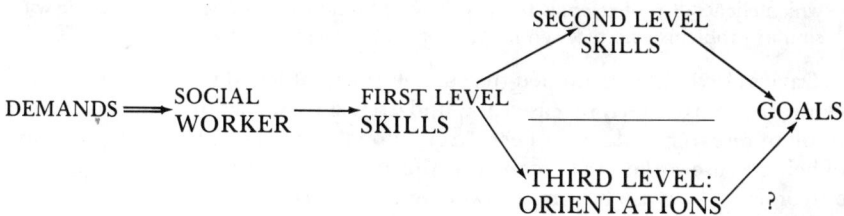

Fig. 11.1

A final question remains before we examine more closely in Chapter 12 the relationship between social work skills and levels of analysis. That final question is one of effectiveness. How effective are those skills, of whatever level that are currently available to social workers?

11.3 The Effectiveness of Social Work Skills

Social work practice is under-researched. CCETSW (1980) established a working party to promote research since '. . . research into the personal social services . . . has not contributed as it should to raising the quality of the service which is provided' (p. 1). This is perhaps a suprising state of affairs as most social services departments have followed the Seebohm recommendation to employ their own research staff. Harbart (1977) found that 90% of the 116 social services departments employed researchers. Part of the explanation lies in the functions that the researchers have taken to constitute their main priorities. As Philip *et al.* (1975) indicate: 'Although social work departments have established research sections, their products have been almost exclusively of an operational nature. This activity, while useful for policy formulation, has contributed little to the enhancement of social work practice and professional knowledge.' There is not, therefore, a substantial body of critical research which has concentrated on social work practice.

Such research studies as have been carried out on the effectiveness of social work practice, and indeed on the effectiveness of the helping professionals in general, have been largely critical, consistently having difficulty in establishing that the majority of clients benefit from the involvement with the practitioner. Fischer (1973) examined controlled research into the effectiveness of casework and concluded that '. . . at present lack of evidence of the effectiveness of professional casework is the rule rather than the exception'. In 50% of all the studies cited, clients receiving casework 'skills' did in fact tend to deteriorate. In a rather desperately entitled paper 'Does Anything Work', Fischer (1978) reviewed research on the effectiveness of a whole range of 'helping' activities, including social work, psychotherapy and counselling. His conclusions were more concerning than in his original survey:

> In all these areas the research indicates that, at best, professionals are operating with little or no empirical evidence validating their efforts, since lack of effectiveness was the rule rather than the exception. In addition, a pattern of deterioration was found in which clients of professionals frequently were found to do less well than people with similar problems who received no professional services whatever.

Davies (1976) also examined the current status of social work research, concentrating particularly on casework, and drew similar conclusions: 'The prime result of research to date has been an emotional one: to highlight the problems of being a caseworker, to demonstrate the difficulties of demonstrating positive outcomes.' On a slightly more positive note, Truax and Carkhuff (1967), having reviewed the evidence on the effectiveness of counselling and psychotherapy concluded that:

(i)   therapy, on average, is ineffective;
(ii) therapy itself is a diffuse and splintered phenomena;
(iii) helpful therapy can be identified;
(iv) helping therapists, regardless of the therapy used, exhibit:
    (a) genuineness,
    (b) non-possessive warmth,
    (c) empathy;
(v)   each trait is a skill that can be learned.

Essentially then, Truax and Carkhuff minimize the value of most existing second level skills and third level orientations and stress the personality trait approach as the way forward.

From such research as is available, then, and it is so far no more than piecemeal and episodic, a general picture emerges of ineffective third level orientations and second level skills, with some support for the development of effective first level skills. In a sense, of course, the research findings are no more than might be predicted. Techniques that do not prescribe actions are unlikely to result in the effective achievement of goals. Perhaps the main value of the research is to dispel a few myths. Techniques that have been considered to constitute second level skills are obviously nothing of the sort. Psychotherapy, for example, seems to be nothing more than an aggrandized third level orientation. Where does this leave social work? The answer to this must be that social work should be in the business of capitalizing on its first level skills to develop true second level skills that are of direct relevance to the demands made on the profession. The value of the SPA in placing the development of effective social work skills within a theoretical context is a central theme throughout this book. In the next chapter we look more closely at the form this might take.

Part IV
Theory Use

12
Levels of Analysis in Social Work

The central and universal demand that is made of social workers is that they should solve 'problems'. The nature of the problems varies: they may be the problems of a community or the problems of a single member of that community: they range from the sociopolitical dilemma to the psychological trauma. Something of the nature of these problems and the skills available to social workers in their solution have been described in Chapter 11. The purpose of this chapter is to examine what SPA can offer in the analysis and solution of a problem. Problems can be analysed at many levels and the level of analysis adopted will have an important influence upon the definition of the problem, upon the solution preferred and upon the methods chosen to achieve that solution.

12.1   The Problem Orientation

The problem orientation in social work is easily described. It assumes that the social worker is a problem solver. This means that the social worker must identify the problem and understand its structure and ramifications. Having done this, the next stage is to decide what would be the most desirable solution. Strategies for attaining this solution are then considered and, if feasible, are put into operation. In this model of social work, the social worker is the definer of the problem, the definer of the solution, the definer of the action strategy and the change agent who acts upon that strategy. There is no real belief that the social worker does all this alone, collaboration with the clients in defining the problem and the feasibility of strategies and alliances with other professionals in order to execute the strategies is expected.

The general systems theory approach is archetypical of the problem orientation in social work. Pincus and Minahan (1973) in their seminal work clearly outline what they consider are the stages in 'problem assessment' (Chapter 6): identify the problem; analyse the dynamics of its social situation; establish the goals and targets; determine the tasks and strategies; and stabilize the change effort. As it stands, of course, this five stage recipe for 'problem assessment' is not very useful. It is a formalized, abstract description of the process rather than a substantive description of it. It is rather like a recipe which says: take a fish, prepare it, cook it, serve it, and eat it. The aspiring but ignorant cook needs to know more. How do you recognize a fish and which are edible? How do you prepare it and do you use the same method with all fish? How do you cook it and how far do different fish demand different modes of cooking? How do you serve it and under what conditions? Of course, most recipe books can count on a certain amount of prior knowledge on the part of the prospective cook but they are also normally quite specific in their instructions. It is not likely that the young cook would be presented with the sort of meaningless example given above. Unfortunately, social workers frequently are given equivalently meaningless recipes for practice. How do you identify the problem? How do you analyse the dynamics of its social situation? How do you establish goals and targets? How do you determine tasks and strategies? How do you stabilize the change effort? These are questions which must be answered if the problem orientation in social work is really to be put into practice. Unlike others who promote the problem orientation, Pincus and Minahan did try to answer some of these questions. However, their answers are limited and incomplete.

Their definition of what constitutes a problem is a particularly useful starting point nevertheless. They define 'a problem as a social situation or social condition which has been evaluated by someone as undesirable' (p. 104). Thus 'no social situation is in itself inherently a problem' (p. 104). Child battering, by this token, is not inherently a problem; it becomes one when someone says it is undesirable and should end. This might account for the sudden appearance of the 'problem' of child battering in the mid-1960s. A problem can be seen, according to Pincus and Minahan, to have three related parts:

(i)   the actual social condition or situation labelled a problem;
(ii) the people who evaluate it as problematic;
(iii) the reasons or bases for that evaluation.

Each of these three components needs to be understood in order to comprehend the 'problem'. The implication of this sort of definition is that the problem should not be viewed as the property of 'a given person or persons, but as a characteristic of their interactions' (p. 105). A further implication, important for practice, is that the 'presenting problem', which first occasioned the intervention of the social worker, is only the starting point for the problem assessment. From it, the social worker must trace the source and nature of the problem.

154

This form of detective work demands the analysis of the social situation, the second stage in problem assessment. Pincus and Minahan indicate that the dynamics of the social situation should be seen primarily in terms of the individual's and group's (those presenting the problem) interactions with resource systems. Resource systems are simply the agents or agencies (formal or informal; large or small) which give some help. If resource systems are inadequate and help, of whatever kind, is withheld problems arise. By analysing what has happened to the resource system/s, the social worker can understand the nature of the problem. The social worker is advised to use theories of social work and social science in the analysis of resource systems and the problem. What theories is a choice left to the social worker. Finding out how to use them is left to the social worker. Evaluating them and learning how to use them is left to the social worker. More importantly, perhaps matching theory to problem is also left to the social worker. Consequently, the general systems approach seems capable of telling the social worker what to analyse but not how to do it.

The same could be said for each of the remaining three stages of problem assessment as outlined by Pincus and Minahan. The third stage requires the social worker to establish goals and targets. At this point, the social worker is effectively determining what are the desired consequences of intervention and mapping the route to the ultimate achievement of those consequences through any necessary sub-goals. This entails pinpointing who or what needs to be changed as part of this process. A hierarchy of priorities for change has to be established and the feasibility of changes has to be calculated. Again, stage three is described in terms of what should be done but not how it should be done. Should goals and targets be determined by the social worker in a dictatorial fashion without consulting the client? If consultation is essential, as it would appear to be, how would it work? And, most importantly, how does the social worker decide who or what is the effective target for change?

These questions carry us straight into queries about stage four of the problem assessment. This entails the development of strategies that will bring about the desired changes. These strategies constitute the 'intervention plan'. Pincus and Minahan consider what these strategies might be but they offer no prescriptions for action. They engage in a taxonomic rather than a descriptive exercise. There are three approaches to intervention mentioned: education, facilitation and advocacy. This tripartite classification system is useful in itself. It encourages realization that there is a vast array of options open to the social worker when dealing with a problem. It demands that the social worker is open to various approaches. However, it is clear that the classification system is rather superficial: the same activity could be said to be simultaneously education, facilitation and advocacy. The categories are neither mutually exclusive nor constant in their referents. Nevertheless, the classification is an heuristic device. The major problem, of course, is again the failure of Pincus and Minahan to indicate how intervention tactics should be matched to problems. This is associated with their failure to indicate how the social worker should actually go about educating, facilitating and advocating. It is,

155

moreover, also true that their system is by no means exhaustive. Less pleasant forms of intervention must also be considered. For example, techniques of control. A social worker may need to have an individual placed into a mental hospital in pursuit of an established hierarchy of goals. Sectioning that person under the Mental Health Act 1959 would be a legitimate strategy. Without further specification of how strategies might be put into operation and what strategies might be available, the invocation to decide upon an intervention plan seems rather empty. So does the instruction to stabilize the change effort in stage five of the plan for problem assessment. How is stability to be achieved? Through maintenance is the reply from Pincus and Minahan. But the question remains: what form should maintenance take?

It may seem that these criticisms harp upon the obvious: that the general systems approach gives a formal analysis but no prescription for action. The approach says what social workers should achieve but not how to achieve it. Yet it is important to labour the point because it means that the most vital issues in social work are not addressed: the issues that surround how to decide upon the means to achieve any end. Social workers need to know how to get what they want to achieve but this is just what no one tells them.

The problem orientation to social work seems particularly open to this sort of flaw: it carries the message that the problem has to be analysed but has no message about the tools of analysis that might be used. The fact that general systems approaches (and this includes Goldstein's, 1973, model) typify the problem orientation is the only reason that they have been the focus of concern above. They typify the absence of prescriptive messages. The SPA to social work is also founded upon the problem orientation but, unlike the general systems approach, after exhorting the social worker to analyse the problem the SPA offers the means to do so. The SPA offers theories which seek to elucidate the evolution of the problem in its social context and which indicate how change might be brought about most effectively. At this point it seems appropriate to examine the analysis of a problem from the SPA perspective.

12.2 The SPA and the Levels of a Problem

The sort of problem with which social workers deal most frequently lies within the matrix of interactions between people and between individuals and social institutions or agencies. Such interactions are not 'problems' until they are evaluated as such and the reason for that evaluation may be an integral part of the problematic interaction. However, this perspective on the problem, akin to that of Pincus and Minahan, lacks important elements vital to the understanding of the problem.

Any problem exists at a series of different levels simultaneously. At any one time a problem may manifest itself at a single level or at any or all of these levels. Across time, the problem may move and become manifest at levels where it was not initially apparent. When not manifest at all levels, the problem is nevertheless present in a latent form at all levels. A problem latent at a particular level may be triggered by changes in the context and become manifest.

These levels at which the problem exists, and which are described in Chapter 8, are:

(i) the intrapsychic — in the thoughts and feelings of individuals;
(ii) the interpersonal — in the interactions and relationships between people;
(iii) the intragroup — in the structure and dynamics of the group;
(iv) the intergroup — in the relationships between groups.

An example of how the problem actually exists at all four levels simultaneously — whether manifest or latent — might help here. Take the imaginary case of Abel Cain. Cain believes that he is John the Baptist returned to Earth to save the people. He wanders the streets of his town preaching and praying. His wife, with whom he was happily married before the onset of the delusional system, becomes distraught. His employers of many years' standing cannot understand his behaviour and fear for the reputation of their firm. His workmates are ashamed or pity him. Within the broader community, there are those who consider his activities blasphemous and others who really think he might just be the reborn herald of the second coming. The behaviour of the individual has its ramifications across all levels: for himself, for his family, for his friends and his community. The problem to which it gives rise thus exists across all four levels. It exists in the thought and feelings of the individuals involved, in their inter-actions and relationships, in the group structure and in the relationships across groups (e.g. the believers versus the cynics). The original presentation of the problem may be at the intrapsychic level — in the thoughts and feelings of Cain but it grows outwards. It invades his relations with his wife and hers with others. It seeps into the community and its activities. It may take time for the problem to manifest itself at all levels but the point is that as soon as Cain developed his delusional system (if that is what it is), the problem had a latent existence at all four levels. Its manifestations could have been prevented but the potential was there due to pre-existent social configurations and belief structures. This last point emphasizes something which should always be acknowledged, this is that a problem has social history.

This example should not be allowed to mislead the reader into thinking that problems always work from the intrapsychic level outwards. In fact, the process of manifestation can be totally reversed: a war between nations, a family split by civil strife which follows, the parents die, the children steal to live and lose respect for life in the process, degenerating into dissatisfied self-seekers.

The difference between the latent and manifest levels of a problem's operation is important because the analysis of the problem must encompass both. In practice the social worker is likely to be presented with a problem that seems to operate at a single level. In the Cain example, the social worker might have been asked to help when relations between the family members became fraught. The social worker would need to consider the problem at all its potential levels of operation without the benefit of complete information. Of course, the social worker should seek information about each level. However, it

157

might be impossible to establish that if Cain continues to preach he will gain a following. Nevertheless, the social worker might be able to hazard a guess on the basis of knowledge about the community and its dynamics seen through the filter of social psychological theory. The use of the SPA should enable the analysis manifest levels of the problem and to anticipate something of the latent potential. This analysis would be in terms of the processes of construal, consistency, comparison, and conformity associated with constructs of identity, relationships, groups and environment. The operation of analyses is exemplified in Part V: on the application of SPA to social work problems. Choosing the right social psychological theory to use upon a particular problem is difficult. The choice of theory is important because it has a twofold purpose:

(i) to lay bare the dynamic processes of the problem at each level;
(ii) to indicate what means of change might be best suited to the problem.

Chapter 13 deals with how to choose a theory to fit the problem. Here it is enough to say that several different theories may serve to elucidate the sort of problem with which the social worker is faced and a choice has to be made. Essentially, the criterion for evaluation has to be efficacy: the theory has to elucidate the nature of the problem in such a way that the appropriate action on the part of the social worker becomes obvious. The appropriate theory may be one which is centred on intergroup relations even when the problem seems to be focused upon interpersonal relations. Alternatively, the theory and the problem may be both at the same level of analysis. The level at which the theory is pitched is not important just as long as it serves the twofold function of theory in the social work process: elucidation and guidance. The SPA theories can do this. Effectively, the SPA offers the substantive, prescriptive information lacking in the general systems approach to problem analysis and strategy evolution.

Because the SPA assumes a problem exists at four levels simultaneously, either manifestly or latently, it is not easy to break the SPA orientation to the analysis of a problem down into a linear process. The process is too fluid to impose any unidirectional stage-structure upon it. The process is more a matter of oscillation among the component parts. The social worker needs to move back and forth within the process like the juggler who keeps 20 or 30 plates spinning on sticks and who must constantly maintain their speed of rotation.

The components of the process can be delineated as follows.

(i) The problem should be defined at each of the four levels and both its manifest and latent characteristics should be established — this is bound to entail the social worker in information-gathering exercises which are sometimes simple (a matter of observing reactions) and sometimes more complex (social workers could benefit from the implementation of techniques of attitude measurement and surveying used extensively in social psychology — these methods are easy to learn, see Breakwell et al., 1982).

(ii) Without preconceptions, the social worker should try out a series of different types of explanation for the problem — the SPA would indicate that the central target zones for analysis at each of the four levels would be identity, relationships, groups and environment; the central explanatory constructs would be construal, consistency, comparison and conformity. These are all explained at great length in Part II.

(iii) The social worker should be wary of a particular problem: the explanation for the problem will introduce particular ways of construing the problem and may change the ways in which it is defined. This means that definition and explanation of the problem should go hand in hand and any assumption that there is a single correct definition of the problem should be carefully avoided. The definition should be transient and responsive to analytical tools at work. The choice of tools should in turn be responsive to the social worker's objectives in dealing with the problem.

(iv) The analysis and explanation thus achieved will tend to imply what type of change strategies should be used to affect the problem.

(v) The SPA findings about inducing personal and social change have been described in Chapter 7 — having identified the objective, an appropriate method may be shaped on the basis of these findings. It should be noted that techniques for inducing the desired change also operate at the four levels: intrapsychic, interpersonal, intragroup and intergroup. Moreover it should be said that a technique operating at, say, the interpersonal level may have consequences at each of the other levels; the repercussions of a managed social change can be extensive. The social worker therefore has to monitor how the managed change influences the problem at all levels.

(vi) The SPA demands one final component to this process of analysis: the social worker must understand his or her part in the problem at each of the four levels; it is only by knowing this that the change introduced can actually be managed predictably. The SPA demands that the social worker is self-conscious in the best possible way: knowing the impact of the role and its occupant upon the intervention tactic. It is not assumed that the social worker can be an unbiased objective observer in the course of the analysis. Bias is assumed to be an inherent part of the analysis. Asking the social worker to monitor his or her impact is one means of bringing that bias to the fore. The bias cannot be eradicated but if it can be identified the social worker can be said to have achieved a minor triumph. Such identification is, after all, the first step towards counterweighting those biases in the analysis. Perhaps, to console those who feel maligned by this assertion about the inevitability of bias, it should be added that the bias is often by no means intentional or even within the control of the social workers nor is it always in their own interests. Nevertheless, the bias is there and if detected it may mean that other aspects of the analysis have to be recalculated.

These then are the components of the process of analysis as conceived within the SPA framework. They have elements in common with the general systems theory approach but the similarities are limited. In substance, the SPA requires a specific sort of analysis tied clearly to a body of theory and a methodological corps. Moreover, the SPA explicitly avoids any simplification of the process of problem analysis. It is complex and cannot be arrayed along tidy straight lines:

it is a cybernetic process, with continual feedback loops channelled through the social worker's own self-monitoring.

12.3 Conclusion

This chapter should end not merely with a summary of the arguments presented but with a statement of what still needs to be said. In this chapter, the central arguments have been that social workers should be told by theorists not just what they should achieve but how they should achieve it; that simply telling social workers to identify problems and work out strategies to deal with them does not tell them *how* to do either or these things; that the analysis of problems is a complex affair since the problem exists, actually or potentially, at four different levels and so must the analysis; that the form of analysis and the form of explanation of the problem are intimately connected; that the SPA leads to a particular sort of process in problem analysis; and that this process is multi-levelled and not unidirectional. Implicit in the SPA analysis of problems is the use of social psychological theory and method (both of data collection and inducing change). What still needs to be said is how the social worker decides upon the theory to use and how it is translated into strategies for intervention. Answers to these questions are given in Chapter 13 and in Part V.

13
How to Use a Theory

The object of this chapter is to point out some of the pitfalls which surround the use of theory. In the chapters in Part II of this book, various social psychological theories were portrayed. Each of these theories seeks to explain, causally or rationally, some form of social phenomenon. Sometimes theories compete to explain the same phenomenon. When they are not in direct competition, still the domains they explain frequently overlap, though this is obscured because they operate at slightly different levels of analysis or explanation. Among such a plethora of criss-crossing theoretical threads, when all may have some relevance, the greatest problem facing the practitioner is choice. The practitioner needs to be able *to evaluate* the relative merits of theories in order *to choose* the most appropriate for the task in hand. Many myths have grown up around the evaluation of theories and they are responsible for a number of the pitfalls which surround the use of theory. Some of these myths and a few of their pitfalls will be described below with instructions for avoidance tactics.

In the use of theory, the first traps to sidestep are those attached to evaluation and choice but there are other snares. These are associated with *the extended use* of any particular theory. Again, an attempt is made below to lay bare these dangers.

It should be acknowledged from the outset that the higher reaches of philosophical or epistemological speculation will be avoided here. The prime objective is to forewarn and thus forearm those intrepid enough to use theory by describing its little tricks and quirks. Those who develop a taste for such delicacies might read Breakwell (1982a).

13.1 The Problem of Evaluating a Theory

In what follows the terms theory and model are used interchangeably. This is because there is no consensus about how they should be differentiated; what one person would call a theory, another would call a model and vice versa. The important thing to be remembered is that both terms are used to label *a system of ideas* explaining something.

A theory can be evaluated in two ways:

(i) the formal evaluation;
(ii) the pragmatic evaluation.

Both types of evaluation need to be performed before a theory is used.

The Formal Evaluation

The formal evaluation entails taking a theory and assessing it in terms of its own premises. In the formal evaluation, the theory is not compared with any competitive theories; instead, it is examined against independent criteria which a 'good' theory should satisfy. These criteria lie on a number of dimensions; the theory should be evaluated on each:

*In terms of its **internal consistency***. If propositions and constructs used in the theory are contradictory or mutually exclusive then it is said to lack internal consistency. Freud's theory of psychoanalysis is a masterpiece of internal consistency: each of the jigsaw pieces fits every other, there is no awkward piece which does not quite fit — the picture is smooth without marring incongruities.

*In terms of its **parsimony***. The theory should be free of propositions or constructs that fail to contribute to the explanation. Theories containing redundant loops of argument should be clearly identified and their worst excesses avoided.

*In terms of its **external validity***. The theory should be able to predict phenomena or interpret them effectively. The theory's proponents should be able to show evidence to this effect. The notion of external validity is also tied to the notion of *falsifiability*. Popper (1963) has argued that for a theory to be considered 'scientific' it must be open to refutation. If a theory is so constructed that it can explain and potentially predict all possible outcomes in the situation with which it is concerned, it cannot be refuted. It cannot be shown to be wrong because it can explain all possible eventualities but, by the same token, it cannot be shown to be right because no test for it can be erected. An unfalsifiable theory is not scientific, it is just a story told about events, it could be right or wrong but it is impossible ever to establish which. Psychoanalysis is the perfect example of the unfalsifiable theory; from its multitudinous network of concepts all outcomes can be explained. Each tenet of the theory is unassailable because it is covered and protected by others: if a prediction on the basis of one tenet is shown to be wrong because people do not behave in the way anticipated, another tenet can be invoked to explain their behaviour.

Some psychologists argue that a 'good' theory in psychology need not be 'scientific' and therefore need not be falsifiable. They argue that as long as a theory is *heuristic*, acting as a stimulus for new discoveries and insights, that theory is good. Indeed, this is a standard criterion of formal evaluation.

*In terms of its **ease of communication*** and the *stimulus for further insights* it provides.

*In terms of its **responsiveness to new evidence***. A theory which is actually a closed system, disregarding new evidence, is moribund.

A 'good' theory should therefore be internally consistent, parsimonious, and heuristic; it should be responsive to new evidence and be externally valid. Now, of course, not all theories possess all these characteristics. This does not mean that they are 'bad' theories, but it does mean that in formal terms they are not perfect. Most theories are not perfect. They have some of these characteristics in strength, others more weakly. The value of any particular theory will depend on the importance that the evaluator places on each characteristic. Not all characteristics will have equal value all of the time — even for one evaluator. Though it seems a fair enough bet to say that most practitioners will place greatest emphasis on external validity. A practitioner will want a theory which has been shown to have the capacity to predict and explain behaviour accurately. Though in the pursuit of this, it is really inadvisable to ignore completely the other criteria of a good theory. The practitioner about to use a theory should perform a complete formal evaluation of the theory first and only then weight the evidence consistently with the task in hand. That might mean ignoring whether the theory is heuristic or parsimonious but at least knowledge about these things will then form the backdrop to the theory's use and may halt inappropriate usage.

The Pragmatic Evaluation

The pragmatic evaluation of a theory is purely in terms of how far it helps you to achieve a particular desired result. The practitioner decides on the objective and the theory is measured against this objective. The evaluation is purely utilitarian. This means that a theory will have no constant value. Its value is conditional upon the objective of the evaluator and the time and space which is the context of its evaluation. Objectives change over time and the relative utility of a theory will change with them. Even when the objective remains the same over time, a different context may well mean that the value of a theory changes. For instance, the objective may be to prevent child abuse and this may remain constant. However, one may wish to do so in a context where social work departments have plenty of resources and in times when economic stringencies deplete those resources. In times of plenty, a theory which prescribes actions on the part of the social worker that eat up resources (whether material or in terms

163

of labour) might be considered most effective. In times of cutbacks, a theory that minimizes expenditure is likely to be preferred. The objectives are the same, the theories are the same. The only thing which has altered their relative attractiveness is the economic climate — the context. One of the great dangers in the use of theory is to forget that a theory has no constant pragmatic value. Dogmatic adherence to a theory because it once served the purpose is an error which is easy to make. The advice here is to be ever-critical, especially of old allies.

So far it has been assumed that the practitioner who wishes to evaluate a theory pragmatically can do so. In fact, it is not quite so easy. An effective evaluation is dependent upon relevant information. The evaluator needs to know what there is to know about the implications of the theory for the achievement of the objective. Such information may not be available to all who wish to use it. The flow of such information can be controlled in order to bias the conclusions drawn by an evaluator. Moreover, as long as information about the implications of a theory is imperfect, there is room for propagandists of a theory to manoeuvre. Tasty titbits are thrown to the amassed hoards of practitioners who wait for a theory that will direct their actions and give dividends in results. These bits and pieces seem to work but information about their foundations and long-term effects is either withheld or, more frequently, just not known. These criticisms can certainly be levelled at theories of behaviour modification and social skills training which are so popular. The practitioner deprived of appropriate information cannot make adequate pragmatic evaluations. The obvious way around this problem is for practitioners to vocalize their demands for more information and be explicit that they are not satisfied with titbits any longer. Practitioners need to make it clear that they see no need to fall into the trap of adopting a theory hook, line and sinker; they are, after all, a fish big enough to pull the fisher into the pond.

Even when adequate information is available, there remain problems in the pragmatic evaluation of a theory. Let us postulate the ideal world in which the practitioner knows the objective and knows what actions are prescribed by the theory and their outcomes. Even in that situation, the practitioner has the problem of establishing exactly what will constitute the successful attainment of the objective. In some cases this is not so difficult. For instance, if the objective is to stop a man battering his baby, the method is successful if he stops. However, non-total success is more difficult to measure. Which is more successful, the method which results in the man beating the child just as frequently but less severely or the one which results in less frequent but equally severe attacks? If the two methods, based on different theoretical frameworks, have to be assessed relatively then a judgement about what constitutes the greater success is necessary. Obviously, the judgement in the last resort will be subjective: the practitioner or those with whom he or she works will decide. Even in those more enlightened establishments where the client may be consulted, the decision remains subjective.

Achieving consensus on what constitutes success is further hampered by the fact that adherents to different theoretical systems have built into their theories very different conceptions of success. The proponents of one theory will claim that it gives rise to methods that generate outcomes that are different from the outcomes of methods derived from other theories. They will resist attempts to introduce standardized measures of success in any specific domain. For example, one can imagine only with difficulty a psychoanalyst and a behaviourist agreeing upon what constituted success in the treatment of a neurotic. Removal of a symptom might satisfy the behaviourist who would argue that its origin in the level of conditionability of the central nervous system is unalterable. Nothing less than a reworking of unconscious motivation would satisfy the psychoanalyst. For one, the removal of the symptom is success; for the other, only removal of the cause of the symptom would be success. The philosophy determining their methods also determines their values. There is, therefore, little real chance of establishing a common criterion for the measurement of their success.

In reality, as long as the practitioner resists the temptation to become a faithful adherent of any particular theory, there should be no need to face this problem of establishing a common criterion. A subjective criterion of success against which the outcomes of each theoretical orientation can be measured is sufficient. The effective pragmatic evaluation of a theory demands a stringently objective subjectivity. That is to say, the theory itself should never be allowed to determine what is thought to be success. That should only be determined by the individual who understands the objectives.

A further trap in this vicinity should be identified. The theory can try to dictate what is considered success and this is a danger to be seen and precautions should be taken against it. But more importantly, the theory can attempt to determine the objectives and this is even more dangerous. This is a trap which is difficult to avoid because it operates slowly. The sequence goes something like this: the practitioner has an objective, a theory is chosen and used, the theory is tied to a method, the method proves effective in attaining the initial objective, but then, having found an effective method, the practitioner carried on using it looking for objectives amenable to the method. For instance, this might happen to the social worker who is faced with a child who truants repeatedly. When systematic desensitization is used the child no longer truants. The social worker has found an effective technique based on a firm theoretical orientation. There is then a strong temptation to use the technique with other clients, to see their problems in the light of the technique and define intervention objectives in terms of the technique. The technique is ultimately predisposing if not predetermining what are seen to be the objectives with new clients. This may sound improbable but it is a very real trap. It is a particularly attractive trap because if the technique only encourages objectives it is designed to achieve, success is almost assured.

There is one further important difficulty that the practitioner is likely to encounter when pragmatically evaluating a theory. Theories are designed to explain or interpret phenomena; they do not normally entail prescriptions for use by a practitioner. The psychological theories which have techniques or methods attached to them are still rare. Having explained a phenomenon, the theory does not go on to explain how the phenomenon can be altered though this may be implicit in the explanation. Most often, the practitioner has to extrapolate from the explanation what might be effective in changing or controlling the phenomenon. The practitioner translates theory into action. In so far as this is true, the pragmatic evaluation of a theory is intimately tied to the ability of the practitioner as a translator. One practitioner might be able to transform theory into action, another might fail in this abysmally. The former is likely to consider the theory valuable, the latter is unlikely to do so. At this level, the practitioner is evaluating himself or herself at the same time as the theory is evaluated. Of course, there is nothing intrinsically wrong with this as long as it is done consciously and no self-delusion is involved.

The process of translating theory into action is not simply determined by the capacities of the individual practitioner involved, though these are of fundamental importance. The process is also moulded by the location of that individual within professional and institutional constraints. The notion that it is the practitioner who ultimately decides how theory is put into practice is simplistic. It ignores the enormous structural constraints which are laid upon any practitioner. The individual who contravenes those structural limits is unlikely to have the opportunity to do so a second time. Thus a practitioner translates the theory into action but only within the bounds of professional or institutional propriety. The pragmatic evaluation of a theory must, therefore, build-in these restrictions which will affect its ultimate utility. For instance, a theory which explains delinquency in terms of the symptoms of interclass conflict might propose that the solution lies in social workers seeking to promote class consciousness and radical change within the capitalist system. The value of such a theory for the fieldworker might be limited by his or her recognition that acting in such a way would only lead to one more radical on the dole. There is no intention here to dissuade the social worker who values a theory which is unacceptable to the establishment from using it. Again, the focus of concern lies in trying to pinpoint the pitfalls which surround evaluation. Here the unwary end up in the snare if they forget that the value of a theory at the pragmatic level is dependent upon how far you are permitted to put it into practice.

To summarize the problems facing the practitioner in evaluating a theory. The evaluation should be both formal and pragmatic. In the formal evaluation, the practitioner must face problems of imperfect information and, perhaps, inadequate skills in that type of analysis (the practitioner may not be trained to assess the validity of evidence amassed to support a theory). The pragmatic evaluation poses other problems: of establishing objectives and criteria of success; of translating theory into action; and of resisting the temptation to succumb to the dictatorship of the theory. All of these problems can be overcome and need to be overcome if the practitioner is to choose a theory with which to work on the basis of rational evaluation.

166

13.2 The Problem of Extended Use of a Theory

Theories embody and transmit ways of conceptualizing the social world. They show how it should be broken into bits and how these bits look and how they are related to each other. Effectively, theories encapsulate 'world views'; they carry assumptions about the right and the wrong ways to see the world. Once adopted, a theory can become a way of thought which preselects what is perceived and how it is analysed. For some unfortunates the theory becomes a self-fulfilling prophesy. It is important that the practitioner avoid such total adherence to a single theoretical framework. It annihilates the possibility of rational evaluation.

It is interesting to note that the after-effects of adherence to a theory can be as important as its initial impact. The individual may publicly recant and deny the value of the theory but its exorcism is never really complete or total. Even after its rejection, it continues to channel thought if only because abhorrence of it leads to fanatical adherence to anything which opposes it. The imprint remains, it become more dangerous in many ways because it has gone underground. The covert influence of past theoretical enthusiasms can be very potent. Like the past agnostic, past Catholic, current atheist; the past Freudian, past behaviourist, current ethnomethodologist has a history that needs to be considered; it is certainly likely to affect current affiliations. Rational evaluation of theories currently requires an understanding of the 'theoretical past' of the evaluator. That is to say that rational evaluation is dependent on a certain amount of self-knowledge on the part of the evaluator. This requires some considerable sophistication because it demands that the practitioner evaluating a theory asks searching questions about his or her own presuppositions and preconceptions that may have been imprinted during training or through practice. But it is vital if the subjective and inconsistent influences of these imprints are to be brought under control.

Since the extended use of a theory may bring such problems it seems relevant to consider why a theory may be used beyond the time when it ceases to have any utility in achieving the initial objective. Anachronistic allegiance to a theory often occurs because the theory is a rationalization for habit or inactivity. Abandoning the theory would mean having to change and this is undesirable. Alternatively, sometimes a theory is upheld after it becomes redundant because it provides a jargon, what some would call a 'universe of discourse', which cloaks ignorance. The initiate when faced with a difficult problem can bluff by wrapping the issue in layers of impenetrable jargon. The jargon can also be a symptom of other benefits which continued adherence to the theory might provide. By accepting and 'using' the theory, the practitioner may be gaining entry to a group which has coalesced around that theory. Membership of this group of like-minded people, if it is important enough to the practitioner, may actually prevent him or her from abandoning the theory. Use of the theory's jargon symbolizes membership of the group and, because it can mystify outsiders, can superficially legitimate the group. The importance of habit and group membership in determining the continued use of a theory should not be underestimated. It is certainly not easy to provide any simple advice which, if taken, would ensure a practitioner would avoid the foibles of habit and group affiliation. The only antidote is critical self-awareness.

The use of a theory may be extended beyond its natural lifetime because it develops into a form of propaganda. The relationship between theories and the rhetorics dominant within a society is complex; they are certainly often inter-dependent. Different theories thrive in different social and economic climates. For instance at times of high unemployment when female labour is not needed it is noticeable that theories of optimal child rearing practices tend to emphasize how important the presence of the mother in the home is during childhood; at times of low unemployment when women are needed in the labour force, this emphasis declines. Some theories at least can be seen to rationalize what are existing social pressures. Such theories are maintained as long as they serve this purpose. Other theories can be seen to act in order to change existing social norms. These theories are virtually rhetorics designed to change society. The Szaszian model of mental illness (Szasz, 1961, 1970) could be said to fall into this category. Szasz argues that mental illness is a fabrication of society, a matter of arbitrarily imposed labels. Because people behave in particular ways, they are labelled as mentally ill and then treated appro-priately. In fact, he argues, there is no such thing as 'mental illness', there is only the process of stigmatization. Mental illness is as much a myth as witchcraft. The object of Szasz's theory is to change the entire conceptualiza-tion of mental illness and change the social institutions that surround it. It is an ideology as much as it is a theory. It is thus interesting as propaganda in itself but also because it pinpoints the extent of propaganda and vested interests involved in the other models of mental illness (like the medical, psychoanalytic and behaviourist models). The importance of power structures in determining which theories are heard and which are maintained over time cannot be overestimated. Recognition that the popularity of any particular theory may be in large part determined by factors quite independent of the formal or pragmatic value of it may go some way towards deterring naive acceptance of any theory.

It is perhaps time to move on to a different sort of problem that arises with the extended use of a theory. Theories in the social sciences are unique because they have the power to influence the phenomena they seek to explain. This may mean that a theory which initially offered a valid explanation of a phenomenon can so influence that phenomenon as to invalidate itself. As the existence of a theory becomes broadly known among those whose behaviour it is designed to explicate, they are likely to change their behaviour. The theory, because it was not designed to take into account its own effects, will no longer predict their behaviour. A good theory needs to be reflexive; to grow and develop with the changes it initiates. A good example of the impact of theory must be psycho-analysis. The insights of psychoanalysis have altered the societal conception of sexuality to the point where a theory founded on concepts of repression and denial of sexuality has much less relevance. The organic nature of psycho-analysis means that it has weathered the ravages of its own impact on society

168

rather well. Psychoanalysis is a theory which has grown to accommodate to the changes it was influential in instigating. All too frequently theories do not possess this important reflexivity. Yet they are maintained. The result is inappropriate adherence to the theory.

To summarize, the extended use of a theory has various problems. These centre on the power the theory has to predispose the user to see and accept only what is amenable to the theory; on the way in which the theory becomes embedded in habit and group allegiances; on the tendency that the theory has to become enmeshed in dominant societal rhetorics; and on the potential the theory has to change the phenomenon it explains. Safe usage of a theory for any extended period is therefore unlikely. The reasons for using a particular theory rather than others should be under continual review. To take the value of a theory for granted is to be led up the garden path.

13.3 The Practitioner Theorist

Thus far there has been an unwritten assumption that the practitioner chooses a theory to use from among those made available by theorists. It has been taken for granted that the practitioner has no part in the production of the theories. In fact, there is no reason why this should be the case. There is no logical or pragmatic reason why there should be a cut and dried distinction between the theorist and the practitioner. Both roles could be occupied by a single person.

Theory building by someone who is primarily a practitioner is, of course, likely to have a slightly different emphasis from that done by someone who is solely a theorist. It is more likely to be oriented towards specific objectives and to be delineated in terms of what actions might achieve those objectives. The objectives and the possible actions, that is to say, are likely to influence what are taken to be basal phenomena and what theoretical premises are used in elaborating the explanation. Theory building of this sort would be an integral part of practice and practice an integral part of theory building. The entire process would have a cybernetic nature. The flow chart (Fig. 13.1) captures

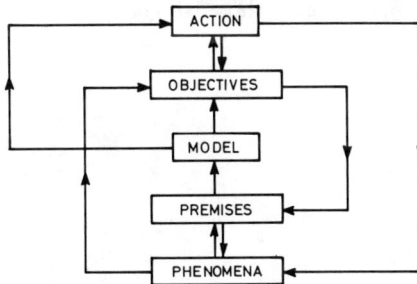

Fig. 13.1 Theory building in practice. (Reproduced from G.M. Breakwell (1982) *Threatened Identities*, by permission of John Wiley.)

some of this process of continual feedback between theory building and practice.

The sooner practitioners become theory builders the better. It should mean that theories begin to include prescriptions for action and become tied to method. It should also mean that they are less likely to ossify because they will be used in situations which demand reflexivity. More than all of this, it should mean that theories are relevant, even if that relevance is transient.

Other valuable tangential consequences of theory building by practitioners can be envisaged. If a practitioner is involved in theory building, that practitioner should be monitoring the outcomes of actions and interventions predicated by the theory in order to evaluate it. Any move which means that the effects of interventions are systematically examined is of great value. It is only showing systematically the effects of their intervention that will enable social workers to prove their value to the cynics.

13.4 Concluding Remarks

Anyone reading this chapter might conclude that using a theory is like walking through a pit full of vipers. Anyone doing so would be right. The use of theory is hazardous but it can have large payoffs. The person walking through the nest of vipers, because it results in high rewards, is no fool. At least, that person is no fool as long as there is snake serum handy in case of mishaps. Where the person has been forewarned of the need to perambulate among ophidia, there is even the chance to take the antidote first. In a way, this chapter is encouraging the practitioner to take the risk and jump into the pit by using theory. At the same time, it is forewarning of the dangers and suggesting what sort of critical self-awareness might operate as the magic serum. The practitioner who actively engages in theory building is effectively taking the antidote before jumping into the pit. Of course, like many antidotes, this one has its own dangers which have to be weighed against the eventual returns. The scales will undoubtedly come to rest in different positions for different people. Not everyone can be a theory builder and not everyone will self-consciously use theory. It is nevertheless useful to know the dangers facing those who can and do.

Part V
The SPA in Practice

14
Disablement

The concept of disablement is complex. There are many types of disablement, ranging from the slight to the severe, the physical to the psychological, and the material to the social. Similarly, the needs of the disabled are diverse, and depend upon the precise nature of their disablement and on the dynamics of the social situation in which it is experienced.

By definition, the disabled are not normal. Yet their abnormalities differ in visibility. Gross and permanent disabilities are obviously visible, however some disabilities are only perceptible under specific conditions. Compare, for example, amputees and epileptics. The more visible disabilities have an impact both on those who come into contact with the disabled and upon the disabled person themselves. Such disability tends to generate feelings of anxiety, repulsion and avoidance among the non-disabled. The impact of the less visible disabilities is primarily upon the disabled themselves. Regardless of the actual visibility of their disablement, the disabled may find their identity, relationships, and group memberships, not to mention their physical environment, radically affected by the form of their disability. This chapter is concerned with how the SPA might provide a route to the analysis and explanation of some of the problems that face the disabled, and with how these problems may be ameliorated. Obviously it should be emphasized that the SPA is only one way of looking at the dynamics of disablement, and no claim is being made here that other perspectives should be ignored. It should also be mentioned that only one small part of the plethora of issues generated by disablement can be examined here. Much of the background information described when applying the SPA model to the process of social work with the disabled has been based on the following source texts:

Mittler (ed.) (1970)
Anderson (1973)
Byrne and Padfield (1978)
Disability Alliance (1978)
Harris (1971)
Young and Ashton (1956)

Here the intention is to provide a brief and selective overview of the field, a case history, and then to show how this case would be analysed in terms of the SPA. The format will be as follows:

(i)   Overview:
   (a) Terminology
   (b) History of provision for the disabled
   (c) Current services available
   (d) Some issues
(ii) Case history (Rowena)
(iii) SPA and disablement:
   (a) Problem analysis
   (b) Data collection
   (c) Targets for intervention
   (d) Problem explanation
   (e) Techniques
   (f) Reflexive analysis

14.1 Overview

Terminology

Being physically or mentally different from most other people has generated a plethora of descriptive terms over the years, which remain fairly confused in common usage. Thus we have disablement, handicap, impairment, defect, deformity, limitation and so on. Sometimes the terms refer only to those with physical problems, sometimes to the mentally subnormal/handicapped and sometimes to the mentally disordered; at other times they can be applied to any combination of the three. The definitions adopted depend largely on the perspective and purpose of the compiler of the definition. Thus the Disabled Persons (Employment) Act 1944 defines a 'disabled' person as:

> A person who, on account of injury, disease or congenital deformity, is substantially handicapped in obtaining or keeping employment, or in undertaking work on his own account of a kind which, apart from that injury, disease or deformity would be suited to his age, experience and qualifications.

Disablement is here seen in terms of thwarted employment potential. On a more global tack, the United Nations Declaration of the Rights of Disabled Persons (1975) offers a definition in terms of the necessities of life:

> The term 'disabled person' means any person unable to ensure by himself or herself

172

wholly or partly the necessities of a normal individual and/or social life, as a result of a deficiency, either congenital or not, in his or her physical or mental capabilities.

The disabled are here explicitly defined in terms of departure from a 'normal individual and/or social life'. Presumably therefore the purpose of working with the disabled is to help them to reach or become as close as possible to a normal individual with a normal social life.

A valuable definition of disablement is proposed by Harris (1971). Harris defines disability as 'the loss or reduction of functional ability' and differentiates it from handicap which is 'the disadvantage or restriction of activity caused by disability'. A disability is what you have; a handicap is a consequence of what you have. This distinction seems to have received fairly general acceptance and has the advantage of being couched in both behavioural and attitudinal terms, facilitating the application of the SPA.

History of Provision for the Disabled

Byrne and Padfield (1978) present a view of the development of provision for the disabled which seems fairly consistent with the views of other writers on the subject. They aver that throughout the Middle Ages, provision was made primarily by the disabled person's family or neighbours, supplemented by the activities of the organized Christian Church who took a particular interest in the more visible and readily understandable disabilities such as blindness, deafness, lameness and chronic sickness. The 1601 Poor Law Act generated the involvement of the local authority in providing basic subsistence requirements for the sick, needy and homeless. By the nineteenth century, the development of medical services and their dissemination on a wider basis than before made basic medical care and hospitalization more readily available. However, hospitals were usually dirty and unhygienic, 'doctors' did not have to register as medical practitioners until the 1858 Medical Registration Act, and treatments continued to be based on mythology and superstition rather than on science.

The middle and end of the nineteenth century saw a change of attitudes towards the disabled. No longer were the disabled so totally the hopeless product of malevolent fate; rather they were slowly becoming viewed as individuals with particular needs who might achieve a degree of integration in society. Although legislation did exist to try and ensure that blind, deaf, mentally handicapped and epileptic children received an elementary education, most of the involvement with the disabled came from medical practitioners and voluntary workers.

The different forms of disability — mainly the blind, deaf, mentally defective, insane, epileptic and crippled — attracted their own group of interested non-disabled people. As Young and Ashton (1956) put it: 'Because each class of handicapped person had to be fought for separately, there grew up distinct services for each, and distinct groups of workers with their own training, skill and function.' The services remained distinct despite the impetus created by the two world wars to provide more systematic and widespread rehabilitation and treatment techniques. Young and Ashton asserted that the

173

different specializations did in fact rest on common skills and therefore a common basic training for the workers should be evolved, supplemented by 'specialised knowledge concerning the kind of defect and its psychological implications for the sufferer . . . according to the branch of work chosen'. This notion of integration was given structure initially by the 1948 National Assistance Act but most forcefully by the Seebohm Report (1968) and the 1970 Chronically Sick and Disabled Persons Act, two major extant pieces of legislation affecting the disabled.

Current Services Available

The 1948 National Assistance Act recommended but did not require each welfare department to devise and submit for approval a scheme for the development of services for the handicapped within its area; it stated that services should only be supplied to registered disabled people, with the responsibility for registering being placed on the individual rather than the department; and failed to allocate adequate resources to the departments to carry out these suggestions.

Seebohm (pp. 100–106) considered that the services for the physically 'handicapped' existing at the time went some way towards meeting their needs. Most areas identified young children with handicaps, arranged for their medical treatment, educated them in ordinary or special schools, and had a register of persons resident in their area who were blind, deaf, dumb or in other ways substantially and permanently handicapped. Voluntary organizations were seen as providing the bulk of the input: 'Public authorities have been mainly concerned to cooperate with voluntary effort in developing the services and extending their average' (p. 100). However, acknowledgement was made that major gaps still remained: social care of children and families had not developed to the same extent as medical care; handicapped school leavers had few facilities; services for disabled adults varied between areas; the Disabled Persons' Register was incomplete and apparently indicated uneven distribution of the handicapped; housing was generally poor and incomes low; some forms of disability elicited little interest; and no major research programme had been taken to indicate numbers involved and the extent and type of needs exhibited (this deficit was to be met by Harris, 1971).

Seebohm was clear in general terms where the needs of the disabled fitted into the functions of the proposed generic social service departments: 'the Social Service Department should take over responsibility for social work and occupational therapy with physically handicapped people and their families, the provision of residential and day centres for them, as well as providing home helps, meals on wheels, holidays and a sitters-in service' (p. 102). Other services were to retain existing functions: health services provide medical diagnosis, treatment, medical rehabilitation, home nursing and health visiting; education services provide education in ordinary schools wherever possible, failing this in day or residential special schools, psychological services, speech

174

therapy, and further education; the youth employment service and the Department of Employment in the form of disablement resettlement officers were to find suitable work; and the Ministry of Social Security, now the DHSS, was to provide adequate financial income for the disabled who were unable to work. Although all these service agencies were to be involved, it fell to the social services department (SSD) to be responsible for long-term involvement with the disabled, more specifically '. . . for the social care of the handicapped individual and his family'. Seebohm was careful to list those needs with which the SSD should have a particular concern:

(i)   mobilization of services for the handicapped school leaver;
(ii) helping those handicapped living in poor housing conditions to achieve a better or more appropriate living environment;
(iii) assisting the middle-aged wage-earner incapacitated through chronic illness or accident;
(iv) providing interest and relief to the permanently incapacitated;
(v)   meeting the particular needs of the elderly disabled and their families — laundry service, day-care, sitters-in.

The 1970 Chronically Sick and Disabled Persons' Act, with a few exceptions and additions, largely transformed the recommendations of the Seebohm report into mandatory duties for the SSD. SSDs must survey the number and needs of the disabled in their area, have at least one disabled person on their Social Services Committee, and provide services to the disabled ranging from the provision of wirelesses to the blind, housing adaptations, and meals on wheels, to recreational facilities and holidays. Stroud (1975) in outlining the provisions of the Act (pp. 58–63) argues that social workers have become involved in four key areas — provision of physical and of practical help (though this is being delegated to more specialized personnel), dealing with the

Table 14.1   Number of Physically Handicapped of All Ages Registered with Local Authorities in 1967

(Reproduced from Seebohm Report (1968) *Report of the Committee on Local Authority and Allied Personal Social Services, Cmnd. 3703.* © Crown copyright. Reproduced by permission of the Controller, Her Majesty's Stationery office.)

Blind	103 000
Partially sighted	34 000
Deaf	25 000
Hard of hearing	16 000
Other physically handicapped	184 000
Total:	362 000

emotional concomitants of disability ('uselessness, loneliness and boredom'), and in 'problems of relationships'. These latter two areas will be developed more fully in the later section on the SPA analysis of Rowena's case history.

As a final piece of background information, some of the estimates of the current numbers and types of disability can usefully be presented (Table 14.1). These enable the extent of the potential social work involvement to be conceptualized and give some indication of the range and profundity of the needs likely to be presented to the social worker.

Of course, one of the central problems in developing policy, and hence provision for the disabled, concerns the time lag between the collection and the analysis and publication of relevant data, and in the shifting types of categories within which the data collection is framed. Thus the COI (1975) estimate of the numbers of disabled in Britain over the age of 16 quotes a total of over three million; more recent data collection has concerned England only and has used different categories. Whatever the precise totals, the fact remains that there is a considerable difference between the number of registered disabled, and the total number of people who might reasonably be considered to be disabled.

Finally, Anderson estimates that the number of disabled children under school-leaving age is something in the region of 22 000 (Anderson, 1973, p. 11). Although there are obvious discrepancies in the definition of disablement used in these various estimates, they give some idea of the potential demand that could be made on social service departments, a demand probably far in excess of that which is actually being made.

Some Issues

Two interlinked issues will be considered here. Firstly, the examination of what is involved in enabling the disabled to live a 'normal' individual and social life. Secondly, initial consideration will be given to the perspective provided by the SPA to the analysis and understanding of some of the problems facing the disabled in their struggle for this goal.

Disablement and normality. Two of the major parameters along which 'normality' is assessed are the individual's physical appearance and general social behaviour. The disabled, particularly the more chronically sick, are often visibly physically abnormal — their physique is inconsistent with a racial phenotype — and they experience a range of social handicaps as a consequence: in general terms the disabled do not fit many of the behavioural templates imposed by society and suffer discrimination in such areas as employment, recreation, transportation and housing design.

The United Nations Declaration (United Nations, 1975) co-sponsored by the United Kingdom, argues that the disabled as a right should have: respect for their human dignity; the right to enjoy a decent life, as normal and full as possible; the same civil and political rights as others; measures designed to help them to become a self-reliant as possible; medical, psychological and functional treatment to develop capabilities and skills and hasten the process of integration or reintegration; economic and social security and a decent standard of living; to have their special needs considered at all stages of economic and social planning; to live with families or foster parents and participate in all social, creative and recreational activities.

Eventually then, the disabled want a larger share of what the majority of non-disabled already have and have so far refused to cede to the disabled. It might therefore be worth conceding that the disabled, like many other groups, are competing for some of the icing on the normality cake. Competition and conflict are closely related. Later in this chapter, we look at some of the techniques that a social worker might be able to utilize in working with a specific disabled person. It is worth making the point that the general principles underlying those particular techniques can be made to apply to the needs of the disabled as a whole in their fight for their rights. More importantly they are techniques available directly to the disabled themselves, and do not necessarily require the intervention of a professional and usually non-disabled practitioner. It might indeed be a prime concern of the disabled to attempt to change the attitudes and/or behaviour of the practitioner as well as those of the wider public.

Basic SPA concepts and the disabled. The next section contains a detailed outline of how the SPA might be used in one particular case. The point worth making here, is to stress that the SPA offers a perspective to a whole range of problems and is not something that only applies to any particular case, problem or social context. The more obvious possible implications of SPA concepts with the disabled are:

Identity. Chapter 4 stressed the importance of a positive sense of identity and how the assessments of others are therefore potentially threatening. The disabled are more likely than most to experience spoiled identities, where social approval is not forthcoming and identity is discredited. The disabled are classically stigmatized, usually visibly but also more covertly. Playing the disabled role or redefining the self are likely tactics for dealing with visible stigma: where the stigma is less visible, attempts at passing as normal are possible. Of the three most threatening situations to a sense of positive identity — alienation, role conflict and marginality — the disabled are likely to experience most acutely alienation and role conflict. Alienation might be manifested in feelings of powerlessness, meaningless and isolation (see Stroud, *op. cit.*), generated by behaviours that conflict with identity ideals or reflect dissonant self-concepts. Conflict may be generated, for example, when a disabled person has a stereotype of disability as being 'in need of care' while being aware that other disabled people hold the stereotype of disability as 'being deprived of our rights'. To a lesser extent, marginality may be experienced by those with less obvious disabilities, such as epilepsy: as long as they do not have a fit in public they are effectively normal, a fit in public places them in the disabled, and therefore stigmatized, group.

Relationships. The processess of impression formation and attribution by and of the disabled are fundamental in conceptualizing and explaining the behaviour of the disabled towards other people and the behaviour of others toward the disabled. More than most groups, being disabled is conducive to having stereotypes and prototypes made of them: being seen as less capable than they are, or inherently incapable of competing with the non-disabled. It might also be anticipated that interpersonal attraction may cause difficulties for the disabled; not only in being perceived as attractive by non-disabled, but also in perceiving attractiveness in the fellow-disabled.

Groups. The 3 million or so 'disabled' people in this country have developed an increasingly cohesive group and powerful voice over the last 50 or 60 years. Group memberships for the disabled offer an unusual array of benefits, both material and psychological. Numerous small-scale voluntary groups, have, from time to time, been incorporated into large federal groups such as the Disability Alliance, and have campaigned for such things as adequate incomes, and provision of benefits according to degree rather than type of disability and handicap. Disabled groups require clear external criteria of membership and offer benefits sufficient to satisfy the individual's internal criteria of membership. Ironically perhaps, whether the generation of such clear-cut group memberships and boundaries jeopardizes the very thing the members are seeking — membership as near as possible of the dominant non-disabled group — remains to be seen.

Environment. The disabled live in a largely alien environment: most of the territory in which they move 'belongs' to the larger group of the non-disabled. If they are fortunate, their primary territories may have been adapted specifically to suit them; but most of the secondary and 'public' territories available to them will not be. Not surprisingly, it might be reasonable to assume a tendency for the disabled to remain within their primary territories. On a more intimate level, personal space may be rather more extensive than the disabled person desires: disabled men in wheelchairs may find it particularly frustrating. The environment can have a more powerful influence on the problems of the disabled than on most of the other groups making demands on social workers: indeed, not only may it be the variable to alleviate a particular problem, it may be the determiner of the problem. At the very least, it will almost certainly be part of the context of the analysis of the problem.

Obviously these brief notes do no more than hint at the range and depth of possible applicability of the SPA to work with the disabled. Inherent in the SPA is the assertion that any particular problem presents a unique constellation of dynamic events meriting individual analysis and explanations at different points in time. The generalizations are no more than a few general pointers. Below, a particular case history is given to provide something of the other side of the coin — a flavour of work with one individual. Now, case histories themselves present their own problems — they are not readily generalizable, a written account cannot conjure the reality, and probably no two practitioners will see the case in the same way. The balance between the general and the specific must be performed in the mind of the reader, influenced by whatever prejudices, theories, experiences and beliefs rest therein.

14.2 Case History: Rowena

Rowena is a 16-year-old girl suffering from spina bifida with associated hydrocephalus. She is confined to a wheelchair and has an ileostomy; that is, her bladder empties into a bag she has tied to her waist. Verbally fluent, she gives an impression of being more intelligent than she is. Most of her life has been spent in hospital or residential special school, though since she reached school leaving age, her care has devolved to her parents. She has been living at home for the past nine months, on a full-time basis, other than the occasional visit to a local hospital for a check-up or a short-stay to provide her parents with a respite. She has always had learning difficulties, and although she can read and write both these skills are rudimentary, and she does not use them unless prompted. She takes great pride in her appearance, makes up her attractive face carefully, has a well-coiffured hairstyle, and encourages her parents to buy her fairly expensive dresses. She spends most of her time at the window of her parents' house, which looks on to a busy road, with the colour television going on in the background. Her relationship with her parents is one of tolerance: they are used to her temper tantrums, screaming fits and verbosity; she has adapted to their tendency to treat her as a young child and give way to her will. Although the parents have a number of friends who call in and see them from time to time, Rowena has no friends of her own.

The house is not adapted to the wheelchair, and she has to be carried down the three front steps leading to the front of the house. Although her parents sleep on the first floor, lifting Rowena up the 20 steps necessary to get there has proved to much for them and she therefore sleeps on a single bed in a corner of the front room where she spends most of her day. The nearest shops are 200 yards away via a pavement long in need of repair. Neighbours call in from time to time but being at work all day are unable to help with Rowena's transport difficulties.

Rowena's parents are both comparatively elderly. Her father is in his 60s, her mother in her early 50s. They have had no other children and Rowena has brought them near to separation on a number of occasions. Although her mother has a fierce devotion to her, her father is worn out with the physical and emotional effort needed to look after her.

Rowena's parents have contacted the local SSD to ask for help with her. Their initial wish is to discuss Rowena's long-term future in the light of her father's 'advancing years': her father would like her removed from home as

179

soon as possible; her mother wants her to stay at home but says she cannot manage Rowena without her husband's help.

14.3   The SPA and Rowena

Problem Analysis

Intrapsychic level   (a) Manifest. Rowena's mother says that she is devoted to Rowena and that as long as her husband is alive and able to help, Rowena could stay at home if she wishes. She tends to treat Rowena as a young child and at moments of crisis will give in to her.

Rowena's father is tired of her. An old man, he no longer feels he has the physical energy to carry her about or the emotional strength to face the occasional tantrums. He has in the past said he would leave his wife and daughter to their own devices but has never carried out the threat.

Rowena does not like being on her own most of the time. She says that she wants friends, particularly a boyfriend, and would like to go to discos and socials. She is embarrassed by her ileostomy but says she has got used to being in a wheelchair. She thinks she is pretty and would like other people to think so too. She does not want to go back into a hospital and has not considered what might happen to her on the death of her father. She likes her mother but her father annoys her because he does not talk to her very much.

(b) Latent. It seems likely that Rowena is experiencing some of the fairly usual pangs of adolescence — bright enough to realize she is different to her contemporaries, she nevertheless wants to experiment with most of the things a normal girl of her age might be expected to desire. Having spent most of her life in institutions, it seems reasonable to assume that much of her behaviour fits an institutional environment rather better than it does a family one. Feelings of isolation, alienation and hopelessness may well still be mixed at this stage with the more positive drives and optimisms of youth.

Rowena's parents may have feelings of resentment and even hatred towards Rowena that have not been expressed. Though her mother professes devotion, the virtual sacrifice of the marriage on Rowena's behalf, may have generated a range of repressed antagonisms. Rowena's father seems to have only a barely concealed despair and disinterest in his daughter, and might be predicted to support any attempt to move Rowena from the family even before his own death.

Interpersonal level   (a) Manifest. Rowena is a problem to her parents because she has temper tantrums, is heavy to carry about, and is not going to lead an independent life. She demands enormous amounts of their time and energy, and gives back little in return.

Rowena's parents are a problem to her only because they are not very much fun.

(b) Latent. The relationship between Rowena's parents has been strained to

near breaking point for some years but has never led to a parting: their explanation for the disharmony rests with Rowena, but this need not necessarily be the real reason. Removing Rowena from home may not lead to the harmony anticipated by the father.

Rowena throws more temper tantrums when the father is present, perhaps having recognized a weaker character. The removal of father, either by his death, or her parting, may result in a diminution in the frequency of tantrums.

Intragroup (a) Manifest. At the moment, neither Rowena nor her parents have sought membership of any particular group. They are obviously, however, members of the 'disabled' and 'family of disabled' group whether they like it or not. Manifest problems are, perhaps, surprisingly obvious to the family. Rowena and her parents express a number of complaints they see as deriving directly from their imposed group memberships. Such complaints centre on the lack of resources for the disabled, lack of interest, stigmatization, stereotyping and resulting isolation.

(b) Latent. Rowena's awareness of the gap between her access to social goals and those of contemporaries in the non-disabled group is likely to become more acute, leading to perhaps an increased sense of frustration and undirected aggression.

Removal of Rowena will largely place the parents back into the normal group, and may therefore be supported, however unacknowledged, by the mother as well as the father.

Intergroup (a) Manifest. Rowena is a member of a different group to her parents. Her parents can move largely at will between the groups of 'family of disabled' and 'normals'; Rowena is disabled and will always be disabled.

(b) Latent. Both Rowena and her parents, though not formal members of groups for the disabled are, nevertheless, influenced by their activities. Currently, the drive from these pressure groups is towards normalization: it might be anticipated that, should the parents attempt to encourage Rowena's removal from home, they will stand to be criticized by these groups.

Data Collection

Problem analysis is obviously dependent on the collection of comprehensive relevant data. Although the information required by the SPA is different to that required by other approaches, the means of its collection remains largely the same. For a detailed account of data collection see Pincus and Minahan (*op. cit.*, Chapter 7).

In Rowena's case, data may have been provided by:

(i)   informal but structured conversation with each member of the family, together and separately. Particular foci of interest would be
   (a) existing support systems
   (b) the marital relationship in Rowena's absence
   (c) perceived stigmatization.

(ii) eliciting Rowena's constructs of the significant people in her life. Use of a repertory grid (Kelly, 1955) with significant people as the elements. Rowena is asked to indicate one way in which any two elements (people) of a triad are similar and thereby different to the third. Thus all the significant people are presented to her in triads. Rowena provides the criteria with which she evaluates them. She might afterwards be asked to work them in order of, say, liking. This would give some idea how significant both of her parents are to her, compared to each other and to significant other people in her life, and an indication of *how* she evaluates people in general.

(iii) asking Rowena to write her own 'autobiography' or establish whether she has kept a diary and would allow the diary to be perused. Particular interests would be in:
    (a) relative importance she attaches to hospital v. home on her identity
    (b) manifestation of social comparison processes
    (c) consistency or otherwise of both behaviours and attitudes.

(iv) asking parents to collect baseline information, on a daily basis over a period of time, on the frequency, cause, type, duration and aftermath of Rowena's tantrums.

These are obviously not the only means of collecting data useful to the SPA. In the various practice chapters reference will be made to a number of data collection methods.

Targets for Intervention

(a) What do the problems imply for the identity of those involved? Rowena. Although Rowena has a considerable amount of self-esteem, repeated contact with other people has indicated that the necessary social approval of others with whom to compare herself has not been forthcoming. It seems likely that she has developed a spoiled identity. She is unable to deal with this by 'passing' because her stigma is visible. Two tactics are left to her — playing the assigned role and redefining herself.

Suffering from a congenital disability, she is well socialized into the assigned role, the stigmatized identity. So far, she has not shown the awareness and control necessary to redefine herself, though in later years and with guidance, it may be possible for her to do this by joining a group for the disabled. In the interim, her spoiled identity is eased by the role play.

Rowena's father has found the burden of assimilating an ascribed social role into a previously satisfactory personal identity too difficult to bear and is attempting to cope by eliminating the source of the problem. In some ways, he has shown some of the components of alienation that may later be anticipated to develop in his daughter.

Rowena's mother, the character with the strongest sense of personal and social identity, seems to have adapted to the new role of 'mother of a disabled child' with considerable vehemence. If anything, the new role has been perhaps rather too forcibly assimilated into her personal identity and she has, in her

182

husband's eyes, lost something of her previous identity as 'wife', 'lover' or whatever.

(b) What do the problems mean for the relationships of those involved? *Rowena* is having considerable difficulties in forming relationships with anyone. A ready victim of stereotypes, she is disadvantaged in the struggle for contact with others. Though wanting to be seen as 'attractive' she has few of the attributes usually involved in the process of interpersonal attraction: geographically close, competent, pleasant, intelligent and so on. It is unlikely she will develop long-term committments as she has little opportunity to reach even the sampling phase. Her parents are her only close contacts and rejection by them is likely to force her to return to institutional living on a long-term basis. It may be that such a move will in fact enable her to develop more numerous and intense relationships, and these are most likely to be with other disabled people.

Rowena's parents. The central presenting problem — the removal of Rowena — seems fundamental to the return to a satisfactory relationship. If Rowena goes, her father will remain with her mother, though both will have to reinterpret their long-term committment in terms of the act of rejection. If Rowena stays and all things else remain equal, the relationship between them is likely to deteriorate and reach crisis point as Rowena's struggle to resolve her own feelings of self-denigration become more acute.

(c) What group structures and processes are involved? Currently, group processes are only peripheral to the family. Membership of the disabled group is ascribed rather than sought, and is operating largely at the manifest level.

(d) What role does the physical environment play? The environment provides an essential contextual backdrop in the analysis. Rowena has little privacy — her bedroom is the living room. She has scant opportunity for personal autonomy, emotional release or self-evaluation. She has minimal personal territory, and restricted access to secondary and public territories. She may feel she has an excess of undesired social contact — her family — and may be psychologically crowded, a phenomenon that correlates with high anxiety and stress and greater hostility to others.

A substantial portion of the father's stress seems to focus on the physical strain involved in carrying Rowena, and her wheelchair, about the house, and in transporting her out of the house and along the potholed pavement outside.

(e) What processes of change are involved? *Physical change.* Change of home, or alteration to the existing one. Installation of a lift to the first floor, and building of a ramp to the outside. Provision of a separate bedroom for Rowena. Contact with the local council to have the pavement repaired. Possible provision of a motorized wheelchair and consideration to assessing whether Rowena would be capable of learning to drive some form of adapted car.

Economic change. The family receive their full entitlement of benefits. Con-

183

sideration to the use of sitters-in, provision of holidays, together and separately and the installation of a telephone.

Political change. Pressure on the SSD, Education Department, and Department of Employment to make a greater range of work and recreational provision available for disabled school leavers.

Psychological change. Rowena to be put in touch with a group for the disabled to facilitate a more positive redefinition of self. Needs objective referents to justify her self-esteem.

Rowena's father must assimilate the ascribed role of father of a disabled child more positively into his personal identity and avoid the perceived response to the conflict manifested in his flight/fight reaction to his wife and daughter.

Rowena's mother must try to loosen the hold that one particular social role — 'mother of a disabled child' — has over her social and personal identity. Her personal identity is bound up in one social role as to exclude a number of other social roles — wife, neighbour, gardener or whatever.

Social change. The attitudes of the three members of the family to each other and the attitudes of the neighbours to the family are imbalanced and therefore seek consistency. Techniques for attitude change are outlined in Chapter 7.

Problem Explanation

The four key processes of construal, consistency, comparison and conformity have been touched on throughout the problem analysis, without being clearly labelled as having explanatory power. The way in which Rowena and her parents construe the world has been considered: techniques for eliciting a comprehensive impression have been outlined.

Rowena probably sees the world with a particularly restricted perspective. Congenitally disabled, she has had comparatively scant opportunity to broaden her experiences; neurologically damaged, her ability to assimilate and categorize information is limited; stigmatized, she has not been given the ready opportunity to develop a strong sense of self-worth.

Rowena's parents seem to have developed very different superordinate construal systems. Her father interprets much of his current experiences in the light of the change brought about by Rowena's birth, particularly how it deprived him of a wife and membership of a number of social groups from which he derived a positive social identity.

Rowena's mother, similarly affected by her birth, has elevated her role as mother to a position of dominance within her social and personal identity structures, to the extent of excluding social roles she had previously filled quite happily.

None of the three family members is stable: each has a particular imbalance of thought, feeling and action, manifested in various forms of distress: Rowena in her tantrums; her father in his threatened flight; and her mother in her over-protection.

Little is known about the success or failure of attempts by Rowena's parents to compare their understanding of their situation with the views of others,

184

though it seems likely from their isolation that they have not fared very favourably. Rowena is unlikely to have had much opportunity to compare herself with others who are not handicapped.

All three try to conform to dominant social norms — they live in an identical house to their neighbours, do not upset the sensibilities of others by leaving the house very often, and adopt the same criteria of success and failure as others. They are not, however, capable of generating conformity in the behaviour and attitudes of each other.

Each exhibits a degree of unison and conflict between these four key processes. Thus Rowena's mother construes her world largely in terms of her involvement with her daughter, acts consistently with this view, but finds difficulty in finding outside agreement with her understandings and is unsure quite what is the 'best', most conforming response, society would want her to make. Rowena's father sees the world much as he did before Rowena's birth which he views as being something of a curse; he fails to act consistently with his views; receives inadequate information from others to justify his failure to adopt a principled stance one way or the other; and though conforming to the wishes of his wife, fails to regain the social approval he valued prior to Rowena's birth. Rowena sees the world fairly simply at the moment as best she can, but without having developed an adequate stable construal system is unable to act consistently; she has little information on which to compare her understanding with that of others, and is as yet unable to grasp the correlations between conformity and social acceptance.

Techniques

Techniques vary with the individual social worker and the context in which they are used. In Rowena's case, a number may be postulated:

(i)   Establishing a working relationship with Rowena and each of her parents. (Relationship skills — Chapter 11.)
(ii) Attitude change techniques (Chapter 7) to facilitate a more cohesive family unit.
(iii) Personal construct techniques (Chapter 11) to elicit the construal processes.
(iv) Identification of identity support systems (Chapter 4).
(v)   Behaviour modification (Chapter 11) as a temporary relief from Rowena's temper tantrums.

Each of these techniques can be related to the SPA process outlined above. Each rests on its own value bases and theoretical assumptions and will usually be consistent with the social worker's own values, and be appropriate for the demands placed upon it. They must obviously be used with the other forms of change, particularly the economic and physical, outlined earlier.

Reflexive Analysis

Throughout the analysis, the social worker should look at his or her own biases,

185

values and prejudices, and own involvement in the situation, and try and decide whether the resulting distortion has gone beyond acceptable limits.

In Rowena's case, it might be postulated that the social worker, being aware of the financial cutbacks experienced by his or her employer, has placed perhaps less emphasis on the importance of changing Rowena's physical environment than he or she should have. Alternatively, it may be that the social worker is happier working at a particular level of analysis or using a particular technique, and has edged the analysis in its favour at the expense of an open and as rational approach to the analysis as possible. Whatever the bias, it rests with the social worker to have a sufficient degree of self-knowledge to identify it, and allow for it.

14.4 Conclusion

This chapter has concerned itself with the application of the SPA to disablement. Though largely neglected until the present century, the disabled have become one of the most powerful pressure groups in contemporary society. Presenting as they do a challenge to the concept of normality in their search for equivalent rights, some of the social psychological concepts thus generated have been outlined. By the use of a case history, such fundamental processes as identity formation, group membership and personal change have been considered within a SSD context. The problem description, analysis and explanation generated a number of areas where change might be striven for, and some of the techniques likely to be involved in the change process were mentioned.

15
Group Homes

Group homes for both mentally ill and mentally handicapped adults are in fashion. Such unusual bedfellows as Local Authority Social Service Departments, Regional Health Authorities, MIND, the Mental After-Care Association and the Rotary Club of Great Britain are seemingly united in their liking for this particular form of community care. MIND, in a booklet entitled *Starting and Running a Group Home** (1972) asserts that:

> Interest in group homes has increased dramatically in recent years. Enquiries come from all parts of the United Kingdom and from overseas. It is a scheme which has snowballed in less than twenty years. (p. 4)

It is impossible to establish with any degree of accuracy the number of people who now live in group homes in this country. However, in *Priorities for Health and Personal Social Services in England* (DHSS, 1976) it was noted that there were some 9500 places in local authority homes in 1974 for the mentally handicapped, with a recommendation that some 22 000 beds be made available by 1985. It is therefore perhaps not too unreasonable to suggest that taken together with group home provision for the mentally ill, some 20 000 people currently live in group homes. It is also likely that a sizeable number of these group homes will receive some form of support/supervision/guidance/control from an outside agency, usually in the form of a social worker or community nurse. If we estimate that a group home on average will have five residents then perhaps some 1000 social workers are currently involved in one way or another with group homes. In this chapter we want to examine group homes in a little more detail, and look at some of the implications of an SPA analysis for the supervising social worker.

*This booklet is now ten years old and out of print and the quotes taken from it do not necessarily reflect MIND's current policies in this area.

Let us begin by asking a few basic questions. What is meant by the term 'group home'? What is the purpose of a group home? How effective is it? And, perhaps the most important and also the most neglected question of all, if it does work, how? To try to achieve a fair cross-section of opinion in reply to these questions, five main sources will be used: *Priorities for Health and Personal Social Services in England* (1976); MIND's *Starting and Running A Group Home* (1972); the views of MacAndrew *et al.* (1980) who surveyed some 26 group homes in the Prestwich area; Ryan (in Wing and Olsen, 1979) who interviewed 39 residents who live in group homes in North London; and Thornicroft (1979) who studied 11 group homes with a combined total of 52 residents in the Cambridge area.

15.1 What is a Group Home?

The government policy document, *Priorities for Health and Personal Social Services in England*, though advocating group homes as a low cost form of community care, contains no clear definition of what constitutes a group home, although a section on the desirability of utilizing low cost forms of community provision contains a recommendation for: 'The use of group homes and other forms of housing suitable for those who need an environment providing some support rather than a substantial degree of care' (p. 58).

MIND, in its manual for the setting up of group homes (1972, *op. cit.*) considers that: 'Strictly speaking group homes have no resident staff, and residents either live communally in small groups of from four to eight, sharing cooking and housekeeping or they have bedsitting rooms, usually with a communal TV room and sometimes a shared utility room with washing facilities.' (p. 5) The property suitable for a group home is 'A family house with two to five bedrooms which has easy access to shops and public transport' (p. 9).

MacAndrew *et al.* have a broadly similar opinion: 'Ordinary leased houses in the community where a small group of ex-patients, usually three to five, can live a virtually independent life.' (p. 1) Ryan is also keen to emphasize the notion of self-sufficiency: 'An environment where a small group of three to five former patients could live together and give each other friendship and support needed to live outside hospital.' Finally, Thornicroft, with a fairly categorical statement, offers a concise definition: 'By group home, I mean a house where three to six former psychiatric patients live together without residental supervision.'

Thus, to tie the various threads together, a group home is an ordinary family house where some three to eight ex-patients live together with a minimum of outside support. This is an important statement in that the emphasis on independence would seem to preclude the possibility of having resident staff in the home, the consequences of which will be discussed later in the chapter when we look at the social psychological implications of group-home living.

15.2 What is the Purpose of a Group Home?

Views on the purpose of group homes vary according to the attitude of the agency or writer concerned. Government policy, for example, encourages cheap alternative forms of community provision for those patients needing only minimal support in order 'to be integrated as fully as possible into the local community'. Cheapness and integration are the key words, though no attempt is made to specify in any detail what is meant by integration. MIND sees group homes as having a variety of purposes not just for the residents themselves but also for the community and government. Thus group homes enable the residents to 'learn to be independent and become integrated into the community' (p. 6), 'to return to normal living, and in many cases to normal employment' (p. 5); the community also benefits since the residents 'as good neighbours . . . can show the community that recovery from mental illness is possible' (p. 5), and of course they 'save the taxpayer money' (p. 4).

MacAndrew is of the opinion that group homes were set up to meet a specific need — to provide accommodation for a number of long-term patients ready for discharge from hospital but with nowhere to go:

> They may have no family or at least no family who want to have an ex-patient living with them and, after many years of institutional life, it may be asking too much of patients to live on their own or to re-establish themselves in the community on their own. One solution to this problem which has been adopted in various parts of the country has been the setting up of group homes.

Ryan echoes this notion of providing substitute families, thus: 'What was required, in fact, was to create "artificial" families for a group of people who had lost contact with their own. This is what group homes were created to provide.' Thornicroft takes a more individualistic prospective arguing that the purpose of a group home is 'to offer a chance for those severely disabled people to become reunited with the community . . . we can see this in three types of achievement:

(i)   individual independence of welfare agencies;
(ii) how well the group members get on together;
(iii) how independent each group becomes.'

Group homes do not, therefore, seem to have any one particular purpose. Although it seems generally agreed that they are a cheap form of provision, whether they are intended to provide a substitute family or whether they are a means for an individual to become once again a full member of the community remains open to negotiation. There is also an additional note, sounded by MIND, of group homes being a means of dispelling myths over the untreatability of mental illness. In effect group homes are good public relations. Since the use to which a group home is put is so dependent upon the views of the originators, it is not surprising that when the time comes to evaluate how effective a group home is in meeting its purpose, there is considerable diversity in the means of evaluation.

15.3 How Effective are Group Homes?

There has been no systematic large-scale controlled analysis of group homes, and it has only been in the last few years that attempts have been made to evaluate their effectiveness. Such studies as have been performed tend to look for behavioural correlates which might justify the initial purpose of the home as defined by the group home's instigators.

MacAndrew (1980), seeking to establish whether a degree of 'virtually independent life' had been achieved administered a self-rating questionnaire to 48 of 100 residents living in 25 group homes affiliated to Prestwich Hospital, Manchester. The sample was largely female (70%) and single, with a mode age in the 51–55 age group; 15 of the sample had been in a psychiatric hospital for 5 years or less, 26 had been in for over 10 years, and 7 had been in for over 30 years. They had been living in the group homes for between one and seven years. Using a number of evaluative parameters the essential findings convey an image of a group of people pleased to be no longer in hospital and managing to survive in the community. However, the majority of residents continue to remain dependent on medication, have a limited range of outside interests and activities, are unemployed and have limited involvement in the routine upkeep of their home.

Graham Thornicroft attempted to evaluate how well the 52 residents of 11 group homes in the Cambridge area achieved the desired goals of individual independence from welfare agencies, getting on well with other residents, and the independence of the group as a whole. Although he did not specify his means of evaluation, his conclusions were that those residents with long histories as psychiatric in-patients were less dependent but tend to get on better in the group. He commented:

> The common claim for group homes is that they offer a path towards normal life for otherwise hopelessly institutionalised people. On the basis of my study, this claim is over-exaggerated. Group homes re-locate severely emotionally and socially disabled people. Most are then dependent, in the long term, upon drugs and professional support. This is not how we usually define normality.

Peter Ryan interviewed 39 'tenants' of 11 group homes in South London. 90% of the tenants were over the age of 45, most were women who had spent long periods in psychiatric hospitals and were largely diagnosed as being schizophrenic. Two-thirds had been living in the group home for more than two years at the time of interview. The majority were unemployed. Ryan construed effectiveness of the group home in terms of the tenants' autonomy, quality of life and weekly running costs. He found that about half of all decisions were taken on tenants' own personal responsibility, the remainder being group decisions or decisions made by staff. There was some relationship between professional supervision and decision making autonomy; homes supervised by social workers having more individual decision making than did homes supervised by community nurses.

Quality of life was assessed in terms of participation in community affairs, richness of interpersonal contact, degree of autonomy and degree of satisfaction. Ryan concluded that group homes are no more a part of the community than are local hospitals, that social contacts within group homes are not very close (53% are brief formal conversations with staff or fellow residents), and seemed to assert that the social withdrawal typically associated with schizophrenia had in the context of the comparatively free lifestyle of the group home resulted in a degree of underactivity in the tenants.

Costs are not however as difficult to assess. In 1976, when Ryan conducted his survey, the cost per hostel resident in a parallel survey ranged from £41.96 to £61.21 per resident week: in group homes the running costs per resident week were £1.11.

Finally, Pritlove (1976) carried out an extensive and detailed analysis of one eight-bedded group home in Leeds between 1973 and 1975. The residents were men, most of whom had been moved from a local authority staffed hostel for ex-psychiatric patients, aged 40−60, single, without family and with diagnoses ranging from subnormality and brain damage to manic depression and schizophrenia. Criteria for evaluation were generated from both staff and residents and were allied to the original objectives of the home which were:

1. To provide a secure environment for men with a history of psychiatric disorder, where they can grow to their fullest level of independence in terms of work, relationships and self-care. This level may be either within the home or beyond it.
2. The function of the house is also preventive in that it seeks to avoid the situations of loneliness and lack of support that have led to breakdowns in the past. (p. 367)

Pritlove scored descriptive accounts of changes in individual situations to evaluate independence levels, and assessed the preventive component by counting the number of residents who required to be admitted to a staffed hostel or to a psychiatric hospital. His conclusion was that:

. . . the group home, while not increasing residents' independence, appeared to preserve it at current levels, and this was associated with no significant group solidarity among residents, and with a consistent element of 'institutional' dependence on supervisors.

Group homes, then, regardless of the criteria of effectiveness taken by the assessors, are not noticeably effective at achieving their stated goals. They are, however, much cheaper than comparable forms of community provision. But should cost be the major factor in deciding on a particular form of care for this group of people? Before we conclude that group homes are ineffective but cheap let us go back one stage in the analysis and have a look at the research itself, for it is our contention that the research does not in fact provide any sort of satisfactory account of the effectiveness or otherwise of group homes. It fails to do this for three main reasons. Firstly, methods used are fairly unsophisticated, tending to rely on self-report questionnaires and largely avoiding the use of control groups. Secondly, the assumption is made that the behavioural measures taken are relevant to the success of a group home. Yet there is no evidence, for example, that sheer frequency of contact with a community is actually indicative of integration with that community. And thirdly, the blanket concepts used, such as 'integration', 'independence' and 'autonomy' are notoriously difficult to define and have no formally agreed meaning.

If the research is on the wrong track where should it be redirected? We would suggest that the inappropriate direction has resulted from researchers addressing the wrong question.

All the studies mentioned attempt to *describe* behaviours which have *a priori* been taken to indicate some particular parameter such as integration or independence. Although it is therefore possible on a frequency basis to establish how many residents perform certain acts, it does not answer the question of why some individuals and homes achieve high levels of independence whereas others do not. In other words there is no adequate attempt to *explain how* group homes work. It is why people behave in the way they do when they are placed in groups that is important, not how well these people can justify other people's essentially moralistic rationale for putting them in small groups in the first place. It is one thing to put a number of middle aged men and women with mental handicap or a history of psychiatric disability in a largely single-sex home and expect them to behave like a two-generational mixed sex family next door, it is quite another thing altogether to then try to evaluate how close they come to this ideal without taking into account how small groups work, how marginals survive, how group norms are established, how leaders evolve, how friendships are made and how groups interact with other groups. It is our contention therefore that any attempt to analyse group homes must take account of their working dynamics, and this must include an analysis of both the role of the supervisor and of the community. It is here that the SPA has relevance.

15.4 SPA and Group Homes

An initial difficulty centres on the question of terminology. 'Group home' conveys very little of what group homes are actually like. Perhaps if we were to reverse the term and call it a 'home for a group' it becomes clear that we are dealing with a fairly complex entity, consisting of the deliberate creation of a small group of stigmatized individuals, their placement in a 'typical' house next to identical houses containing 'normal' people, and then attempting to influence the dynamics of the situation to ensure that their lives are improved in the way in which the home's instigators originally intended. In order to clarify some of the major issues involved the analysis will be divided into three sections:

1. Formal analysis of the problem.
2. Statement of the objectives of the social worker.
3. Outline of the techniques used by the social worker.

Formal Analysis

Let us begin by making a fairly arbitrary but nevertheless useful distinction between manifest and latent problems. Manifest problems are those facets of group home membership which are readily observable to outsiders and which can generate immediate feelings of 'difference'. They have traditionally been a centre-point for social work intervention. Latent problems refer to those inter-personal and intergroup dynamics which underlie the genesis of these feelings of 'difference, prejudice and stigmatization' unrecognized by those outside the situation and unlikely to be recognized by those in it. It is in this area of latent problems that the SPA provides its main thrust.

Manifest v. latent problems. Manifest problems are easy to identify. Poverty, poor dress, unusual physical appearance, and different social skills are common presenting problems of the group home residents which the supervising officer is typically expected to influence. The supervising officer obviously takes considerable time and trouble to try to ameliorate these manifest problems encouraging residents to become more like those around them. This demanifestation of the visible difference has recently become insti-tutionalized, in that an increasing number of psychiatric hospitals are seeing it as part of their brief to carry out this work with the potential residents prior to discharge. However, even if all potential group home residents walk through the hospital gates for the last time with no visible stigma and with sufficient money to maintain appearances, this will not necessarily facilitate integration, since the crucial problems are those inherent in actually being a group home member. These dynamic latent problems in the group home process can be divided into four types:

(i)   The relationship between group members.
(ii) The relationship between the social worker and the group members.
(iii) The relationship between the group home and the community.
(iv) The relationship between the group home plus social worker and the community.

Intragroup relationships. A commonly held desire for group home membership is that members should like each other. On the basis of social psychology data one might be forgiven for believing that this should in fact be the case. Group home members have been thrown together in close physical proximity and several studies (Festinger *et al.*, 1950; Byrne, 1961; Priest & Sawyer, 1967; Segal, 1974) have shown that mere proximity is a powerful influence on interpersonal attraction. Furthermore, the residents have led fairly similar lives and other studies have shown that perceived similarity leads to liking (Berscheid & Walster, 1969; Insko & Schopler, 1972; Rubin, 1973). Moreover these processes would presumably be accelerated in group homes since there is a tendency to select potential residents on the basis of how complementary their skills are likely to be, and again complementarity in the context of a fairly intense relationship where mutual needs can be satisfied,

193

typically leads to friendship formation (Wagner, 1975; Winch, 1958). In MàcAndrew's sample, 37 out of 48 residents did in fact say that they got on well with the other residents; however, 11 obviously did not. It would be interesting to have had some idea of what went wrong in these 11 cases — whether the problems were in initial selection, whether any particular incident had occurred to generate ill-feeling, whether it was associated with psychiatric illness itself, whether or how the supervisor dealt with the situation, and what plans had been formulated to change the intragroup dynamics.

As the group evolves a variety of phenomena can be predicted on the basis of social psychological research on small groups. The residents will participate differentially in the life of the group (Bales, 1950), and this social differentiation may well lead to the creation of one and possibly two group leaders — a task leader whose energies are directed towards getting things done, and a socio-emotional leader who is more concerned with maintaining affable relationships between the group members (Burke, 1968). Such sharp differentiation occurs most frequently in groups of four to five and upwards where there is a fairly low degree of structure, and as such is of *prima facie* relevance to group homes.

Members of groups conform to group norms (Sherif, 1936), where a norm is a 'socially devised standard that provides a framework for interpretation and evaluation' (Harrison, 1976). Different groups develop different norms and norms developed in group settings will continue to influence a group member even when he is alone. Such conformity is influenced by personality traits, the properties of a particular task, and the properties of the group. Conforming individuals tend to be young and unskilled or to have a history of conforming behaviour (Tuddenham, 1959; Allen & Newtson, 1972). A conformity-inducing task is one which is difficult and ambiguous (Deutsch and Gerrard, 1955), and a group conforms more which has a higher number of conforming members (Gerard *et al.*, 1968). As ex-patients, group home members will have been part of one of the most conformity inducing of all institutions — the psychiatric hospital. They will almost certainly transfer these induced norms of behaviour to the group home, norms which will be different from, if not in direct contrast with, those of the outside community — dependence on staff, adherence to a strict daily routine, dormitory sleeping arrangements, homosexuality, and the avoidance of conflict. The supervisor is typically held responsible for either changing these norms or for monitoring their consequences.

The group home and the supervising social worker. Social workers who supervise group homes frequently talk of the conflict such a role creates for them. It is not easy to decide whether to try to become a member of the group home, the group leader, or whether it is more desirable to merely be an outside adviser. There is some evidence to indicate that unless the social worker identifies with the group and adopts the norms of the group members, he will never be accepted as part of the group. On the other hand, given that the norms the group members retain from their time in psychiatric hospital contain an element of dependency on outside staff, there may well be a strong drive from

194

the residents to force the social worker to remain an outsider, yet responsible for their decisions. Pritlove comments that this was the case in his sample, and added that there is also a tendency for staff to prefer to give advice and to oppose attempts by the residents to make their own decisions.

The social worker then is in a marginal situation, attempting to identify with and support the group home members without actually becoming a member himself, and simultaneously being a member of the same outgroup who placed the group members in the stigmatized situation in the first place. It is perhaps worth noting that only the social worker has this choice, the residents can only adhere to the group contained within the home and have no opportunity to hide behind membership of other groups, such as a professional group, or a peer group.

The group home and the community. Being a member of any group creates feelings of ingroup preferential bias (Tajfel, 1970), in other words all things being equal, the group member will attach greater value to his own group than to an outgroup. When the ingroup is characterized by strong negative views of the outgroup, prejudicial attitudes can be evoked, that is feelings that are irrational, unjust and cold hearted. Membership of a group home typically implies membership of a subordinate and in this case highly stigmatized group. Since a group member's very identity is itself highly dependent on this sense of belonging to a group (Breakwell, 1982), then any threat to the group is all the more painful. Once an individual has been identified as a member of a particular group a number of unfavourable personality traits can be attributed by the perceiver. These stereotypes are fixed attitudes about the psychological and social attributes of the members of the given group. They are prejudicial in that they are irrational and unjust in that they generalize about people as members of a group rather than as individuals (Signall & Page, 1971).

Potentially, then, the setting up of a group home is an act which can generate feelings of prejudice and stereotyped attitudes which can lead to discrimination, making desired resources inaccessible to the group home residents. Such resources might be employment, access to social activities and membership of élite subgroups such as the Rotary Club. This in turn can lead to a self-fulfilling prophesy, when the residents behave in the manner the community expects them to behave (as 'typical' mental patients).

What we have then when we attempt to establish a group home is a recipe for potential if not actual strife between group home members and sections of the larger community. Account must be taken of such intergroup conflict (discussed in detail in Chapter 5) in any analysis of group homes and as such should be part of the brief of the supervising social worker.

The social worker, the group home and the community. Social work involvement with group homes is under-researched. When social workers publish accounts of group homes the tendency is simply to outline the major events in the life of the home without mention of the form their own interventions have taken. This might be modesty, though given the low 'success' rate of group homes is perhaps more likely to reflect the lack of precise formulation of what constitutes relevant and useful information. An attempt will be made later to outline both the objectives and possible techniques of social work intervention, though it might be useful to make a few initial comments.

Firstly, it is apparent that any supervisor of a group home has to be prepared to grapple with an enormous range of manifest and latent problems, from establishing satisfactory intragroup relationships to resolving intergroup conflict.

Secondly, conventional social work training takes little account of the sort of issues we have outlined (see Chapters 9 and 10), and therefore social workers probably operate on either a common-sense level dealing with problems as best they can as and when they arise, or they attempt to operationalize, perhaps inappropriately, techniques they were taught in training, notably casework. It is perhaps because neither approach has been shown to be effective that there is a dearth of practical information on what social workers actually do with group homes.

And thirdly, when there is an indication of actual practice methods, they do not always seem to have been appropriate. It is fairly common, for example, for social workers to attempt to prevent possible intergroup conflict by organizing public meetings for the dissemination of general information prior to the formal opening of a group home. Unfortunately, these are also often a forum for the expression of prejudicial views and can focus discrimination more accurately than might otherwise be the case. A slightly different approach to preventive work is implicit in Dutton and Lake's (1973) theory of reverse discrimination. They argue that if people consider themselves unprejudiced then they will actively seek to give preferential treatment to members of the minority group to prove to themselves that they are not prejudiced. To a hard pressed social worker this might indicate that the advertising for public meetings should seem to attract those members of the community in favour of the notion of a group home, whose support should then be gently threatened, in anticipation of useful spin-offs thereafter.

It might also be worth mentioning at this point that a number of studies have attempted to derive strategies for the resolution of conflict once preventive techniques have failed. Although no firm conclusions have been reached, Amir (1969) and Pettigrew (1971) argue that intergroup contact can reduce conflict, particularly when there are a number of similarities between the groups. Culbertson (1957) favoured role playing of minority group membership by members of the outgroup, while Cook (1970) emphasized among other factors that interaction might usefully occur in a situation where goodwill and harmony might reasonably be anticipated — tea or drinks at the group home or attendance by the group home members at community parties or celebrations might be appropriate.

The second stage of the analysis is to look in more detail at the parties involved in the creation and maintenance of a group home, at their motives, their objectives and at the sources of power, for it is only by looking at the complete nexus that appropriate and effective strategies of intervention can be postulated. The diagramatic summary in Table 15.1 conveys the essentials of the analysis.

196

Table 15.1

The parties involved	Their motives	Their objectives	Power ?
The creators	Political ideology Financial 'Humanistic'	Cheap resources Good public relations Integration	Yes
The producers	'Political' 'Humanistic'	To realize ideology	Yes
The cast	'Individualistic'	Freedom Independence Employment Marriage, etc.	Yes
The audience	Moralistic Pragmatic	Readmission	Yes

The parties involved. The theatrical format adopted is similar to that used by Goffman (1959). Group homes have been developed as a response to a combination of governmental policy preference for community care and pressure group influence to close down large asylums: the creators are therefore a number of governmental policy committees and such voluntary bodies as MIND.

By producers we refer to those organizations and individuals who convert the idea into reality. The house itself is generally made available by the local Housing Department or by a Housing Association; the residents are provided by the local psychiatric or mental subnormality hospital; the DHSS provides the basic living expenses in the form of benefits; frequently a voluntary body such as the Rotary Club provides the furnishings and the Social Services Department or hospital provides a supervisor. The resource provided by each of the producers is crucial, and it is likely that without any one of them the home could not begin to work.

The cast consists of a number of ex-long-term patients who either want to leave hospital or have been persuaded to do so (MacAndrew, 1980). They may or may not have received preparation beforehand, they may or may not have been deliberately selected to constitute a working group, it is fairly likely that they all lived in the same institution for a considerable number of years, and fairly unlikely that their general views and behaviour are similar to those of the majority of the members of the community in which they are going to live.

Finally, we have the observing audience, consisting largely of a number of mixed sex, two generational families living in similar houses on the same estate. It is likely that the majority are passively indifferent to the presence of a group of ex-patients in their midst as long as they are not adversely affected either pragmatically or 'emotionally' by the home's existence, a number of individuals will be actively opposed to the presence of the group home members, and hopefully there will also be some individuals who will do what they can to help the group home members settle into the community.

Their motives. The motives underlying both the act of caring and the act of rejection are difficult to establish with any degree of certainty, since not only are they rarely committed to print, but they tend to remain largely unrecognized by the parties involved and often fall under the banner of latent problems mentioned earlier. They are nevertheless important since they should influence the objectives and also give some indication of how likely a particular party is to be influenced by a certain form of intervention.

Government policy forming bodies tend to be influenced by the combination of ideology, practicality, cost and public acceptance. At the time when the group homes were first mooted on any scale, in the 1960s, this form of care seemed to meet all the criteria. Although it is probably fair to say that faith in the ability of the community to care has diminished in the light of experience, nevertheless group homes remain practical to establish and cheap to run.

Voluntary bodies, notably MIND, seem to be driven by a rather more missionary zeal. MIND remains committed to the notion of community care and has remained apparently untroubled by research findings indicating that group homes are perhaps not as effective as they were originally believed to be. In this light it would be interesting to know whether MIND's apparent belief that group homes would act as a means of encouraging the public to believe in the curability of mental illness has retained its strength.

By way of contrast the producers do not seem to have any particularly strong driving force. They seem to see their function as operating as the paid staff of the creators, assisted by some enthusiastic volunteers. Assuming some congruence with the motives of the creators, it could be said that they too exhibit ideological and humanistic drives, though in practical terms they merely oil the wheels. Without the cooperation of any one of them, however, it is likely that any particular scheme could not progress.

The motives of the cast are not easy to establish with any degree of conviction. It is commonly argued that group home members, being ex-long-term patients, will exhibit a low degree of drive and motivation to do anything, a combination of their mental illness itself and of many years in total institutions, where thinking for oneself is not always required. However, MacAndrew asserts that in his sample the cast wished to leave the hospital in order to achieve greater freedom and independence. Whether they actively preferred to seek this in a group home as opposed to some other form of community care remains an open question.

Audience motivation is similarly difficult to establish. Some members of the community will indeed actively strive to support successful 'integration' of the group home members into the community, while experience indicates that more powerful factions are prepared to go out of their way to oppose the establishment or continued presence of a group home classically justifying their opposition in terms of the effect of the group home on housing prices or of the danger of the group home residents to the children of the neighbours. The

198

mechanics underlying these feelings of stereotyping and prejudice have been discussed earlier.

Their objectives. The presumed objective of government policy is to create an extensive network of cheap community-based provision for the 'old' and 'new' long-term chronic patients, so that large, expensive and outdated asylums and mental handicap hosptials can be gradually run down. It would probably be somewhat realistic to assume that community integration is seen as less of an objective and more as an added bonus should it happen.

MIND's support of group homes seems to be part of a larger objective which is to improve the lot of the psychiatric patient in general by returning the patient to the community from which he or she came as quickly as possible and hence to reduce the amount of time to a minimum that the psychiatric patient spends in the many large traditional asylums.

More prosaically such producers as the DHSS, Housing Department, and to an extent the Social Services Department, are concerned with enabling the creators, the cast and the audience to develop a working relationship. Objectives, if they are formulated, are imprecise and largely unpublished, and tend to reflect indecision.

The objectives of the residents are a matter for conjecture. Escaping the asylum? Independence? Marriage and a family? Employment? Or perhaps more likely, they have no real objectives at all, and the group home simply offers a touch of variety within a troubled life.

Finally, of course, we have the audience. Objectives are rarely explicit and have to be assumed from behaviour. The minority will do all they can to encourage the residents to settle in the community, the majority will remain passively indifferent, and a minority will actively seek to harm the residents in an attempt to force them to return to the hospital from whence they came.

Their power. Pritlove argues that in a group home power has two facets, control and support and that 'this is a vital problem in a situation where different groups have different expectations of each other, and one man's independence may mean another man's loss of face, dependence, or even breakdown'. He goes on to apply this to what he sees as being the two sources of power — the residents and the staff, and concludes that there are eight types of group home in terms of the use of power (see Table 15.2).

This raises a number of issues. Firstly, the staff referred to by Pritlove actually live in the home, and there is some doubt about whether he is in fact talking about a group home or a staffed hostel. Secondly, his account of power is essentially dyadic and takes no account of the larger power base within which group homes have their place. Both the residents and staff are controlled or supported by what we have called earlier the creators, the producers and the audience.

If we adopt Lukes' (1974) definition of power a different and perhaps more useful picture of the power structure inherent in group homes is created. Lukes asserts that '*a* exercises power over *b* when *a* effects *b* in a manner contrary to *b*'s

199

Table 15.2 Models of Accommodation in Terms of Staff Power and Residential Support (with Analogous Residential Settings)

		Staff power			
		Coercive	Normative	Utilitarian	Absent
Residents support for each other	Positive	(POW camp ?)	Therapeutic community		'Happy family'
	Negative	'Institution'	Paternalistic hostel	Bedsit	'Problem family'

interests'. Looked at in this way power is multifaceted and each of the parties involved is capable of exerting some power over one or more of the other parties. From the point of view of the supervising officer it could be argued that true power lies in the ability to identify where the seat of power is in the group home nexus and to be able to manipulate it.

Considerable power is inherent in the role of the creators. A shifting government policy or preference for a new form of community care would threaten the continued expansion of group homes and might possibly, by shifting resources elsewhere, lead to extensive closure of existing group homes. This is a very real possibility unless group homes can be shown to be effective in what they purport to do.

Each of the producers controls a particular resource which if withdrawn would have severe repercussions for the residents, particularly since each resource is largely dependent upon the other resources to be of value. There is no point in having a house if you cannot pay the rent or do not have any furnishings. The role of supervisor is largely wasted at the moment though potentially the supervisor could be a key figure in the network of power. The role might range from the more traditional one of assessing whether the resident is showing 'satisfactory progress' and as a consequence he should be readmitted to hospital, to negotiating the boundary between the ingroup and outgroup and, as such, influencing the likely extent of integration with the community.

The residents can and do exert power over each other and over the quality and extent of relationships with the outside community. Residents can be skilled manipulators, who if for what ever reason take a dislike to one of their fellow residents, are quite capable of creating or capitalizing on situations to incriminate their colleague with the aim of rejecting him from the home (Rowett & Dews, 1979).

The greatest power perhaps rests with the community. In theory at least complete community rejection of a group home would lead to an intolerable situation for the residents and to their readmission to hospital. Although this is most unlikely to happen, variations on the theme of acceptance/rejection seem to be present in most communities where group homes have been established.

Power in this situation is vested in the dominant group which is determined by such factors as local press coverage, preparatory work from the producers, and the actual behaviour of the residents.

The Objectives of the Social Worker

Given that we have a complex mixed-power situation resting on dynamics ranging from the interpersonal to intergroup levels, with the prime responsibility being thrust on the social worker to handle the situation, what are the objectives of the social worker? MIND (1972) doubts neither the importance of having a social worker, 'It is essential for the residents in a group home to have adequate social work support', nor the role the social worker should adopt:

> The social worker in consultation with the general practitioner in many cases, should be responsible for any professional matters concerning the residents, such as readmission to hospital if this becomes necessary, difficulties over supplementary benefits or personality clashes among residents. The social worker will encourage the residents to function as a group and co-operate with the rent collecter in dealing with practical problems. The residents may need additional help in integrating with the community and in finding new interest.

The objectives of the social worker are therefore to liaise with the GP, deal with the money, create a smooth group and facilitate integration with the out-group (that is to resolve intergroup conflict with the ultimate aim of changing the group membership of the residents from that of being a member of a group home to being a member of the community).

Gardham *et al.* (1977) are a little more adventurous in the objectives they attribute to homes for the mentally handicapped residents, allying them with those of the more general objectives of services for the mentally handicapped — 'A satisfying environment . . . social education and stimulation, purposeful occupation and employment . . .'

Young (1977) adheres to a somewhat more traditional and perhaps a more generally accepted view of social work involvement with residential communities — 'Social workers have a particular skill in understanding and correctly interpreting . . . crisis situations/personal upset . . . to try and resolve such reactions and exclude external social causes before it can be assumed that the problem requires medical treatment.'

Social work objectives therefore seem to range from dealing with anxiety to collecting the rent, from creating a 'good group' to facilitating integration with the community. Now it seems to us that this means in effect that the fate of the residents rests with the particular social worker who happens to be allocated to the home. Social work credibility might be better served by the adoption of a clearer statement of objectives, achievable by the adoption of suitable techniques and strategies. These objectives are:

(i) To facilitate the development of relationships between three to eight ex-patients living in a conventional house in the community acceptable to each resident and consistent with community norms.

201

(ii) To prevent or resolve conflict between group home members and the community.

(iii) To enable the residents to change successfully group membership, from being a member of the group home to being a member of the community.

The Techniques Used by the Social Worker

Social work methodology has traditionally taken the form of casework, with excursions into group work and community work and a more recent liking for the unitary or integrated approach (Chapter 12). The SPA leads to techniques based on the ability to locate the sources of power in conflict situations and to manipulate them to achieve the desired goals consistent with the available predictive data. Thus the actual work performed by the social worker will vary according to the specific nature of the problem, the parties involved and the peculiar nexus of power. The approach is empirically based and essentially rational; this, together with the emphasis on large-scale dynamics makes it fundamentally different to conventional forms of social work intervention.

We offer below a procedural plan with allied techniques designed to achieve the three objectives mentioned earlier:

(i)   On referral, decide on your particular moral/value stance towards group homes. If these are congruent with the likely demands from the referring agencies, proceed with your involvement; if not refer elsewhere.

(ii) Establish with all relevant parties the precise objectives of the group home and how you are going to evaluate these objectives. This might involve a meeting of all parties and the recruitment of an outside specialist familiar with empirical methods. This might involve a link with a university department, a teaching college or a CQSW course. It could be appropriate to establish a base line of behaviour, that is to observe and evaluate the behaviour of residents while in the hospital with a view to comparing chosen parameters with their subsequent behaviour while in the group home. There are a number of variations on this scheme, for example, comparing the behaviour of the experimental group in the group home with a control group who remain in hospital, alternatively discharging the residents to a group home which has a social work supervisor as opposed to a community nurse supervisor.

(iii) Select a stable group and establish a high degree of affiliation and liking prior to discharge. Selection might necessitate the involvement of a hospital psychologist or occupations' officer to evaluate the complementarity of skills and interest. It might be possible to create situations in the hospital where the residents are able to spend time together in pleasant unstressful surroundings, perhaps in task oriented small groups with appropriate rewards.

(iv) Reduce the manifest differences between the potential group home members and the community outgroup. This will involve the buying of a range of modern clothing, training in personal hygiene, and possibly retraining in social skills.

(v)   Decrease or deflect potential prejudice and discrimination from the outgroup by actively encouraging supporters rather than critics to public meetings and limit the amount of general information provided to the outgroup. Use this meeting to identify key supporters from the community and involve them subsequently.

(vi)   Locate the leader or leaders within the group home and encourage the development of appropriate new group norms. Pre-discharge preparation should have given some idea of the likely leaders, though this might be confirmed by behaviour in such allocated tasks as cleaning, gardening and shopping. Of the many new norms that might be developed, having one's own money, own frontdoor key, own outside interests, own friends and own group memberships might be emphasized.

(vii)   Locate the power source in the group home community nexus and decide whether it is in your power to manipulate. If it is not, liaise with agencies more capable of influence. It might, for example, be appropriate to involve the local press, the local community worker, local teachers if children are stone-throwing, and possibly the chairman of the local Working Men's Club.

(viii)   Encourage interaction between the group home members and the outgroup in settings conducive to feelings of well-being, and be present yourself as you are the negotiator between the boundaries of group home membership and outgroup membership.

Finally, remember that your ultimate objective is to create a happy group living self-sufficiently in the community with the minimum of attributed marginality, a long-term ideal is to change their group membership from being a member of a group home to being a member of the community. We believe that the procedural plan outlined above, tailored to a particular situation and backed by research will make a contribution to the understanding of why people behave as they do when a number of ex-patients are placed in a house in the community. If we can understand why people behave in a certain way then perhaps we stand a chance of influencing the situation and can be a little more optimistic about the fate of group home residents than existing research would indicate.

15.5   Conclusions

In this chapter we have looked at the application of the SPA to the study of group homes, with particular interest in the role of the social worker. Although fashionable and increasingly numerous, with backing from most relevant agencies, such research as has been carried out on group homes seems to indicate that they are largely ineffective in meeting their stated objectives. This statement, however, remains unproven in that research has tended to look at the frequency of a number of behaviours performed by the group home members, prejudged to constitute a manifestation of the required behavioural objective. Little if any account has been taken of the mechanisms that cause a group home to work or to break down. By analysing the phenomena from the SPA we have concentrated on a number of areas that have so far been neglected in a study of group homes — friendship formation, group membership, group differentiation, prejudice, discrimination and intergroup dynamics — areas which we contend are crucial for the supervising officer to examine and manipulate if any significant contribution is to be made to influence the lifestyle of the group home member. Finally, by looking at possible objectives of the social worker and techniques that might be utilized by the social worker, we have given some pointers towards the practice methods a social worker might use if he chooses to adopt the SPA.

16
Child Battering

A substantial portion of the coverage given by the media to social work has concentrated on cases where social workers have been involved with children who have been beaten or killed by their parents. At times, social work has been virtually synonymous with unsuccessful intervention on behalf of the child. This intense media interest perhaps reflects a more widespread change of societal expectations towards the behaviour and attitudes parents 'should' adopt to their children. Although children do not have an identity in law (Ford in Smith, 1978), it has increasingly been recognized that they have a right to those requirements considered necessary for the development of a positive personal and social identity. Explicitly or implicitly, much of the energy of those numerous practitioners involved in work with battered children has been directed towards this end. The purpose of the present chapter is to examine in what ways the SPA might be of use to a social worker with a battered child on her or his caseload. The structure of the chapter is as follows:

(i)   Historical background
(ii) The battered child syndrome
(iii) Current societal response
(iv) Use of the SPA

16.1   Historical Background

Detailed accounts of the history of parental ill-treatment of their children are contained in a number of texts (Carver, 1978; Walters, 1975; Smith, 1978). They portray a consistent picture, accurately miniaturized by Smith (1978):

It is a fact that throughout recorded time, the killing, maiming, abandonment, starving, neglect, cruel punishment and sexual exploitation of children have been a feature of the life experience of every generation. Sometimes it has been given sanction by tradition and ritual usage; more often, it has been a matter of private acts committed in shameful secrecy. Only very recently, in historical terms, has any concern been voiced about the problem of maltreated children.

Analyses of the various changes of perspective developed by parents towards their children are plentiful: explanations of the changes are less easy to come by. Jobling (in Carver, 1978) argues that Graeco-Roman culture considered babies to be 'hardly human, more of a little animal'. They were sacrificed to the gods, to various lower deities and mythical figures, and if deformed, were left to die in exposed places to increase the strength of the bloodline. The Middle Ages reflected an attitude of benign indifference to children: they were seen as small immature adults who were expected to adopt the full adult role — work and marriage — as soon as possible. Children could be apprenticed at the age of seven or eight and sold in marriage in their early teens. The sixteenth and seventeenth centuries saw a perception of the child coloured by the stained glass of religion. The child was a potential repository of both good and evil: the parental role was to ensure, by physical discipline, that goodness held sway. The Industrial Revolution of the eighteenth century correlated with a period of increased interest in the subjective experience of childhood, heightened by the liking of the Romantics for the notion of childhood innocence. The Victorians, spiced by guilt, continued the tradition of harsh discipline of their children, but were slowly influenced by the growth of 'scientific' interest in childhood, later to be given a focus by the work of Darwin and Freud. The current century witnessed greater concern for the quality of mother-child relationships, and a happy and united family has become the desired goal. Physical punishment of children remains generally acceptable; though Britain is the only European country that legally permits corporal punishment of schoolchildren.

Obviously, the above is nothing more than an extended caricature of the changes in parent – child relationships that may have taken place over the years, based largely on analyses of a select number of written accounts. The purpose of the presentation is to indicate the perceived contrast between current concepts of the needs of children and those that have gone before. Child 'battering' is not only a new term, it is a new concept, and seems to reflect a fundamental change in the normative expectations of society about the way parents should treat their offspring. The social worker, perhaps more than other practitioners, has been vested with the role of ensuring that these normative expectations are upheld.

16.2 The Battered Child Syndrome

The first legal challenge to the parents' absolute rights over their children was made in 1870 in New York by the Society for the Prevention of Cruelty to Animals. A church missionary, working in the Hell's Kitchen district, came upon a young girl — Mary Ellen — who sufferred fierce and frequent beatings from her parents. Receiving no help from the authorities as there were no legal grounds on which to protect a child from the parents, the missionary presented the case to the SPCA, who took the child to court and asked that action be taken to protect her as an 'animal'. The court accepted the motion and the parents were convicted and imprisonned. Shortly thereafter, a society for the protection of children was formed in New York and various other American cities. In England, Liverpool followed suit in 1883, and in 1891 31 societies amalgamated to form the National Society for the Protection of Cruelty to Children.

Tardieu, a French forensic scientist, was the first — in 1860 — to describe child ill-treatment in medical and social terms. The first case description in England was presented by West in 1888 who attempted to explain the existence of 'acute periosteal swellings in several young infants of the same family'. Though his original diagnosis of rickets seems to have been incorrect, the case generated an amount of medical interest in the phenomena of unexplained bruising and swellings in young children.

Although the X-ray was discovered in 1895 it was not until 1946 that Caffey and his associates began gradually to develop the view that cases of multiple fractures in various stages of healing, in the long bones of some infants referred to them, were caused by trauma rather than disease. Caffey received general support from his colleagues but public dissemination of the information was largely constrained until 1962 when Kempe, an American, deliberately coined the emotive term 'the battered child syndrome'. He had surveyed 749 children who had experienced some form of non-accidental injury, and found that 78 of them had died and 114 had suffered permanent brain damage. Kempe was in no doubt that physical abuse by parents or caretakers was a major cause of the death and maiming. The British Paediatric Association circulated a memorandum to doctors in 1966 summarizing the current information on the syndrome. Kempe's (1962) definition of the phrase was generally accepted:

> . . . a clinical condition in young children who have received serious physical abuse, generally from a parent or foster parent. The syndrome should be considered in any child exhibiting evidence of fracture of any bone, subdural hematoma, failure to thrive, soft tissue swelling or skin bruising, in any child who dies suddenly, or where the degree and type of injury is at variance with the history given regarding the occurrence of the trauma.

Though differing terminologies have been proferred and used, for example child abuse, non-accidental injury, Tardieu's syndrome, parent — infant traumatic stress syndrome, they have all referred to substantially the same entity. Once established, the syndrome was sought and found throughout the world (see, for example, West Australian Department for Community Welfare, 1975), and research studies proliferated, examining all possible aspects of the phenomenon and attempting to devise means of ensuring its eradication. It is probably fair to say, however, that research has been bedevilled by differing sampling techniques, and methodological approaches;

results and opinions have become intermingled, and the development of effective intervention skills confounded. What has occurred, however, is the rapid development of formal procedures for dealing with child abuse cases, procedures that involve a plethora of disciplines and the notions of shared responsibility and a nominated 'key worker'.

Estimates of prevalence indicate that some 4000–5000 children per annum are probably battered in Britain, with a 10% mortality rate (Smith, 1975, p. 33; Hall in Franklin, 1975, p. 11). Hall asserts that:

> Both the hospital and police figures suggest that between 4000 and 5000 children every year . . . will require legal action to be taken by the hospital or social services . . . An equal number will also require close supervision for their protection as the evidence will be insufficient to support an application for a care order.

In other words, 450 children may be killed each year, 4000–5000 sets of parents will be involved in legal proceedings and a further 4000–5000 children and parents will receive close supervision. The proportion of social work time spent on such cases can only be conjectured but must be considerable.

One of the most interesting and concerning expositions of the state of research findings on the battered child syndrome is contained in Smith (1975). After reviewing previous studies, and in the light of his own extensive controlled study of 134 battered infants in the West Midlands, Smith came to a series of conclusions not calculated to reassure professionals involved in such cases. Among the more significant of his concluding comments (pp. 217–219) were the following.

(i) The tendency to perpetuate child abuse in successive generations is not diminished by supplying extensive medical and social help to battering parents.

(ii) 60% of children who return home are re-battered.

(iii) Baby batterers are far less handicapped in social and economic terms than previously believed.

(iv) Battering parents have not necessarily experienced poor parenting themselves.

(v) Baby battering is strikingly similar to other forms of deviant behaviour in that it occurs with other social inadequacies or failures of adaptation, rather than in isolation.

(vi) 'No study has convincingly shown that any treatment of battering parents is effective.' (p. 218)

16.3 Current Societal Response

Contrary to many of the images portrayed in the media, the formal societal response to child battering has not been to delegate all responsibility to social workers. Rather, there has been general agreement in both theoretical and procedural terms that a number of different practitioners should be involved with each such case as a matter of course. Thus in any particular case all or any combination of the following may be involved: social worker (social services) social worker (NSPCC), health visitor, general practitioner, paediatrician, midwife, teacher, police, magistrate, solicitor. Overseeing all, is the watchful myopic eye of the press. Although this does ensure that each of the various perspectives represented by the numerous practitioners has an opportunity for expression, it also ensures that the inherent conflict generated by incompatible perspectives has to be resolved. There may well be, for example, need for considerable negotiation between a policeman who considers battering primarily as a crime and that 'There should never be a case where an abused child . . . is returned to the same domestic environment' (Mounsey in Franklin, 1975, p. 127); and the social worker whose view is that 'If children are hastily removed from parental care and no attempt is made to treat or modify the parents' problems, not only may these problems discharge themselves on the next baby, but the parents may carry forward . . . hostility to and suspicion of social workers, health visitors, and so on' (Stroud in Franklin, 1975, p. 96). Tension might also be predicted to exist between the doctor and the social worker: the doctor perceiving the phenomenon as primarily medical; the social worker aware that he or she is likely to be the key worker asked to intervene without the benefit of valid medical techniques. Occasionally the doctor may question the involvement of non-medical staff: '. . . it almost seems as if the medical profession may have abdicated its responsibility to Local Authorities and voluntary organisations . . . Both agencies rely heavily upon inexperienced and possibly inadequately-trained social workers' (Smith, 1975, p. 218). It is hardly surprising that case conferences contain an enormous potential for conflict, and demand a high level of skill from whoever, usually a social worker, functions as chairperson. However, in some senses, the legal framework now dictating reactions to child abuse cases has achieved pre-eminence and in many ways functions as a means of rough riding the white water of interdisciplinary 'cooperation'. To clarify the likely procedures involved a brief example can be given.

Case: Jonathan

A neighbour telephones the local SSD to complain that the noises of a child, Jonathan, screaming have been heard in the house next door on a number of occasions. A social worker visits the home concerned, speaks to the parents and notices that the child, a one-year-old boy, has a black eye. Checking with the office, the social worker finds that the family are not previously known to the department and are not on the Non-Accidental Injury (NAI) register. The social worker persuades the mother to take the child to the local GP for examination, who finds more extensive bruising to the child's back and buttocks. Both parents vehemently assert that the bruises are the result of the child bumping into furniture around the home, and deny absolutely the neighbour's assertions about the child's frequent screaming bouts, saying that the noise must have been mistaken for crying which the child does most nights before he has to go to bed. Apart from the physical bruising there is no other evidence that the child is in any way failing to thrive. The social worker consults senior staff, and a decision is made to call a case conference, to be chaired by the area officer and to which all parties with a possible interest are invited. Options available to the conference might include:

(i) Accept the parents' story at face value and close the case.

(ii) Place the child's name on the register and adopt a watching brief, but without formal intervention.

(iii) Offer the family contact with a particular practitioner.

(iv) Ask for police investigation to be pursued.

(v) If there is sufficient evidence and the damage to the child is sufficiently serious seek to prosecute the parents under section 1 of the 1933 Children and Young Persons Act on the grounds that they are over the age of 16 and have wilfully assaulted, ill-treated, neglected, abandoned, or exposed Jonathan in a manner likely to cause unnecessary suffering or injury to health. Alternatively, if the assault is particularly serious, the accused parent or parents may be charged with grievous bodily harm with intent to injury under section 18 of the Offences against the Person Act, 1861.

(vi) Alternatively, and occasionally simultaneously, legal action may be taken to protect the child under the 1969 Children and Young Persons Act if the court is of the opinion that:

(a) the proper development of the child is being avoidably prevented or neglected or his health is being avoidably impaired or neglected or he is being ill-treated; *and also*

(b) that he is in need of care or control which he is unlikely to receive unless the court makes an order, then the court may make a care order or supervision order for the child.

(For greater elaboration of these and other forms of possible legal action, such as place of safety orders, wardship proceedings, hospital or guardianship orders, and interim care orders, see Hall and Mitchell (1978).)

The decision of this particular case conference is to place the child's name on the NAI register and nominate the social worker originally involved to make further assessment of the case with an immediate brief to arrange, with the parents if possible, for the child's more extensive examination by a consultant paediatrician. Other practitioners, particularly the health visitor and the local GP, indicate that they will take a closer interest.

Obviously such an outline merely scratches the surface of an actual case, and charts only one of the innumerable courses of action that might have been taken by such a conference. However it does permit a number of initial generalizations to be made.

(i) The initial assessment is usually made by a practitioner who visits the child's home and forms an opinion in one visit. At the outset, it is unlikely that the family will have a historical context as far as the practitioner is concerned: what is happening at or about the time of the home visit is crucial. *The practitioner forms impressions and attributes reasons for actions on limited*

210

information. The possible consequences need to be clearly acknowledged.

(ii) *The practitioner, deliberately or unintentionally, is actively pursuing a process likely to discredit aspects of the social and perhaps personal identity of one or both parents.* In doing this, the social worker will perceive the problem through his or her own prejudices or biases, and will select information on that basis. 'Parenthood' is currently held in high esteem: being 'bad parents' can be a fundamental threat to identity. The potentially stigmatized are likely to adopt a number of self-defence tactics which need to be anticipated: ostrich, chameleon and lemming tactics have been outlined in Chapter 4. The practitioner needs also to bear in mind the likely differences in the ability to control impression management techniques between middle class and working class clients.

(iii) *A case conference is a group and its proceedings can be understood in terms of intragroup dynamics.*

(iv) *Leadership of the case conference is likely to be crucial*; a number of differing and potentially conflicting perspectives are represented, and the group has been artificially imposed upon its members.

(v) *The key worker is expected to change attitudes and behaviours, probably against the will of the people concerned.* Attitude change, persuasion techniques, and possibly methods of coercion may be crucial.

There are many other areas that may be considered, but the five mentioned have a particular interest for practitioners wishing to adopt the SPA. Each area has possible SPA inputs, some of which have been mentioned. In this final section, the use of the SPA in child battering cases will be considered, with a particular focus on these five areas. Although the local authority social worker will be given primary consideration, the SPA has potential value for any of the other practitioners involved.

16.4   Use of the SPA

The SPA should be used whenever possible in its full format: part of its value rests in the comprehensive nature of the approach, its concern with describing, analysing and explaining the problem at its multiple levels focused on the key targets of identity, relationships, groups, the environment, and their corollary changes; and in utilizing effective intervention techniques based on the power of the processes of contrual, consistency, comparison and conformity. Occasionally, expectations of the social work role may attempt to predetermine the findings of the SPA. In child battering cases, for example, a primary expectation of the social worker seems to be that he or she will act as the nation's conscience. Sometimes this is stated explicitly: 'The local authority social worker represents the public conscience and must therefore take account of public attitudes' (Drake in Franklin (ed.), 1975, p. 88). Precisely what is meant by the public's conscience and attitudes is not specified but broad limits are given: 'SSDs, in conjunction with other agencies and departments, can give the sort of help and support to a unitary family in the lower income group that

211

might be available to a middle class home or an extended family' (Drake, *op. cit.*, p. 92).

The normative framework to be adopted by the social worker is presumably to be that of the middle class home. The obvious danger of such an approach is that both assessment and 'treatment' may be based on a stereotyped perception that may or may not be relevant to a particular case. The adoption of the SPA will never eradicate this bias: what it will do if used properly is to identify the form the bias takes and examine how it has influenced the analysis. Once completed, the SPA analysis is available for others to comment upon and the reasons for the adoption of particular techniques are identified: research and cross-case comparisons are therefore feasible. Arguing from the normative perspective, the worker may wish to adopt the SPA to facilitate a more thoroughly-based assessment leading to the use of effective control or coercion techniques with the parents.

First Impressions

In terms of the possible repercussions for both the child and parents, the impressions formed by the practitioner and the *attributions* given to events are crucial. Although it is unlikely that a child will be removed from a family upon immediate contact by the practitioner without the most obviously justified reasons — frequently concerned with severe physical maltreatment of the child — nevertheless pressure on the worker to form rapid impressions is considerable in most child abuse cases. Consideration needs to be given to those influences that impinge on the formation of impressions. Three such influences were outlined in Chapter 3: assumptions about human nature, stereotypes and prototypes, and personal constructs. In Jonathan's case it might be, say, that the worker operates on the assumption that 'children need to be cared for at all costs' or 'all children are innocent and must not be corrupted' or that 'parents have rights too'. The assumption held will influence what the worker 'sees', as will whatever stereotypes and prototypes are being used. A fairly common stereotype might be that: 'child batterers all come from the working class' or 'all child batterers have been battered when they were children'. A prototype might be that battering mothers are 'inadequate' — weak, ineffectual, not very bright, beaten in turn by their husbands, and so on. More fundamental perhaps, and certainly more accessible, the worker's own construct system will help determine how well he or she will be able to understand the construct systems of the battering parents. As they are likely to be dissimilar, the likelihood of shared understanding is diminished.

One of the key components of the social worker's interaction with the battering parents centres on the concept of attribution: how the worker explains the actions of the parents. Though such causal schemata as 'parents who hit children are responsible for their actions' may be involved in Jonathan's case, what happens if both mother and father hit Jonathan regularly but neither ever hit his older sister, Helen? Has Jonathan done something to evoke punishment? The worker needs to consider carefully the dynamics of

212

impression formation and attribution processes in the stressful situation of assessing what has gone on in battering cases, and more importantly, who is responsible and how context shapes the behaviour.

Identity

Jonathan's parents have had no contact with the SSD before, and have never been referred to any other agency. They are 'model citizens' apart from their possible treatment of Jonathan, which would not be considered a desirable attribute of model citizenship at the moment. The worker by evaluating them as battering parents, whether rightly or wrongly, has proferred a major blow to their sense of social identity, their public self. Regardless of whether or not the actions of the parents 'deserve' such consequences, the form those consequences will take must be taken into account. As we saw in Chapter 4 'spoiled identities' are a particularly powerful phenomenon. Jonathan's parents, from the time of first contact with the worker, have a potentially discredited social identity, which may or may not be formally discredited by the outcome of the case conference, over which they have no control. Such spoiling of identity may range from imprisonment, to having compulsory contact with a social worker, to simply being aware that other people believe they are 'batterers'. It might be anticipated that 'innocent' parents are at least as likely, if not more likely than guilty ones, to make vehement attempts to retain their identity as non-batterers. In a sense the innocent parents, knowing their behaviour is consistent with their social identity, face the most intense form of stigma, that which is unmerited. The guilty parents on the other hand, know they have to deceive the worker, to 'pass' as non-batterers, to be part of a cat and mouse game. The latter realize they have spoiled aspects of their social identity and have therefore to pass: the former realize they might also be forced to pass without, in fact, needing to do so. Trauma may be confounded if failure to pass has repercussions for other roles performed by the parents. As an active member of the Women's Institute, and a member of the local baby-sitting group, Jonathan's mother may have large segments of her personal as well as social identity threatened. Strategies to overcome such role conflicts are commonplace to most social workers' experience: the father or cohabitee who immediately leaves his wife or girlfriend (a lemming); the mother who denies everything in spite of unequivocal evidence against her or her husband (an ostrich); and the chameleon, the parent who presents the 'appropriate' role to everyone, but still batters the child.

The Case Conference

The conference is probably the crucial factor in the procedure developed to deal with cases of child battering: it is the forum where information is produced and shared, the problem is evaluated, and decisions taken that determine the action to be evoked. Stevenson (in Carver, 1978), from a small study of such conferences, points out areas where conference members indicated particular concern: the location of the conference — another profession's territory is likely to generate feelings of anxiety and insecurity; the language used — communication is hindered by the use of idiosyncratic jargon; and the frames of reference adopted — those professional and personal perspectives which channel attitudes towards the problem behaviour. If the conference is examined more closely — as a particular form of group — a number of additional factors are seen to have a potential for generating inadequate or distorted communication.

The conference as a group. A case conference is a group of some 6 to 20 people, lasting for a number of hours; all members are invited because of their professional role; minutes are carefully taken; it has a leader who may or may not be of a higher social status than the members; cohesion is likely to be poor, with a low level of allegiance to the group; communication is largely verbal face to face; it has been generated to meet a number of complex goals, of differing duration from a variety of sources.

Group membership. For some members, the internal and external criteria of group membership will be incompatible. The police, for example, may consider it perfectly appropriate to attend the conference, but may find it disconcerting that the majority of other members do not share the view that child battering is a crime and should be treated as such. The police may resolve the clash by re-evaluating their perspective, or may decide to try and change the external criteria. At least some of the pressures within the group may arise from a series of such conflicts of varying degrees of intensity, with the sufferers trying out different means of resolving the difficulties. In fact, much energy, which ideally should be channelled into the immediate goal, may be devoted to largely futile attempts to redefine the external criteria.

Norms and conformity processes. It will be fairly unusual for such a group to develop collective norms and exert effective conformity pressures. Opinions are usually discrepant, the overall decision does not necessarily affect each member, the group is not particularly cohesive, personality types are mixed but probably of a fairly independent disposition, and there is little reason for deindividuation to occur. However, paradoxically, pressures to conform are likely to be powerful since the overall function of the group has social importance and the consequences of an error of judgement are so profound and extensive for the members.

Decision making. Pressure towards achieving a positive group experience may lead to 'groupthink' among some group members — a greater concern with the group than with the problem — particularly the less experienced, younger or more passive ones. Influence hierarchies are already fairly highly developed: the view of the consultant paediatrician is likely to have a higher accredited status than that of the health visitor. It might be anticipated that a series of closed communication systems will operate within the larger group: consultants conversing with senior police officers and the area officer, social workers orientating towards NSPCC workers, health visitors, and the district nurse. Alternatively, the bulk of communications may be channelled from the lowest status upwards, minimizing contact between those workers likely to have the greatest contact with the family. Further, having a conference chairperson, and later on a 'key worker' may militate against the successful analysis of a complex problem and the carrying out of agreed tasks: integrating a mass of information presented by individuals with differing perspectives is a stressful task when left to one person. Thus the quality of decisions made by such case conferences may be suspect:

(i)   It is unlikely that a common goal will be agreed.
(ii) Tasks are not usually divided and shared.
(iii) Status differentials may cloud judgements.

Conference Leadership

Clearly conference leadership is a stressful and demanding role. The leader must have the respect and trust of the group members; be capable of listening to all views and integrating information on the basis of its value rather than its source; be task-oriented; and be able to clarify goals and specify solutions. Given that a number of the members will be themselves experienced leaders in their own spheres, pressure may be considerable in the direction of leader-match, the process of matching the leader to the task. Since there is considerable potential for change of leadership within a child abuse conference, pressure for leadermatch may impinge upon the leader's functioning, and the leader may become more concerned with retaining his status than with the task in hand.

Change Techniques

Once nominated, the key worker's fundamental task is likely to be with changing the attitudes and behaviour of the parents, against their will. Usually the notions of persuasion and coercion are little discussed in such situations. Rather, the social worker is dealing with 'difficult relationships' or is in the course of developing 'treatment techniques'. Chapter 7 outlines some of the principles of effective techniques of persuasion and coercion that may be of use to a social worker in such a situation. In Jonathan's case the social worker may wish to adopt the following:

(i)   Provide new information about child rearing or handling techniques which clearly shows the current techniques to be wrong.
(ii)   Make clear the consequences should Jonathan develop further unexplained bruising, and the benefits to the parents of his remaining unbruised and healthy.
(iii) State the power vested in the social worker's role.
(iv)   Adopt a two-sided rather than fear-arousing presentation in discussing what has happened. Go some way towards acknowledging the parents' view in the first instance, while presenting a much

215

stronger argument in favour of their view being incorrect.

(v) Be aware that the parents have been forewarned of your intention and that your intention if not your techniques are open from the outset.

(vi) Visit and speak with other practitioners.

(vii) Do not be too worried if there are a number of distractions during your 'crucial' visits if you are only wanting to make a few simple points. If what you have to say is complex, have the television turned off and put the dog in the next room.

(viii) Do not assume that the partners can only be influenced by yourself. Assess whether one or both partners might be better influenced by an opinion leader — the father's brother, the chairwoman of the Women's Institute, or whoever.

The most obvious form of coercion in a child abuse case is to remove one or both parents, usually by imprisonment or hospitalization, but it might involve semi-official 'deals' whereby the parents 'agree' to undergo a period of behaviour modification or join a group of Parents Anonymous in return for a less punitive disposal.

Whatever tactical approach the worker chooses to adopt, and no moral judgements have been made about their 'rightness' or 'wrongness', the techniques of persuasion described above work. But they have consequences for the worker which need to be anticipated. How would BASW, for example, react to the notion that one of its members was seeking to change a client's attitudes and behaviour against the client's will? What about client self-determination?

Perhaps the major virtue of the SPA when applied to child battering cases lies with its comprehensiveness, its flexibility and its honesty. 'Social controller' is a difficult role to fill; BASW (1977) acknowledges that it *is* a social work role; various writers cited earlier, agree wholeheartedly. However, social control is usually described as some form of 'tension' between control and relationship formation, as though relationships are always positive and control can always be integrated. The SPA points out the distinctions between the two and specifies their component parts.

17
Community Work

Together with casework and groupwork, community work is usually seen as one of the three basic 'methods' available to social workers. Chronologically the most recent, it is taken to represent a reaction to the essentially individualistic orientation of casework and groupwork. With its greater interest in the role of social structures in both generating and determining the form of certain types of individual problems, it has from time to time been viewed as a means of saving social work and social workers from the tunnel vision generated by working for lengthy periods with problems presented purely at an individual level. More importantly, it has contained an implicit and sometimes explicit assumption that social work clients are not having their best interests served by contact with social workers who favour purely casework or groupwork 'methods'. The argument is that caseworkers are more likely to 'pathologize' the client, that is, see the source of the problem as lying within the client, rather than in the larger social structures that surround the client. Community work is accredited with a more visionary zeal, a greater readiness to grapple with some of the more fundamental issues in contemporary society. Rein (1970) was in no doubt about where the future of social work should lie:

> Redistribution, social justice, and participatory democracy are the crucial issues for change today. Social work must find its contribution to these ideals. It cannot rest content by working with the institutional fallouts of an inequitable system or by seeking to reduce public dependency by the use of social services.

Community work was about the generation of fundamental change within society, using whatever means were available and acceptable within a democracy. At the same time, community workers were largely expected to act according to those values and principles traditionally associated with social

217

work as a whole. This zest for value-based change proved irresistible to a number of qualified social workers and a greater number of others simply interested in the idea, but without formal qualifications. A proportion of community workers, then as now, did in fact consider that community work and social work did not have enough in common for them to be bracketed together in any way. For this group, community work was to become a new self-contained discipline. CCETSW (1974) outlined their position clearly:

> They fear that the orientation of social work, its bureaucratic controls, and the power of greater numbers will swallow up the radical initiatives of community work and emasculate the driving force which is associated with an independent identity.

Though fundamentally divided among themselves from the outset, community workers of the 1960s and 1970s entered into the new role with considerable energy, rapidly amassing practice knowledge of the trials and tribulations of working within their particular perspective. Craig (1974) collected together a series of case studies which bring out vividly the feelings of impotence, frustration, complexity and enthusiasm that seem to be the hallmarks of working in a community framework.

Not far behind the gut experiences came the warnings. Thus Cheetham and Hill (1973) commented:

> The community worker, like many other social workers, may be committed intellectually to fundamental political changes and yet be unconvinced of the likelihood of these. His contribution may therefore be limited to improving marginally the circumstances of some of the most deprived, and this only by compromise. Inevitably he is faced with a gap between his personal ideology and his working principles. It is possible that the problems of living with the gap lead community workers to hope for more from their activities than is realistic.

Community workers had not apparently begun to achieve the fundamental change they had been hoping for. Reasons were already being postulated — the employing agencies, largely social services departments, were not taking kindly to their own workers identifying them as targets for intervention; workers were having difficulty in gaining access to sources of power; workers did not themselves have a particular power base; some workers were reluctant to adopt conflict strategies but were finding that a policy of non-directive involvement was getting neither themselves nor the community very far; communities did not seem to be the integrated units they were supposed to be; workers had few principles on which to base decisions to support particular factions within the community at the expense of others; they were typically being called in after a community had begun to disintegrate; there was some surprise that the most successful community projects seemed to occur in predominantly middle class communities or sections of the community; and some concern at the apparently low level of involvement of the 'community' in work and projects intended to be to their benefit.

Seebohm (1968, Chapter XV1) had had a much more practical reason for emphasizing the importance of the community in social work. He argued that:

218

'the community is both the provider as well as the recipient of social services and
. . . orientation to the community is vital if the services are to be directed to
individuals, families and groups within the context of their social relations with
others'. Since social services are the result of negotiations between groups of
actual or potential providers within the larger community, then the larger
perspective has to be taken into account in the provision of those services. Not
surprisingly, the social services department was not to be a self-contained unit,
but rather a part of a network of services within the community. Whether
community workers involved in the 12 Community Development Projects
established by central government in 1969 were helped by this fairly benign
view of interlinked groups working for the benefit of the community as a whole
remains open to doubt. Largely unsuccessful, the projects were intended to
identify and meet 'social needs, especially within local communities within
older urban areas, through close co-ordination of central, local, official and
unofficial effort, informed and stimulated by citizen initiative and involvement' (Noble in Craig, 1974). Ideals were plentiful, but there was a shortage of
advice on the techniques that might be used to meet the goals generated by
those ideals.

Although techniques were hard to come by, there was no shortage of
attempts at model-building. Leissner (1975), for example, outlined four
models for community workers, intended to provide 'basic guidelines and a
frame of reference'. The models were:

(i)   *The community need and response model.* Here the community are
      ready to participate in attempts to meet a particular need. The
      community worker helps identify the need, discusses policies, identifies
      and mobilizes resources, initiates contacts, helps the community run the
      service, then drops out of the scene. This model is taken to be partic-
      ularly applicable to such projects as the provision of play groups, youth
      clubs, community transport schemes, tenants' associations and social
      action groups.

(ii) *The direct-service model.* The community agree that they do have a
      particular need but are not prepared to participate in the planning and
      provision of services to meet the need. The community worker sets up
      the service and then gradually encourages the community to participate
      until they achieve autonomy in providing the service.

(iii) *The interagency model.* Two or more statutory or voluntary agencies
      are trying to meet a specific community need but are failing to provide
      an adequate service — a result of poor coordination, failure to reach
      those in most need, and so on. The community worker adapts,
      coordinates and rationalizes the services while increasing the level of
      involvement of the community. This model is seen as relevant, for
      example, where a number of agencies are seeking to provide advice and
      information in a redevelopment area.

(iv) *The community effort coordination model.* Based on the same
      principles as the previous model, this model differs mainly in the target

219

of interest. Here the community worker is concerned with uncoordinated attempts by community groups to meet their own needs.

Without wishing to dally overlong on the questionable value of models that fail to explain anything, the sort of approach outlined above merely aggrandizes confusion. A practitioner feeling like a cork bobbing about on the storm tossed waves generated by a plethora of community groups in state of conflict is unlikely to be greatly served by the realization that he or she is operating within the 'community effort coordination model'.

There are perhaps two particular difficulties that have dogged community work. The first has already been touched on, and applies equally to casework and groupwork: they are not methods, they are declarations of interest in adopting a particular perspective, and as such do not prescribe techniques. The second difficulty, related to the first, is in defining what constitutes the focus of interest — the community — in a way that facilitates theory building and leads on to the development of effective means of intervention. In both these areas the SPA has something to contribute.

17.1 What is a Community?

There has been no shortage of opinions about what constitutes the defining characteristics of a 'community'. Hillery (1955) for example, discovered 94 different definitions. These definitions range from the purely geographical — whoever happens to live within a certain ground space — through sociological notions of people living in social systems, to unashamedly sentimental notions based on memories of the community 'spirit' alleged to abound in small rural settings. Ironically perhaps, sentimentality probably comes closer to most people's experience of community living — that essentially psychological sense of being privileged to belong to a particular group or groups. If the notion of community is seen as an essentially psychological concept, then psychology should have something to offer. The SPA has a particular interest in meeting the sort of plea made by Rein (1970): 'we are impelled to make a choice between personality and social structure, although it is obvious that what we require is not choice, but an integrated theory'. In SPA terms the notion of 'community' might usefully be abandoned, and substituted by the concepts of personal identity, social identity and group memberships. In other words it might be productive to stop looking for 'communities' and concentrate on locating and manipulating those forces that underly feelings of personal worth, social identities and group memberships — concepts that have been dealt with in detail in Part II.

It is when people have experienced these forces in a positive sense — when they have a positive sense of self-worth and social identity and derive value from their group memberships — that the superordinate expression of their desirability — 'community' — comes into play. Of course, once these concepts are adopted, linked as they are to a theoretical base, there is an increased likelihood that they will lead to techniques able to influence effectively the under-lying processes.

17.2 What is the Relationship between Community Work and the SPA?

Community work reflects a particular interest in the intragroup and intergroup levels of analysis (Chapter 12). The SPA emphasizes that all four levels must be taken into account in any problem formulation, analysis and explanation, and as such subsumes the community work orientation. One of the contentions throughout this book is that the three traditional 'methods' (casework, group-work and community work) do not generate effective techniques. The subsuming of the community work orientation within the SPA might lead to a more productive generation of techniques. This is not in any way meant to denigrate the role that community workers have played, and the achievements that some have made.

The case history below attempts to show how the SPA might be used in one particular context. Not all the possible implications and interrelationships are spelt out: rather, the fundamental notions are stressed and the most obvious techniques are discussed. The SPA is always a dynamic process, responding to new demands as and when they arise, and as such only a portion of its potential value can ever be reflected in its application to a problem presented at one point in time on a two-dimensional surface in the medium of the written word.

17.3 Case History: King Street

King Street is a cul-de-sac: two long rows of terraced houses leading to a patch of waste ground filled with rubble and slag from the nearby pit. Built originally by the National Coal Board in the 1920s for miners at the local pit and their families, the 100 houses were sold to the local council some 15 years ago. Initial impressions are that the population of King Street can be divided roughly into three groups: miners and their families still employed by the local pit some 100 yards away from the street; retired miners usually widowed and now living on their own; and a group of families imported by the council most recently, usually couples with large families, high unemployment and multiple problems — low income, few recreational opportunities, numerous debts and so on. The general standard of the housing is now poor; most of the houses still have an outside toilet, only a few have an inside bathroom. The council has made repairs only on those houses with the most serious cases of dry rot, damp, missing slates, and general structural weaknesses. Within the last few months the council has made it known that it intends to demolish King Street; all the houses are to be flattened and the residents moved permanently elsewhere.

An office of the local SSD is sited within half a mile of King Street, and has received a number of individual residents calling in and expressing concern about the proposed redevelopment. In general, the retired miners wish to

221

remain in King Street; working miners and their families accept that they will have to move, they do not want to go too far away from the pit but would appreciate better housing; the most recent residents do not mind where they go but are keen to try and ensure that they get the best possible housing for themselves. The social work team decides to delegate one social worker to take a particular interest in the residents of King Street.

17.4 The SPA Process

Problem Statement

Intergroup level (a) Manifest. Three subgroups seem to have developed, each presenting a different type of problem. Initial evidence for this stemmed from the drop-in referral patterns, backed up by the impression of the worker in talking to people in the street. The worker later confirmed the accuracy of these impressions by conducting a small street survey to elicit and measure attitudes (see Oppenheim, 1966). All the subgroups form the larger group of King Street residents. The major problem of the large group is that all its members have to be rehoused. Subgroup problems are that one group wants to stay, one to move locally, and one wants better housing anywhere.

(b) Latent. Since there is no overall agreement about reaction to the demolition, there may be inherent conflict between the subgroups not as yet expressed. An additional problem is that a local councillor wants to condemn the housing department for their policy, and might wish to use the social worker for his own political ends.

Intragroup level (a) Manifest. Members of two of the three groups value group membership, one to the extent of not bearing to move. Each group is sizeable, some 30 households, but only the working and retired miners' groups are noticeably cohesive. None of the groups is organized. Permeable boundaries exist between the two miners' groups, but not with the third group.

(b) Latent. There may be tension between the two miners' groups: the retired group feeling that the working group should not be leaving them; both groups may combine to try and ensure that the third group gets the worst share of any deal. Group leaders are likely to be generated.

Interpersonal level (a) Manifest. There is some feeling that those residents who have contacted the SSD are trying to get a better deal for themselves on the 'quiet'.

(b) Latent. As the deadline for demolition draws near, it is likely that existing interpersonal tensions will be heightened: possible scapegoating, jealousies and resentments may occur.

Intrapsychic level (a) Manifest. The retired miners dread having to part with familiar houses where they have spent most of their adult lives, brought up their children, and perhaps seen their wives die. The working miners and their wives want a better deal for their children but are unsure about the repercussions of a move for the family as a whole, particularly the fathers. The imported group feel anger and despair that they are continually being moved into poor properties: they would like to get themselves out of the cycle, but believe that it is 'every man for himself'.

(b) Latent. Increased referral rate to the local GP for tranquillizers and increased numbers of short-term hospital admissions among the retired miners, may be linked with these feelings of anxiety and constant ruminations.

Problem Analysis: Targets

The environment. The environment has a crucial role; the potential change of the environment is generating most of the problems. However, there is some ambiguity in how the threat is perceived: a struggle to balance fear of losing what is available while simultaneously hoping for better things. There is a high degree of interaction between residents facilitated by the housing design: at times the interaction has resulted in dependency, for example, some of the retired miners give their washing to the wives of the working miners; a number of the wives go on joint shopping expeditions because the nearest shops are a mile away; the mine, the only employer, is so close to the street that any move away has repercussions in terms of additional travel time to the husbands' work or even the necessity to purchase a means of transport. Moving people to what policy makers see as 'better' environment is not always successful. Environment is more than bricks and mortar (Chapter 6).

Groups. To an outsider, King Street residents form one group; in fact there are three subgroups. Large group membership has been imposed by planners; sub-group membership has been determined by jobs and the policies of the housing department. The two miners' groups have strong interrelationships: the third group is rejected and stigmatized. Norms are well established, conformity is largely expected and given. There is no evidence of unity in decision-making processes, and no leaders are as yet identifiable. There is a conflict of interest between the three groups.

Relationships. Demolition potentially means the complete dissemination of relationships developed over many years. Large numbers of the same family live close to each other: family ties are valued within the traditional mining community, where family members were hired to work in gangs down the pit. For some, virtually all their relationships are with people who live in the street.

Identity. Particularly for the older miners, much of their identity has been derived from interaction with people in the street and people at the pit only 100 yards away. The environment has acted as a prop for the development of identity. Work, family membership and the neighbour role have achieved pre-eminence. There are few attachments elsewhere. A positive social identity,

223

constantly reinforced, has provided a sound bedrock for a strong sense of personal identity.

The imposed group has had very different experiences. A high proportion of spoiled identities have developed, largely as a result of stigma. The effects of marginality and alienation processes are apparent. They cannot 'pass', have insufficient time to redefine the self, and there is some evidence of playing the stigmatized role.

The working miners are more mobile, younger, have a wider range of outside contacts and hence potential sources of social identity. Street membership is less central to their personal identity.

Change. There is no possibility that the housing department will reverse its policy: the street *will* be demolished. Change will happen at all levels — physical, economic, social, psychological and political. There is a need to decide — a value judgement — which change is acceptable and which is not, and whether and how intervention should take place to influence the form the change will take. Initial thoughts of the worker might be that there is a need to try and ensure that the sense of personal and social identity of the retired group is as little changed as possible; that some consideration needs to be given to try and unify the three groups to reduce anger and recriminations; that the imposed group should be treated fairly by the housing department and given the best deal possible; and that the working group should have a clearer idea of the sort of change they are likely to experience. Negotiation over placement should be an important part of the worker's role, though acknowledgement needs to be made of the enormous power vested in the housing department.

Problem Explanation: Key Processes

Construal. A largely self-contained entity, King Street has provided the medium of primary experience to a large proportion of its residents. Construal processes are fairly similar among the members of the two mining groups, though differences are growing. The imposed group has a less cohesive view of the world, is more inclined to categorize negative experiences and anticipate stigmatization, with no investment of meaning in the life of the street.

Consistency. The retired miners are held in the grip of consistent patterns of thoughts and actions, rehearsed endlessly over many years. The possibility of having to break their routines, both physical and psychological, is creating feelings of acute anxiety. Here consistency has been achieved and has generated positive emotions: it has to be retained. For the imposed group, consistency is not likely to have been achieved to the same extent. It would be reasonable to predict histories of conflict between acts and aspirations, thoughts and behaviours. The projected move reinforces their inconsistencies — they may well hide behind a few behaviours usually guaranteed to provide a beneficial payoff. The working group are somewhat less homogeneous and show larger internal differences. Mobility has given them greater awareness and aspirations. Hopes and ambitions are more idiosyncratic, largely only detectable by direct contact with individual families. They may well respond differentially to the proposed move, depending on how disconcerting it is to their achieved or aspired consistency.

Comparison. Referrals to the SSD are likely to be an attempt to achieve objective validation of understandings. Each group has gross differences in understanding, and each individual within each group finer differences. The response of the social worker must be carefully judged: by validating one perception there may be an invalidation of another. It is likely that extensive informal comparison is occurring, part of the negotiation process to seek reassurance. As it stands, at least one group, the retired, look like being invalidated in that they are adopting a stand that must ultimately lose — staying where they are. Is it worth importing other retired people who have experienced a similar move, and giving them the opportunity to compare views?

Conformity. A lifetime's conformity for the retired miners is being threatened. Perhaps for the first time they are risking social disapproval. They are also not receiving conformity to their views from the working miners. Expect an entrenchment of views and an unwillingness to consider alternatives. The imposed group have never achieved social approval or persuaded others to conform to their perspectives. They are unlikely to put up any resistance to the move or assist those who want to stay. The working group assess social approval as likely to be positive for their aspirations to better themselves: they do not need conformity from other street members. They are likely to operate to wider social norms than the others.

Change and Techniques for Change

See Table 17.1.

Reflexive Analysis

Has the worker's sympathy and affection for the mining community influenced the analysis? Is the division of the street into three groups itself a form of stereotyping? How will the employing agency respond to attempts by the worker to coerce another agency? Is it right for the worker deliberately to try and persuade colleagues to act on the analysis? Is the worker a member of a group that helps to stigmatize the imposed group? Do the worker's colleagues see things differently? How does the worker's involvement with Mrs Digby at number 53 and her battered children influence the worker's views of the needs of the residents as a whole? Are the worker's middle class background, academic training and professional aspirations distorting what is actually happening to an unacceptable extent?
   Has the worker missed anything?

Table 17.1   Change and Techniques for Change

Change	Techniques
1. The retired group should be rehoused locally and together.	1. Lobby housing department. If resistance, 2. Persuasion: decide on the source of the message, its content, the context and the recipients.
2. The imposed group should have an opportunity to develop a more positive social identity. They should not be rehoused as a group, but placed within existing neighbourhoods in small numbers, with any visible differences eradicated or reduced to a minimum.	Lobby and persuade as above; contact DHSS for full benefits and disretionary payments.
3. The working group seem capable of acting in their own interests, and can be left to their own devices.	Calculated neglect.
4. Once rehoused the retired group may need help in developing a positive attitude to their new area.	Attitude change techniques; reduction of dissonance.
5. Contact with social workers in the areas where the imposed group are placed to provide throughput.	Locate colleagues, adoption of persuasion techniques.
6. Contact the housing department for prior warning of the next area for demolition.	1. Persuasion. More probably 2. Coercion. Use of rhetoric and propaganda.

17.5   Conclusion

This chapter has concerned itself with a brief look at one or two of the issues generated by the notion of community work. From an SPA perspective, community work is an orientation, an interest in one or two levels of analysis, which does not in itself lead to the use of prescriptive techniques. The levels of analysis approach, fundamental to the SPA, can subsume community work and by providing the theoretical link between the individual and some aspects of the social context go some way towards facilitating the development of change points and outlining possible techniques for intervention. A case history was used to show how *some* elements of the SPA might be invoked in practice.

18
Mental Illness

Few would query the assertion that there are people who behave in ways which are unpredictable or inexplicable to the majority. Such people are the epicentre of the phenomenon of mental illness. Their thoughts, feelings and actions are considered abnormal by those around them. The use of the word 'considered' emphasizes the central feature of 'mental illness': it is not a static, concrete concept. The concept refers to a category of phenomena which change with changing societal expectations and beliefs, with social norms and legal restrictions. What constitutes mental illness is negotiated among the power sources in the community.

The WHO (1974) *Glossary of Mental Disorders* lists some ten categories of 'psychosis', a further ten categories of 'neurosis, personality disorder and other non-psychotic mental disorder', and five types of mental retardation (under English law mental retardation is currently classed as a mental disorder but not as a mental illness). Thus sub-category 298.3 'acute paranoid reaction' refers to a psychotic condition attributable to a recent life experience. It 'includes mental disorders apparently provoked by some emotional stress that is misconstrued as an attack or threat. Such states are particularly apt to occur in prisoners or as acute reactions to a strange and threatening environment, e.g. in immigrants.' Whatever behaviour the patient is exhibiting, the doctor is obviously having some difficulty in explaining it! The foreword to the *Glossary* acknowledges this fact:

> . . . since diseases are in any case abstract concepts, it is no wonder that the disease constructs which psychiatrists work with have shimmering outlines and overlap. Observer variation is disconcertingly in evidence; reliability is too low for scientific comfort; discrepancies may be in some cases lessened, in others minimized, depending

on whether they arise from inexact perception, personal bias, or divergency of the nosological systems or terms used. (p. 7)

Although the struggle for construal goes on at this superordinate level, it would be fallacious to believe that this is merely a battle for classification and that the 'actual' phenomenon is not open to dispute. Schizophrenia for example, is usually described as some form of:

fundamental disturbance of personality, a characteristic distortion of thinking, often a sense of being controlled by alien forces, delusions that may be bizarre, disturbed perception, abnormal affect out of keeping with the real situation, and autism. Nevertheless, clear consciousness and intellectual capacity are usually maintained. (WHO, *op. cit.*, p. 27)

Such a description reflects the construal system of the onlooker, and may have no relation to the subjective experience of the sufferer. Indeed, even if the form of construal above is 'correct', it can never be corroborated by the reported experience of the schizophrenic who is, after all, within the terms of the description, operating within a different set of meanings. Schizophrenics throughout the world are often said to provide more or less the same 'symptoms', usually known as 'first rank symptoms' after Schneider (1959), though the reliability of these FRSs is open to doubt (Koehler, 1979). The purpose of the elicitation of symptoms is to facilitate diagnosis. In other words, the phenomena are selected and finely tuned to the taste of the diagnostician: with the paucity of effective curative techniques, such an activity may well be of more value to the diagnostician's own sense of self-esteem and identity than to the patient's welfare.

18.1 Models

The potential of the concept of 'mental illness' for the generation of models is and has been considerable. Maher (1970) and Siegler and Osmond (1966) between them list seven models, there are many more:

The Medical Model

Usually restricted to the notion of 'disease', medical models concentrate on the identification of a syndrome and the generation of means of explaining the syndrome. Thus, in schizophrenia, the syndrome may consist of all or some of the FSRs; explanation must be construed in terms of finding whatever causes those symptoms to be generated. There seems to be an amount of evidence accruing to indicate that schizophrenia has a genetic component, is ameliorated by certain psychotropic drugs, and can be generated 'artificially' in alcoholic psychosis and in various forms of epilepsy. None of these findings, as yet, has explanatory power.

The Moral Model

Here, madness is a sin or merely unacceptable behaviour. The person concerned is behaving irresponsibly or in a way that the particular society concerned finds unacceptable. Their behaviour has, therefore, to be changed, either by holding them to be responsible for their actions (punishment) or by engaging in some form of behaviour modification. The behaviour is construed in normative terms (social comparison processes), and responsibility for the achievement of change is usually delegated to clerics, lawyers or various sorts of behaviour therapists.

The Psychoanalytic Model

Reduced to a caricature: behaviour is the result of balance or imbalance between various intrapsychic innate energy systems. When these energy systems block each other or are blocked by outside factors then a 'deviant' behaviour may develop. These systems exist on three topographic levels — the unconscious, preconscious and conscious — and are therefore available differentially to normal awareness; they operate mechanically through such mental apparatus as the ego, id and superego. Psychoanalytic concepts have pervaded Western culture, and have generated a multiplicity of variations, spin-offs, misinterpretations and 'therapies'. Psychoanalysis is not based on premises that acknowledge the usefulness of empirical validation. To a holder of an empirical model, psychoanalysis is ineffective. To a psychoanalysist, psychoanalysis works.

The Family Interaction Model

Here the role of the family in generating the illness among one of its members is emphasized. In schizophrenia, particularly, the family as a whole is seen as being sick: the patient merely externalizes the symptoms. Successful treatment occurs when the family itself construes the 'illness' in this way, acknowledging that the ill family member was expressing the family pathology, and exhibiting insight into the patterns of family interaction that may have generated this condition.

The Conspiratorial Model

Mental illness is a myth: it is a means of obscuring problems in living. At best, individuals experiencing such problems are being degraded and humiliated, for example by being placed in total institutions (Goffman, 1961). At worst, the process represents an attempt by the dominant social and political ideologies of a given society to maintain the status quo (Szasz, 1961). Psychiatrists are those people delegated by society to carry out the act of labelling particular people as being 'undesirable' (Scheff, 1975).

The Social Model

Sick individuals are the product of a sick society. Those people who exhibit mental illness are made particularly vulnerable by such things as social isolation, anomie, marginal status, role strain, psychological stress, and

230

excessive competition and culture conflict. The hospital is seen essentially as a refuge for those people who are too battered by the process of living to manage outside.

The Statistical Model

This model is essentially descriptive and classificatory, and consists largely of compiling frequency and regularity counts of various patterns of behaviour. The focus of interest is usually at a factorial level: seeking to identify those factors which may be used to describe an individual's behaviour (for example, Eysenck, 1960), or to identify those factors which 'define' a particular sub-type of deviant behaviour.

These models are largely conflicting, based on different premises, and are each interested in only one or two levels of analysis. The practitioner has to accept either a particular model and operate within it, generate some form of composite model, ignore all the models and use more informal models such as the 'common-sense' model, or has to be able to select models on the basis of demands made. (The notion of composite models seems to be gaining credence. Wing (1978) advocates that all professionals working in the field of mental illness should use a series of such models as 'disease, impairment, social disadvantage, and adverse psychological reaction'.)

The SPA would advise the practitioner to:

(i) take cognizance that problems operate on multiple levels, in both manifest and latent formats;

(ii) be aware that most existing models operate on only a portion of these levels;

(iii) select models in terms of their own premises and in their pragmatism (Chapter 13);

(iv) attempt to develop models of their own which relate to the demands made on the practitioner, and relate those demands to effective intervention techniques via the processes of analysis and explanation utilized within an SPA framework.

18.2 Social Work and Mental Illness

Keidan and Hughes (1979) argue that current mental health social work has its origins in two somewhat disparate roots: the pre-1948 relieving officers and welfare officers who filled a largely controlling function, and the psychiatric social workers operating under essentially psychoanalytically based precepts. Both aspects are now combined in the functions of the generic social work team devised by the 1970 Social Services Act. Thus the local authority social worker is required to fill two potentially conflicting roles — controller and clinician, each based on different models. Much of the literature on the history of mental health services concentrates on the clinical perspective, and consists of descriptions of the applications of particular levels of analysis, techniques or

231

orientations. Thus the volume edited by Olsen (1976) and entitled *Differential Approaches to Social Work with the Mentally Disordered*, contains papers on 'methods of psychodynamic therapy', 'behavioural social work', crisis intervention, group work, the unitary approach, family work, and so on. In many ways mental health social work is now one of the most 'advanced' forms of social work, having more alternative techniques from which to choose, and a higher proportion of second level skills among them. Whittaker (1974) portrays 21 different treatment approaches and provides guidance for their selection. These guidelines operate on six levels:

(i) length of treatment (short-term treatment is at least as effective as long term);
(ii) focus of treatment (which should be 'the real life problems of the client as they are being experienced by the client');
(iii) accountability of treatment (the treatments must be amenable to evaluation);
(iv) ecological validity: the treatment must work in the client's natural life milieu;
(v) orientation: the treatment should stress growth rather than deficit;
(vi) client involvement: clients should be involved as full and equal partners in the helping process (quoted in Olsen, 1976).

Again, however, this is a selecting rather than an integrating approach. It assumes that a problem is rather like a rare plant: once it is identified and classified it can be added to the collection. When the next rare plant comes along the collection is thumbed through until the relevant page is reached. The process that generates the act of classification is not considered. Moreover, despite telling the practitioner what should be done, advice on how to do it is not readily forthcoming.

It might be argued, of course, that the demands made on social workers operating in the field of mental health can *never* be met by any particular approach. A finger is pointed to the sheer number of other professionals with whom the social worker has to interact; the range of settings where the social worker might operate, and the type of formal and informal role expectations imposed. Table 18.1 contains details. For detailed elaboration of the current role of the social worker, see Hoggett (1976), Olsen (ed., 1978) and Harris (1978).

If the range of explanatory models that has generated this response to the phenomenon of mental illness is also borne in mind, it is clear that the majority of social workers are unlikely to have developed an integrated approach that subsumes all or most of the various demands made on them, and which leads to effective practice. Although the SPA will not meet this need, it will provide indicators about how the need might be met. We end this chapter with an example of how the SPA might be used in one small part of the mental health social worker's practice.

Table 18.1

People with whom the social worker might have to interact on behalf of a mentally ill client:

clinical psychologist	clergy
psychiatrist	rehabilitation specialists
psychiatric nurse	art therapists
other social workers	dance therapists
administrators	music therapists
occupational therapists	technicians
nursing auxiliaries	home helps
residential care workers	community nurses
disablement resettlement officers	probation officers
teachers	police
housing department officials	voluntary agency workers
social security officers	landlords

Places where social workers might have to operate:

hospitals	rehabilitation workshops
o/p departments	hostels
GP clinics	group homes
day units	

Employing agencies:
SSDs
voluntary organizations
probation departments

Some formal role expectations:
1. committal powers under the 1959 Mental Health Act
2. supervision of restricted patients in the community
3. emergency powers of inspection of premises and the removal of mentally ill persons
4. apprehending absconders

Some informal role expectations:
1. providing practical assistance to the client and to the family
2. providing background reports to other disciplines
3. engaging in treatment programmes
4. arranging community support systems

18.3   Case History: Herbert

Herbert has been seen wandering about the fields, sleeping rough in sheep huts or in cow barns. He seems to spend most of his time muttering to himself, is generally unkempt, and is reported as having a 'wild' look about him. He is

233

currently sleeping in a pig shed, and the wife of the farmer who owns the pig shed has complained to the police that he takes no notice of her when she asks him to move away, merely continuing to mutter and staring in the opposite direction. The local police constable has visited the scene, and considers that Herbert is 'mad as a hatter'. He has managed to elicit the man's name from documents in his pocket, and has found that Herbert does not have a police record. The constable has contacted the local SSD with whom he has a good relationship, and asked that a social worker be sent to make an assessment. The duty social worker checked that the SSD had no records on Herbert, and subsequently visited the scene. For some reason, the social worker finds Herbert in a talkative mood, and Herbert explains that he is staying in the pig shed because the pig shed is his property. He is married to the farmer's wife, and he owns the land. The wife wants him off the land because she has developed a relationship with the man she currently calls her husband, but who in fact is not. They are conspiring to deprive him of his property. The lady in question denies Herbert's assertion resolutely. Herbert seems verbally aggressive but there seems no reason to believe that he might be physically violent to anyone. After an amount of discussion, Herbert agrees to spend the next few days in a hostel run by the SSD. During this time he behaves in a manner acceptable to the hostel warden, and takes the opportunity to clean himself up. He still mutters to himself and is resolute in his beliefs about ownership of the farm. The hostel bed is only available for two more days. The social worker has to decide what to do with Herbert: in the first instance, the worker decides to examine the situation from the social psychological approach.

18.4   The SPA Process

Problem Statement

Intrapsychic level   (a) Manifest. Herbert believes that he is the owner of the farm, that he is married to the owner's wife, and that she and her real husband are conspiring to deprive him of his rightful property. These beliefs seem to be false.

The farmer's wife denies Herbert's accusations resolutely and is adamant that she wants him off the land because he is trespassing, and is a nuisance and an embarrassment to her and her husband. The hostel warden considers Herbert to be a satisfactory resident, but there is no possibility of a bed being made available on a longer term basis.

The policeman considers that he has carried out his duty of arranging for Herbert to be moved from the property, but will continue to keep an eye on him to ensure he does not get into any further 'trouble'.

(b) Latent. Herbert may hold other false beliefs, as yet undiscovered. He may decide that he should take further action consistent with his false beliefs.

Interpersonal level   (a) Manifest. Herbert has annoyed and probably

234

frightened the farmer's wife. They have not met before, and Herbert has apparently never met her husband. Herbert seems to have no relatives or friends he might contact. He relates well to the warden but not to the wife or the policeman.

(b) *Latent*. Herbert's isolation means that either he must be left to wander about, or accommodation must be found for him. Little information as to whether his isolation is his own choice or has been imposed upon him.

Intragroup level (a) *Manifest*. Herbert has no apparent group memberships, though the policeman referred to him as 'crazy' and a 'tramp'. The policeman, the warden and the social worker are involved by virtue of their membership in professional groups. The farmer's wife is a well-respected member of the rural community.

(b) *Latent*. Herbert will have no supporters initially for any action he might choose to take in the situation. Power is vested in those groups who have intervened; the consensus is that Herbert should be 'dealt with', that is, placed in a setting where his behaviour is tolerated.

Intergroup level (a) *Manifest*. There is general agreement among the representatives of the various groups concerned that Herbert cannot be permitted to continue pestering the farmer. Suggestion has been made that a member of the psychiatric group should become involved.

(b) *Latent*. Involving a psychiatrist may 'solve' the problem by removing Herbert to a hospital; and would involve little effort on the social worker's part. The psychiatric group is usually dominant in dealing with mental disorder. Should Herbert not receive a psychiatric disposal and become violent or self-punitive, the social worker may well be held responsible.

Problem Analysis: Targets

The environment. The environment has a fairly central role in the situation. The farmer's territory is being invaded without justification. Herbert seems to enjoy the opportunity of having a degree of privacy in the hostel. It seems likely that Herbert has been wandering about for some weeks, always staying in accommodation intended for animals.

Groups. A powerful alliance has developed to ensure Herbert's conformity to social norms. The social worker is currently the nominated leader but only by virtue of the role, particularly in having access to resources. Decision making has been delegated to the worker with considerable freedom to manoeuvre, but within the expectation that the worker will ensure that this or a similar situation will not recur. Should the worker fail, considerable pressure will be exacted by other members of the group to remove the practitioner as the delegated worker, probably through informal channels in the worker's employing agency.

Relationships. Herbert is seen as a 'crazy but harmless tramp' — a powerful stereotype, perhaps blocking closer examination of Herbert as an individual. Would the worker be as sure in the assessment of him on the information available if Herbert were the local magistrate?

In attributing a reason for Herbert's actions, the worker has concentrated almost solely on Herbert's character: no one else to the worker's knowledge has made the same allegations and Herbert repeats his assertions despite evidence to the contrary. However, the worker has not checked whether he has made this allegation about anyone else. (If he has not, why this couple?) The worker's causal schemata have perhaps completed too short a circuit.

Identity. Herbert has a visible stigmatized identity. He seems to vary between playing the role and successfully passing. He can obviously pass at will, but under what conditions and for what reasons? In his contact with the worker, he has always seemed capable of adequate impression management, which may indicate that he does seek social approval. What little he says about his background indicates that fairly recently he was employed in some form of responsible capacity. He seems to be somewhere along the process linking role conflict and marginality with alienation.

Change. Potential exists for change on a substantial level — particularly financial, social and psychological. The worker can provide accommodation, social security benefits and a form of social contact (? supervised bedsitter): but Herbert would have to exhibit an amount of psychological change before he would benefit, though this may well occur as *as a result of* these other forms of change taking place first. Herbert intends to stay in the area but pressure is apparent that he should either move elsewhere or stay locally under supervision. Some work might be necessary to persuade the farmer and policeman to tolerate Herbert's presence in the interim.

Problem Explanation: Key Processes

Construal. Aspects of Herbert's construal system conflict with social 'reality', and are not amenable to disconfirmation. The generation of this 'unacceptable' construal system is unknown. A decision needs to be made whether this should be controlled, treated, ignord, or redirected. At the moment, Herbert does not wish to be 'treated' and has done nothing to merit formal control. His unacceptable construals need to be either ignored or redirected. The construal systems of the others involved are identical in evaluating him as 'mad'.

Consistency. Herbert is consistent in his assertions: his thoughts, feelings and actions are balanced and not amenable to internal threat — it seems likely he has held the beliefs for some time.

Comparison. His beliefs receive no confirmation. In fact the more he asserts his beliefs, the greater the attempts at invalidation by others. How much does his belief stem from an attempt at differentiation? Why does he need to? Is he receiving confirmation of his belief from any source?

236

Conformity. Herbert readily conforms to environments imposed upon him. He also insists that others conform to his unacceptable views. If people are continually exposed to his views and fail to conform, will his construal be ultimately invalidated, particularly if alternative and more acceptable construals are offered in their stead?

For Herbert, massive potential conflict exists between his construals, his search for comparison and his drive for conformity. Potential for change is also therefore considerable.

Change and Techniques for Change

See Table 18.2.

Table 18.2   Change and Techniques for Change

Change	Technique
1. Place Herbert in a supervised bedsitter with adequate social contacts.	Negotiate with housing association and voluntary agency.
2. Reinforce the acceptable aspects of his construal system.	Develop structured relationship.
3. Provide opportunity for unacceptable constructs to be continually invalidated.	Persuade farmer and wife to continue contact, but in Herbert's own environment.
4. Develop series of hypotheses about the factors that maintain Herbert's behaviour and put them to the test.	Theory building.
5. As interim measure, consider keeping Herbert away from the farm by developing reward/sanction system.	Behaviour modification techniques.
6. As long-stop prepare way for hospital admission should his behaviour become dangerous.	Anticipate the possible need to use coercion, and select the means least damaging to Herbert *beforehand*.
7. Seek information about previous group memberships and attempt his reintroduction to those or similar groups.	Attitude change techniques: focus: (i) Herbert (ii) leaders of relevant groups.

Reflexive Analysis

The worker has found it difficult to examine Herbert's behaviour without looking through a stereotype of the sort of people who become 'tramps', and has an inclination to adopt one of the medical models as an explanatory frame. However, at the moment, the worker has no reason or need to interpret Herbert's behaviour as 'schizophrenic', 'personality disorder' or whatever — such attributed concepts may distort rather than add to the analysis, given the actual behaviour observed and the information available. The worker's experience indicates a pessimistic view of the likely outcome of the interventions, based largely on previous failures to change the attitudes of enough colleagues to assist in such planned change. The sense of pessimism may also stem, in some measure, from the worker's fear of being seen as a non-conformer or an idealist by colleagues. Should the worker attempt to work jointly with one particular colleague, perhaps a social work assistant, from the outset of this case?

18.5 Conclusion

This chapter has been concerned with an examination of the value of the SPA to practitioners working in the mental health field. Particular emphasis has been placed on model selection and explanatory frames. Mental illness, a particularly negotiable form of 'deviant' behaviour, has generated a plethora of responses, both in terms of views and in terms of practice, a considerable portion of which is of a particularly high standard. The SPA is offered as a different way of looking at some of the problems faced by the mental health practitioner, but is by no means considered the only or primary one. The major virtues of the SPA in this field are its comprehensive approach, and its encouragement for the *practitioner* to link techniques with goals generated from within a theoretical base.

19
Use of the SPA by the Client

Throughout this book stress has been placed on the role of the social practitioner as a problem solver. The client experiences a problem of one form or another and at some point becomes involved with the social worker who is expected to solve or ameliorate the difficulty. It has been proposed that under these conditions the adoption of the SPA may be a fruitful activity for the social worker. Particular emphasis was given to the value of multiple levels of analysis and the adoption of effective intervention techniques stemming from relevant theories. It might be assumed from this that the SPA, like most other forms of problem analysis, makes a clear distinction between the person making the analysis and the individual experiencing the problem. The worker makes the analysis on behalf of the 'client' and attempts to ensure that goals generated by the analysis are met. Such a distinction would be consistent with much current practice in the fields of social work, psychotherapy, and psychology. The 'appropriate' form of contact between the worker and the practitioner goes something like this — the worker maintains distance, makes an objective analysis, formulates a diagnostic opinion, prescribes a treatment and monitors the effects of the treatment. Such contact *is* no doubt appropriate for clients who are unable or unwilling to offer an opinion about their own welfare, or for those whose problem is recognizably physical and for whom there is little doubt about the required form of treatment. However, for those whose difficulties are a little more nebulous, or for whom there are a variety of treatments from which to choose, or simply for those who take an active interest in understanding the solutions to their particular problems, such an approach loses a lot of its appeal, and can generate considerable hostility from the client concerned. Partly to meet this need, the notion of developing a more equal form of

239

interaction with clients/patients has begun to develop. Equal not only in the sense that the client is made aware of the practitioner's views as the analysis progresses, but also in that the client is included in the negotiation over what constitutes the problem and which form of intervention strategy should be attempted. The recent campaign by BASW under the banner 'Clients are Fellow Citizens' reflects something of this mood and indicates the desirability of a more equitable relationship between client and social worker. Such an idea would probably receive an amount of support on moral grounds. Difficulty may arise, however, in attempting to put it into practice. There is a considerable difference between taking care to elicit the views of the client, and giving the client the means to channel those views in a form that permits adequate self-analysis. And, perhaps most crucial of all, one which enables the client to act on his or her own behalf.

Giving the client the means to act on his or her own behalf is a particularly interesting concept. What in fact would most social workers do if a client made explicit a desire to be given the opportunity to exercise on their own behalf the social worker's 'effective techniques'? As we saw in Chapter 11, very few such effective techniques are in fact generally available. Moreover, those practitioners who do utilize second level skills may be a little reluctant to, in a sense, have the tables turned on them by the client. For example, would a social worker who devoutly believed in behaviour modification wish his clients to be able to use behaviour modification techniques on their own behalf, particularly if the clients decided that it was the response pattern of the social worker which needed changing?

To return to the question posited earlier, the SPA does not in fact make a distinction about who uses it. The SPA is a body of integrated theory and technique resting within an overall conceptual framework. It is a tool, and like all tools as good or as bad as its user. There is no reason, then, why those clients who are capable of using the SPA and wish to utilize it, should not do so. It would be arrogant to assume otherwise. The purpose of this chapter is to examine more closely this notion of the clients' use of the SPA. Its format will be as follows:

(i)   Identifying the client
(ii) Communication between client and practitioner
(iii) Predisposing conditions for the use of the SPA
(iv) Use of the SPA
    (a) collaboration v. self-help
    (b) individual clients v. groups
    (c) use in whole or part?
(v)   Repercussions for the practitioner

19.1 Identifying the Client

In the first instance, a client is whoever fits into a particular practitioner's perspective. If the worker uses exclusively a particular technique — psycho-therapy, counselling or behaviour modification — then a client is the person who exhibits the problem the worker believes he or she can treat or ameliorate. On a slightly broader front, the worker concentrating on a particular orienta-tion — casework, groupwork or community work — will deal with clients whose problems can be encompassed by the orientation. From a more holistic view-point, the integrated methods followers will search for 'client systems', that is 'the individual, family group, organization or community that, in addition to being the expected beneficiary of the service, is a system that asks for help and engages the services of a social worker as a change agent' (Pincus and Minahan, 1975, p. 56). Pincus and Minahan also stress that individuals only become clients when a working contract is established with the practitioner/change agent. Thus the client can be anyone from an individual to an organization, as long as they are seeking help and a contractual agreement has been reached over the form the social work input will take. In the absence of effective skills to put such fine words into practice they shrink under the cold water comments of Haines (1975, p. 16):

> For the most part, clients are in varying degrees of subjection to the social worker, pay nothing directly for the services they receive, have no contract . . . and are often not free to withdraw from the relationship.

Haines' comment serves as a reminder about who actually *are* the most common clients of social workers — the elderly, the mentally disturbed, and those whose involvement is predicated upon some form of legal control by the social worker manifested in supervision orders, care orders, life licences, and so on. For most social workers, there is little say in negotiating who to have as a client; and a substantial portion of those clients have no wish for the involve-ment or are incapable of expressing a view one way or another. Thus, discus-sion of the use of the SPA by clients may be viewed with considerable scepticism by most practitioners; and rightly so. The assertion here is, hopefully, a realistic one: there are *some* clients on the caseloads of *most* social workers who will be sufficiently educated, interested, motivated, and capable of making a free choice, who will benefit from the opportunity of grasping the principles of the SPA and putting into practice some of its prescriptive techniques on their own behalf. It is to this group alone that this chapter is directed.

19.2 Communication between Client and Practitioner

Sharing knowledge implies adequate communication. There is little reason to believe that the current level of client/practitioner communication is of a high enough standard to enable such sharing to take place. This is obviously a crucial area for all social workers, regardless of their orientation, place of work or professional status. Certainly, the notion of shared use of the SPA is pre-dicated upon an adequate level of communication.

Mayer and Timms (1971) examined the interactions between social workers

241

employed by the Family Welfare Association and 61 clients. The clients were categorized into four groups on the basis of the expressed need and the degree of satisfaction the client experienced with the service:

(i) Those clients seeking help for someone else and expressing dissatisfaction with the service were usually dealt with by 'insight-orientated' social workers. Misunderstandings arose because the social worker did not share the client's interpretation of the problem.

(ii) Those clients seeking help for someone else who expressed satisfaction were dealt with by 'supportive-directive' social workers, i.e. the worker listened to the client, supported them, and offered suggestions and advice.

(iii) Satisfied clients requesting material assistance had received the desired assistance with a minimum of fuss and distress.

(iv) Dissatisfied clients requesting material assistance had, perhaps unsurprisingly, failed to receive the requested assistance from insight-orientated workers.

Putting aside any comment over the use of the labels 'insight-orientated' and 'supportive-directive', the basic point from Mayer and Timms' study seems to be that however vaguely you describe your orientation, a fairly high degree of mismatch seems to occur between it and the needs of the client, blocking communication. In SPA terms, the workers had stuck resolutely to a particular level of analysis, failing to take into account that the problem may not only be construed by the client on a number of different levels but may actually therefore 'exist' on a multiplicity of levels. Adequate communication is founded upon the acknowledgement of this fact, and it is here that the SPA has a particular contribution to make.

There are, of course, a number of other sources of inadequate communication between worker and client. Rees (1978), compared the perceptions of 38 social workers and 90 clients of their interactions in one Scottish town in 1974. He found that half of the clients considered that they had received no help from the worker, and that the worker had not seemed to perceive their problem in the same way as they did. The absence of an empirical base to the interaction, the imposing nature of the office buildings, the passive role expected of the client, and the limited perspectives of the social workers ('casework', 'service' or 'relief') were put forward as contributing factors to the perceived poor communication.

A rather more profound critique of the current form of interaction between worker and client has been put forward by Robinson (1978). The nub of Robinson's argument is contained in his comment:

as a result of his professional socialisation, organisational concerns and often general social background differences from his clients, the professional becomes encapsulated in a different subjective world from his client.

More specifically, Robinson believes that client dissatisfactions can be pinned down and classified under a variety of overlapping headings. Although he distinguishes communication from other factors, each of the factors can probably be construed as being part of the communication process:

(i) Communication. Clients feel they have insufficiently frequent contact with the worker, who does not treat them as an equal, give them sufficient information or listen to their point of view.

(ii) Balance of power. Clients feel, and usually are, powerless. The growth of client support groups is an attempt to counterbalance the power distribution.

(iii) Professionals as people. Though well intentioned, practitioners do not fully understand the nature of the client's problem, do not exhibit genuine sympathy or concern, and in some cases are frankly incompetent.

(iv) Inadequate or inappropriate services. The proferred service was irrelevant to the problem and the worker was more concerned with professional boundaries than with helping the client.

(v) Feelings of discomfort or threat. Stemming from formal communications, imposing buildings, and having their 'meanings' reinterpreted.

Robinson has a particular concern with this notion of reinterpreted meanings — a notion central to discussion of communication breakdowns. He lists seven areas where such phenomenon occurs — what constitutes the central or most important feature of the problem; the meaning of time; triviality v. seriousness; what constitutes adequate information and advice; how costs and rewards are evaluated; probabilistic v. individual interpretations; and what constitutes 'reasonable progress'.

Any practitioner interested in the notion of sharing, collaborating or teaching the client the means for independent action must take cognizance of these findings and feelings. The SPA will not surmount them. What it will do is give the worker a better chance of anticipating them, and including them in the analytic and explanatory process.

19.3 Predisposing Conditions for the Use of the SPA

Adequate communication is crucial. Various suggestions can be made, ranging from increased participation by clients in social work training, policy making and management to the physical redesign of offices, to greater awareness of the complex and multi-layered phenomenon of shared subjective experiences, what Cox (1978) has termed 'mutuality'. That social workers should be involved in power- and decision-sharing has been suggested by BASW (Code of Ethics, Principle 4): the social worker is ethically obliged to 'help his clients increase the range of choices open to them and their power to make decisions'. Here BASW seems to be thinking along similar lines to Goldstein (1973). Goldstein's social learning approach to client/social worker interaction construes them as uniting to form the change system, bonded together by the development of a 'relationship' whose instigation and supervision is the responsibility of

243

the worker. Although this notion gives the client a greater share in the exercise, it does not provide for a situation where the client operates independently of the social worker once a technique for 'thinking' about the problem has been provided.

Thus there are three predisposing conditions for the use of the SPA:

(i)   adequate communication;
(ii) motivated, capable 'clients';
(iii) a worker who is prepared to leave those clients who are capable of doing so to operate on their own behalf.

19.4 Use of the SPA

Collaboration v. Self-Help

The interaction between a social worker and a client wishing to utilize the SPA may take one of two basic forms — collaboration or client self-help.

In the collaborative style, the worker operates jointly with the client throughout the SPA, clearly outlining all the fundamental precepts and theoretical underpinnings. The entire process is a shared experience; problem definition, analysis, and explanation, identifying change and deciding on techniques. The social worker is essentially a skilled resource working jointly with the client, probably under some form of mutually agreed contract. The practitioner operates more like an architect than a doctor or therapist: assisting the client to clarify a particular design, helping to select the building materials, overseeing the construction of the edifice, and ensuring that it is habitable. The final building is a combination of the client's original specifications and the social worker's expert advice on how those specifications can be met; or, if they cannot be met, what the next best type of construction might be. Working closely together, the most complex SPA concepts can be used.

The client self-help style assumes the client wishes to utilize the SPA on his or her own behalf and is capable of doing so. The notion of self-help among clients is usually restricted to situations where clients, dissatisfied with the level of professional service provided, develop mutual support groups. Not untypically, these groups contact their 'own' independent experts, find out as much as they can about their shared problems, then return to do battle armed with their new-found independence. Part of the reason for professional reluctance to disseminate crucial information may rest with the notion of 'responsibility', acting on behalf of the client in the client's own interests. After all, the client is on the practitioner's 'caseload', with the connotations of being a 'burden'.

Self-help among clients wishing to use the SPA is of three main types:

(i)   The social worker teaches the client how to carry out the process, then leaves the client to act.
(ii) The social worker provides the client with indirect support; the worker's knowledge of the SPA is used to change the client during the course of the interaction.

(iii) The social worker deliberately clarifies only the simpler problems and leaves the client to find his or her own solutions.

Note that no moral stance is being taken here. Manipulation is inevitable and acknowledged: but it is recognized that such manipulation is likely to be a two-way process.

Individual Clients v. Groups

Some of the more powerful SPA findings are concerned with groups of people rather than individuals. The SPA is likely therefore to be of particular value to groups of clients rather than to particular clients. Client collectivities based, for example, on having a disabled member of the family, may wish to use the SPA to clarify the tactics that might usefully be adopted to influence local politicians to ensure better access for wheelchairs in municipal buildings; or to adopt rhetorical styles at a national level; or to help ensure that their own group is functioning at an optimum level; or to press for unification with another group expressing similar concerns, and so on — the permutations are considerable. On a more pragmatic level, client groups will almost certainly start from a stronger power base than the individual client, and will therefore have something of a head start on which to base their interventions. One might envisage a future situation when groups of clients and teams of social workers unite to devise the most effective intervention techniques, having agreed on the necessary change.

In Whole or Part?

The SPA is an integrated, dynamic whole, constantly shifting and changing, assimilating and accommodating to new information as and when it arises. For full value to be derived, it must therefore be viewed as a whole. However there are obviously certain aspects of it that may have a particular relevance to certain client groups, such as: the notion of multiple levels of analysis, and the relation of techniques to theory; specific concepts such as spoiled identities, friendship formation, group dynamics; and techniques such as attitude change and persuasion tactics. Here the client may wish to extract and extrapolate: care must be taken, however, to do as little damage as possible to the superstructure during the dismemberment.

19.5 Repercussions for the Practitioner

Enabling clients to solve their own problems, though a well-documented aspect of the social work role, may not receive the universal acclaim that might be anticipated. What happens, for example, if the client or client group decides to engage in techniques of coercion directed at a high political level? How disconcerting might it be for social practitioners to be faced with clients who are attempting to manipulate *them*, not out of some pathological and easily deflected personality trait, but based on empirically validated techniques?

245

What if a pressure group decides to utilize the attitude change findings to ensure that all potential clients of the local Social Security Office take up the benefits to which they are entitled?

The answers are of course in the area of morals and values. Social workers may wish to select carefully those clients to whom the SPA is taught: others may consider any concealment of research findings to be immoral. Some social workers may consider themselves exclusively as social controllers and the notion of collaboration with the client to be anathema; others may be social radicals, wishing to see structural social change, for whom the notion of sharing with clients has a certain appeal. At the end of the day, the use to which the SPA might be put is in the hands of the social workers who choose to use it.

The purpose of this chapter has been to point out some of the issues involved in utilizing one aspect of it — its facility for being shared with clients. As in all branches of social work, social workers face the repercussions of their actions on a daily basis. Using the SPA in accord with one's personal beliefs, values and style, is unlikely to generate more acute repercussions than does the use of those techniques, orientations or approaches that are currently being utilized. In fact, the SPA itself would predict that it will be construed in a manner consistent with a worker's previous behaviour patterns and will be used in a manner that receives social approval!

20
Student Supervision

Behaviour modification is a second level skill, that is, it is a prescriptive technique linking demands with the achievement of appropriate goals. As such, it should be part of the skill armoury of most if not all social workers. Indeed a number of social work courses teach the rudiments of learning theory and a selection of the various skills that may be derived from it. There is no shortage of publications to enhance further the student's knowledge of the theory (Jehu, 1967; Jehu et al., 1972; Herbert, 1981). A crucial period occurs in the life of most social work students when, having decided that a particular technique is relevant to the job, they decide to put that technique into practice, and hopefully convert it into a skill. Of course, this applies equally well to, say, personal construct therapy and various forms of psychotherapy, as it does to behaviour modification. If sufficiently courageous, the student may risk attempting to apply the technique while on placement, where it is assessable.

Usually the interaction between student and fieldwork tutor is in the teacher – pupil mould. In the case of behaviour modification, the principles of learning are used to teach the principles of learning. Once the student has learnt the agreed amount and put the principles into practice at a certain level of expertise, the relationship is deemed to have reached a satisfactory conclusion, at least for the student. The tutor, however, may have learnt very little about either the student or the process of supervision from the placement. The tutor has of necessity to call on other skills or orientations to provide insights. The purpose of this chapter is to examine how the SPA might be used by a fieldwork tutor intending to teach a particular technique, in this case behaviour modification, to a student on placement.

20.1 The Scenario

The tutor, Cliff, is employed by a social services department. The director of the SSD has received a request from the course director of the applied social studies course of a nearby university requesting a placement for a student, Zoe, who is in the second year of a two year CQSW course. Zoe is particularly interested in being taught behaviour modification. She has had two or three lectures at the university on the general topic of learning theory. The director of the SSD has sent the letter to the leader of the area team of which Cliff is a member. This was discussed at a team meeting and Cliff, who has not had a student on placement before, but has been on a student supervisors' course, has agreed to accept Zoe for a 12-week placement.

Cliff, Zoe and Zoe's personal tutor, Brian, have met in advance of the placement to develop a 'contract' specifying the sort of workload Zoe is likely to have. It was agreed that Zoe will have six cases selected on the basis of their apparent suitability for the use of behaviour modification — one child abuse, two agoraphobics, one rebellious teenager, and two couples with marital difficulties.

20.2 The Players

Cliff is in his mid-30s, married with no children. He qualified with a CQSW seven years ago, and is unusual in that he has spent nearly all his career in one SSD. He is now a senior practitioner (career grade). He has used behaviour modification techniques on numerous occasions with reasonable success, and considers it to be one of the more effective skills he has available. His overall perspective to social work practice is one he has derived from the SPA.

Zoe is in her mid-20s, married with two young children. Between her degree in English Literature and enrolment on the CQSW course she worked as an unqualified social worker in a voluntary agency primarily concerned with the needs of the elderly. Currently seconded by an SSD, she has found the training course distressing in its apparent vagueness, lack of relevance to her impending job, and emphasis on presenting a multiplicity of theories, some of which conflict and few of which are actually linked to relevant techniques. She has decided to try to ensure that she has at least one highly developed technique before she qualifies, and opted for behaviour modification on this, her final placement.

Brian, a single man in his early 40s, is a sociologist. He does not hold a CQSW, but has acted as a consultant to a number of community projects. His particular interest is in the development of a structural-functionalist critique of the role of government funded welfare departments operating within a capitalist system. He considers behaviour modification to be an unacceptable form of social control, and psychology as an introspective blinkered discipline.

20.3   The Task

Cliff has to teach Zoe the basics of behaviour modification and supervise her practice with six clients. Having found the SPA useful in his own practice he decides to apply it to his contact with Zoe and Brian.

20.4   SPA: The Process

Problem Statement

Intrapsychic level   (a)   Manifest. Zoe seems keen to participate in the learning process. However, she has little scientific background, and shows few signs of actually preferring an empirical approach to a more humanist one. Her obvious interest in other people's subjective experiences, usually focused through literature, may have difficulty in resolving itself with a more objective behaviourist approach.

(b)   Latent. Integration of the new approach may cause her some need to revise her world view, with a degree of intellectual stress. Some speculation that she may be less interested in the technique itself than in finding a concrete counterpart to her apparently nebulous course input. Possible conflict as a result of having her self-deceit confronted might be predicted.

Interpersonal Level   (a)   Manifest. Though Zoe and Cliff probably have enough in common to develop a reasonable working relationship, both of them have difficulties in relating to Brian. Brian and Cliff have a clash of perspectives; while Zoe perceives Brian as a theorist uninterested in or unable to teach effective skills relevant to the social work role. She has already expressed her disillusionment with Brian's attitude toward her performance in previous placements (where he felt that she showed 'insufficient interest in structural problems and the generation of social change').

(b)   Latent. Possible attempted 'unconscious' collusion between Zoe and Cliff to exclude Brian; some tension for Cliff as an agent of the university.

Intragroup Level   (a)   Manifest. The three of them form a task-centred group. However, each has different backgrounds and existing group memberships influencing the conduct of the task. There is, indeed, some doubt as to whether Brian perceives the task as being valid — he attends the group because his role as 'tutor' dictates it even though it is at odds with his role as 'sociologist'.

(b)   Latent. Minimum involvement from Brian can be anticipated or, alternatively, he may initiate attempts to wrest the leadership of the group from Cliff. Full cooperation between the leading protagonists is unlikely unless lengthy discussions about the areas of similarity and dissimilarity can be arranged. Such discussions are, unfortunately, usually considered unimportant to the student supervision.

Intergroup Level   (a)   Manifest. None of Cliff's colleagues uses behaviour

249

modification and they are unlikely to offer Zoe much practical or emotional support in her attempts to learn it and put it into practice. The team has two other students, both of whom are developing casework 'skills'. Their supervisors and Cliff disagree on what constitutes a 'skill' and they have expressed concern that behavioural modification is inconsistent with the value base of social work. Zoe may therefore experience disapproval from the four of them.

(b) *Latent*. Higher levels of dependency can be expected from Zoe than from the other students. The usual student support groups of other members of the term and fellow students on placement are unlikely to operate. Zoe may seek informed support from other students on her own course that she knows she can trust.

Problem Analysis: Targets

Identity. Zoe is seeking to achieve a significant new component of identity in becoming a qualified social worker and presumably has vested a certain amount of self-esteem in the successful completion of the role induction. She is aware that the university establishes few formal criteria against which the placement supervisor can assess her, he has been nominated assessor with total power to form a judgement. He therefore has considerable significance as a potential threat or bulwark for the nascent identity of Zoe as a social worker. Zoe of course realizes this and is likely to use all the impression management techniques known to her in order to project the image of her that she wishes him to see. Her conversation implies that she is adept at managing her impression. With so much being invested in the successful compliance with role requirements failure can elicit extreme reactions — both legally and emotionally. Failure may represent banishment to a marginal position (that of 'failed social worker') or result in intolerable role conflict (from a clash of actions with expectations).

Relationships. Cliff's first impression of Zoe are that she is something of an introvert (a prototype), a typical caring Christian (a stereotype), and a decent married woman (assumption plus stereotype). It may be worth using the techniques designed to elicit personal construct systems with her in order to clarify his understanding of her construct system.

Speculating about the reasons for her decision to undertake this particular placement Cliff would attribute the cause primarily to circumstances (she has not sought a similar placement before nor has anyone else on her course; she has demonstrated no previous interest in behaviour modification; but she has expressed considerable dissatisfaction about her course in general).

A fairly strong degree of interpersonal attraction is likely to develop between them. Given the high level of personal contact and the need for fairly rapid self-disclosure of one form or another, within a 12 week period, it is probable that sampling, bargaining and commitment stages may be reached but without the opportunity for institutionalization. Terminating the relationship is likely therefore to be problematic.

250

Groups. By coming on placement, Zoe has inevitably placed herself in a position where she can be an actual or potential member of a number of different groups. Such groups might be the placement triad of Zoe herself, Brian and Cliff; the group formed with her fellow students on the course who are also on placement; a member of the group of students who are on placement in the particular SSD; a member of the SSD itself; an aspiring social worker; a colleague; a 'professional'; and so on. Boundaries to some of these groups are permeable; some are concrete, some are conceptual; some cohesive, some diffuse; some demand intense communication, some very little; few have similar goals; membership to some is ascribed, to others achieved. Zoe, then, has a peculiarly fluid set of actual and potential group memberships, and may well show some anxiety about deciding which to join, to what extent, and under what circumstances. The extent of compatibility between the internal and external criteria of memberships of these groups varies enormously: none is likely to generate a perfect match, however, and Zoe's satisfaction with being a member of one, some, or even all of them is likely to be minimal. Some stress can be anticipated while she decides whether to try to bend the groups to her, or herself to the groups, or whether she seeks a hiding place.

Zoe will probably be willing to conform to the norms of some of these groups. (Should Cliff help her to select?) Decision making in the placement triad is potentially good if common goals can be agreed at the outset, if Brian is given a definite task, and if there is no status clash between Brian and Cliff.

Environment. Zoe has a desk in the main office with six workers (Cliff is in a side office), a home help organizer and one of the other social work students. Privacy is minimal, and others in the office have expressed feelings of being overcrowded in the past. A sense of anxiety and veiled petty hostilities pervades the room. Constantly ringing phones and cross-talk across the room heighten the impression of stress.

The room for interviewing clients is small, untidy, poorly furnished, with two hard-backed chairs and an old table. Social work team meetings are held in the team leader's office: all 15 members of the team sit in a circle in the confined space.

It might be anticipated that Zoe will experience the effects of lack of privacy, overcrowding and lack of control over professional territory. Cliff might attempt to ensure that she does have adequate privacy, perhaps by letting her use his room while he is out, ensuring that she is out of the office as much as possible, that her personal space is 'personalized', perhaps by buying her a small gift, such as a tea mug or a diary, and suggesting that she writes most of her reports at home. Cliff might also encourage her to identify the sources of environmental stress, and together they may wish to militate for change in the environment.

Change. Primary change is being sought at a psychological and social level on Zoe's part, though it may have repercussions for both her and Cliff at a political, environmental and economic level. Others may be affected too. In allo-

251

cating the case of Mr. and Mrs. Brown and their marital problems to Zoe, has Cliff taken into account that Mr. Brown is seeking to be elected to the local council? Will a social work student's attempts to change his sexual response to his wife influence his views about welfare provision in general? Does the SSD have the appropriate budget to pay for the rewards of sweets and cigarettes Zoe needs to use with the troublesome adolescent? Has Cliff defined Zoe's required psychological and social change precisely enough, and how does he propose to assess it?

Problem Explanation: Key Processes

Construal. Zoe's construal processes have not been made accessible as yet, and may be worth eliciting more formally. It might be anticipated that current primary constructs are concerned with her social work training, her views of the course, and her feelings of insecurity about the placement. On the other hand, her family, home, or other interests may be construed as being of far more importance than the attempt to become a qualified social worker. It may well be, of course, that Cliff will never have access to her constructs, if Zoe does not consider their elicitation to be relevant to the placement.

Consistency. Zoe has pushed herself into an area that is not consistent with her past, either intellectually or in practice. With no previous contact with an SSD or interest in behaviour modification/empiricism. She has few previously acquired action, thought or feeling patterns to fall back on. She may attempt to deal with this by biasing her response to behaviour modification — perhaps by spending more time with the older clients, or by adopting a 'softer' format than might be indicated. From a slightly different perspective, her wish to achieve a skill may be inconsistent with her (and Brian's) feeling that behaviour modification is morally 'wrong'; her actions may therefore oscillate between interest and repulsion.

Comparison. Zoe has few yardsticks with which to compare her current experience, though the university offers a series of 'return days' to help cope with this need. With the absence of other means of comparison, the return days may be accredited with disproportionate significance, and may in fact inhibit learning if no social support is received from them. It might also happen, on the other hand, that Zoe chooses to use behaviour modification training as a means of differentiating herself from other students, giving the technique a disproportionately high value.

Conformity. Regardless of her individual background of conformity or non-conformity, it is clear to Zoe that she will almost certainly have to conform to the supervisor's and tutor's expectations of her behaviour during the placement, in order to pass successfully. If she fails the placement, she fails the CQSW — a fairly powerful inducement for conformity, however superficial.

Zoe may experience conflict between conformity, comparison and consistency demands. What happens, for example, if Zoe receives no social approval for her placement/skill learning, loses her battle for consistency, and yet knows she has to conform?

Change and Techniques for Change

See Table 20.1.

Table 20.1   Change and Techniques for Change

Change	Techniques
1. Greater awareness of student needs by the team as a whole. Opportunity for privacy, and a certain amount of group support for each student.	Persuasion of team leader. Devise the 'best' message, medium of presentation and source.
2. Zoe's level of disillusionment with the course and social work generally.	1. Measure the state of damage with a repertory grid (personal construct theory), using various professional care workers as the elements. Repeat at the end of the placement. 2. Weight the feedback from her placement performance to resolve her cognitive dissonance (in accord with the cognitive consistency model).
3. Provide Zoe with a more super-ordinate means of viewing social work input and practice.	Teach aspects of the SPA, with a particular emphasis on problem analysis and explanation.
4. Earlier involvement with the university for fieldwork supervisors in the selection of students (and tutors) for particular placements.	1. Persuade course director. 2. Attitude change among fellow supervisors.
5. Increased knowledge of behaviour modification theory and practice, to a level consistent with Zoe's experience and opportunities, and consistent with her own subjective satisfaction of her expertise in the technique.	1. Evaluation of self-esteem methods. Ask Zoe to provide subjective continuum of satisfactory behaviour through to unsatisfactory behaviour, quantify it subjectively, then compare the change in her subjective sense of satisfaction with the technique over time. 2. Compare goals of intervention with each case with what was actually achieved. 3. Simple knowledge questionnaire of behaviour modification theory, with practice problems.

Has Cliff's dislike of Brian influenced the assessment? Is Cliff too calculating in his approach to Zoe, and should he operate more on a guesswork basis? Will Cliff's actions on Zoe's behalf be seen by the team leader as dabbling in low level priorities? What will this mean for Cliff?

Is Cliff's intention to achieve closer contact with the university for Zoe's benefit or for his own? Should Zoe, in fact, be analysed in the same way that Cliff would analyse a client? If there is no distinction, should Cliff tell Zoe what he is doing? Should Cliff attempt to teach Zoe aspects of the SPA, which was not part of the initial contract? Has the SPA added anything to how Cliff would have perceived the placement without adopting the approach?

20.5 Conclusion

This chapter has had a fairly unusual focus — applying the SPA to the experience of supervising a student to whom one is teaching behaviour modification, a second level skill. Some of the more important issues generated have been the complex repercussions for the student, in terms of group memberships, social identity and so on; the importance of the physical environment; and the interlinkage between the attempted role induction and aspects of the student's social, and possibly, personal identity.

Student supervision courses tend to adopt a largely relationship-based or purely introspective approach: by so doing, they miss much of value from other levels of analysis that might be adopted. Once the placement and the act of teaching are placed in context, and the possible psychological consequences elaborated, a clearer if less reassuring vision is provided of the complexity of the rather simple notion of a 'student placement'.

Part VI
Analyst, Analyse Thyself

Preface

Part VI comprises two chapters which represent a change of orientation. So far, in earlier chapters, we have been examining the contribution that the social psychological approach can make to an understanding of the problems of clients and the potential it has for directing feasible strategies of intervention by social workers. In Part VI the focus shifts to an examination of how the social psychological approach can aid the social worker to understand his or her own problems. Here we discuss the attacks that are made on social work as a profession and the threats levelled at individual social workers due to their structural position. We discuss the methods used in the past in attempts to overcome these problems and try to explain why they have failed.

This analysis is predicated on the assumption that it is easier to analyse the problems that others face than to analyse those one faces oneself. Social workers frequently feel under attack. Most frequently they feel outnumbered and powerless and rarely have the chance to consider in abstract terms the reasons for the attack or the possible strategies of self-defence. The object of the two chapters which follow is to examine the problems of the social practitioners who are so busy dealing with the problems of others that they have no time to deal with their own problems.

Any analysis of the problems of social workers would be hopelessly confused if it ignored the distinction between the problems inherent in the position of the social work profession as a whole and the problems involved in the position of individuals within the profession. While recognizing that the position of the individual and the position of the profession are dialectically related, the distinction enables us to clarify many of the misconceptions which arise when these two sources of problems are confused. So, in Chapter 21 the position of the social work profession is discussed and in Chapter 22 that of the individual social worker.

21
The Position of the Social
Work Profession

Some of the history of social work has already been described in Chapters 9 and
10. In those chapters we tried to lay out the facts. Here we want to look at the
implications that these facts have. We also want to examine the currently
changing face of social work and then try to explain why it is changing. We are
thus talking about the dynamics of the relationships between the profession, its
clients and its controllers. The dynamics are analysed in social psychological
terms. As we have stated before, it is possible to analyse the same phenomena
from many other approaches and it is not necessary to claim primacy for the
social psychological analysis. Its primacy or otherwise is irrelevant as long as it
proves catalytic and convincing.

21.1 Social Work Identity

Throughout this volume, it has been acknowledged that there is no monolithic
structure to social work. Its facets have evolved through a slow process of accre-
tion; its duties are a function of the uncoordinated incremental process of
legislation. Over 100 years after their conception, social workers remain a heterogeneous group. Fieldworkers are distinct from residential workers. Qualified are distinct from unqualified social workers. Local authority social workers
are distinct from voluntary sector social workers. The lines of differentiation
appear wherever the eye can focus. If looked at critically the profession is sin-
gularly fragmented: without universal codes of practice; without common
training; without standardized methods or theories; and without a representative professional association.

256

This fragmentation is eminently well recognized within the profession. It is vociferously bemoaned. Yet, it is important to realize that such lines of differentiation or fragmentation are more apparent to those inside the profession than to the rest of the world. To those who are not social workers, a social worker is a social worker. Social workers are viewed as a group. As a group, social workers have an identity ascribed to them by the media, the general public and other professions. The fact that this *ascribed identity*, which is said to be so ubiquitously appropriate, is largely based on the role of fieldworkers in local authorities is not important to those who believe it to be correct. The ascribed identity *is* what social work is — at least to those outside it. It details the traits which characterize social work, the ends it seeks and the masters it serves. The ascribed identity of a group effectively is the image which outsiders have of it.

Not all outsiders will ascribe the same identity to social work, of course, but at any one time there will be a dominant ascription. At any one time there will be an image of the group which is widely held. The number of different ascribed identities attributed to any group is a function of the certainty of that group's social role and power. The greater the uncertainty about the group's role or power, the greater the room for a multiplicity of ascribed identities. The greater the power of the group, the greater its capacity to control the attributes ascribed to it. A powerful group also has more opportunities to control the ascriptions made to other groups. A powerful group can, in other words, control how it is represented in the media and the images people have of it; it can also control the images of other groups. A weak group can neither control its own image nor the images of others. Social work is a weak group. It is weak because it is fragmented and this leads to an inability to make concerted efforts to change the status of the group. The fragmentation, a result of the history of the profession, leaves social workers without a unified voice. It is only by gaining such a voice that social work can begin to control its own image and influence its ascribed identity. The rhetorics which mediate the ascription of identities will be considered below. At the moment, the important point to emphasize is that the ascribed identity imposed on the group coexists with the identity which the members of the group would acknowledge that it has. Outsiders have strong ideas about what social workers as a group are and do and should be but social workers themselves may have quite another view of their group. They have an *acknowledged identity*, one which has traits, duties and rights defined from within the group. Of course, within social work there is no consensus about what social workers are and should be doing. There is, therefore, no unanimity about its acknowledged identity. However, it is clear that no matter how much social workers differ in their definitions of their profession they agree with each other more than they agree with those who would ascribe an identity to social work from outside.

The problem is, in truth, a rather simple one: social workers find that the image that they have of themselves is at variance with the image others have of them. When this happens it is like looking into a mirror expecting to see the blonde, blue-eyed beauty that you believe yourself to be and seeing there an old

257

crone. Self-conception is in conflict with social reflection. The identity acknowledged is not that ascribed. Social workers face an ambiguity in their identity. The theories of social identity and intergroup relations described in Chapters 4 and 5 would indicate that such an ambiguity cannot be tolerated.

The removal of the ambiguity can take many forms but all of them entail some sort of challenge to the parameters of self-definition. To put it crudely, the group will change the way it thinks of itself or it seeks to change the ways in which others think of it. Either way, the object is to bring ascribed and acknowledged identity into line.

Obviously, before dealing with how the group might act to end the ambiguity, something should be said of the sorts of mismatch which can occur between ascribed and acknowledged identities. Essentially, differences between them can be on two sorts of dimensions: the dimension of content and the dimension of value. The content dimension entails the nature of the image attributed to the group; it is comprised of the characteristics that the group is said to possess. For instance, a group might be young, radical and female or old, conservative and male. The content dimension has attached to it a parallel, evaluative dimension which attaches a value to each of the traits characterizing the group: youth is splendid; conservatism is the doctrine of the moribund. Ascribed and acknowledged identities could differ on one of these dimensions or on both. So, one group may say to another: 'You are old, conservative and male.' That group may reply: 'We are young, radical and female.' This would be a pretty obvious clash on the content dimension. Alternatively, one group may say: 'It is good to be young, radical and feminine.' The other may reply: 'It is unpleasant to be young, radical and female.' This, obviously, would be a clash on the evaluative dimension.

It can easily be seen that one of the worst predicaments that a group could be in would arise when it faced an ascribed identity which clashed with its own acknowledged identity on both dimensions. For instance, where it thought that it was an agency designed to help those with social problems and that it was good to do this and where it was being told that it was in truth an agency of social control and that this was a bad thing. The caricature of the position of social work is rather thinly veiled in this example. In fact, social workers find themselves challenged on both dimensions. Social workers, as a profession, have what can be considered a classic case of *threatened identity*.

At this point, something of the nature of this threatened identity needs to be explored. It has been explained earlier that social work was built on the back of casework ideology derived from psychoanalysis (Yelloly, 1980). It constituted a federation of different specialisms including, in the early days, almoners, moral welfare officers, probation officers, psychiatric social workers, child welfare officers and geriatric social workers. However, there was initially some communality of ideology and approach across specialisms fostered by the Association of Social Workers (ASM) which replaced the original British Federation of Social Workers in 1951. The aims of the ASW were to unify the social work profession by encouraging generic training and the casework ideology. The ideology was built on notions of vocational caring allied to

258

voluntary organizations. Most of the early assumptions were based on a medical model of care and a compatible conservatism of aim: the individual was the source of his or her own downfall and the poor and dissolute needed to be saved from themselves. The acknowledged identity of social work revolved around these ideological and methodological assumptions.

But then the enterprise was subject to radical change. The Local Authority Social Services Act of 1970 when taken together with the 1974 Local Government Reorganisation Act which followed the Seebohm Report (1968) broke down old specialisms. All but probation officers were brought under the direction of the local authority social services. Generic training and the introduction of systems analysis (Goldstein, 1973) and integrated methods (Pincus and Minahan, 1973) were predicted to toll the death of casework. Serious questions came to be asked about the value of and values in social work. The multiplicity of the attacks which have been made on social work is rather startling. The attacks are virulent, are carried by all of the media, come from diverse sources and are mutually contradictory to an incredible extent. It would be literally impossible for social work to be all that its critics condemn it for, just as it would be impossible for it to be everything they want it to be. For instance, many on the Left ask whether social workers should be helping the clients to cope or helping them to see the reality of their position and militate for revolutionary change. Meanwhile, on the Right, people query whether social work is necessary at all; it is put to social workers that their clients are misfits and scroungers who should not be represented by public servants at the taxpayers' expense. Whenever their overall value system was not under attack, social workers have been faced with accusations that they are failing in their vital job. They were the ones who were responsible for the baby batterings, the tug-of-loves and the hyperthermia cases. On one hand, they are useless and can achieve nothing; on the other hand, they are so vital that their failures bring disaster. The irony is even greater since both messages often emanate from the same source.

Throughout the ten years since reorganization social workers have been subject to this paradoxical series of attacks. To use the terms employed earlier, they have found that on both the content and the evaluative dimensions their ascribed and acknowledged identities have been in conflict. Even though they have frequently declared the illegitimacy of these attacks which embody the stereotype of the ascribed identity, social workers have taken them seriously. They have responded to the ambiguity in the definition of their identity as a group in the way predicted on the basis of social identity theories. They have engaged in exercises of self-definition. Evidence of this can be seen in every publication on social work in recent years. Anyone who doubts this assertion need only leaf through a few back copies of *Social Work Today* or *Community Care* which are major channels of communication for practising social workers. Repeated 'crisis' conferences held by BASW support the assertion as do the overt efforts which BASW made to define social work in its document *The Social Work Task* (1977). What we want to do now is show what the social psychological approach can offer by way of an explanation of the shape that

259

these efforts after redefinition take. In order to do so, we will examine closely the sorts of claims made in *The Social Work Task*.

21.2 The Rhetoric of the Social Work Task

In 1977, BASW published *The Social Work Task*. This was an attempt to define the task of social workers, the ethics they should employ and the models of manpower deployment which should be adopted. In this document, BASW defined social work:

> Social work is the purposeful and ethical application of personal skills in interpersonal relationships directed towards enhancing the personal and social functioning of an individual, family, group or neighbourhood, which necessarily involves using evidence obtained from practice to help create a social environment conducive to the wellbeing of all.

Repeatedly, BASW claims that 'central to the practice of social work' is the worker's use of self in enhancing a client's personal and social functioning through the medium of interpersonal relationships. BASW does not say exactly how the worker should use the 'self' or the techniques which should be used in 'the medium of interpersonal relationships'. The statement revolves around the desire to establish global definitions of social work rather than a precise theory or method. BASW seems to think that to define social work one needs to define its ideology rather than its practices.

Nevertheless, the ideology outlined indicates fairly clearly what are not to be regarded as social work tasks and practices: social workers are not administrators of legislated provisions of the social services — they should not be dishing out aids to the disabled, carting runaways back to detention centres or sorting out social security claims. Social work, BASW admits, is less to do with materialism and more to do with 'applied love'. Social service workers — the administrators — give practical help, social workers give help with human relationships. Social work 'involves the creative application of skills derived from values to meet individual needs through interpersonal relationships between worker and client' (BASW, 1977, p. 10). Of course, these pronouncements beg major questions like what constitutes need? Where are professional values formulated and deposited and how do they relate to the worker's personal values? What constitutes an interpersonal relationship and how do these relate to group or intergroup relations? And, most important, what are the personal skills which work such wonders? Where the report considers these questions they are evaded by the use of what might be called a taxonomic diversion. The taxonomic diversion entails listing types of need and sorts of social work roles without ever showing how these could work in practice. A taxonomy of the possible is no explanation of the actual.

The big question, of course, is why should the most influential social work organization in Britain be promoting a specious definition of social work. The need to provide some sort of definition is explained by the ambiguities

260

surrounding the threatened identity of social work. But the interesting issue is why this should be the sort of definition proposed. A social psychological analysis provides some of the answer. The theory of intergroup relations initially proposed by Tajfel and his many colleagues (Tajfel, 1978) put at its crudest claims that people need to feel satisfied with their social identity which they derive from their group memberships; if they are not satisfied with it, they will act to make it more satisfying. Depending on the ideological or material circumstances, the person who is dissatisfied may either seek to change his or her group memberships (become socially mobile) or to change the group (initiate social change). Now, it is important to realize that the initial satisfaction or dissatisfaction with a group and the strategies which are chosen in order to remedy any disquiet are tied to social comparison processes such as those described in Chapter 8. Identities are valued in relation to other identities. We compare ourselves with others in order to know how well we are doing. The status of a group is similarly only meaningful in relation to that of others. Where a satisfying social identity cannot be achieved through social mobility — the movement of the individual from one group to another — then social change must involve changing the status of the group in relation to others.

Efforts after social change normally involve unilateral attempts by groups with low status or insecure status to change the criteria of status attribution; the dimensions of intergroup differentiation or the structure of group boundaries. To put this in concrete terms, a group seeking more status can claim that it is worthy of greater rewards because it has characteristics which should now be recognized as meritorious even though they have never been so in the past; or it can claim to have characteristics which it has never been recognized to have and which are generally believed to be meritorious; or it can claim that by admitting new and different people into its midst it eradicates those characteristics which have stigmatized it in the past. These efforts after a changed status in order to provide a positive input to the social identity of members frequently centre upon attempts to make the group distinct from all other groups and then to invest that distinctiveness with a positive ethos. So that a group seeking to improve its status will often focus upon some feature which makes it distinct from other groups as long as this feature can be seen to give the group some advantage over other groups. It is important to note that the advantages attached to any such distinguishing feature can often exist merely in the heads of the leaders of the group. Sometimes the feature has no objective advantage or value but it is invested with all sorts of glorious implications at a subjective level. This distinctiveness is thought to be good, regardless of its objective value, and it is represented to others as being good and, not infrequently, propaganda is produced to encourage others to perceive it in the same way. Given this, it is hardly surprising that a group will cling to dimensions of differentiation which are valuable and which it can call its own: these are the things that make it unique and superior.

Seen in this framework, the stance of BASW becomes more comprehensible. In truth, BASW is marking out the professional domain and ethos of social

261

work. It is engaged in the task of differentiation: making clear what is unique about social work and surrounding that uniqueness with value. The basic problem faced by BASW is that none of the roles occupied by social workers is unique to social workers. Perhaps even more important: where other professionals can point to a technology or an institution they can all their own, social work has neither. In the past, social work possessed no unique method and social workers had no unique system of knowledge to administer. The surgeon has a knife, the doctor has a drug; both have an accumulated wisdom in the use and efficacy of their tools. In seeking an equivalent tool and skill for social workers BASW has come up with the 'self' and 'personal' skill. The very absence of a professional tool or set of skills in any material sense has been made the hallmark of social work. The social worker — having no overt tools — uses the 'self'.

Finding that other 'caring professions' had occupied institutions and took possession of technologies of social problem solving, BASW actually had two alternatives which might have led to a distinctive and positive identity for social work. It might have claimed that social work was unique in its eclecticism — in the breadth of the techniques and tools it was able to employ. In fact, this option was rejected in favour of the claim to élitism through the notion that only social workers use their 'self' to solve social problems. It is interesting, but hardly surprising, that the least tenable alternative was adopted. Since its establishment, social work has been harried by protestations that it could do nothing more than was already being done more efficiently by others. The claim of a specialized tool and skill for social work, no matter how ethereal, at least served to fend off attacks that called social work a scavenger preying on the cast-offs of other professions. BASW has been arguing that social work is not merely an opportunist scurrying around after the clients which others will not treat using methods which are not its own and which it frequently misunderstands. Claims of eclecticism might have provided social work with distinctiveness but they would not have carried that positive ethos which has to be the penumbra of any distinctiveness. In a way, perfectly predictable on the basis of intergroup theories, BASW chose a form of self-definition which established distinctiveness and which, even if it did not immediately impart it, had the potential to be invested with a positive ethos.

Intergroup theories also predict other efforts BASW has made to legitimate social work. Some of these efforts are described in greater detail in Chapters 9 and 10. These efforts largely entail attempts to get more social workers qualified and to get standardization and accreditation of training courses. They reflect a wish, already evident in their definition of social work, to have it seen as a profession with a standardized body of knowledge to pass on to initiates. This is paralleled by the desire to institute manpower deployment which ensures that qualified social workers have different roles to those of the unqualified. The qualified should be dealing with the most complex, important and dangerous cases. In sharpening the distinction between the tasks of qualified and unqualified BASW is careful to attach kudos and significance to the professional.

The emphasis on professionalism has been accompanied by demands for the reintroduction of specialization (Otton, 1974; Birch, 1976). At the moment, only 38% of social workers are qualified and it has been argued that only through specialization can they deal with the range and volume of work they face to the best of their ability and preference. The irony of BASW's support for specialization, of course, lies in the fact that having identified the 'self' as the central tool of social work BASW has difficulty delineating the skills which would differentiate between specialisms.

It is a great pity that BASW's attempts to set up a positively valued professional group seem likely to backfire. By locating the unique essence of social work within the social worker's self and in the intangible interpersonal relations with the client, the very definition of social work militates against the growth of consensual practices or established data in social work. If the tool is the 'self' and there is no theory of the 'self', the tool must be used, if not randomly, then on the basis of intuition. Establishment of the efficacy of social work intervention is a rather remote possibility if the parameters of that intervention cannot be specified and the consequences it has are either indescribable or unidentifiable. The definition of social work makes it immune from any sort of scientific evaluation. There is a hint that social work is closer to magic than social science which is a nice delusion but delusions have a nasty way of disappearing in the face of reality. Certainly, the fact that this magus ideology simultaneously embodies a doctrine which fragments social work, through qualification and specialization, and places the burden of responsibility on the individual social worker, through the emphasis on the 'self', is likely to threaten the social work identity it was designed to evolve.

The object of this section has been to show that BASW has evolved a rhetoric designed to protect social work from the attacks massed by clients, the public and other professions. In discussing this attempt in terms of a social psychological analysis it becomes clear that BASW's actions were predictable. It becomes equally clear that these attempts are likely to be ineffective. They are ineffective for at least two reasons. Firstly, they fail because the rhetoric BASW chose and the self-definition it embodied is so peculiarly abstract and intangible and, consequently, open to multitudinous forms of reinterpretation. Ambiguous self-definition, typified by unverifiable claims, is not good medicine for an ailing social identity. Secondly, they fail because social workers have no social power, whether economic or political. If they had such power, the peculiarities of the self-definition would not matter since power encourages acquiescence. Without power it is necessary to persuade and persuasion is largely dependent upon being consistent and persistent in your message (Brown, 1963; Moscovici, 1976).

The failure, so far, to bring ascribed and acknowledged identities of social work into alignment is important because it has resulted in a kind of identity flux in social work. Social workers, unconvinced of their own propaganda, no longer appear to have an acknowledged identity. As a group they do not know themselves. There is what Erikson (1965) would call identity diffusion. In the face of a multiplicity of new demands and expectations old formulations of

263

social work identity and purpose seem outmoded and the substitute formulations are either unassimilated or inappropriate.

Any practising social worker reading this is likely to say 'So what? I know the problems, give me some answers.' The only response to this enviable pragmatism has two facets. Firstly, answers only mean something if you ask the right questions and asking the right questions is only possible if you really understand the problem. And it is here important to distinguish between understanding a problem and experiencing a problem. Secondly, a clear delineation of this identity problem can lead on to an understanding of how it is connected to other problems experienced by social workers recently. The next section deals with just one of these problems: the 1978–1979 social work strike.

21.3 Conflict and Rhetoric

The prime purpose of this section is to show what happened when social workers took their threatened identity into conflict. The conflict concerned is the social work strike of August 1978 to June 1979. The reasons for the strike and the course it took are outlined below, however the analysis centres on the form of the conflict and the implications this has for the future of social work.

21.4 The Strike: August 1978 – June 1979

Two things should be understood at the outset. Firstly, this was the first time that social workers had engaged in what is called 'indefinite strike' (i.e. for a period unspecified at the outset). There had been one-day stoppages, refusals to do weekend or night duties and restricted practices engendered by demarcation disputes during the preceding year which marked a growing militancy among social workers, but this was their first ever avowed long-term strike. Secondly, the strike was not in pursuit of greater pay but in order to change the machinery of pay negotiation. The methods of future pay negotiation were at the crux of the dispute. The pay negotiating machinery operative at the time is not simple but can be caricatured. Social workers who worked for local authorities were treated as local government officers and the majority belonged to the National Association of Local Government Officers (NALGO) though a few were members of the National Union of Public Employees (NUPE). Accredited unions, effectively NALGO, were responsible for negotiating pay scales with representatives of the local authority employers on the National Joint Council (NJC). Pay scales were established on a national basis for all local government officers through the NJC and social workers were no exception to this rule. This meant that social workers on the same point on the national scales would be paid the same whether they worked in the quietest rural village or the most problematic inner city district. Individual branches of the union had no right to negotiate locally with their own councils for a different rate of pay or conditions of service. Dissatisfaction with these national prescriptive scales was at the root of the dispute. When, in June 1977, NALGO passed a resolution making it the union's policy to abolish such national prescriptive gradings, the official door was opened for social workers to pursue local pay and regrading claims.

The interesting thing is that the employers on the NJC were quite willing to countenance a national regrading of social work scales since a good case could be made for their jobs having changed drastically since the last adjustment of scales in 1971. Social workers were recognized to have taken on greater responsibilities due to changes in legislation and an upgrading resulting in more pay was reasonable. However, the NJC employers were unwilling to allow local negotiations in breach of national scales. They feared that NALGO would use the social workers, if this breach were made, as a precedent to begin local bargaining for all local government workers. They foresaw that this would lead to differential settlements — some areas negotiating a greater rate on the basis of greater social needs or job difficulty. This in itself was not considered too bad but they expected that these higher settlements would then be used as comparitors for inflated claims for the less well paid areas. Section 11 of the Employment Protection Act then in force enabled workers to apply through the Arbitration and Concilliation Service (ACAS) for a 'going rate' adjustment to hitch their wages to the same level as those paid to workers in the same or similar work in another part of the country. This is why the employers were expecting leapfrogging if local negotiations were permitted. They consequently urged local authorities to stand firm on the rejection of the claims.

The local authorities stood firm and the social workers came out on strike.

Of course not all social workers went on strike. By the end of the strike 14 authorities had been extensively affected by industrial action. Newcastle and Southwark were the first out on 14 August 1978. They were followed by Tower Hamlets almost immediately. These authorities saw the virtually total shutdown of social work services and yet neither the union nor the employers took serious steps to end the dispute until mid-October when Lewisham and Liverpool social workers joined the strike. By this stage the social workers were already afraid that NALGO would betray them and engage in a compromise settlement. This fear originated in the fact that NALGO did compromise over claims made by Brent social workers against the wishes of the branch members. This fear welled up in a mess demonstration on 25 October outside the NJC meeting where NALGO representatives were talking to the employers. The national officers of NALGO emerged from this meeting to tell the demonstrators that they had not changed their policy but that a working party with representatives of both sides had been set up to discuss a plan for local negotiations within the national framework.

While this working party held talks Gateshead, Greenwich, Knowsley, Leeds and Sheffield social workers joined the strike. By the end of November the working party had a set of recommendations to which both sides had agreed. However, NALGO put these recommendations to the strikers and they rejected them in their local branches. NALGO was thus obliged to send the proposals back to the NJC where they were accepted by the employers but they could not be instituted until NALGO accepted them and NALGO would not go against the overwhelming sentiments of the strikers at this point.

December saw little change in the situation except that Islington and Cheshire came out on strike and BASW entered the arena with an abortive call for an independent inquiry into pay. By January, 14 areas were on strike, including Manchester and Rochdale. The working party discussions resumed and on 26 January NALGO finally accepted the working party's offer but advised areas not to return to work until 'meaningful progress' had been made in local bargaining. Since the settlement accepted in January was not substantially different from the one rejected in November strikers felt justified in taking the advice about 'meaningful progress' seriously and many places had no intention of returning to work until full local settlements were made. Eleven areas were still on strike in mid-March when NALGO made the strike unofficial and stopped paying strike pay which had been running at 55% of the strikers' normal gross pay. When the final area to return to work, Tower Hamlets, did so on 11 June 1979 only one-quarter of the local authorities in England and Wales had implemented the social workers' complex pay deal. Where agreement had been reached, social workers were not satisfied and many felt betrayed by NALGO.

To put it in a nutshell: social workers got more money out of the strike but they did not win what they had fought so long to get. They still had a cumbersome, inequitable system of national scales produced by negotiation machinery designed to control the pay of dustmen and council clerks.

21.5   Rhetoric of Conflict

The description above merely outlines the chronology of the dispute. It is a colourless image of what was really happening. In truth, the social work profession faced a considerable crisis. It is only by looking more deeply at the structure of conflict that the nature of the threat to the identity of social work can be understood.

Conflict between groups normally takes place on two planes: the physical and the symbolic. The physical plane involves acts of physical aggression — occupying a country or a council house. The symbolic plane entails the aggressive arguments and posturing involved in the conflict. Most industrial conflicts entail minimal physical hostility and maximal symbolic hostilities. This is merely to say that, nowadays, once labour is withdrawn much of the conflict revolves around argument and negotiation processes. Labour and management do not cudgel one another with sticks — they do it with words. Of course, the real power lies in the withdrawal of labour or the control of employment but the arguments lubricate the realization of this power.

In the case of the social work strike, conflict on the physical plane was fairly static in form. The social workers withdrew their labour and picketed social services departments, often disrupting the machinery of local government in doing so. While these industrial actions were reasonably static, the arguments which raged around the dispute were dynamic. These arguments can be called the 'rhetoric of conflict'.

Rhetorics are used by groups in a conflict to manipulate their position and that of other groups. Rhetorics rarely entail a single argumentative proposition. They are more like a mosaic of arguments. Each of the arguments is akin to an attitude; having a cognitive and an evaluative component: the argument proposes that a thing is true and then shows how that thing should be valued. The rhetoric can be like a fine tapestry woven of many threads of argument. The rhetoric is never balanced, it is always biased — serving the interests of the group which creates it. In order to serve group interests, it may evolve and change in the course of the conflict. In its responsiveness to the demands of the conflict rhetoric shows another aspect of its functioning: it is tailored both to influence members of the group which produces it and to influence members of other groups. Rhetoric is a two-edged sword and its effects on both sorts of audience interact. This multiplier effect means that the consequences of rhetoric cannot always be anticipated. Rhetoric designed to serve one purpose may become the slave to another.

In so far as rhetorics are tailored to group interests and objectives they are a function of the group ideology. In many, they are ideology in action; they encapsulate beliefs and objectives and actively seek to inculcate them in others. Of course, rhetorics are consequently context-specific in a way that ideologies are not expected to be. Rhetorics are only efficient in achieving their objective if they take advantage of things of the moment: rhetorics are opportunistic.

Furthermore, rhetorics tend to have a structure characterized by inconsistency in the content of arguments but consistency in the objective of the arguments. The structure encompasses illogical shifts of argument but these arguments are invariably emotive and they are subject to stereotype. Moreover, rhetoric feeds off itself: once the ball is rolling arguments gather their own momentum and ferocity of attacks on the target of the rhetoric builds. It is also the case that rhetorics, while mouthing adherence to moral codes, can be the means of their destruction. Rhetoric enters the ring and the referee is blinded as a precursor to the real business.

Now that the general properties of rhetoric have been outlined the rhetorics of the social work strike can be examined. The rhetorics of the strike are interesting because they show how a group identity can be attacked in a conflict. They also show how rhetoric is a powerful shaper of group identity. In fact, the rhetoric of the strike shows how ascribed identities determine and are determined by rhetoric to a large extent. Certainly, the rhetoric of the strike was founded on the ascribed identity of social work and was instrumental in revising that identity. To the extent that the rhetorics aggravated the disparity between the ascribed and the acknowledged identity of social work they formed a real threat to social work identity.

21.6 Rhetorics of the Strike

Breakwell (1982c) reports a detailed studied of the rhetorics used in the strike. That study, which entailed a systematic content analysis of reports of the strike in the prime social work media, is the foundation of the assertions made below about the rhetorics used by the various groups in the conflict. It is important to realize that the analysis covered the entire period of the strike and mapped how rhetorics developed and changed over time. The results are, therefore, not simple to summarize. The outlines of the rhetorics here are their bare bones.

Six identifiable groups evolved rhetorics during the strike: the employers; the social services directors; the union; the strikers; BASW; and the government. An identifiable group that might have been expected to have something to say about the strike but which was strangely silent was the client group. The silence of the clients is particularly interesting since it became part of the rhetorics of some of the other groups. Perhaps this silence should not be regarded with too much surprise. After all, the clients are not a group in the sense of a corporate entity with representatives to mouth its views. The clients are an amorphous mass — separated by time and space from each other. In fact, if they have a voice at any time, it tends to be that provided by social workers who represent them. Deprived of that voice, they had no means of expressing how much they needed it or what they thought of the strike. The clients were left without an audible rhetoric. The rhetorics of the other six groups can be briefly described.

To deal with the least vociferous first: the government rhetoric. During the period of the strike there was a change of government. David Ennals was succeeded by Patrick Jenkin as Secretary of State for Social Services in the May 1979 changeover. Ennals, in December 1978, made his one and only reported pronouncement on the strike. It had two lines of argument:

(i) Social workers are playing into the hands of their critics by striking — the victims of the strike were the clients whose distress was hidden from sight. He predicted that there would be countless cases of irreparable damage done by the decision of social workers to leave their clients, stranded and in the lurch, unaided. It would destroy worker – client relationships.

(ii) Social work is the second victim of the strike since they are contradicting their own value systems. He argued that they might find 'their present actions merely served the interests of greed, selfishness and ruthless individualism which they normally opposed'.

The second line of argument is a beautiful example of ascribing an identity to the group and then arguing that they are not living up to it even when the group has not accepted the ascription. Having stated his opposition to the strike in terms which make it sound as though his only interest is for social work and its future Ennals refused to do anything about the strike. The government played no further part in the genesis of rhetorics about the strike. Not, at least, until Jenkin took office and then he stated that social work had got nothing but grief from the strike and set up an inquiry into the effects of the strike. This inquiry will be discussed later. For the moment, it is enough to note that the government, whether in Labour or Tory vein, clearly expressed its view that the strike was ill-considered and potently damaging to social work but was extraordinarily unwilling to do anything about it. The unwillingness of the government to intervene in the social work dispute is more marked by the excessive amount of interventions it was making in other industrial disputes during the winter of 1978.

The rhetoric of the employers (the local authorities) although encompassing that of the government was considerably more diverse. The rhetoric of the employers was dependent on the stage at which they were in the negotiating process. Initially they argued that the strike was illegitimate because it was being masterminded by NALGO to break national pay scales and the social workers were merely pawns in this larger battle. The line they took was that the pay increases were available without changes in the national negotiating machinery and therefore social workers should take the money and not fight other people's battles for them. NALGO were, according to the employers, irresponsible and local negotiations would be unfair. Moreover, they protested, the public would not understand nor sympathize with the idea of local negotiations. It was only after the strike had been going for two months that the employers started to change their rhetoric. At the end of September they started to say that the social workers were using the vulnerable for their own ends and the strike would damage client – worker relations. By January, this had evolved into claims that the strike was undermining all social services progress and fueling the fervour of those who think that social work is unnecessary. At the same time they were proclaiming that councils were in no mood to settle and in the future all social work appointments would be 'carefully scrutinized'. Warnings echoed on all sides: priorities will change (reversing the move to employment of qualified workers) and social work methods will be re-evaluated. The employers started the strike with appeals to the strikers' sense of fair play and ended it with appeals to their self-interest. But it is noticeable that the appeals to self-interest are couched in terms finely tuned to reverberate with the doubts that social workers already had about their identity and the values underpinning it.

The third group involved in the dispute were the directors of social services who are the managers of social work. Directors have their own professional body — the Association of Directors of Social Services (ADSS) — which promoted their rhetoric. Though, it should be emphasized that many of the arguments of the directors came from a small number, notably those nearest the action: the directors of Southwark, Tower Hamlets, Newcastle and the Chairman of ADSS (at the time Ted Brown). The directors came into the dispute in full force in August 1978 and their rhetoric exemplifies all of the salient features of the phenomenon. They proclaimed that they deplored NALGO's methods and action; the dispute was not about increased pay but about achieving locally negotiated settlements and these, if instituted, would initiate inequalities of services across the country. Moreover, the strike would damage the image of social work, harm clients and impair the development of the social services. They protested that the long-term effects of the strike would be very serious and, in the same breath, claimed that its effects would never be known. These lines of argument were continued into September and October but gradually became associated with suggestions that cutbacks in social services could be expected and unemployment for social workers would result. Increasing emphasis was placed upon the fact that the serious consequences of the withdrawal of social services was not appreciated by the local authorities as the strike continued. Moral indictments and warnings of future public disfavour were beginning to be juxtaposed by the end of October. So that the directors were telling social workers that people were seriously questioning the need for social workers in the same speech as they were claiming that 'someone has probably died as a result of the strike'. The directors were prophesying doom in other directions too. Not only would there be strife between strikers and non-strikers in the future; residential social workers had a stronger case and were the unsung heroes of the day and fieldworkers would find themselves in conflict with these their more conscientious colleagues. By the end of the period, in August 1979, the directors were arguing that the public and the employers doubted the social workers, they had lost the right to be considered 'dedicated people' and 'must be measured' in their work like others. One director went so far as to say that 'we must see that there are real rules for social workers'.

The directors' rhetoric shows the paradoxical nature of such arguments. They say the social work role is of ultimate, life and death importance and in the same moment claim that virtually everyone regards social work as unnecessary. They say that the effects of the strike are invisible and yet they proceed to claim incalculable damage has been done. The rhetoric is further characterized by its adroit accentuation of existing schisms in social work. Residential workers, also seeking a pay increase at the time but not engaged in industrial action, are painted as the heroes of the piece. Residential workers are good; fieldworkers on strike are bad. They will never be able to work effectively together if they are paid on different systems. The directors' arguments also point to the potential strife between strikers and non-strikers within the fieldwork group. The threat for the strikers is that their own colleagues will isolate them and abandon them. The directors were not only telling the social workers that they were damaging their public image and credibility, they were also predicting that the unity within the social work profession which had been fought for over such a long period was likely to be stillborn. Underlying all of this, there is the emphasis on the fact that NALGO is misleading and using the social workers for its own ends. This theme was dominant in the rhetoric of the employers too and its impact on the strikers is clearly evident in their rhetoric.

The strikers, it should be emphasized, did not get their views well represented in the social work media. There was no centralized voice for the strikers (independent of the union) until the All London Social Work Action Group (ALSWAG) came into existence. ALSWAG coordinated much of the strikers' actions, like rallies and demonstrations, and with the Shop Stewards Strike Committees put the strikers' case to the media. The line of their arguments is simple enough: social workers had no alternative but to strike, the risks to

270

clients of the withdrawal of services are overestimated and responsibility for any suffering that is incurred should be put at the door of intransigent councils; social workers will no longer put up with emotional blackmail which anchors their pay to lowest levels; lack of public concern only means that the public do not understand the social work role; and NALGO mismanaged the strike and bungled the settlement.

The most noticeable feature of the strikers' rhetoric is that it is not self-justificatory or defensive. It does not attack the opponents in the dispute. Instead, most of it is levelled at the union. While the employers and directors belabour the idea that NALGO is using the strike for its own ends, the strikers protest these are just the ends that they seek but are fearful that the union may not go far enough in pursuit of them.

The union itself has a consistent and simple rhetoric. NALGO argued that the strike was justified primarily by the fact that clients will benefit in the long run and any interim damage to clients would be minimized. They steer clear of any comment on the need for social work — *they justify the strike, not the profession*. This is very important since the employers and directors were not simply attacking the strike, they were also attacking the profession. Neither the strikers nor the union sought to defend the profession. The only group left to do this is BASW.

In fact, BASW totally failed to provide a protective rhetoric for the profession. The rhetoric of BASW was strangely ambiguous. BASW condemned the strike yet endorsed the right of social workers to strike. BASW acknowledged that the regrading claim was justified and yet deplored the notion of local negotiations. BASW considered national negotiations necessary and yet believed the NJC machinery inappropriate for social workers. The fact that BASW did not accept that the issue of local negotiations merited strike action encouraged it to produce a code of strikes which indicated what was to be considered the limits of acceptable industrial action. The code served to emphasize how negative its attitude to the strike was. The message was that the strike was unprofessional and damaging to the image of social work. In many ways, BASW bolstered the identity attack embedded in the rhetoric of the directors and employers.

The salient components of the rhetorics used in the strike can now be summarized. The most interesting aspect for an understanding of the dynamics of social work identity was the unanimity of the directors and employers in their attack. If the frequency of usage of each sort of argument is calculated, it becomes obvious that the employers and directors use the argument that the strike is 'damaging to social work' and 'damaging to the clients' much more frequently than any other. The social workers were being told that what they were doing was unethical, dangerous and irresponsible *and* that they were at risk of losing all public belief in their value. They were told that no one understood what their role was and no one felt that they were necessary. They were told that they could no longer be considered a 'caring' profession. Their value and their values were therefore simultaneously attacked. The very root of their acknowledged identity was being dug up, pulled from sustenance and incinerated. The ascriptions evolved in the rhetoric of the employers and the directors were such that social workers might feel their entire future as a profession threatened.

In such a situation, the threatened group should act to protect itself. Yet the strikers and NALGO did not protect themselves except from each other. Their rhetorics were addressed to legitimating the strike not the profession yet the attacks wove the strike around the profession and threatened both simultaneously. The social workers were attacked with their defences down. The vital feature for present purposes is what consequences this had for identity.

21.7 The Effects of the Rhetoric

The strikers and the union on one hand and the employers and directors on the other were using their rhetorics to achieve different ends and influence different audiences. While the strikers and the union strived to consolidate their own group, the employers and directors aimed to compromise the strikers and dissuade them from their course of action.

The failure of the strikers' rhetoric is evident in the settlement made against their wishes by the union. The success of the employers' rhetoric becomes manifest in more complex ways. The rhetoric of the management and employers was tailor-made to influence the strikers; it had barbed shafts which sank deep into the wounds of the social workers' already threatened identity. The rhetorics took each weakness of the profession, highlighted it, and showed that the strike was making people realize that those weaknesses existed. The message was clear — through all the paradox and inconsistencies — the employers were saying 'don't be silly and call attention to the fact that you are worthless and unethical; people won't realize that you are an unnecessary occupational group if you only return to work'.

Of course, the employers' rhetoric did not persuade the strikers to return to work. The effects of the rhetoric can be seen in other directions however. Firstly, the effects can be seen in the changed self-perceptions of the social workers since the strike and, secondly, they can be seen in the means chosen to evaluate the effects of the strike and in the way in which the report of these effects was received. They will be dealt with briefly and in turn.

Researchers working at Liverpool Polytechnic under the direction of Pat Clayton (1979) have investigated the course and the consequences of the strike for social workers in Liverpool. One of their findings is that social workers are reporting a changed self-perception since the strike. Social workers interviewed in Liverpool see themselves as 'workers' not as professionals with a caring vocation as they used to. They believe that they have thrown off the shroud of emotional blackmail associated with professionalism. They have moved closer to other unionized labour during the dispute and now experience solidarity with them — especially since they feel rejected by other 'professionals'. It seems that having been told that they are not a profession of worth, social workers are transforming their self-image. Unionism is being used as the substitute for the

272

ideology of professionalism. Having failed to repel the attack mustered by the rhetorics during the strike, social workers seem to be changing their acknowledged identity. Even BASW, the bastion of professionalism, has opened its membership to unqualified workers and created a union to parallel its activities (British Union of Social Workers, BUSW, created in September 1978). The Liverpool sample may not be representative of the rest of British social workers. The majority may not resolve the threat so easily, though it does seem that the shift to militancy and unionism is developing at some speed (McCarthy, 1980). Of course, the rhetorics of the strike are not the sole cause of these changes. The seeds of the changes were already sown in the threatened identity of social work which preceded the strike and which dictated the form that the rhetorics took. The rhetorics merely encapsulated and accelerated a process which had already begun and without which they could not have come into existence. The rhetorics, by mirroring the weaknesses of social work, oiled the wheels of change.

The second realm of consequences of the rhetorics of the strike can be seen in the report of the DHSS (1980) on the effects of the strike. The effects of the strike were evaluated by DHSS researchers on the instructions of the Secretary of State, Patrick Jenkin. They investigated the effects in only one area, Tower Hamlets, which had been on strike for the longest period and had a reputation as an area with extreme social problems (bad housing, high unemployment and inter-racial tension). The interesting aspect of this investigation for current purposes is that it can be seen to have been considerably influenced by the rhetorics of the conflict. The rhetorics of the conflict, in fact, established the milieu in which the strike effects would be examined and appraised. The rhetorics can be seen to be merely reiterated in the report; they predicated the questions asked and the answers given. This phenomenon can be seen most clearly in the attitude the researchers took to measuring the effects of the strike. One of the dominant rhetorics of the conflict had been that the effects of the strike would be immeasurable. The researchers actually supported this rhetoric by failing to establish any criteria on which the effects could be measured. They reported the opinions of relevant groups: there had been irreparable but invisible damage; there was a loss of confidence in social workers; their public image was spoiled; contacts with clients had been ruined; and association with other professionals was broken. Yet none of these things were measured. Hard data on these changes — if such had been gathered — were not presented. The report is a summary of prevailing attitudes in those very groups which had generated anti-strike rhetorics. It is hardly surprising that these attitudes echo the rhetoric of the strike. One might be pardoned for wondering how much of the report itself is merely rhetoric — even if unintentionally so. It is to be hoped that understanding something of the dynamics of rhetoric will forestall a repetition of this sort of investigative approach. At least understanding rhetoric provides social workers reading the report with the tools to analyse it.

The dynamics of rhetoric would also predict the reception of such a report. To put it mildly, the report was greeted with mixed feelings. *Social Work Today* said that it showed the importance of social work. *Community Care* said

273

that it showed the importance of social work but that it was obvious that the voluntary sector had coped and social workers were not much missed. *New Society* indicated that it showed that home helps and the like were much more important than the social worker who had hardly been missed at all. The *Spectator* ran an article in which June Lait said that the report not only showed how pointless social workers are but also how pointless DHSS researchers are. In the hands of the majority the report has become yet another cudgel with which to beat the social work profession. The report is interpreted to imply that the absence of social workers is not really so traumatic. The message to social workers is clear: we can do without you.

The absence of a self-defensive rhetoric from the social workers during the strike has its effects on the report too. The case of the social workers is not presented in the report. Their perspective on the effects of the strike is missing and yet, in most cases, they are the only ones who would know what has not happened that should have happened during the strike. They lie like the ghost at the feast — one can almost imagine them walking the streets of Southwark or Tower Hamlets head under arm. The consequences of their absence are reported, impressionistically, without reference to them or how they evaluate the effects. But then you would hardly expect the executioner to put his head on the block and the chopper in the hands of the accused. Social workers have been afforded no weapon. The terms of reference for the investigation lay in the rhetorics of other groups — after all the social workers had evolved no protective rhetoric during the conflict.

21.8   Lessons from the Conflict

The analysis of rhetoric above says something about what happens when a group with a threatened identity goes into conflict. If you take a threatened identity into conflict you should expect to get slapped in the very places where that identity is most in doubt. This is true even when those weaknesses look as though they are irrelevant to the issue in hand. It should be remembered that the value, or otherwise, of social work had no real relevance to the dispute over local negotiations. Rhetorics are shaped by the audience and the objective, they are a complex means of attaching values to actions and calling up moral or pragmatic fervour against groups and their actions. They work best when they can tap weaknesses in the identity of the group attacked.

Realizing this is useful if you belong to a group with a threatened identity and are under such an attack. For one thing it can act as insulation against the attack. Knowing that an evaluation of your importance is part of a rhetoric means that it should not be regarded as objective or absolute. If a man tells you that you are worthless, before believing him, it is wise to ask his motives; better still — guess the motive and anticipate the insult before it comes. Being able to predict an insult and knowing why it is made can, though not invariably, draw its sting.

This realization can also advance strategies of self-defence. It is obvious from

274

the analysis above that social work needs a protective rhetoric. This rhetoric, in the future, can take at least two forms: it can be defensive or it can be offensive. A defensive rhetoric could take one of two forms. Defence could entail a change in the self-image of social work which acknowledged the criticisms generated by others. This would effectively mean that social workers made fewer claims about their importance and value and began to pare away the layers of the profession's identity until only the core defining properties were left. These would be a solid base for a rhetoric but would hardly enable members of the profession to gain much kudos from it since the remnants that the criticisms leave are rather sparse. This form of defence might cause more harm than good; it is reminiscent of setting up an inviolable barricade around something which is not valued and not under attack. The second form of defence would entail rejection of the criticisms and the refusal of efforts to redefine social work. This would entail a determined rhetoric which claimed the uniqueness and value of social work and was promoted without the hint of self-doubt. Of course this would not mean that social workers themselves would have to cease doubting the value of their work, it would simply mean that all their doubts were not hung on the line for the world to examine. Other professions (like the medical profession) have certainly taken this line, with considerable success. In this case, the defence builds a strong barricade around something which others are made to believe is valuable and are, therefore, dissuaded from attacking.

Offensive strategies entail attacking those who would attack you. There are many ways of doing this. The offensive rhetoric can go straight into the attack; for instance, social workers could argue that if social work is pointless, so are the managers of social work — a line which might encourage managers of social services to reconsider the paradoxes in their arguments. Alternatively, offensive rhetoric can be circuitous. For instance, social workers could encourage clients to develop a voice for themselves. Social workers could direct their efforts towards building channels through which clients could make their needs heard and then use their rhetoric to make sure that clients used these channels. An integral part of such offensive rhetorics would be the inclusion of an acknowledgement that these rhetorics are being used by other groups. The analysis of a rhetoric can be used to dearm it.

Of course, several of these rhetorical strategies can be used simultaneously. They would then be likely to interact and the consequences may not be predictable. However, the direction of effects in most cases can be anticipated if the rhetorics are tailored to the identity of the group under attack.

Nothing has been said about the organizational structures through which rhetorics are transmitted. To many social workers since the strike it has seemed that the natural channel for social work rhetoric is not a professional association like BASW but a union. Unionization is seen simultaneously as a means to power through unity with other workers in the unions and a means of evading questions about ethics that have to be faced by professional groups. However, it is a fallacy that unionization as a matter of course leads to industrial strength. It can only do this if the union involved is truly a representative organ of social work. Should it ever get on its feet perhaps BUSW will provide the channel for an effective social work rhetoric. Belonging to a less specialized union might give social workers more industrial and political muscle but this would be pointless if they did not determine the use to which this muscle was put.

21.9 Summary

This chapter focused on the identity of social work as a profession. The many attacks on social work were discussed and some of the defences adopted were described. Central to the argument is the notion that a threatened and weakened identity will be problematic in a conflict. The threatened identity will be further attacked in exactly those places that it is weakest. The rhetorics evolved to manipulate the conflict by the groups involved will pinpoint the weaknesses and use them to the greatest advantage. This can be seen to have happened in the strike. Having discussed the effects of the strike and the failure of social workers to evolve self-protective rhetorics, suggestions were made for future strategies which social work might adopt to defend itself.

The value of this chapter for the practising social worker is twofold. It elucidates the motives underlying the continual attempts to redefine social work. It also shows how they fail and what might succeed. The message for the individual social worker is simple: often you will be attacked as an individual merely because you belong to a profession which is under attack — do not mistake an attack on the group for an attack on you and remember that attackers are unlikely to tell you the truth about yourself.

22

The Position of the Individual Social Worker

Having explored the position and sociopsychological dynamics of the profession, it is time to look at the position of the individual social worker. Now, this task obviously entails a basic problem: the position of each social worker is unique. Each social worker will work in a specific locality, in a specific authority or institution, with specific colleagues and administrators and with a specific caseload. These specifics cannot be ignored in portraying the position of the individual social worker but they can be surmounted by looking at what individual social workers share as a consequence of their structural position and the nature of their training and tasks. It is the generalizable features of the condition of the individual social worker which will be considered below. This means that some aspects of the analysis will apply more to some contexts than others but the overall import has relevance for most social workers.

It might be useful to paint the picture of the typical career structure for a social worker. The career tree (Fig. 22.1) does this graphically and indicates alternative career choices and prospects. Doubtless, this tree is not exhaustive and the titles attached to positions in the tree will change from time to time. The major points will be likely to remain the same:

(i)   the higher you go in the profession, the less casework and the more administration you do;

(ii)   the bulk of casework is done by the least experienced (though this may be changed with the introduction of the 'career grade' which is designed to preserve good fieldworkers from being channelled off into administration);

(iii)   generic social work is tied to generic administration (though specialisms are returning);

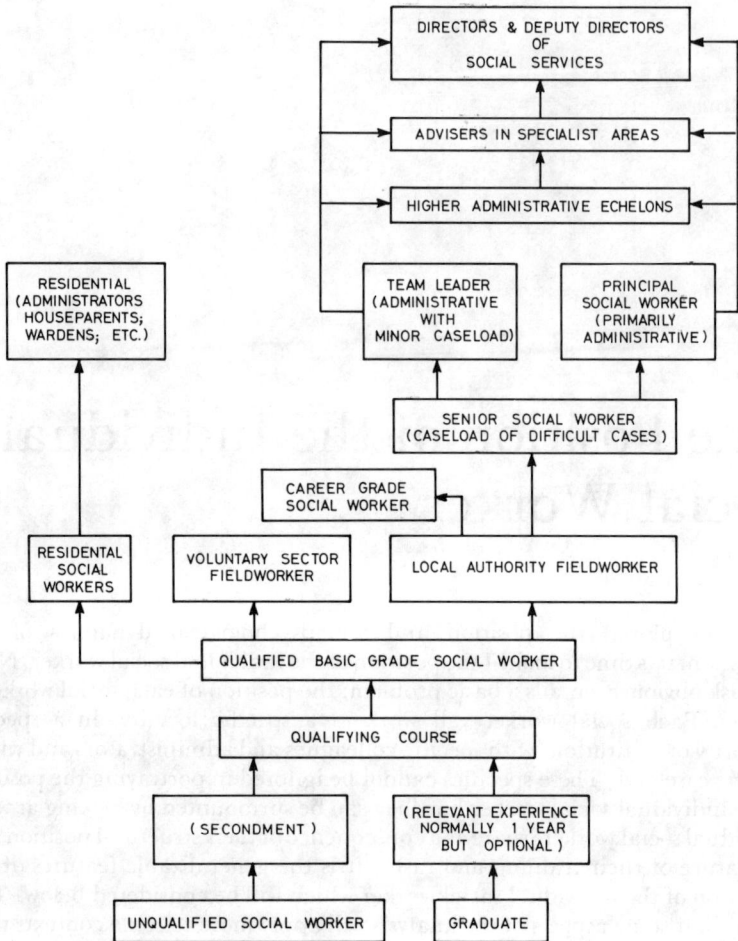

Fig. 22.1   The hierarchy of types of social work job.

(iv) administrators are not trained to administer, they have been trained to social work;

(v) the picture for field and residential workers though different on the ground (e.g. conditions and nature of work) is not different structurally (though since there are less administrative positions, there is less possibility of promotion in the residential setting).

One task for the analysis is to understand the implications of this career structure but this can only be done by acknowledging the broader context of this pattern. Fig. 22.2 indicates what might be considered the standard pattern

278

of contacts between clients, fieldworkers, middle and upper management, and local and national government in a local authority social services department. The position for voluntary sector practitioners is not so very different. In their case, the government representatives are supplanted by the source of their funds.

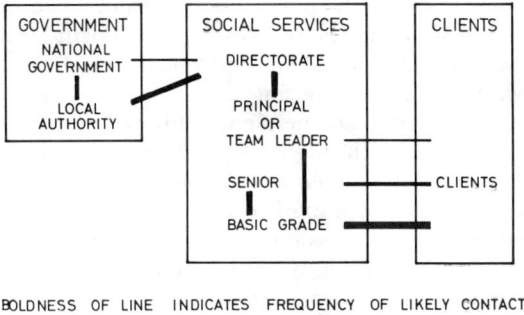

Fig. 22.2 The nature of contacts in local authority social services departments. Boldness of line indicates frequency of likely contact.

Whichever point the individual is at in the career structure, that individual is also part of this nexus of group relations. The point of major importance is that each grouping, no matter how loosely it coheres, has demands to make upon the individual. Government, social services department and clients all make demands upon the practitioner and most frequently they are contradictory.

The position is not eased by the fact that the practitioner is part of the social services group since memberships may be nested within a group. This is simply to say that you can belong to a social services department, to a district team and to a particular clique of 'radical' caseworkers — all at the same time and these memberships may each make contradictory demands on your allegiance and call for quite opposite commitments simultaneously. Moreover, the super-ordinate group, that is the social service department, may be tugged simultaneously in opposite directions by the other groups, that is government and clients. The clients may want one sort of service and the government may be only willing to give something else. Sometimes it seems that social services are the rope in a tug-of-war and the only question is when the rope will snap. Before it snaps, the rope stretches and the individual fibres of which it is composed, the practitioners, feel the strain.

Of course, the strain is borne differentially depending upon one's position within the social service hierarchy. Governmental demands are obviously felt most immediately by upper management; client demands are most immediate for fieldworkers. While it is the case that the whole social services are sandwiched between two hungry opponents, it seems reasonable to assume that the least powerful within the social services — the fieldworkers — are the ones that get most chewed up. They face the clients *and* the higher management daily.

Caseworkers are, in fact, an archetypal marginal group. They stand, or more accurately lie, between the governors and the governed and do a service for both. They are not allowed to consider themselves a part of either group yet they are used by both. Demands from government come in many forms: through legislation; through the prescription of values mediated by training; and through control of financial resources and investment decisions. Demands from clients may be of many sorts but tend to come through a single channel: direct contact with the client expressing need or labelled by some other agency as needy. Government controls the rights, duties and resources of a social worker; the client controls through cooperation or antagonism. While the governmental controls can be seen as tangible and imperative demands, the clients' control rests on the ethics of social work. The unenforceable claims which clients make can be just as imperative as the demands of government because they rest on moral value systems which most practitioners regard as paramount. So, the demands from the two sides may have a different moral or ethical status but they are both real enough. It is the individual social worker who has to negotiate a path between these contradictory demands on a day-to-day basis.

Documentation that this structurally induced strain is subjectively experienced by practitioners is abundant. However, it is rarely articulated as a structurally induced strain. Social workers tend to take upon themselves the blame for being unable to fulfil these contradictory demands as though they failed because they were personally deficient or because social work methods are inadequate. Though it is undoubtedly the case that individual social workers can be deficient and social work methods can be inadequate, the point is that in this situation the most capable with the most apt methods are still doomed to failure. It is not possible to overcome problems induced by one's structural position by changing oneself or one's method. The only way is to change the structural position.

Obviously, some analysts have avoided this trap of assuming that the problems for social work lie in the inadequacies of individual practitioners or the specific methods employed. Masud Hoghugi (1980) is a typical example of that school of thinkers who consider that social work evolved out of society's need to control troublesome members. Hoghugi argues that social workers act as agents of social control providing palliatives for major social problems and tensions. As such social services are just another part of the governmental bureaucracy. In fact, Hoghugi considers the high level of bureaucratization to be a salient characteristic of social services. He goes on to state:

> In the present context, the prime concern of a bureaucracy is maintenance of status quo, rigid power hierarchies and self-protection. The essence of professional work, on the other hand, particularly in social services, is informed risk-taking. To this extent the mere existence of social services within local authority structure is likely to continue to create major tensions.

The message of this is clear: the structural position of the social work profession is antithetical to its professional objectives. Hoghugi concludes that social workers 'have to accept implicitly the blame for any consequential inefficiencies of the organisations which they serve'. This causes resentment.

Hoghugi's approach, though attractive and compatible with the analysis described above, is inadequate. In it there is no attempt to show how social workers are coping with the problems or how they might have better success in coping with them. In fact, while recognizing that the strains are structurally induced, Hoghugi seems to imply that the answer lies in changing social work methods, or, rather, introducing a method since he does not believe that social work has one at the moment. The method he suggests entails the creation of 'empirical social work'. 'The chief premise of this approach is that social work is about solving problems.' (Hoghugi, 1980b p. 28) The approach entails what Hoghugi calls 'a cyclical and progressive process of: determining the problem; acting to alleviate it; evaluating the action; using the evidence of the evaluation to improve dealing with the next problem of the same kind, and starting the process again' (p. 28). The intention is obviously to fit social work into the tradition of experimental enquiry common to the social and physical sciences.

Any call for social work to become more analytic and logical in its self-awareness must be supported. Were ongoing evaluation of the outcomes of social work interventions to become the norm it could only be applauded. Yet it would be over-optimistic to think that by merely adopting the empirical method social work can overcome its difficulties. The introduction of any method could only be a palliative for structurally induced ills. Moreover, the particular method suggested has special weaknesses. Firstly, empirical methods only work well if the parameters of the variables involved can be clearly specified. Most social sciences have found the unambiguous delineation of social variables impossible to achieve even when they can be arbitrarily defined. The method which seems to have such clear-cut appeal becomes murky when one looks at how it might be used in practice. The basic problem, of course, being that the investigator or social worker will have little control over those variables involved. A chemist wishing to know the effects of chemical A on chemical B can measure them and control the circumstances of their interaction, varying temperature, length of exposure, or quantities at will. The same is not the case for someone wishing to understand why a child is battered. It is not possible to manipulate the emotions, physical circumstances and membership of a family in order to discover the optimal conditions for battering. Of course, trial and error rather than controlled problem solving may give some clues as to causes of battering but this sort of fortuitous empiricism is little more than already operates in social work departments. The second weakness of this method is that it is what might be called a meta-method. Many more specific methods would fall under its aegis — in fact, it encompasses any attempt to gather data. To this extent, it is nothing more than an exhortation to the gathering of data. It is certainly not tied to any theory or set of theories which might direct the practitioner in efforts to solve the client's problem. This method does not suggest what might be effective; it suggests that you should measure how effective you are. This method does not tell you how to measure your efficiency; it merely suggests that you should. The method does not tell you how to incorporate findings into future strategies; it indicates that you should. The method entails a list of *shoulds* without any *hows*. The method is an orientation and not an answer. As such it is fairly innocuous.

It remains the case then that social services and the individual social worker face structurally induced problems. The introduction of new methods or new theories, even if they were substantive, could not eradicate those problems. Only a change in the position of social services within the bureaucracy of local government could change those problems. In the meantime, social workers, on a day-to-day basis, cope with the marginal position which they occupy. The next section examines the ways in which individuals cope.

Of course, in some instances the demands of the authority and the demands of the client will not be at variance. But in those cases where they are, it may be impossible to resolve the incompatibility between them. If it is the authority's policy to clear pensioners out of council houses and move them into old people's homes and a client in this situation wishes to remain in a house that they have perhaps inhabited for a lifetime no conciliation is going to be easy. But the social worker has to deal with this clash of purpose. The authority demands that the social worker acts as its agent and assists in the transfer of the pensioner; the pensioner expects the social worker to defend him or her and ensure that the move is not brought about. The social worker needs to evolve strategies for dealing with such mutually exclusive demands.

22.1 Strategies and Rationalizations

One strategy that could be adopted in this situation is to accept and institute the policy of the authority. There are many forms of rationalization which can be employed if this is the strategy adopted: the move is in the interests of the community as a whole; the move is ultimately in the client's best interest; individuals are powerless in the face of social change; etc. A favourite rationalization for this strategy was encapsulated by Bill Utting; chief social work officer at the social work service of the DHSS (Fogarty, 1980):

> The price of salaried employment is that the organisation wants to prescribe what is done and sometimes how it is done. (p. 22)

The authority holds the purse strings and calls the tune. This is a nice form of rationalization because it implies that the social worker is not responsible for the strategy; it implies that they resort to this because they are either coerced by the threat of losing their job or are morally obliged to adopt that strategy if they are to remain 'loyal' to employers who can legitimately expect this of them.

An alternative strategy would be to uphold the client against the authority. Rationalization in this case would be just as easy: social work is about acting as a facilitator for the client and there are enough others to act against the client; the client is old and cannot live much longer anyway so that any interruption of housing policy is only temporary; the right to self-determination is inalienable; etc. The favoured rationalization in this case revolves around the image of the social worker as the chivalrous knight seeking the Holy Grail of individual freedom; the bureaucratic dragon not having met its St. George.

Two things can be said about these strategies and the attached rationalizations:

(i)   strategies tend to become habitual, i.e. practitioners develop strong tendencies either to take one side or the other consistently in conflicts;
(ii) rationalization tend to become habitual.

Rationalizations can be categorized:

(i)   pragmatic, i.e. the 'well he'll die soon anyway' or 'the service will be better in the old people's home and he'll live longer' arguments;
(ii) ideological, i.e. the 'individual freedom' or the 'community welfare' arguments;
(iii) expedience, i.e. the 'I'm powerless in the face of the administration' argument.

The last form of rationalization is, perhaps, the only one which cannot be used to uphold a strategy supporting the client; unless that strategy becomes expedient because, for instance, others in the district team were very strongly in favour of support for the client and placed pressure on the social worker. Indeed, this form of rationalization, bemoaning the powerlessness of social workers, can be used very effectively with clients. There is considerable evidence (Kitchen, 1980; Sainsbury, 1980 provides a good bibliography of studies of client evaluation of social workers) that clients see the social services as a vast monolith of bureaucracy with which 'their' social worker has to battle. Although some clients see social workers as the perpetrators of the system, most see them as its victims. This impression is supported by what they see as the bemusing turnover of workers on a case — social workers change but the social service spectre, with its interminable meetings which engender prevarication and procrastination, does not. So the social workers, who are regarded by most clients as too young and too inexperienced anyway, can use this rationalization of 'powerlessness' quite effectively. It is believed because the stereotypes confirm it. If the clients largely support the social worker's rationalizations, the same can be said of other professionals. They too conceive of the social worker as powerless (Fogarty, 1980). It is no wonder the 'powerlessness' rationalization is so popular.

To some extent, it is necessary to show why these explanations offered for the adoption of any particular strategy should be considered to be rationalizations rather than reasons. They are rationalizations rather than reasons because they tend to be generated *post hoc*. To a large extent they act to excuse the strategy and can be either private or public in their capacity as excuses. The point is that the contradictory demands encountered by the social worker frequently create a true dilemma: the social worker is faced with a decision in which there is no morally 'correct' answer. The dilemma means that whichever decision is taken some value is breached, some ideal marred. In this situation, the individual cannot differentiate between options on rational grounds. The response is to generate a support rhetoric or rationalization for the decision which has been based on any number of other pressures. In fact, the rationalizations merely serve to alter the moral significance of the breaches which the decision inevitably entailed. The rationalization effectively justifies or excuses the breach.

The difficulty with such rationalizations lies in the fact that to be effective they have to be convincing both to others and to the individual producing them. The problem is that few people believe their own rationalizations. At least, they do not do so initially. As a rationalization becomes habitual, and it largely does so because it is more believable than others of its ilk, it gathers greater powers to convince. After all, it has been successful in the past. Indeed, a rationalization can become so habitual and gather such momentum that it can become a reason for adopting a strategy. So that what started out as a rationalization on a *post hoc* basis can become a reason for future action. This means that in order to understand the dynamics underlying the adoption of any strategy it is really necessary to have the history of the individual's strategies and rationalizations. When the rationalizing formula becomes a self-fulfilling prophesy, actually creating those conditions which ensure that it is seen to be relevant and used again, it is obviously likely to be maladaptive and dangerous to rational social work practice. It encourages stereotyped perceptions of problems and stereotypical responses to them. This is a major consideration in arguing for the abandonment of both of the two strategies described above: ultimately, they are antithetical to rational social work.

Faced with the dilemma, there is a third strategy which can be adopted and which *is* rational. This entails allying with *neither* side; remaining independent. This, the 'honest broker' role is one which many social workers fight to maintain. It means that the social worker seeks to mitigate the conflict between the two sides without joining forces with either. The tactics of 'brokerage' have been described in earlier chapters and are crucial to the SPA in the social work process. What is implicit in these earlier descriptions and what should be made explicit here is that the social worker taking this option treads a tightrope. In all likelihood, the 'honest broker' will be seen as anything but honest by those concerned and will find all sides attack. Moreover, they are likely to find themselves picking up the pieces of a client who has fought and failed. The social worker choosing the role of arbitrator, rather than representative, cannot expect to walk away free and clear when the negotiations cease, there is then the aftermath of those negotiations to negotiate.

22.2 SPA and the Dilemma

The SPA has been described in relation to various sorts of social work problems in earlier chapters. But it might be valuable here to examine exactly what SPA can contribute to the social worker facing mutually exclusive demands from employers and clients.

284

The contribution of SPA will be outlined schematically in relation to the example of the pensioner fighting relocation. However, before doing that there are several points which should be made about the use of SPA in the context of such a dilemma. Firstly, it should be said that SPA can be used regardless of which strategy is adopted in face of the dilemma. The social worker choosing to ally with the evicting council can use it just as readily as the social worker who allies with the client or the social worker who chooses the independent role. The SPA connotes a method; it does not tell you who to work for or what end to aim at; it does indicate how to work. The SPA can provide the tactics to pursue any strategy.

Secondly, it should be noted that the SPA can be used in two sorts of ways. On the one hand, it can be used to enable those the social worker deals with to achieve their ends more easily. In this case, the social worker acts as the enabling agent, providing the analysis and the tools to achieve the desired ends but not determining what the ends will be. On the other hand, the SPA can be used by the social worker to achieve ends which the social worker personally specifies. In this case, the social worker is a manipulator of events. As an enabler the social worker is only indirectly responsible for the consequences of the analysis and the action which it suggests; as a manipulator the social worker is directly responsible.

If either of the first two strategies is adopted by the social worker (i.e. alliance with either side in the dispute) then the social worker becomes an enabler for the chosen side. Responsibility for outcomes is thus indirect and this diffusion of responsibility can be part of the attraction of these strategies. The third strategy, remaining independent, can entail the social worker becoming either an enabler or a manipulator. As an enabler, the social worker offers skills indiscriminately to both sides. By doing this, the social worker provides both sides with ammunition and, effectively, makes no moral or practical distinctions about the ends to which the ammunition is used. This contrasts markedly with the use of SPA if the social worker decides to act as a manipulator. The manipulating social worker sets the goals and uses the SPA to achieve them.

Of course, the label 'manipulator' is emotive because it is tainted with connotations of unrestrained control of others which many social workers would not wish to have. They are social workers not because they wish to control but because they believe that people should have the resources that enable them to make their own decisions. For this reason, many would not use the SPA to evolve powers to manipulate. Only individual social workers can make the choice between 'enabling' and 'manipulating'. The point is that the SPA can be used regardless of which alternative is chosen.

The next task is to examine how it can be used in face of the dilemma. The use of the SPA, as in previous examples, entails a four-step process:

(i)   The formal analysis of the dilemma in terms of interpersonal and intergroup dynamics.

(ii)   The determination of objectives.

(iii) The determination of techniques to achieve objectives.

(iv) The implementation of techniques.

Each of these steps will be described below, using the pensioner example to illustrate the process.

Formal Analysis

This entails the following.

(i) Specification of the parties actually or potentially involved in the dispute; the social worker must always be recognized as one of these parties. In the case of the pensioner threatened with eviction, the concerned parties might be the housing department, a local councillor, the pensioner's GP, the pensioner and his or her family, the neighbours, and, of course, the social worker.

(ii) Specification of the objectives of the parties. The GP, neighbours and housing department might want the pensioner moved to supervised accommodation for the elderly. The pensioner, his or her family and the local councillor might wish him or her to stay in the house that he or she currently occupies.

(iii) Specification of motives. The parties may have different motives for the same objective. The GP wants to do less house calls, the neighbours want their married daughter and her baby to be able to move away from home and into a council house and this one looks ideal, and the housing department has a general policy about large council properties which are occupied by single people. The pensioner's supporters can similarly have any number of motives. The social worker has to find out the motives of each of the parties and any belief systems which are attached to them. Interviewing normally provides the basis for reasonable hypotheses about motives and belief systems.

(iv) Specification of how and why the objectives of the parties differ.

(v) Specification of relative power of the parties; this includes identification of rights and duties and the allies that each·is likely to have. For instance, on one side the housing department may have powers to evict if the pensioner is causing a public nuisance; the GP might have the power to section the pensioner if he or she were found to be behaving in an unacceptable manner, or the family might have access to the local press and a particularly fluent and articulate member willing to propagandarize for the pensioner. Variables of this sort are either public knowledge and lodged in statutes or are open to discovery through careful interviewing with regard to intended actions and perceptions of possible courses of action.

(vi) Identification of those elements or features of the dispute which if changed would eradicate the conflict. This might mean looking for areas of compromise; it might mean looking for the weaknesses in the parties; or it might mean looking for a completely new alternative route that none of those involved has considered before. It may mean that on interviewing the pensioner the social worker finds that he or she wants to stay because he or she cannot take his or her animals to the new accommodation and some compromise can be reached with the housing department on that. The weakness may lie in the evi-

286

dence that the housing department has that the pensioner has caused trouble in the area. The new alternative might be the use of a different sort of protected accommodation.

Determination of Objectives

This entails the social worker deciding what it is that should be achieved (if the social worker has allied with one side or the other, this decision will already have been made of course). The objectives should be precisely stated, not general. So the form should be something like this: the objective is to move the pensioner into protected housing with his or her cats within the next two days with the approval of his or her family. It is only by specifying the targets precisely that the techniques can be specified precisely. In this, the SPA has something in common with behaviour modification procedures.

Determination of Techniques

Steps (i) and (ii) allow the social worker to hypothesize about the nature of the problems and to set a target for action. The techniques adopted are obviously shaped by the objectives. Without being blasé, it is as simple as this: if you wish to change an attitude, you use attitude change techniques (the principles of attitude change techniques have been described earlier). There will be limitations on what techniques the social worker can use. If the social worker lacks the power or the knowledge to use a technique then it is effectively ruled out of the repertoire. The choice has to be made within the social worker's repertoire.

Implementation of Techniques

Initially, the implementation of the technique depends on the social worker but it may entail involving other agents. One of the fundamental features of the SPA is the emphasis on the fact that the social worker is part of a social network and should use this network. The use of other professionals is well recognized but others can be used: the community, the media, national lobby groups (e.g. Age Concern), etc. Social workers must learn to choose the appropriate change agent and employ that agent whenever possible. Thereby, the social worker becomes as eclectic in the use of personnel as in the use of techniques.

As in all the other cases described in earlier chapters, the precise nature of the techniques and the agents employing them will depend on the precise nature of the problem and the combatants involved. Also, as in those cases, we are arguing that the SPA is just another weapon in the social work armoury, it is certainly not the only possible weapon. It is however, one which formalizes what many social workers do by intuition. Moreover, it is one which provides not merely a method, or orientation to problem analysis, it also provides suggestions as to how the problem might be solved. The point is that the method is tied to a series of theories about social behaviour; the theories suggest what actions might be effective given a particular context and a specific objective.

To conclude this section it should be emphasized that the individual social worker employing the SPA does not evade the fact that there is a dilemma created by the mutually exclusive demands of clients and employers. The structurally induced problem still exists. The SPA merely helps the social worker to adopt a strategy of independence because it provides an understanding of the nature of the dilemma.

22.3   Training and the Position of the Individual Social Worker

The structural position of the individual social worker also influences the use that can be made of skills and techniques derived from training. This is not the place to go into a review of the effectiveness of social work training. Suffice it to say that there are two indices of the efficiency of training:

(i)   whether techniques are used when they are taught;
(ii) whether techniques which are taught work in practice.

There are few data on either of these indices. The studies of the efficacy of social work (for example, Reid & Shyne, 1969; Fischer, 1973) are fraught with methodological weaknesses. Studies of the transfer of trained skills to practice are the prime focus of attention here.

Parsloe and Stevenson in *Social Service Teams*, 1978, showed that methods taught on courses and used on placements were not used once the students became social workers. Parsloe in a later, unpublished paper (1979), suggested that there were several reasons for the absence of transfer of techniques from courses to practice. Some of the deficiencies could be seen to lie in the content of courses:

Gaps in the Curricula

Topics which prove vital to the practitioner are omitted. For example, Parsloe and Stevenson found that few courses taught students about intergroup dynamics.

Provision of Generic Training rather than the Inculcation of Particular Skills

This becomes important when it is recognized that there is evidence that students taught specific techniques do use them later in practice. For instance, Seligman of the Family Institute, Cardiff, found that students who had been trained in structural family therapy specifically were using it later in practice. Parsloe argues that this transfer is a function of feeling mastery of a technique as opposed to a passing acquaintance with many. Generic training may be producing a Jack-of-all-trades, master of none mentality in students. They, therefore, tend to reject the methods they are taught when faced with the real

288

problems of practice — they are uncertain of their own control of the technique and, perhaps, uncertain of the efficacy of the technique anyway.

Teaching not Related to the Context of Application

This point has several aspects.

(i) On courses, methods are taught in an environment which expects a logical, sequential, intellectual approach to problems assumed to have a single endpoint and unique solution. In practice, emotion, illogical reasoning, prejudice and multitudinous partial possible solutions to an ongoing problem are more likely to be the order of the day. It is hardly surprising that methods taught and learnt in the first context fail to be transferred into the second. Moreover, courses rarely explain how the methods taught will work when the practitioner is faced with a monstrous caseload. Caseload management and the interaction between cases has to influence the feasibility of any practical application of methods. To some extent this issue of the impact of caseload on methods has been discussed in earlier chapters and cannot be re-examined here.

(ii) The application of any method is dependent upon the individual using it. The individual invests the method with his or her own style. Yet, the fact that people have their own distinctive styles is largely ignored on courses. This becomes important when the style dictates that the method cannot be used. Take the example of behaviour modification: the effective use of behaviour modification necessitates a rational, unemotional and analytic approach to clients, someone who wishes to understand and empathize with the client may find the underlying demands of the behaviour modification techniques unacceptable. Style, self-image and ethical beliefs are all important determiners of a social worker's choice of technique. If the teaching of a technique fails to take this into account it seems likely that the technique will not be taken up and used by the student once outside of the supervisory constraints of the course.

(iii) Techniques are taught as if they were applicable to any social milieu, little consideration is, for instance, given to the problems of cross-cultural applications. Transactional analysis might work (though even this is not proven) for the products of Western industrialized monogamous families, to suggest it is relevant to other groups is obviously ludicrous. The point is that some methods which are more subtly culture-specific are taught as if the group on whom they are used is irrelevant and as though they were universally applicable. The practitioner in the field soon finds that this is not the case and techniques which might work in one context are rejected because they are not universal balms.

(iv) A student on a course learns a method with other students, they leave the course to find employment in disparate social work departments and work with people who were not trained with them, are unlikely to have been trained by the same people or in the same place and are certainly unlikely to have been trained in the same techniques or to have the same personal styles as their new recruit. The incoming student-practitioner is unlikely to be able to continue to use techniques taught on his or her course if the people around are antipathetic to or uninterested in their use. It has been shown that the transfer of techniques into practice is significantly more likely if those working together were trained as a team. The fact that it is not feasible to train social services teams together normally means that the problem has to be overcome in a different way. Certainly, one way to mitigate the effects of the move into the new context is to teach the student about the internal dynamics of a group of people working together. Many of the earlier discussions in this volume about group dynamics and interpersonal influence processes can be seen to be of relevance here.

The failure to recognize these four types of problem (and there are others) can be seen as a deficiency in the structure of social work courses but there is another side to the coin. The values of teaching institutions are rarely identical to the values of the institutions destined to employ their output. Social services departments tend to be hostile to the courses and take an anti-intellectual stance. It is hardly surprising in this atmosphere that techniques learnt on courses do not get transferred into practice. The whole attitude of the organization indicates how worthless the training enterprise is. The message to social workers is simple: you learn your trade on the job, not in an ivory tower.

The problem for individual social workers is then obvious enough. Stripped of the slender defence of the methods that training provided, the social worker faces the mutually exclusive demands of the employers and the clients without armour. The answer to the problem lies outside of the remit of the individual suffering it. Course structures should, of course, be changed to include the sorts of things outlined above. This would not be a difficult task. If the courses change there is some hope that attitudes to them will change. This is, obviously, dependent upon those who run courses becoming more responsive to employers and having closer contacts with them. The courses must be seen to be relevant before they will become capable of directing social work practice. However, this process of attitude change on the part of employers will take time. In the interim, individual social workers have two options. Firstly, they can, as individuals, choose between the strategies outlined earlier and fit in methods that they have learnt as best they can. Secondly, they can seek to develop within the group with whom they work a common orientation and a set of compatible methods. The second option effectively involves a recognition of the marginal position of social workers and attempts to unite within the existing bureaucracy to form a self-defence group. Existing team structures could form the foundations for such groups. It would be impossible here to outline the structure or operations of social work teams. There are many different groupings within social services that are entitled 'teams'. Their organization, hierarchy and mode of operation differ across authorities and systematic evaluations of their efficacy are only now beginning. The fact that each team is unique makes any generalizable evaluation rather problematic. Nevertheless, regardless of their current structure and mode of operation, social work teams could be the means of insulating the individual social worker from the difficulties of his or her position. Some teams obviously already act in this way. Unfortunately, as yet, we do not know how they work or why they succeed. Certainly, the dynamics of social work teams need to be examined. Meanwhile, individual social workers can apply the SPA to examine how their own team works; the techniques for doing it are precisely those which we have advocated for use with clients who find themselves in problematic group contexts.

In saying all this, it becomes obvious that this book describes techniques which can be used to help the client or the social worker. The self-analysis, no matter how gross or lacking in detail, which these last two chapter have presented to social workers is designed to promote an exercise in self-revelation and engender change. The knowledge of social dynamics, if not perfect, is available if social workers are willing to grasp it and use it. Deprived of that self-knowledge and bereft of self-control, social workers could be doomed to a purgatory between the heaven of fulfilling the demands of all and a hell of requiting the demands of none. Even if self-control does not blossom from self-knowledge at least individual social workers should be able to recognize their predicament is shared by others. Purgatory is structurally determined for the practitioners of social work.

22.4 Summary

This chapter focused on the position of the individual social worker. The career structure of social workers and the drift from practice towards administration which occurs with promotion were briefly described. This led to a discussion of the problems of fulfilling the demands of both clients and employers when they are mutually exclusive. The strategies and rationalizations frequently adopted by individual social workers in this dilemma were examined. The contributions of the SPA in this situation were considered and it was suggested that only rational independence allows the social worker to survive the dilemma. The difficulties created by the structural position of social workers for the transfer of skills learnt on training courses were then outlined. It was suggested that the courses should be changed in a number of directions. But it was also suggested that individual social workers could use the SPA to analyse why their use of their skills is thwarted. The SPA, it was further suggested, could provide the tools for an analysis of how the individual social worker's team functions and how it might be changed to create a self-defence group against the pressures emanating from employers and clients alike.

The value of the chapter for the practising social worker is twofold. Firstly, the difficulties which are structurally induced are explicitly described. It is shown that the social worker is a buffer between the two interest groups: clients and employers. To ignore the fact that this structural position is not altered by any method that the social worker can employ is dangerous. The pressures introduced by the position of the social worker can only be alleviated by changing that position. The methods that are employed while still occupying that position will not eradicate such pressures. Theorists arguing that social workers should change their methods and will thereby eradicate the real ethical and pragmatic difficulties created by their bureaucratic position are misguided. The value of this recognition is that it indicates a course of action. Social workers should not chase after their own tails seeking new methods. The frantic rush from one method to the next can cease because none can ameliorate the structural pressures. The second implication of value to the practitioner is that the SPA provides simultaneously a means of analysing the problem and techniques for maintaining rational independence within the constraints of the structural position. The immediate value of this analysis can be seen in the possibilities of changing the teams within which the individual has to work. The suggestion is that the individual social worker uses the forms of analysis and the skills engendered during training to ensure that the skills can continue to be used in the future. The message here is clear: skill protect thyself.

Conclusion to Part VI

Chapters 21 and 22 are, by the standards of this book, unusually long. However, they are the only ones devoted to the position of the social worker and the social work profession. As it is, they cover only parts of what would be needed for a total analysis. The intention has been to give an indication of how the SPA would be used to analyse those who should be using it. In doing this it becomes clear that the SPA is just as readily used to inform the social worker about his or her own difficulties as about those of clients.

In fact, a major implication is that social work does not take place in a vacuum: the social worker is part of the system in which the clients live, the social worker is subject to similar forces and any understanding of the client entails self-understanding for the social worker. Part of this recognition is awareness that social workers do not, cannot, work alone. They are part of a system and it is the functioning of the system which determines how much the individual can achieve. Thus understanding the system becomes important if you are to achieve your own ends. These two chapters provide signposts in the road to that understanding.

Part VII
Theory into Action

23
Theory into Action:
A Conclusion

The emphasis thus far has been upon the exposition rather than the evaluation of the SPA to the social work process. In Chapter 1 the bones of the SPA were examined and each subsequent chapter has served to drape the skeleton in flesh. Part II described the nature of social psychology: its character and history, and the key findings and theories on the fundamental targets for analysis — relationships, identity, groups, the environment, and social and personal change. In Part III, the structure of social work and the demands placed upon social workers; the organization of their professional groups; and the types of skills available to them were discussed. Part IV focused upon the sort of problem analyses social workers engage in and the implications of the SPA for the development of analytic skills. It also contained a chapter which was designed to lead the practitioner through the pitfalls which surround the choice and use of theories from the social sciences. Part V comprised a series of chapters which exemplified how the SPA might actually be used with cases from central areas of social work: disablement, group homes, child battering, community work and mental illness. That part also included two further chapters: on the use of the SPA by the client and the use of the SPA in student supervision. In the penultimate part of this book, the SPA is used to analyse the position of the social work profession within Britain and the position of the typical social worker within that profession. Throughout the emphasis has been upon showing the value of the SPA rather than any of its disadvantages. The object here is to rectify the balance somewhat and give a fairly unbiased catalogue of the major strengths and weaknesses of the SPA.

The major strengths and weaknesses of the SPA are listed in Table 23.1. It will be seen that the first four pros of the SPA are paired with the first four cons: each of these first four advantages has its own built-in problems.

Table 23.1 The Advantages and Disadvantages of the SPA to the Social Work Process

Pros of the SPA	Cons of the SPA	
1. Dynamic — it is designed to be responsive to a changing problem.	1. Requires flexibility on the part of the practitioner — rigidity is very destructive.	These disadvantages can be largely overcome with growing expertise in the SPA
2. Comprehensive — all aspects of the problem are examined and its context assessed.	2. A comprehensive analysis is complex; expertise is required for success.	
3. Offers techniques and strategies effective in bringing about personal and social change.	3. The social worker needs to make a decision between various techniques — choosing the right one may be difficult. Also, the social worker may know which technique would bring about the desired end without being in a position to put it into practice for ethical, legal or other reasons.	
4. Offers methods for gathering information necessary to an appropriate analysis and explanation of the problem.	4. Information gathering methods have to be learnt by the practitioner — expertise in these is required.	
5. Offers not simply the means of analysing the client's problem but also the problems of the individual social worker and the social work profession.		
6. Reflexivity is in-built.		

Firstly, the SPA is dynamic. Its forms of analysis and explanations are meant to be used continually during the course of dealing with a problem; new information can be assimilated to old understandings and thus they can develop. The SPA is a continuous process in which new understanding is likely to lead to altered strategies for intervention because the strategies are predicated upon social psychological principles. The corollary disadvantage inherent in this feature of the SPA is relatively simple: users of the SPA cannot afford to be rigid in their approach or dogmatic, they must be flexible and responsive to new variables in the problem situation. Secondly, the SPA is comprehensive: the problem is analysed at multiple levels, each of four target zones for analysis (relationships, identity, groups and environment) are examined, and then attempts at explanation using the process of consistency, construal, comparison and conformity are made. The SPA requires that the problem be seen in total context and the solutions generated be seen to operate only in that context. To this extent, the SPA answers Peter Townsend's (1981) call for methods of social work practice which consider large-scale social processes and place the client problem against the broader backdrop of societal problems. However, such an orientation demands much from the practitioner: the comprehensive nature of the analysis and the vast scope of the social processes involved can be intimidating. The social worker needs to be well trained in order to cope with such complexities. Thirdly, the SPA is no mere moral exhortation about what the social worker should achieve, it actually offers prescriptions on how to achieve desired goals through the use of techniques of personal and social change. Of course, this too leads to problems. The social worker may be presented with an array of change techniques and be faced with a single problem which requires intervention; that social worker has to be able to choose appropriately among an arsenal of techniques. This is not easy without practice and guidance — largely because different techniques may lead to the same outcome even though they are very different in substance. Moreover, even when the social worker knows which technique is the best for his or her purposes, there is every chance that there will be some obstacle preventing or limiting its usage. There is a world of difference between being able to choose an appropriate technique and satisfactorily putting that technique into practice. The fourth advantage of the SPA is that it carries within it methods of data or information collection. In this volume it has been impossible to describe all of these methods. There are many texts available which serve this purpose (including Breakwell et al., 1982). The point is that social workers, in the past, have relied on relatively haphazard methods of collecting information and there is really no reason why this should be allowed to continue. Methods which systematize information collection and enable information, once gathered, to be validated are vital for social work if it is to progress towards self-evaluation and truly planned change. The disadvantage at the moment associated with the presentation of such methods of information gathering is that few social workers have expertise in these areas. However, this can be rectified with practice. In fact, most of the disadvantages associated with these first four advantages of the SPA are not immutable, they can be eradicated or ameliorated by practice in the use of the SPA.

Table 23.1 also includes two advantages of the SPA which seem to have no troublesome counterparts. These are the advantages of the provision of a means of analysing the problems of both clients and the social work profession besides the individual practitioner; and those associated with insisting that all analyses entail as a matter of course the examination of the role of the social worker in the problem.

To counterbalance these undoubted advantages there are two rather important disadvantages which have not yet been considered. These lie at two distinct levels: in the responsibility the social worker has for using methods which are effective in inducing change and in the nature of collaboration between social workers and social psychologists. To take the latter first: if social psychology is to become more useful to social workers, they must become involved in shaping the sort of research and theory that social psychologists produce. Social workers need to become actively involved in the process of research and theory building. At the moment, this is difficult — few social workers have either the training or inclination to get involved in these areas. This is sad because it means that the products of social psychology, though they may continue to be of interest to social workers, are unlikely to be tailor-made to fit the purposes of the practitioner. Clothes off the peg do not need to be ill-fitting but they are more likely to be so than the garments cut and sewn specially. There is no intrinsic reason why social workers should not become researchers and theorists or collaborate with those who are. Until they do so more extensively the SPA to the social work process will lack something of the style of bespoke tailoring. The second problem is less an inherent disadvantage of the SPA and more an inherent disadvantage of any profession which takes it upon itself to institute change. People with the power to wreak change carry the responsibility for those changes. Social workers have until quite recently avoided the responsibility for their actions since there has been an underlying belief that their efforts were ineffectual anyhow: they were not responsible because they had little power, except statutory powers for which they were a channel rather than a controller. In so far as the SPA actually offers the social worker effective means of inducing personal and social change, it also lays the burden of real responsibility upon the social worker's shoulders. This can, of course, be regarded positively or negatively; either way the use of the SPA adds a new dimension to the social work process.

Having explored the advantages and disadvantages of the SPA it becomes clear that the only way in which the social worker can really ascertain its value is by putting it into practice and assessing its effects. It is certain that only in this way its weaknesses be eradicated and its strengths fortified. In this case, it is probably true to say that practice makes perfect.

References

ADORNO, T.W., FRENKEL-BRUNSWIK, E., LEVINSON, .D.J. and SANFORD, R.N. (1950) *The Authoritarian Personality*. New York, Harper.

AJZEN, I. and FISHBEIN, M. (1980) *Understanding attitudes and predicting social behaviour*. New Jersey, Prentice-Hall.

ALBERT, S. and DABBS, J.M. (1970) Physical distance and persuasion. *J. Personality & Soc. Psychol.*, **15**, 265–270.

ALGIE, J. (1971) Managing the Social Services — Merger Objectives. *Hospital J. and Soc. Science Review*, 10 July 1971.

ALLEN, V.L. and NEWTSON, D. (1972) Development of Conformity and Independence. *J. Personality & Soc. Psychol.*, **22**, 18–30.

ALLPORT, G.W. (1954) The Historical Background of Modern Social Psychology. In: G. LINDZEY (Ed.) *The Handbook of Social Psychology, Vol. 1*. Cambridge, Mass, Addison-Wesley.

ALLPORT, G.W. (1968) The Historical Background of Modern Social Psychology. In: G. LINDZEY and E. ARONSON (Eds.) *The Handbook of Social Psychology, Vol. 1*. Reading, Mass., Addison-Wesley.

ALTMAN, I. (1975) *The Environment and Social Behaviour*. Monterey, California, Brooks/Cole.

AMIR, Y. (1969) Contact Hypothesis in Ethnic Relations. *Psychological Bulletin*, **71**, 319–342.

ANDERSEN, E.M. (1973) *The Disabled Schoolchild: A Study of Integration in Primary Schools*. London, Methuen.

ANTAKI, C. (Ed.) (1981) *The Psychology of Ordinary Explanations of Social Behaviour*. London, Academic Press.

ANTONOVSKY, A. (1956) Towards a refinement of the marginal man concept. *Social Forces*, **35(1)**, 257–262.

ARGYLE, M., FURNHAM, A. and GRAHAM, J.A. (1981) *Social Situations*. Cambridge, Cambridge University Press.

297

ARMISTEAD, N. (Ed.) (1974) *Reconstructing Social Psychology*. Harmondsworth, Penguin.

ARONSON, E. (1976) *The Social Animal*. San Francisco, Freeman and Co.

ASCH, S. (1956) Studies of independence and conformity: I. A minority of one against a unanimous majority. *Psychological Monographs*, **70** (9, Whole No. 416).

BADIA, P., HABER, A. and RUNYON, R. (Eds.) (1970) *Research Problems in Psychology*. Reading, Mass., Addison-Wesley.

BALES, R.F. (1950) *Interaction process analysis: a method for the study of small groups*. Reading, Mass., Addison-Wesley.

BANNISTER, D. (1981) Knowledge of Self. In: M. HERBERT (Ed.) *Psychology for Social Workers*, London, BPS & Macmillan, pp. 112–125.

BANNISTER, D. and FRANSELLA, F. (1971) *Inquiring Man: The theory of personal constructs*. Harmondsworth, Penguin.

BARKER, R.G. (1968) *Ecological Psychology*. Stanford, Calif., Stanford University Press.

BASW (1981) Submission to The NISW Working Party on the Role and Tasks of Social Workers. BASW, Birmingham.

BASW (1977) *The Social Work Task*. Newcastle, BASW Publications.

BAVELAS, A. (1950) Communication patterns in task oriented groups. *J. Acoustical Society of America*, **22**, 725–730.

BEM, D. (1967) Self perception: an alternative interpretation of cognitive dissonance phenomena. *Psychological Review*, **74**, 183–200.

BEM, D. (1972) Self-perception theory. In: L. BERKOWITZ (Ed.) *Advances in experimental social psychology*, Vol. 6. New York. Academic Press, pp. 1–62.

BERNE, E. (1964) *Games People Play*. New York, Grove Press.

BERSCHEID, E. and WALSTER, E. (1969) *Interpersonal Attraction*. Reading, Mass., Addison-Wesley.

BIRCH, R. (1976) *Manpower and Training for the Social Services*. HMSO.

BOTT, E. (1957) *Family and Social Network*. London, Tavistock.

BRAGINSKI, B., BRAGINSKI, D. and RING, K. (1969) *Methods of madness: The mental hospital as a last resort*. New York, Holt.

BREAKWELL, G.M. (1976) *The mechanisms of social identity in intergroup behaviour*. Unpublished Ph.D. Thesis, University of Bristol.

BREAKWELL G.M. (1978a) Some effects of marginal social identity. In: H. TAJFEL (Ed.) *Differentiation between social groups*. London, Academic Press, pp. 301–339.

BREAKWELL, G.M. (1978b) Groups for sale. *New Society*, **45(823)**, 66–68.

BREAKWELL, G.M. (1979) Illegitimate group membership and inter-group differentiation. *Br. J. Soc. & Clin. Psychol.*, **18**, 141–149.

BREAKWELL, G.M. (Ed.) (1982a) *Threatened Identities*. Chichester, Wiley.

BREAKWELL, G.M. (1982b) 'Models in Action: The Use of Theories by Practitioners. In: P. STRINGER (Ed.) *Confronting Social Issues: Applications of Social Psychology*. London, Academic Press.

BREAKWELL, G.M. (1982c) Social workers: a group with a threatened identity. In G.M. BREAKWELL (Ed.) *Threatened Identities*. Wiley, Chichester.

BREAKWELL, G.M. FOOT, H. and GILMOUR, R. (1982) *Social Psychology: A Practical Manual*. BPS/Macmillan, London.

BROWN, J.A. (1963) *Techniques of Persuasion*. Harmondsworth, Penguin.

BURKE, P.J. (1968) Role Differentiation and the Legitimation of Task Activity. *Sociometry*, **31**, 404–411.

BURNS, R.B. (1979) *The self concept*. London, Longman.

BYRNE, D. (1961) The Influence of Propinquity and Opportunities for Interaction on Classroom Relationships. *Human Relations*, **14**, 63–69.

BYRNE, D. (1971) *The attraction paradigm*. New York, Academic Press.

BYRNE, D. and CLORE, G.L. (1970) A reinforcement model of evaluative responses. *Personality: An International Journal*, **1**, 103–128.

BYRNE, A. and PADFIELD, C.F. (1978) *Social Services Made Simple*. W.H. Allen, London.

CANTOR, N. and MISCHEL, W. (1977) Trait as prototypes: Effects on recognition memory. *J. Personality & Soc. Psychol.*, **35**, 38–48.

CANTOR, N. and MISCHEL, W. (1979) Prototypes in person perception. In: L. BERKOWITZ (Ed.) *Advances in Experimental Social Psychology*. New York, Academic Press, pp. 4–52.

CAPLAN, G. (1960) *An Approach to Community Mental Health*. London, Tavistock.

CARTWRIGHT, D. and Zander, A. (1968) *Group Dynamics* (3rd Ed.). New York, Harper & Row.

CARVER, V. (Ed.) (1978) *Child Abuse, A study text*. Open University Press.

CCETSW (1974) *Social Work Curriculum Study: The Teaching of Community Work — A Study Group Discussion Paper*. CCETSW Paper 8, December 1974.

CCETSW (1980) *Research and Practice: Report of a Working Party on a research strategy for the personal social services*. CCETSW/PSSC.

CCETSW (1976) *Values in Social Work*, CCETSW Paper 13, April 1976.

CHEETHAM, J. and HILL, M.J. (1973) Community Work: Social Realities and Ethical Dilemmas. *Br. J. Social Work*, **3**, 331–348.

CHRISTIE, R. and GEIS, F.L. (Eds.) (1970) *Studies in Machiavellianism*. New York, Academic Press.

CLAYTON, P. (1979) What did you do in the strike volunteer? *Community Care*, 7 June 1979.

COMER, R.J. and PILIAVIN, J.A. (1972) The effects of physical deviance upon face-to-face interaction: The other side. *J. Personality & Soc. Psychol.*, **23**(1), 33–39.

COOK, M. (1977) The social skill model and interpersonal attraction. In: S. Duck (Ed.) *Theory and Practice in Interpersonal Attraction*. London, Academic Press, pp. 319–339.

COOK, S.W. (1970) A Preliminary Study of Attitude Change. In: M. WERTHEIMER (Ed.) *Confrontation: Psychology and the Problems of Today*. Glenview, Ill., Scott Foresman.

COOLEY, C.H. (1902) *Human nature and the social order*. New York, Scribner.

COX, M. (1978) *Structuring the Therapeutic Process: Compromise with Chaos*. Oxford, Pergamon.

CRAIG, G. (Ed.) (1974) *Community Work Case Studies*. Association of Community Workers.

CULBERTSON, F. (1957) Modification of an Emotionally held Attitude through Role Playing. *J. Abnl. & Soc. Psychol.*, **54**, 230–234.

DAVIES, M. (1976) The Current Status of Social Work Research. *Br. J. Social Work*, **43**, 281–303.

DAVIES, M. (1981) *The Essential Social Worker: a guide to positive practice*. Heinemann Educational Books, The Chaucer Press, Suffolk.

DEUTSCH, M. and GERARD, H.B. (1955) A Study of Normative and Informational Social Influences upon Individual Judgement. *J. Abnl. & Soc. Psychol.*, **51**, 629–636.

DISABILITY ALLIANCE (1978) *Disability Rights Handbook*. Disability Alliance.

DHSS (1976) *Priorities for Health and Personal Social Services in England*. HMSO.

DHSS (1980) *An Investigation into the effects on clients of industrial action by social workers in the London Borough of Tower Hamlets*. HMSO.

DOISE, W. (1978) *Groups and Individuals: Explanations in Social Psychology*. Cambridge, Cambridge University Press.

DOISE, W., CSEPELY, G., DANN, H., GOUGE, C., LARSEN, K. and OSTELL, A. (1972) An experimental investigation into the formation of intergroup representations. *Eur. J. Soc. Psychol.*, **2**, 202–204.

DOISE, W. and SINCLAIR, A. (1973) The categorization process in intergroup relations. *Eur. J. Soc. Psychol.*, **3**, 145–157.

DOUGLAS, T. (1978) *Basic Groupwork*. London, Tavistock.

DOUGLAS, T. (1979) *Group processes in social work*. Chichester, Wiley.

DUCK, S. (Ed.) (1977) *Theory and Practice in Interpersonal Attraction*. London, Academic Press.

DUHAMEL, T.R. and JARMON, H. (1971) Social schemata of emotionally disturbed boys and their male siblings. *J. Consulting and Clin. Psychol.*, **36(2)**, 281–285.

DUTTON, D.G. and LAKE, R.A. (1973) Threat of Own Prejudice and Reverse Discrimination in Inter-racial Situations. *J. Personality & Soc. Psychol.*, **28**, 94–100.

EISER, J.R. (1980) *Cognitive Social Psychology*. London, McGraw-Hill.

ELLIOT, G.C. (1979) Some effects of deception and level of self-monitoring on planning and reacting to a self-presentation. *J. Personality & Soc. Psychol.*, **37**, 1282–1292.

EPSTEIN, I. (1968) Social Workers and Social Action: Attitudes Toward Social Action Strategies. *Social Work* (USA) **13**, 2.

EPSTEIN, I. (1970) Specialisation, Professionalisation and Social-Worker Radicalism: A Test of the 'Process' Model of the Profession. *Applied Social Studies*, **2**, 155–163.

EYSENCK, H.J. (1960) *The Structure of Human Personality*, 2nd Edn. London, Methuen.

FARINA, A., GLIHA, D., BOUDREAU, L., ALLEN, J. and SHERMAN, M. (1971) Mental Illness and the Impact of Believing Others know about it. *J. Abn. Psychol.*, **77**, 1–5.

FAUCHEUX, C. and MOSCOVICI, S. (1967) Le style de comportement d'une minorité et son influence sur les responses d'une majorité. *Bulletin du Centre d'Études et Recherches Psychologiques*, **16**, 337–360.

FESTINGER, L. (1954) A theory of social comparison. *Human Relations*, **14**, 48–64.

FESTINGER, L. (1957) *A theory of cognitive dissonance*. Evanston, Ill., Row Peterson.

FESTINGER, L., SCHACHTER, S. and BACK, K. (1950) *Social Pressures in Informal Groups: A Study of Human Factors in Housing*. New York, Harper & Row.

FIEDLER, F.E. (1967) *A Theory of Leadership Effectiveness*. New York, McGraw-Hill.

FIEDLER, F., CHEMERS, M. and MAHAR, L. (1976) *Improving Leadership Effectiveness: The leader match concept*. New York, Wiley.

FISCHER, J. (1973) Is Casework Effective? A Review. *Social Work* (USA) **18**, S1, 5–20.

FISCHER, J. (1978) Does Anything Work? *J. Social Service Research*, **1**, 3, 215–243.

FISHBEIN, M. and AJZEN, I. (1972) Attitudes and opinions. *Annual Review of Psychology*, **23**, 487–544.

FISHER, R.L. (1967) Social Schema of Normal and Disturbed School Children. *J. Educational Psychol.*, **58**, 88–92.

FOGARTY, M. (1980) What the other professions think. *Social Work Today*, 10 June 1980.

FORGAS, J. (1979) *Social Episodes*. London, Academic Press.

FRANKLIN, A.W. (Ed.) (1975) *Concerning Child Abuse*: papers presented by the Tunbridge Wells Study Group on non-accidental injury to children. Churchill

Livingstone, Edinburgh.

FREUD, S. (1975) *Introductory Lectures on Psychoanalysis*. Harmondsworth, Penguin.

FRIED, M. and GLEICHER, P. (1972) Some sources of residential satisfaction in an urban slum. In: J.F. WOHLWILL and D.H. CARSON (Eds.) *Environment and the social sciences: Perspectives and Applications*. Washington, DC, American Psychological Association.

FROMM, E. (1955) *The Sane Society*. New York, Rinehart.

GARDHAM, J.H., WARDELL, K.D. and MCKEOWN, K. (1977) Community Care for the Mentally Handicapped. *Social Work Service*, **14**, 31−34.

GERARD, H.B. WILHELMY, R. and CONOLLEY, E. (1968) Conformity and Group Size. *J. Personality and Soc. Psychol.*, **8**, 79−82.

GERGEN, K. (1971) *The Concept of Self*. New York, Holt, Rinehart and Winston.

GLASSER, W. (1965) *Reality Therapy: A New Approach to Psychiatry*. Harper, Colophon Books.

GOFFMAN, E. (1959) *Presentation of Self in Everyday Life*. New York, Anchor Books.

GOFFMAN, E. (1961) *Asylums: Essays on the Social Situation of Mental Patients and Other Inmates*. New York, Anchor Books.

GOFFMAN, E. (1971) *Relations in Public*. New York, Basic Books.

GOFFMAN, E. (1976) *Stigma: Notes on the Management of Spoiled Identity*. Harmondsworth, Penguin.

GOLDBERG, M. (1941) A quantification of the marginal man theory. *American Sociological Review*, **6**, 52−58.

GOLDBERG, P., GOTTESDIENER, M. and ABRAMSON, P. (1975) Another put-down of women? Perceived attractiveness as a function of support for the feminist movement. *J. Personality & Soc. Psychol.*, **32**, 113−115.

GOLDBERG, E.M., WARBURTON, R.W. MCGUINNESS, B. and ROWLANDS, J.H. (1977) Towards Accountability in Social Work: One Year's Intake to an Area Office. *Br. J. Social Work*, **7**, 3, 257−283.

GOLDSTEIN, H. (1973) *Social Work Practice: A Unitary Approach*. University of South Carolina Press.

GOLOVENSKY, D. (1952) The marginal man concept. *Social Forces*, **30(3)**, 333−339.

GREER, S. (1955) *Social Organisation*. New York, Random House.

HAASE, R.F. (1970) The relationship of sex and instructional set to the regulation of interpersonal interaction distance in a counselling analogue. *J. Counselling Psychol.*, **17**, 233−236.

HAINES, J. (1975) *Skills and Methods in Social Work*. Constable, London.

HALL, J.G. and MITCHELL, B.H. (1978) *Child Abuse: Procedure and Evidence in Juvenile Courts*. London, Barry Rose.

HARBART, W.B. (1977) Organising Research and Evaluation. *Municipal and Public Services J.*, 1 July 1977.

HARRÉ, R. (1982) Identity Projects. In: G.M. BREAKWELL(Ed.) *Threatened Identities*. Chichester, Wiley.

HARRÉ, R. and SECORD, P. (1972) *The Explanation of Social Behaviour*. Oxford, Blackwell.

HARRIS, R. (1978) Social work and the schizophrenic − some dilemmas of theory and practice. *Social Work Today*, 17 January 1978.

HARRIS, A. (1971) *Handicap and Impaired in Great Britain*. HMSO.

HARRISON, A. (1976) *Individuals and Groups*. Monterey, Calif., Brooks/Cole.

HEIDER, F. (1946) Attitudes and cognitive organisation. *J. Psychol.*, **21**, 107−112.

HEIDER, F. (1958) *The Psychology of Interpersonal Relations*. New York, Wiley.

HEIMSTRA, N.W. and McFARLING, L.H. (1978) *Environmental Psychology*, 2nd Edn. Monterey, Calif., Brooks/Cole.

HERBERT, M. (1981) *Psychology for Social Workers*. Basingstoke, BPS/Macmillan Press.

HEREFORD, S.M., CLELAND, C.C. and FELLNER, M. (1973) Territoriality and Scent-Marking: a study of profoundly retarded enuretics and encopretics. *Am. J. Mental Deficiency*, **77(4)**, 426–430.

HILL, C.T., RUBIN, Z. and PEPLAU, L.A. (1976) Breakups before marriage: The end of 103 affairs. *J. Social Issues*, **32(1)**, 147–168.

HILLERY, G. (1955) Definitions of Community. *Rural Sociology*, **20**.

HINDE, R. (1979) *Towards Understanding Relationships*. London, Academic Press.

HITCH, P. (1982) Social Identity and Marginality. In: G.M. BREAKWELL (Ed.) *Threatened Identities*, Chichester, Wiley.

HOGGETT, B.M. (1976) *Social Work and Law: Mental Health*. Norwich, Sweet & Maxwell.

HOGHUGI, M. (1980) Social Work in a Bind: Which Way Welfare? *Community Care*, 3 April 1980.

HOGHUGI, M. (1980b) Social Work in a Bind: The Nature of the Task. *Community Care*, 10 April 1980.

HOLLANDER, E.P. and HUNT, R.G. (Eds.) (1976) *Current Perspectives in Social Psychology*. New York, Oxford University Press.

HOLLANDER, E. and JULIAN, J. (1976) Contemporary trends in the analysis of leadership processes. In: E. HOLLANDER and R. HUNT (Ed.) *Current Perspectives in Social Psychology*, 4th Edn. Oxford, Oxford University Press, pp. 474–483.

HOMANS, G.C. (1950) *The Human Group*. New York, Harcourt Brace, pp. 1 and 84.

HORNEY, K. (1950) *Neurosis and Human Growth*. New York, Norton.

HOROWITZ, M.J. (1968) Spatial behaviour and psychopathology. *J. Nervous and Mental Diseases*, **146**, 24–35.

HOROWITZ, M.J., DUFF, D.F. and STRATTON, L. (1964) Body-buffer zone. *Archives of General Psychiatry*, **11**, 651–656.

HUNT, R.G. (1976) Role and role conflict. In: E.P. HOLLANDER and R.G. HUNT (Ed.) *Current Perspectives in Social Psychology*, 4th Edn. New York, Oxford University Press, pp. 282–288.

HUSTON, T.L. (Ed.) (1974) *Foundations of Interpersonal Attraction*. New York, Academic Press.

INSKO, C.A. and SCHOPLER, J. (1972) *Experimental Social Psychology*. New York, Academic Press.

ISRAEL, J. and TAJFEL, H. (1972) *The Context of Social Psychology*. London, Academic Press.

JACKA, A.A. (1973) *The Acco Story* (Association of Child Care Officers) The Society for Promotion of Education and Research in Social Work. Distributed by BASW.

JACOBSON, M.G. and KOCH, W. (1978) Attributed reasons for support of the feminist movement as a function of attractiveness. *Sex Roles*, **4**, 169–174.

JAMES, W. (1890) *The Principles of Psychology*, Vols. 1 and 2. New York, Holt.

JANIS, I.L. (1976) Groupthink. In: E. HOLLANDER and R. HUNT (Eds.) *Current Perspectives in Social Psychology*, 4th Edn. Oxford, Oxford University Press, pp. 406–411.

JEHU, D. (1967) *Learning Theory and Social Work*. London, Routledge & Kegan Paul.

JEHU, D., HARDIKER, P., YELLOLY, M. and SHAW, M. (1972) *Behaviour Modification in Social Work*. London, Wiley.

JOHNSON, T.J. (1972) *Professions and Power*. London, Macmillan.

JONES, E.E. (1964) *Ingratiation*. New York, Appleton-Century-Crofts.

JONES, E.E. and DAVIS, K.E. (1965) From acts to dispositions: The attribution process in person perception. In: L. BERKOWITZ (Ed.) *Advances in Experimental Social Psychology*, Vol. 2. New York, Academic Press, pp. 219–266.

JONES, E.E. and NISBETT, R.E. (1972) The actor and the observer: Divergent perceptions of the causes of behaviour. In: E.E. JONES, D. KANOUSE, H.H. KELLEY, R.E. MESBETT, S. VALINS and B. WEINER (Eds.), *Attribution: Perceiving the Causes of Behaviour*. Morristown, NJ, General Learning Press, pp. 79–94.

KAKABADSE, A.P. and WORRALL, R. (1978) Job Satisfaction and Organisational Structure: A Comparative Study of Nine Social Service Departments. *Br. J. Social Work* 8, 1, 52–70.

KATZ, D. (1960) The functional approach to the study of attitude change. *Public Opinion Quarterly*, 24, 163–204.

KATZ, E. and LAZARSFELD, P. (1955) *Personal Influence*. Free Press of Glencoe.

KATZ, D. and STOTLAND, E. (1959) A preliminary statement to a theory of attitude structure and change. In S. KOCH (Ed.) *Psychology: A Study of Science*, Vol. 3. New York, McGraw-Hill, pp. 423–475.

KEIDAN, O. and HUGHES, Z. (1979) Roots: Reflections on the 1878 Select Committee on Lunacy Law. *Social Work Service*, 21, 49–54.

KELLY, G.A. (1955) *A theory of personality: The psychology of personal constructs (2 vols.)*. New York, Norton.

KELLEY, H.H. (1951) Communication in experimentally created hierarchies. *Human Relations*, 4, 39–56.

KELLEY, H. (1967) Attribution theory in social psychology. In: D. LEVINE (Ed.) *Nebraska Symposium on Motivation*, Vol. 15. Lincoln, Neb., University of Nebraska Press, pp. 192–238.

KELLY, G.A. (1955) *The Psychology of Personal Constructs*, Vols. 1 and 2. New York, Norton.

KELMAN, H.C. (1958) Compliance, identification and internalisation: three processes of attitude change. *J. Conflict Resolution*, 2, 51–60.

KELVIN, P. (1977) Predictability, power and vulnerability in interpersonal attraction. In: S. DUCK (Ed.) *Theory and Practice in Interpersonal Attraction*. London, Academic Press, pp. 355–379.

KEMPE, C.H., SILVERMAN, F.N., STEELE, B.F., DROEGEMUELLER, W. and SILVER, H.K. (1962) The Battered Child Syndrome. *J. Am. Medical Association*, 181, 17–24. © 1962, American Medical Association.

KERCKHOFF, A.C. and DAVIS, K.E. (1962) Value consensus and need complementarity in mate selection. *American Sociological Review*, 27, 295–303.

KINZEL, A.S. (1970) Body buffer zone in violent prisoners. *Am. J. Psychiatry*, 127, 59–64.

KITCHEN, M. (1980) What the Client thinks of You. *Social Work Today*, 3 June 1980.

KLECK, R.E., BUCK, P.L., GOLLER, W.C., LONDON, R.S., PFEIFFER, J.R. and VUKCEVIC, D.P. (1968) Effect of stigmatising conditions on the use of personal space. *Psychological Reports*, 23, 111–118.

KNOX, R. and INKSTER, J. (1968) Post-decision dissonance at post time. *J. Personality & Soc. Psychol.*, 4, 319–323.

KOEHLER, K. (1979) First Rank Symptoms of Schizophrenia: Questions Concerning Clinical Boundaries. *Br. J. Psychiatry*, 134, 236–48.

KRECH, D., CRUTCHFIELD, R.S. and BALLACHEY, E.L. (1962) *Individual in Society*. New York, McGraw-Hill.

LAMM, H. (1967) Will an isolated individual advise higher risk-taking after hearing a discussion of the decision problem? *J. Personality and Soc. Psychol.*, 6, 467–471.

LAPIERRE, R.T. (1934) Attitudes vs. actions. *Social Forces*, 13, 230–237.

LEISSNER, A. (1975) Models for Community Workers and Community Youth Workers. *Social Work Today*, **5, 22**, 6 February 1975.

LERNER, R.M. (1973) The development of personal space schemata toward body build. *J. Psychol.*, **84(2)**, 229—235.

LEVINGER, G. and SNOEK, J.D. (1972) *Attraction in relationship: A new look at Interpersonal Attraction*. New York, General Learning Press.

LE BON, G. (1896) *Psychologie des foules*. London, Unwin.

LINDEMANN, E. (1944) Symptomatology and Management of Acute Grief. *Am. J. Psychiatry*, **101**, 141—148.

LIPMAN, A. (1967) Chairs as territory. *New Society*, **9(238)**, 564—565.

LIPMAN, A. (1968) Building design and social interaction. *Architect's J.*, **147(3)**, 23—30.

LITTLE, J.C. and BURKITT, E.A. (1975) *Psychiatry and the Social Worker*. London, Smith, Kline and French Laboratories Ltd.

LUKES, S. (1974) *Power: A Radical View*. London, Macmillan.

MAHER, B.A. (1970) *Principles of Psychopathology: An Experimental Approach*. McGraw-Hill, Yugoslavia.

MAYER, J.E. and TIMMS, N. (1971) *The Client Speaks*. London, Routledge.

MEAD, G.H. (1925) The genesis of the self and social control. *International J. Ethics*, **35**, 251—273.

MILGRAM, S. (1970) The experience of living in cities: a psychological analysis. In: F.F. KORTEN, S.W. COOK and J.I. LACEY (Eds.) *Psychology and the Problems of Society*. Washington, DC, American Psychological Association.

MILLERSON (1964) cited in MCCARTHY (1980) *op. cit.*

MIND (1972) *Starting and Running a Group Home*. London, MIND.

MITA, T.H., DERMER, M. and KNIGHT, J. (1977) Reversed facial images and the mere-exposure hypothesis. *J. Personality and Soc. Psychol.*, **35**, 597—601.

MITTLER, P. (Ed.) (1970) *The Psychological Assessment of Mental and Physical Handicaps*. London, Methuen.

MORAWSKI, J.G. (1979) The Structure of Social Psychology Communities. In: L. STRICKLAND (Ed.) *Soviet and Western Perspectives in Social Psychology*. Oxford, Pergamon.

MOSCOVICI, S. (1972) Society and Theory in Social Psychology (p. 17—68). In: J. ISRAEL and H. TAJFEL (Eds.) *The Context of Social Psychology*. London, Academic Press.

MOSCOVICI, S. (1976) *Social influence and social change*. London, Academic Press.

MOSCOVICI, S., LAGE, E. and NAFFRECHOUX, M. (1969) Influence of a consistent minority on the responses of a majority in a color perception task. *Sociometry*, **32**, 365—380.

MURSTEIN, B.I. (1977) The stimulus-value-role (SVR) theory of dyadic relationships. In: S. DUCK (Ed.) *Theory and Practice in Interpersonal Attraction*. London, Academic Press, pp. 105—129.

MACANDREW, C.H., OVERTON, N.K. and WHITE, M. (1980) *Life in the Community: A Survey of the Prestwich Hospital Group Homes*. London, Psychiatric Rehabilitation Association, Occasional Paper No. 5.

MCCARTHY, P. (1980) *Unionism and Professionalism in Social Work*. Unpublished M.Sc. Thesis, Linacre College, Oxford.

MCDOUGALL, W. (1908) *Social Psychology*. London, Methuen.

MCLEOD, D.L. and MEYER, H.J. (1967) A Study of the Values of Social Workers. In: J.E. THOMAS (Ed.) *Behavioural Science for Social Workers*. New York, The Free Press.

MCGUIRE, W.J. (1969) The nature of attitudes and attitude change. In: G. LINDZEY and E. ARONSON (Eds.) *The Handbook of Social Psychology*, 2nd Edn., Vol. 3. Reading,

Mass., Addison-Wesley, pp. 136–314.

NEWMAN, O. (1973) *Defensible Space*. New York, Collier.

NEWMAN, R.C. and POLLACK, D. (1973) Proxemics in deviant adolescents. *J. Consulting & Clin. Psychol.*, **40(1)**, 6–8.

NEWCOMB, T.M., TURNER, R. and CONVERSE, P. (1975) *Social Psychology*. London, Routledge & Kegan Paul.

NISBETT, R.E. and BORGIDA, E. (1975) Attribution and the psychology of prediction. *J. Personality & Soc. Psychol.*, **32**, 932–943.

OLSEN, M.R. (Ed.) (1976) *Differential Approaches in Social Work with the Mentally Disordered*. BASW/University College of North Wales, Dept. of Social Theory and Institutions, Occasional Papers No. 2.

OLSEN, M.R. (Ed.) (1978) *The Unitary Model*. BASW.

OPPENHEIM, A.N. (1966) *Questionnaire Design and Attitude Measurement*. London, Heineman.

OSGOOD, C.E. (1962) *An alternative to war or surrender*. Urbana, Ill., University of Illinois Press.

OSGOOD, C. and TANNENBAUM, P. (1955) The principle of congruity in the prediction of attitude change. *Psychological Review*, **62**, 42–55.

OTTON, G. (1974) *Social work support for the health services*. HMSO.

PARK, R.E. (1928) Human migration and the marginal man. *Am. J. Sociology*, **33**, 881–893.

PARSLOE, P. and STEVENSON, O. (1978) *Social Service Teams*. HMSO.

PAULUS, P., COX, V., McCAIN, G. and CHANDLER, J. (1975) Some effects of crowding in a prison environment. *J. Appl. Soc. Psychol.*, **5(1)**, 86–91.

PETTIGREW, T.F. (1971) *Racially Separate or Together?* New York, McGraw-Hill.

PHILIP, A.F., McCULLOCH, J.W. and SMITH, N.J. (1975) *Social Work Research and the Analysis of Social Data*. Oxford, Pergamon.

PILISUK, M. and SKOLNICK, P. (1968) Inducing trust: a test of the Osgood proposal. *J. Personality & Soc. Psychol.*, **8**, 121–133.

PINCUS, A. & MINAHAN, A (1973) *Social Work Practice: Model and Method*. Illinois, F.E. Peacock.

POPPER, K.R. (1963) *Conjectures and Refutations*. London, Routledge & Kegan Paul.

PORTEOUS, J.D. (1977) *Environment and Behavior*. Reading, Mass., Addison-Wesley.

PRIEST, R.F. and SAWYER, J. (1967) Proximity and Peership: Bases of Balance in Interpersonal Attraction. *Am. J. Sociology*, **72**, 633–649.

PRITLOVE, J.H. (1976) Evaluating a Group Home: Problems and Results. *Br. J. Social Work*, **6**, 3.

PROSHANSKY, H., ITTELSON, W. and RIVLIN, L. (Eds.) (1970) *Environmental Psychology: Man and his physical setting*. New York, Holt, Rinehart and Winston.

PROSHANSKY, H. and SEIDENBERG, B. (Eds.) (1970) *Basic Studies in Social Psychology*. New York, Holt, Rinehart and Winston.

RAPOPORT, A. (1977) *Human Aspects of Urban Form*. Oxford, Pergamon.

RAVEN, B. and RUBIN, J. (1976) *Social Psychology: People in Groups*. New York, Wiley.

REES, S. (1978) *Social Work Face to Face: Client and Social Workers' Perceptions of the Content and Outcomes of their Meetings*. London, Edward Arnold.

REGAN, D.T., STRAUSS, E. and FAZIO, R. (1974) Liking and the attribution process. *J. Exp. Soc. Psychol.*, **10**, 385–397.

REID, W.J. and SHYNE, A.W. (1969) *Brief and Extended Casework*. Columbia, Columbia University Press.

REIN, M. (1970) The Cross-roads for Social Work. *Social Work*, **27, 4**, 18–27.

ROBERTS, G. (1978) *Essential Law for Social Workers*. London, Oyez.

ROBINSON, T. (1978) *In Worlds Apart: Professionals and their Clients in the Welfare State*. London, Bedford Square Press.

ROGERS, C. (1951) *Client-centered Therapy*. Boston, Houghton Mifflin.

ROKEACH, M. (1971) Long-range experimental modification of values, attitudes and behaviour. *Am. Psychol.*, **22**, 453–459.

ROSS, E.A. (1908) *Social Psychology*. New York, Macmillan.

ROSS, L. (1977) The intuitive psychologist and his shortcomings: Distortions in the attribution process. In: L. BERKOWITZ (Ed.) *Advances in Experimental Social Psychology*, Vol. 10. New York, Academic Press, pp. 173–220.

ROWAN, J. (1976) *The Power of the Group*. London, Davis-Poynter.

ROWETT, C. and BREAKWELL, G.M. (1982) Up Against the Beast. *Social Work Today*, 12 January 1982.

ROWETT, C. and DEWS, E. (1979) The Story of Billy. *Social Work Today*, 30 October 1979.

RUBIN, Z. (1973) *Liking and Loving: An Imitation to Social Psychology*. New York, Holt, Rinehart and Winston.

RUBIN, Z., PEPLAU, L.A. and HILL, C.T. (1978) *Loving and leaving: Sex differences in romantic attachments*. Unpublished manuscript, Branders University.

RYAN, P. (1979) Residential Care for the Mentally Disabled. In: J.K. WING, and R. OLSEN (Eds.) *Community Care for the Mentally Disabled*. Oxford, Oxford University Press.

SCHEFF, T.J. (Ed.) (1975) *Lebelling Madness*. New Jersey, Prentice-Hall (Spectrum).

SCHERER, S.E. (1974) Proxemic behaviour of primary school children as a function of their socioeconomic class and subculture. *J. Personality & Soc. Psychol.*, **29(6)**, 800–805.

SCHJELDERUP-EBBE, T. (1938) Social behaviour of birds. In: C. MURCHISON (Ed.) *A handbook of Social Psychology*. Worcester, Mass., Clark University Press, pp. 947–972.

SCHNEIDER, D.J. (1969) Tactical self-presentation after success and failure. *J. Personality & Soc. Psychol.*, **13**, 262–268.

SCHNEIDER, K. (1959) *Clinical Psychopathology*. Grune & Stratton.

SECORD, P. and BACKMAN, C. (1964) *Social Psychology*. New York, McGraw-Hill.

SEEBOHM REPORT (1968) *Report of the Committee on Local Authority and Allied Personal Social Services*. HMSO Cmnd. 3703.

SEEMAN, M. (1959) On the meaning of alienation. *American Sociological Review*, **24**, 783–791.

SEGAL, M.W. (1974) Alphabet and Attraction: An Unobtrusive Measure of the Effect of Propinquity in a Field Setting. *J. Personality & Soc. Psychol.*, **30**, 654–657.

SHAW, M.E. (1976) *Group dynamics: the psychology of small group behaviour*. New York, McGraw-Hill.

SHERIF, M. (1936) *The Psychology of Group Norms*. New York, Harper & Row.

SHERIF, M. (1966) *Group conflict and co-operation: their social psychology*. London, Routledge & Kegan Paul.

SHERIF, M., HARVEY, O.J., WHITE, B., HOOD, W. and SHERIF, C. (1961) *Intergroup conflict and co-operation: The Robbers Cave Experiment*. Norman, Okla., University of Oklahoma Book Exchange.

SHERIF, M. and HOVLAND, C.I. (1961) *Social judgement: assimilation and contrast effects in communication and attitude change*. New Haven, Conn., Yale University Press.

SHERROD, D.R. (1974) Crowding, Perceived control and behavioural after-effects. *J. Appl. Soc. Psychol.*, **4(2)**, 171–186.

SHERWOOD, J., BARON, J. and FITCH, H. (1969) Cognitive dissonance: theory and research. In: R. WAGNER and J. SHERWOOD (Eds.) *The study of attitude change*. Monterey, Calif., Brooks/Cole, pp. 56–86.

SHIBUTANI, T. (1961) *Society and Personality*. New Jersey, Prentice-Hall.

SIEGLER, M. and OSMOND, H. (1966) Models of Madness. *Br. J. Psychiatry*, **112**, 1193–1203.

SIGALL, H. and PAGE, R. (1971) Current Stereotypes: A little fading, a little faking. *J. Personality & Soc. Psychol.*, **18**, 247–255.

SKINNER, B.F. (1959) *Cumulative Record*. New York, Appleton.

SMITH, D.H. (1967) A parsimonious definition of 'group': toward conceptual clarity and scientific utility. *Sociological Inquiry*, **37(2)**, 141–167.

SMITH, E. (1961) The power of dissonance techniques to change attitudes. *Public Opinion Quarterly*, **25**, 626–639.

SMITH, G. (1970) *Social Work and the Sociology of Organisations*. London, Routledge.

SMITH, S. and HAYTHORN, W. (1972) Effects of compatibility, crowding, group size, and leadership seniority on stress, anxiety, hostility, and annoyance in isolated groups. *J. Personality & Soc. Psychol.*, **22**, 67–79.

SMITH, S.M. (1975) *The Battered Child Syndrome*. Butterworths, London.

SMITH, S.M. (Ed.) (1978) *The Maltreatment of Children*. Trowbridge, MTP Press.

SNYDER, M. (1979) Self-monitoring processes. In: L. BERKOWITZ (Ed.) *Advances in experimental social psychology*, Vol. 12. New York, Academic Press, pp. 85–128.

SNYDER, M. and MONSON, T. (1975) Persons, situations and the control of social behaviour. *J. Personality & Soc. Psychol.*, **32**, 637–644.

SNYDER, M. and URANOWITZ, S.W. (1978) Reconstructing the past: Some cognitive consequences of person perception. *J. Personality & Soc. Psychol.*, **36**, 941–950.

SOMMER, R. (1969) *Personal Space*. Englewood Cliffs, NJ, Prentice-Hall.

SOMMER, R. and SOMMER, B. (1980) *A Practical Guide to Behavioural Research: Tools and Techniques*. New York, Oxford University Press.

STAATS, A. (1968) Social behaviourism and human motivation: principles of the attitude-reinforcer-discriminative system. In: A.G. GREENWALD, T.C. BROCK and T.M. OSTROM (Eds.), *Psychological foundations of attitudes*. New York, Academic Press, pp. 33–66.

STEINER, I. and FISHBEIN, M. (1965) *Current Studies in Social Psychology*. New York, Holt, Rinehart and Winston.

STOGHILL, R.M. (1974) *Handbook of leadership: a survey of theory and research*. New York, Free Press. © 1974 by the Free Press, a Division of Macmillan Publishing Co., Inc.

STOKOLS, D. (1976) The experience of crowding in primary and secondary environments. *Environment and Behaviour*, **8(1)**, 49–86.

STONEQUIST, E.V. (1937) *The Marginal Man*. Scribners, New York.

STRICKLAND, L. (Ed.) (1979) *Soviet and Western Perspectives in Social Psychology*. Oxford, Pergamon.

STROUD, J. (1975) *Where to get help: a guide to the support services*. Glasgow, Ward Lock Educational.

SUEDFELD, P. and RANK, A. (1976) Revolutionary leaders: long term success as a function of changes in conceptual complexity. *J. Personality & Soc. Psychol.*, **34**, 169–178.

SWENSON, C.H. (1978) Love, problems and the development of the marriage relationship. Unpublished manuscript, Purdue University.

SZASZ, T. (1961) *The Myth of Mental Illness.* New York, Hoeber-Harper.

SZASZ, T. (1970) *The Manufacture of Madness.* New York, Harper & Row.

TAJFEL, H. (1970) Experiments in intergroup discrimination. *Scientific American,* **223(5)**, 96–102.

TAJFEL, H. (Ed.) (1978) *Differentiation between Social Groups.* London, Academic Press.

TAJFEL, H. (1981) *Human Groups and Social Categories.* Cambridge, Cambridge University Press.

TAJFEL, H., and BILLIG, M. (1974) Familiarity and social categorisation in intergroup behaviour. *J. Exp. Soc. Psychol.,* **10**, 159–170.

TAJFEL, H., BILLIG, M., BUNDY, R. and FLAMENT, C. (1971) Social categorisation and intergroup behaviour. *Eur. J. Soc. Psychol.,* **1**, 149–177.

TAJFEL, H. and FRASER, C. (Eds.) (1978) *Introducing Social Psychology.* Harmondsworth, Penguin Education.

THIBAUT, J.W. and KELLEY, H.H. (1959) *The social psychology of groups.* New York, Wiley.

THORNICROFT, G. (1979) Group Homes — a Success? *Nursing Times,* 11 January 1979, pp. 84–85.

TOREN, N. (1972) *Social Work: The Case of a Semi-Profession.* London, Sage Publications.

TOWNSEND, P. (1981) Social Work teaching 'needs revamp'. *Times Higher Educational Supplement,* 18 September 1981, p. 2.

TROWER, P., BRYANT, B. and ARGYLE, M. (1978) *Social Skills and Mental Health.* London, Methuen.

TRUAX, C.B. and CARKHUFF, R.R. (1967) *Toward Effective Counselling and Psychotherapy.* Chicago, Aldine.

TUDDENHAM, R.C. (1959) Correlates of Yielding to a Distorted Group Norm. *J. Personality,* **27, 2**, 72–284.

UNITED NATIONS. *Declaration of the Rights of Disabled Persons.* General Assembly Resolution 3447 (XXX) 9 December 1975.

VALINS, S. and BAUM, A. (1973) Residential group size, social interaction and crowding. *Environment and Behaviour,* **5(4)**, 421–439.

VEBLEN, T. (1958) *The theory of the leisure class.* New York, Mentor.

VERNY, T.R. (1974) *Inside Groups.* New York, McGraw-Hill.

VIDEBECK, R. (1960) Self-conception and the reaction of others. *Sociometry,* **23**, 351–362.

WAGNER, R.V. (1975) Complementary Needs, Role Expectations, Interpersonal Attraction and the Stability of Working Relationships. *J. Personality & Soc. Psychol.,* **32**, 116–124.

WALSTER, E., WALSTER, G. and BERCHEID, E. (1978) *Equity: Theory and Research.* Boston, Allyn and Bacon.

WALTERS, D.R. (1975) *Physical and Sexual Abuse of Children: Causes and Treatment.* Indiana University Press.

WATSON, P. (1980) *War on the Mind.* Harmondsworth, Penguin.

WATSON, O.M. and GRAVES, T.D. (1966) Quantitative research in proxemic behavior. *American Anthropologist,* **68**, 971–985.

WEGNER, D.M. and VALLACHER, R.R. (1977) *Implicit Psychology.* New York, Oxford University Press.

WEINSTEIN, L. (1965) Social schemata of emotionally disturbed boys. *J. Abnl. Psychol.,* **70**, 457–461.

WEIR, S. (1981) What do people think about social workers? *New Society*, 7 May 1981, pp. 216–218.

WEST AUSTRALIAN DEPARTMENT FOR COMMUNITY WELFARE (1975) The Battered Child: Proceedings of the First National Australian Conference, 25–28 August 1975. W. Aust. Dept. Comm. Welfare.

WESTIN, A. (1970) *Privacy and Freedom*. New York, Atheneum.

WETTON, K. (1976) *The Cheltenham Intake Team: An Evaluation*. Clearing Home for Local Authority Social Services Research No. 2, University of Birmingham.

WILENSKY, H.L. (1965) The Professionalisation of Everyone? *Am. J. Sociology*, **70**, 137–158.

WILTSHIRE SOCIAL SERVICES DEPARTMENT RESEARCH UNIT (1975) *Intake Referral Study*. Wiltshire SSD.

WINCH, R.F. (1958) *Mate Selection: A Study of Complementary Needs*. New York, Harper & Row.

WING, J.K. (1978) Diagnosing Schizophrenia. *New Society*, 8 June 1978.

WITKINS, H., DYK, R., FOTERSON, H., GOODENOUGH, D. and KARP, S. (1962) *Psychological Differentiation*. New York, Wiley.

WOLFGANG, J. and WOLFGANG, A. (1971) Explanation of attitudes via physical interpersonal distance toward the obese, drug users, homosexuals, police and other marginal figures. *J. Clin. Psychol.*, **27**, 510–512.

WORLD HEALTH ORGANISATION (1974) *Glossary of Mental Disorders and Guide to their Classification*. WHO, Geneva.

WRIGHTSMAN, L.S. (1972) *Social Psychology in the Seventies*. Monterey, Calif., Brooks/Cole.

WRIGHTSMAN, L.S. and DEAUX, K. (1981) *Social Psychology in the 80s*, 3rd Edn. Monterey, Calif., Brooks/Cole.

WYLIE, R. (1961) *The self concept*. Lincoln, Nebr., University of Nebraska Press.

YELLOLY, M.A. (1980) *Social Work Theory and Psychoanalysis*. London, Van Nostrand Reinhold.

YOUNG, A.F. and ASHTON, E.T. (1963) *British Social Work in the Nineteenth Century*. London, RKP.

YOUNG, M. (1977) Treating the Long-term Mentally Ill. *Social Work Today* 1 November 1977, pp. 11–12.

ZANDER, A., COHEN, A. and STOTLAND, E. (1957) *Role relations in the mental health professions*. Ann Arbor, Institute for Social Research, University of Michigan.

ZILLER, R.C. (1973) *The Social Self*. Oxford, Pergamon.

ZIMBARDO, P. (1969) The human choice: individuation, reason and order versus deindividuation, impulse and chaos. In: W.J. ARNOLD and D LEVINE (Eds.) *Nebraska Symposium on Motivation*. Lincoln, University of Nebraska Press, pp. 237–308.

Index

310